THE ATLAS OF
ART CRIME

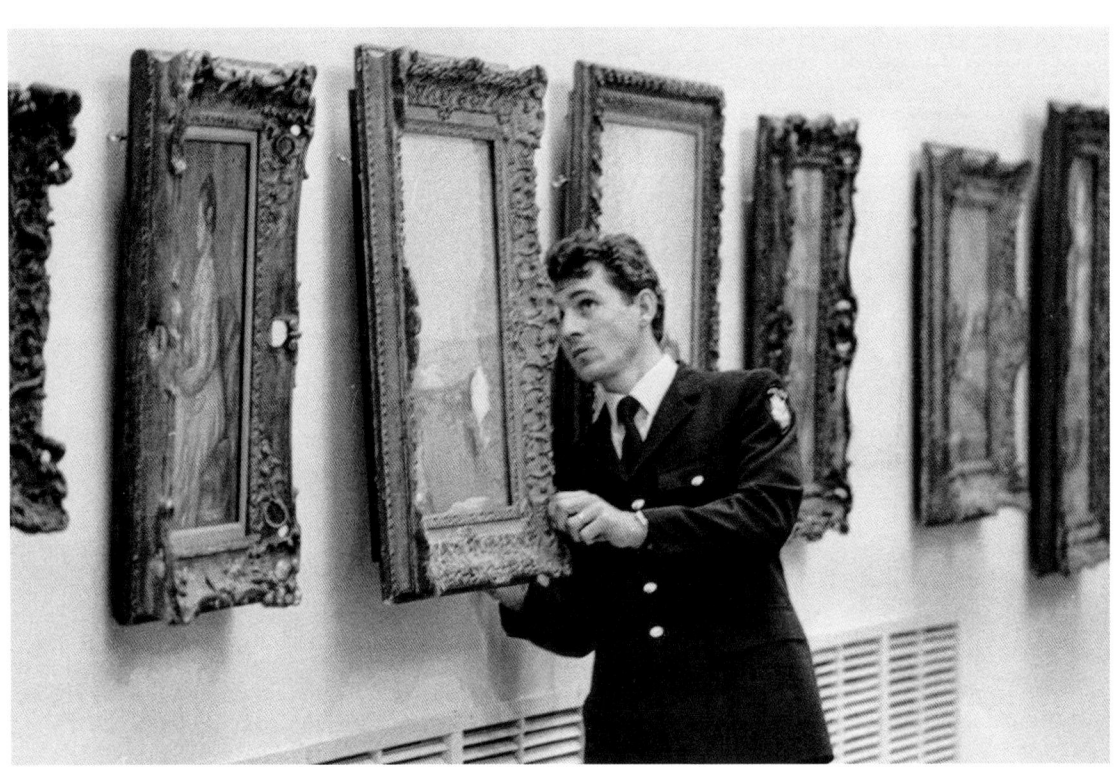

LAURA EVANS

THE ATLAS OF
ART CRIME

THEFTS, VANDALISM,
AND FORGERIES

PRESTEL MUNICH · LONDON · NEW YORK

To Sean, my partner-in-crime, and to the Evanses, who helped me forge my path. You are all one of a kind.

And, to Terry, my mentor and friend. Rest in peace.

Prestel Verlag, Munich · London · New York 2024
A member of Penguin Random House Verlagsgruppe GmbH
Neumarkter Strasse 28 · 81673 Munich

Published in association with
Quintessence Editions
1 Triptych Place, Second Floor
London SE1 9SH

This book was conceived, designed and produced by
Quintessence Editions.

For Prestel Verlag:
Editorial direction: Katharina Haderer
Production management: Cilly Klotz

For Quintessence Editions:
Senior Commissioning Editor: Eszter Karpati
Senior Editor: Emma Harverson
Design: Ocky Murray
Senior Designer: Rachel Cross
Picture Research: Sara Ayad
Production Manager: David Hearn
Associate Publisher: Eszter Karpati
Publisher: Lorraine Dickey

Printed in Dubai.

ISBN 978-3-7913-7711-7 (English edition)
ISBN 978-3-7913-7712-4 (American edition)

www.prestel.com

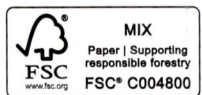

CONTENTS

SEEKING INFORMATION

BY THE FBI

The FBI is seeking information in the theft of thirteen works of art from the Isabella Stewart Gardner Museum in 1990.

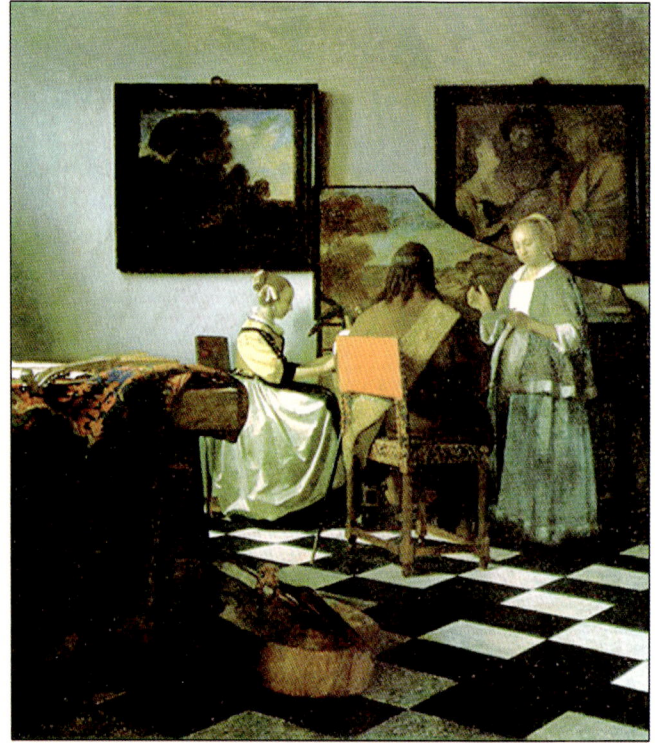

The Concert
VERMEER, 1658 - 1660

Oil on canvas, 72.5 x 64.7 cm

$5 Million Reward

The FBI encourages anyone who may have information on the whereabouts of the artwork to contact the FBI at 1-800-CALL-FBI or submit online at Tips.FBI.Gov.

WHY ARE WE DRAWN TO ART CRIME?

Whether it is a dramatic and cinematic heist, a cheeky but self-destructing forger, or a social issue-inspired vandal, art crime stories titillate and intrigue us. I see and feel this sense of enthrallment in both my audiences and myself when I lecture about art crime around the world. But why?

My own fascination with art crime started early in life with a steady diet of Scooby-Doo as a child. My first art crime movie was *The Great Muppet Caper*. I was beguiled when Miss Piggy, in her shimmery silver jumpsuit, crashed through the stained glass windows of the Mallory Gallery on her red motorcycle to save the famed Baseball Diamond from the evil clutches of the movie's villain. As an undergraduate art history student, I was both intrigued and repelled after learning about the 1990 theft at the Isabella Stewart Gardner Museum (p. 98). While on a visit to the Gardner in graduate school, I was haunted by the museum's empty frames—tombstones marking the graves of the stolen paintings. I was also hooked. My love for crime, storytelling, and art coalesced and developed into a full-blown obsession with learning about and sharing art crime tales.

A Boom in Art Crime

The communications theorist Marshall McLuhan once wrote, "Art is anything you can get away with." In turn, art crime is anything you can't get away with. Art crime has a simple, generally accepted definition first put forward by criminologist J. E. Conklin in his 1994 book *Art Crime*. According to Conklin, art crimes are "criminally punishable acts that involve works of art."

In terms of scale, art crime and antiquities trafficking is often cited as the third-highest-grossing illicit trade after drugs and guns, though the validity of this statement and the careless use of it has been recently called into question by art and antiquities crime scholars Donna Yates and Neil Brodie, who argue that we don't need to quantify how illicit the market is to understand its irreparable damage to society. Still, numbers can make an impact; in the early 2000s, the FBI's Art Theft Team (established in 1992) believed that each year $4–6 billion worth of art is stolen around the world. Regardless of its ranking, it is clear that art crime is booming, not just as an illicit industry but within popular culture as well. With an influx of books, movies, and podcasts about trafficked, forged, stolen, or vandalized art, art crime has certainly captured the public imagination.

But *should* we be so drawn to stories about art crime? Shouldn't we be outraged? It's complicated. The art world itself is not exactly a squeaky-clean place. In fact, as you'll see in the following pages, it can be downright sleazy. Many museums are contemporary battlegrounds for contested objects of cultural heritage. Some proudly display stolen art that was wrongfully taken during times of conflict or colonialism. Auction houses are often accused of neglecting their due diligence, turning a blind eye and authenticating a forgery or overlooking an object with dubious provenance to make a stratospheric sale that benefits the auction house over humanity. Who are the bad guys? The lines can get a bit blurry.

Some think art crime is a victimless crime. It's true that there are few tales of art crime (within the parameters I am writing about) where people get physically hurt. But art is certainly hurt. In some cases, art disappears or is irreparably damaged or obliterated. In these ways, we are all victims of art crime: anyone who could have been touched by that work of art no longer has that opportunity.

Sharing Stories

In this book, I try to tell stories of wronged works of art and of the people, both heroes and villains, involved in their histories. I write about true tales of relentless opportunism (both on the part of criminals and art-world emissaries) and try to highlight the seediness of the art world—a $67.8 billion-a-year industry that masquerades as being above the law.

As a narrative researcher, I share stories to connect us as human beings. The stories in this book are sometimes humorous, oftentimes shocking, and frequently ridiculous. My goal in telling them is to make you lean in, to make you want to know something more about the art, the artist, the time period in which the artist created, or anything that piques your interest. You need not know anything about art history to appreciate the motivations, the conflicts, and the emotions that swirl around these stories. Ultimately, I believe that stories about art crime are human-interest stories, and the ones you'll read here reflect this sentiment. You'll find a range of motivations for art crime: greed, validation, revenge, power, and fame, but also love, equity, and idealism.

This book is divided into three categories of art crime: theft, vandalism, and forgery. I've concentrated on visual arts—art made with the express purpose of being seen and appreciated as art, with two exceptions: Tucker's Cross (p. 110) and the objects at the center of the vandalism at the Dallas Museum of Art (p. 166), which included several ancient Greek vessels, along with a piece of contemporary sculpture. In all other entries in this book, the attention is on visual arts as defined in the traditional Western sense: paintings, drawings, sculptures, golden toilets (p. 28), and bananas (p. 170).

I chose not to include trafficked antiquities or art looted or destroyed during times of conflict or confusion because these are enormous problems with far-reaching and extremely serious consequences. There are many excellent books and articles about these tragedies, and I encourage you to seek them out and read deeply.

About half of the vandalized and stolen works covered in this book have been rescued or returned. I love these happy endings, but they are usually the exception when it comes to art crimes. Some estimates suggest that less than 10 percent of stolen art will ever be recovered. I hope you will contemplate what happens, or what can't happen, when art is not recovered. We lose a thread from our collective humanity, and a connection to our past is untethered forever, damaging our sense of identity and trust.

So why are we drawn to stories of art crime? Is it wrong to enjoy reading about it?

When I lecture about art crime, I like to call it "historical gossiping." Psychologists have found that gossip plays a role in maintaining the social cohesion of groups, and allows us to learn from the success and failure of others. Thus, I think that being enthralled by art crime and engaging in "historical gossiping" about the triumphs and misadventures of it all serves an evolutionary purpose: we learn what not to do, how not to behave, how to better appreciate art, and why, more than ever, we should strive to protect, care about, and support art and artists throughout the world.

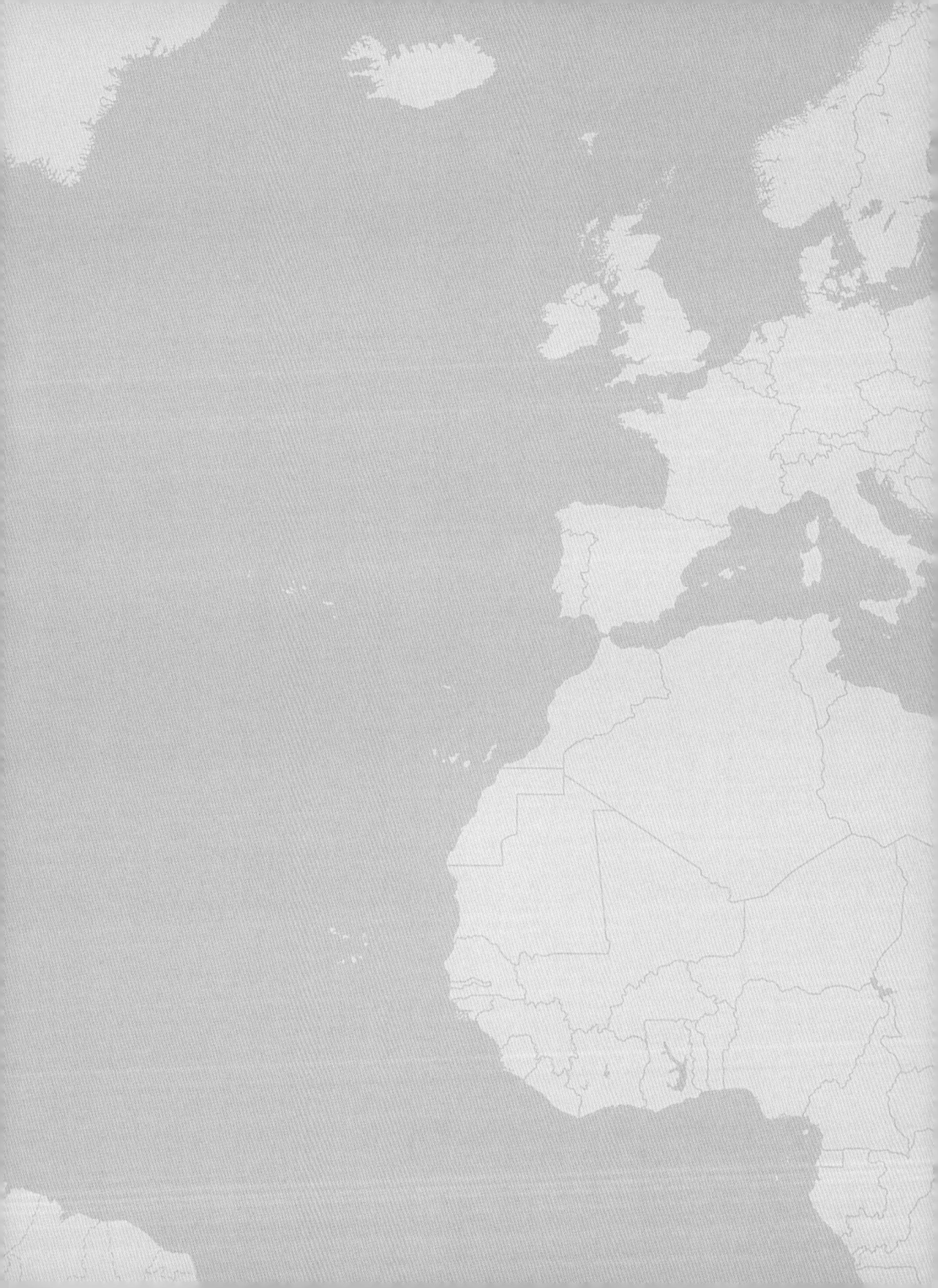

CHAPTER ONE
THEFTS

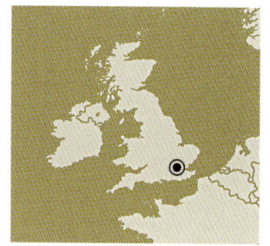

THE DISAPPEARING DUCHESS: A LOVE STORY

This art theft is a love story. One of the romantic leads is Georgiana Cavendish, the 5th Duchess of Devonshire, seen here in her portrait by Thomas Gainsborough. The other is criminal mastermind Adam Worth, who stole her portrait seventy-one years after her death.

Georgiana is easy to love. With her creamy ivory skin and her blushing cheeks, she is the epitome of an English rose, holding two in her hands: one bud and one mature, allusions to her beauty and sexuality. She raises her left eyebrow suggestively, knowingly admired. Her hair is long, feathery, curled, and abundant. With hairdressers' help, she spent hours building the "hair towers" that were her hallmark, adding horsehair and decorative ornaments to complete the style. Georgiana could ride in a carriage only by sitting on the floor, the cabin full of hair and fabric. On top of her tower of hair is an extravagant hat, which popularly became known as a Gainsborough chapeau and could incorporate whole stuffed birds, toy ships, and other ornaments.

By the time this painting was made, Georgiana was twenty-nine years old and had been married for around twelve years. Her life was one of extreme highs and lows, which continued after her death. Her portrait mysteriously disappeared from Chatsworth House (the residence of the Duke and Duchess of Devonshire) and reappeared in the 1830s in the home of an elderly teacher, who purportedly trimmed the portrait to fit above her fireplace; Georgiana now appeared only from the hips up. In 1841, the schoolteacher sold the duchess for just £56. Upon that art collector's death, the painting was auctioned in 1876 and bought by William Agnew, a prominent gallery owner in London, for the highest price ever paid for a painting at the time.

Opposite: Princess Diana and her fourth great aunt, Georgiana Cavendish Spencer, suffered similar tragedies: they married young to men who pined for someone else, they were thrust early into positions of power, and their lives ended too soon.

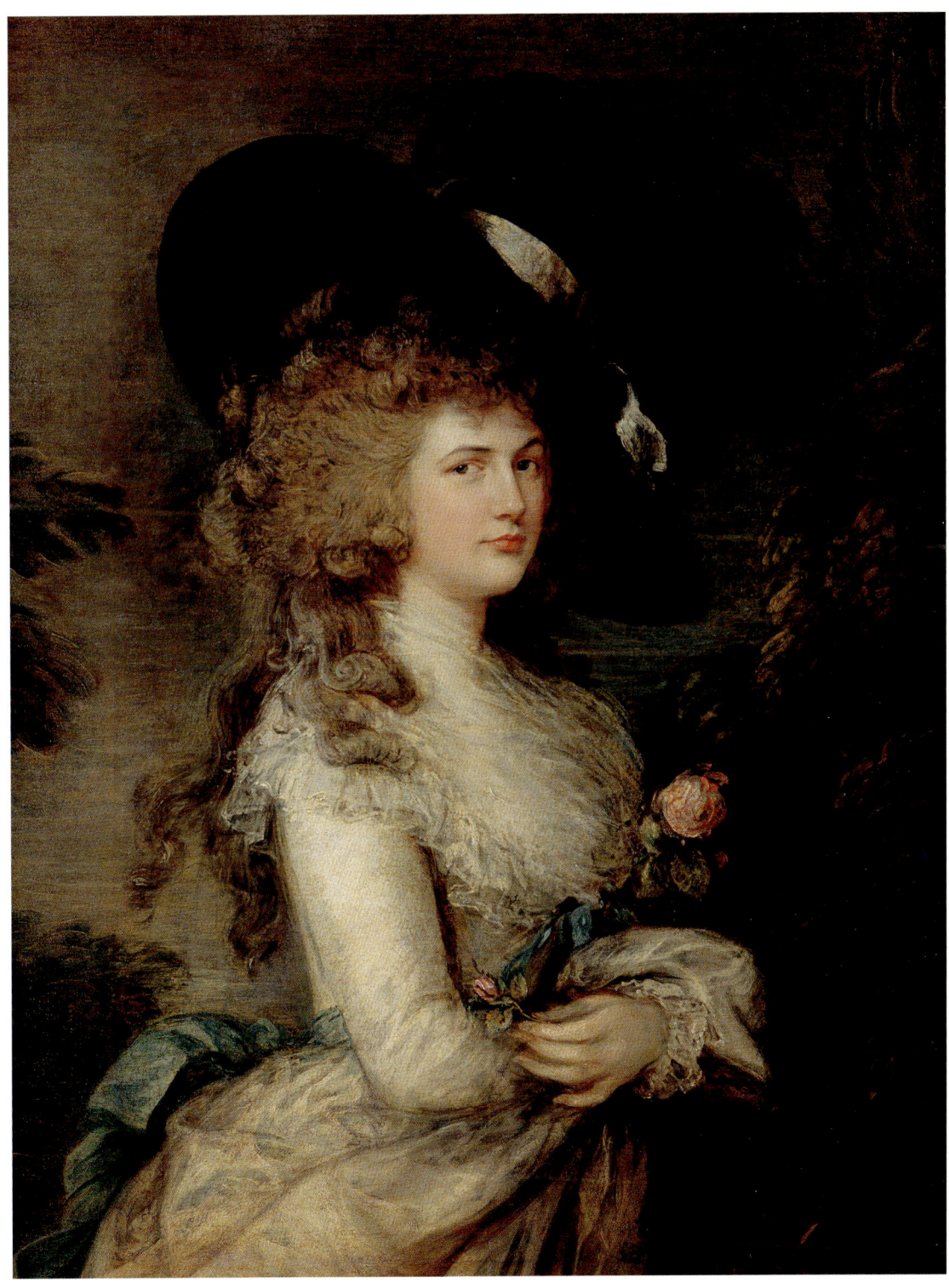

When displayed at Agnew's gallery, the *London Times* reported, "All the world had come to see a beautiful Duchess created by Gainsborough, and so far as we could observe, they all came, saw and were conquered by the fascinating beauty." Two Americans were among the admirers. The first was banker Junius Spencer Morgan, who had agreed to buy the painting for his art collection. The second was Adam Worth, a big-time criminal, who wanted to steal it. This bounty jumper, pickpocket, and petty thief had hotfooted it to England after robbing a Boston bank of $400,000 (around $8 million today). In the UK, he developed a vast criminal network stretching from Europe to Turkey and South Africa.

At the same time that Georgiana was on display at Agnew's gallery, Worth's brother was in jail for forgery. Worth planned to hold the portrait for ransom to post his brother's bail. Around midnight on May 25, 1876, using his butler and bodyguard as a human ladder, Worth scaled the gallery building and cut the duchess from her frame. Unbeknownst to Worth, his brother was already out of jail on a legal technicality. Morgan and the rest of the world were flabbergasted. No longer needing to ransom his "noble lady," as he fondly called her, Worth kept the duchess to himself, sheltering her in a false-bottomed trunk and carrying her around the globe on his criminal escapades.

Ten years later, Worth was arrested in Belgium for an unrelated crime. Police suspected he had the painting and pressured him to give it up, but Worth had his network spirit the duchess off to a Brooklyn warehouse, where she remained until he got out of jail five years later. He rushed to the duchess's side, a broke and

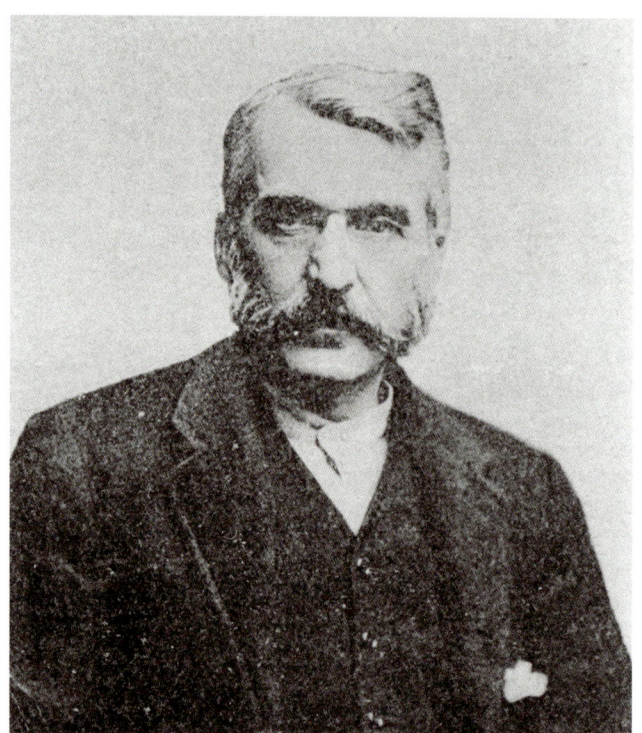

Left: The thief, Adam Worth, was known by many pseudonyms. On his gravestone, he is "The Napoleon of Crime," but he may also be the inspiration for Sherlock Holmes's nemesis: the criminal mastermind Professor James Moriarty.

Opposite: A carte de visite (visiting card) announcing the theft of Gainsborough's *Duchess of Devonshire.* This card might have functioned like an early social media post to get the word out about the robbery.

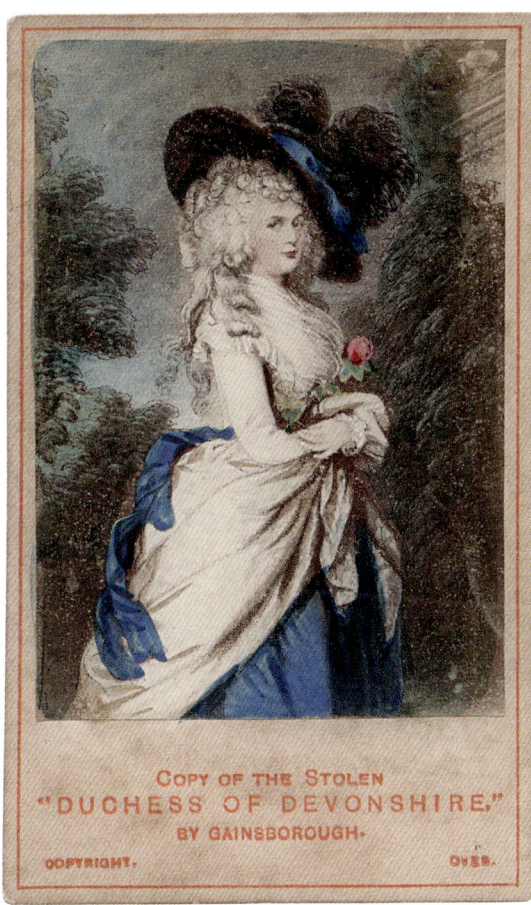

COPY OF THE STOLEN
"DUCHESS OF DEVONSHIRE."
BY GAINSBOROUGH.

COPYRIGHT.

OYES.

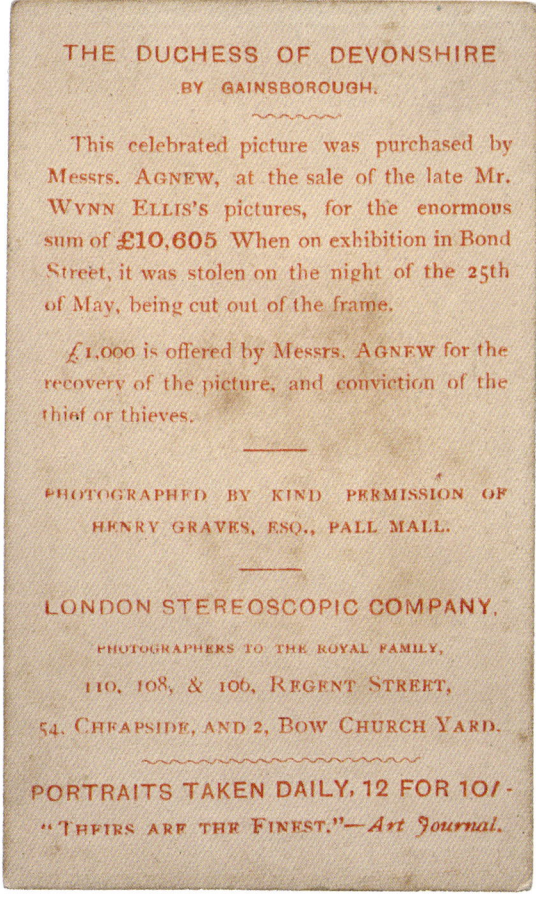

THE DUCHESS OF DEVONSHIRE
BY GAINSBOROUGH.

This celebrated picture was purchased by Messrs. AGNEW, at the sale of the late Mr. WYNN ELLIS'S pictures, for the enormous sum of £10,605 When on exhibition in Bond Street, it was stolen on the night of the 25th of May, being cut out of the frame.

£1,000 is offered by Messrs. AGNEW for the recovery of the picture, and conviction of the thief or thieves.

PHOTOGRAPHED BY KIND PERMISSION OF HENRY GRAVES, ESQ., PALL MALL.

LONDON STEREOSCOPIC COMPANY,

PHOTOGRAPHERS TO THE ROYAL FAMILY,

110, 108, & 106, REGENT STREET,

54, CHEAPSIDE, AND 2, BOW CHURCH YARD.

PORTRAITS TAKEN DAILY, 12 FOR 10/-
"THEIRS ARE THE FINEST."—*Art Journal.*

broken man. He could not give her the life she deserved, so he orchestrated a sale back to the son of the art dealer from whom he originally stole it. Through an intermediary, Worth sold the painting to Morland Agnew and probably delivered her to him in disguise, savoring his last moments with her. In turn, Agnew sold the painting to the son of the man who originally intended to buy it at his father's gallery: J. P. Morgan. In 1901, Morgan paid $150,000 for the duchess, three times what his father was planning to pay in 1876; at the time, he wouldn't reveal the amount publicly because, he said, "If the truth came out [about how much I paid], I might be considered a candidate for the lunatic asylum."

Before heading back to America and into J. P. Morgan's art collection, the duchess's portrait was shown one last time in London. A week after the exhibition closed, Worth passed away. Though his burial certificate says he died of "chronic habits of intemperance," it may be that Worth died broken-hearted at his separation from the love of his life, Georgiana.

Today, Georgiana lives on at Chatsworth House. And Adam Worth lives on too—he is purportedly the inspiration for Professor James Moriarty, the art connoisseur and archenemy of Sherlock Holmes in the popular crime series by Sir Arthur Conan Doyle.

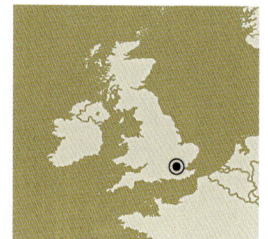

LUCK OF THE IRISH

If we look at this black and white photograph taken during the theft of a Berthe Morisot painting from the Tate Gallery in London in 1956, we can see a young man hustling down the stairs of the museum, intent on putting one foot in front of the other. He's disheveled and looks like he's having a hard time holding onto the painting he has wrapped between two pieces of cardboard. There is a couple, arm in arm, walking up to the front entrance of the museum. Because there are no backward glances at the young man coming down the stairs, we can presume the couple is not aware of anything suspicious. There aren't any security guards tearing after the thief and we can assume there are no alarms blaring.

If we could press "play" on this photograph, we'd see the man at the top of the stairs (his torso and legs are just visible in this image) race down to join the man with the painting. They hail a cab because they hadn't anticipated that they would get away with the theft, so they haven't planned for a getaway car or destination. They ask the driver to take them to Piccadilly Circus, where they end up in one of the busiest intersections in London with a painting that would now be valued at around $10 million. The boys manage to keep the painting hidden for four days at a friend's flat before handing it over. The Tate Gallery and Scotland Yard chose not to press charges, which is interesting, if not suspicious. What more is behind this photograph from the scene of the crime?

The stolen painting was part of Sir Hugh Percy Lane's collection. Lane was born in Ireland in 1875 and achieved great success with several commercial art galleries, first in London and then in Dublin. He was a discerning connoisseur of modern art, especially the work of the Impressionists. While Lane was working to establish a gallery of modern art in Dublin where he could house his collection, he ran into considerable roadblocks with colleagues, the government, and corporations in Ireland. In frustration, Lane agreed to donate his

Opposite: The moment Paul Hogan runs down the stairs of the Tate Gallery with the stolen Berthe Morisot painting, *Jour d'Eté*. His accomplice in the theft, Billy Fogarty, stands at the top of the stairs.

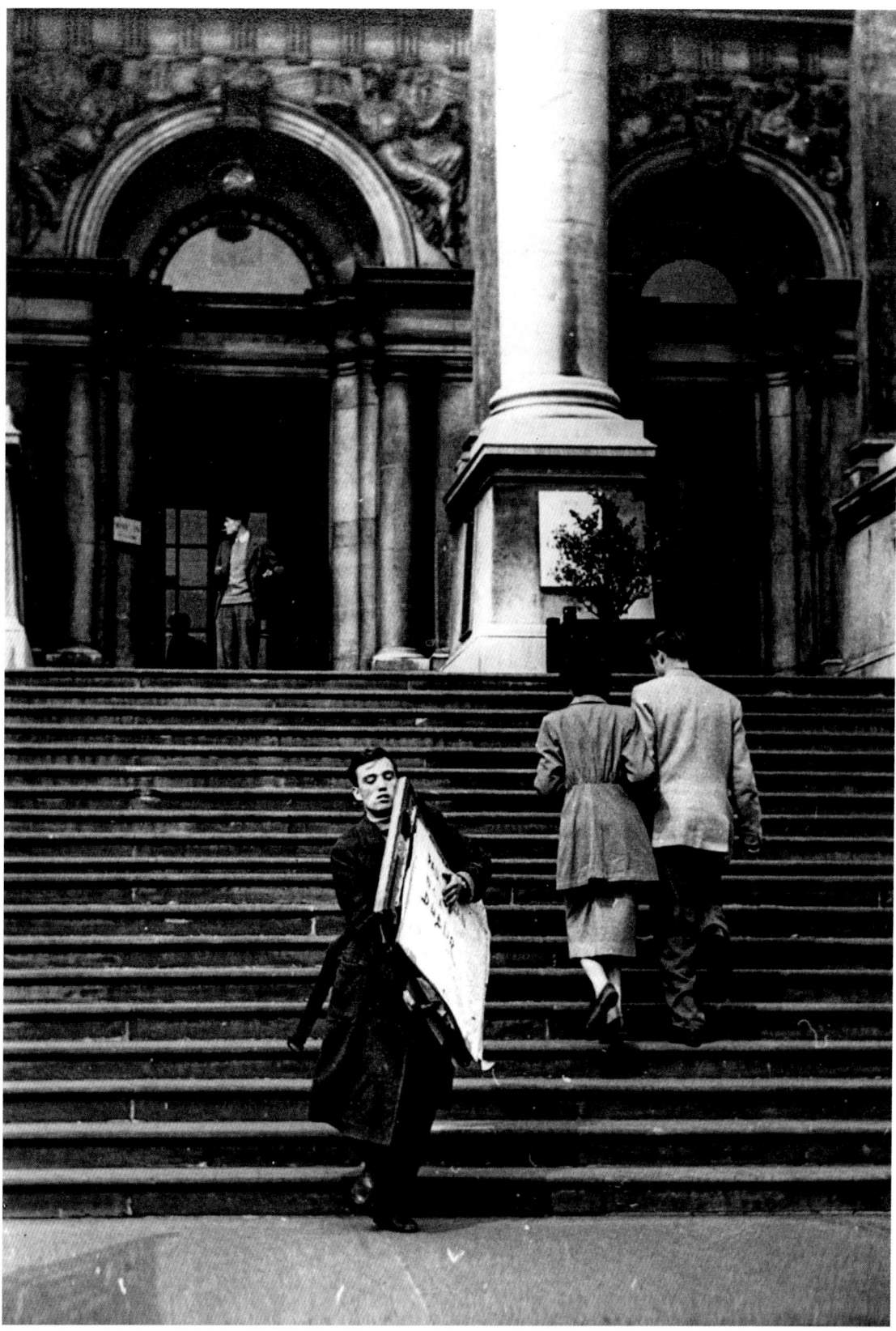

personal collection to the National Gallery in London upon his death. At some point, Lane regretted his decision and reversed the agreement in a codicil in his will, so that his collection would stay in Ireland. Though Lane made his intentions known, he didn't have the amendment witnessed. Presumably, he was going to take care of that right after getting home from a cruise on the HMS *Lusitania* in 1915. Tragically, Lane perished on the ship after it was torpedoed by a German U-boat.

Because Lane's amendment of his will had not been witnessed, London's National Gallery refused to turn the paintings over to Ireland. The Irish were furious at the turn of events, and Lane's aunt and others campaigned, in vain, to have his collection returned. William Yeats even penned some memorable poems about it. But the Lane collection—some thirty-nine works of art—lingered in storage at the National Gallery until being moved to and displayed at the Tate Gallery. It would remain there for more than thirty years until two plucky young Irishmen stole one of the paintings as a political statement.

Let's return to the photo we started this story with now that we know this added context. Billy Fogarty, aged twenty-five and from Galway, and Paul Hogan (the one racing down the stairs in the photo), aged twenty-one and from Dublin, were two idealistic Irish lads who knew their history and were aware of the controversy of the Lane Collection at the Tate Gallery. They decided to steal a painting as a political shot across the bow to reignite the conversation about bringing Lane's art back to Ireland.

The boys cased the gallery for a few days to acquaint themselves with the space and with the guards' habits. Hogan was an art student (Fogarty was a veterinary student), so he brought a giant drawing pad with him to the museum and would spend time sketching in the Lane galleries. Hogan had one of his professors write

him a letter explaining that he was going to be sketching Morisot's *Jour d'été* for a school project. Hogan quickly flashed this letter at a guard as he sat down to draw. When the guards went on their tea break, Hogan lifted the painting off of the wall, placed it between the pages of his giant sketchpad, and walked out of the gallery.

Hogan and Fogarty had called the Irish news agency beforehand and told them that there was going to be a political protest happening on that day outside of the Tate Gallery. The boys expected that the photographer might capture an image of them fighting with the security guards as they tried to seize the painting. But, instead, the photographer captured this image of Hogan running out of the museum with the painting under his arm, thanks to Fogarty yelling "TAKE THE PICTURE!"

The photographer had no idea what he had captured until the story broke that the Morisot painting had been stolen from the museum. When the photographer realized what he had on his camera roll, he handed over his film to Scotland Yard. Soon, Hogan's face was splashed across newspapers around the world, sharing the front page with Grace Kelly, who was preparing for her marriage to the Prince of Monaco.

After stashing the painting at a friend's home, they asked her to drop it off at the Irish Embassy. The boys dressed up as priests to get out of London, while the paintings were returned to the Tate. Hogan and Fogarty were allowed to return to Ireland with charges dropped, presumably because the museum did not want to encourage copycat thefts or to highlight the suboptimal security. One has to wonder how Paul Hogan's father reacted when his son returned home. Sarsfield Hogan was a senior adviser to Éamon de Valera, who had twice been Ireland's prime minister and who would go on to serve a third term, a year after the theft.

There is a somewhat happy, but not perfect, ending here. In the end, the protest worked. The

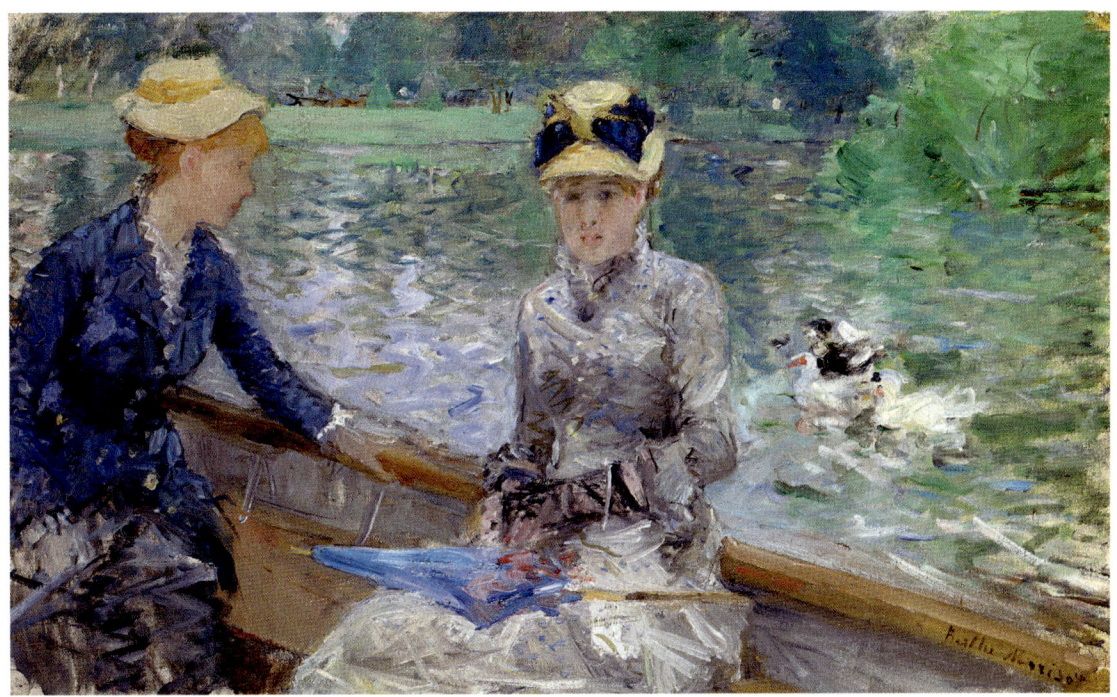

Above: In *Jour d'Eté* (1879), Berthe Morisot, one of the few women welcomed into the Impressionist group of painters, captures two women enjoying a summer's day in a rowboat in the Bois de Boulogne.

Tate eventually agreed to share the Hugh Lane collection with Dublin, and the paintings are rotated between Dublin and London, though the Tate still retains ownership of the pictures. As the National Gallery's website says, "The sharing agreement first brokered more than sixty years ago in 1959 has permitted audiences in the two cities where Lane spent most of his life to enjoy the remarkable collection of pictures that he assembled over a hundred years ago." That short sentence doesn't do justice to what really happened. Billy Fogarty and Paul Hogan's audacious theft is the only reason Lane's collection has a presence in Ireland.

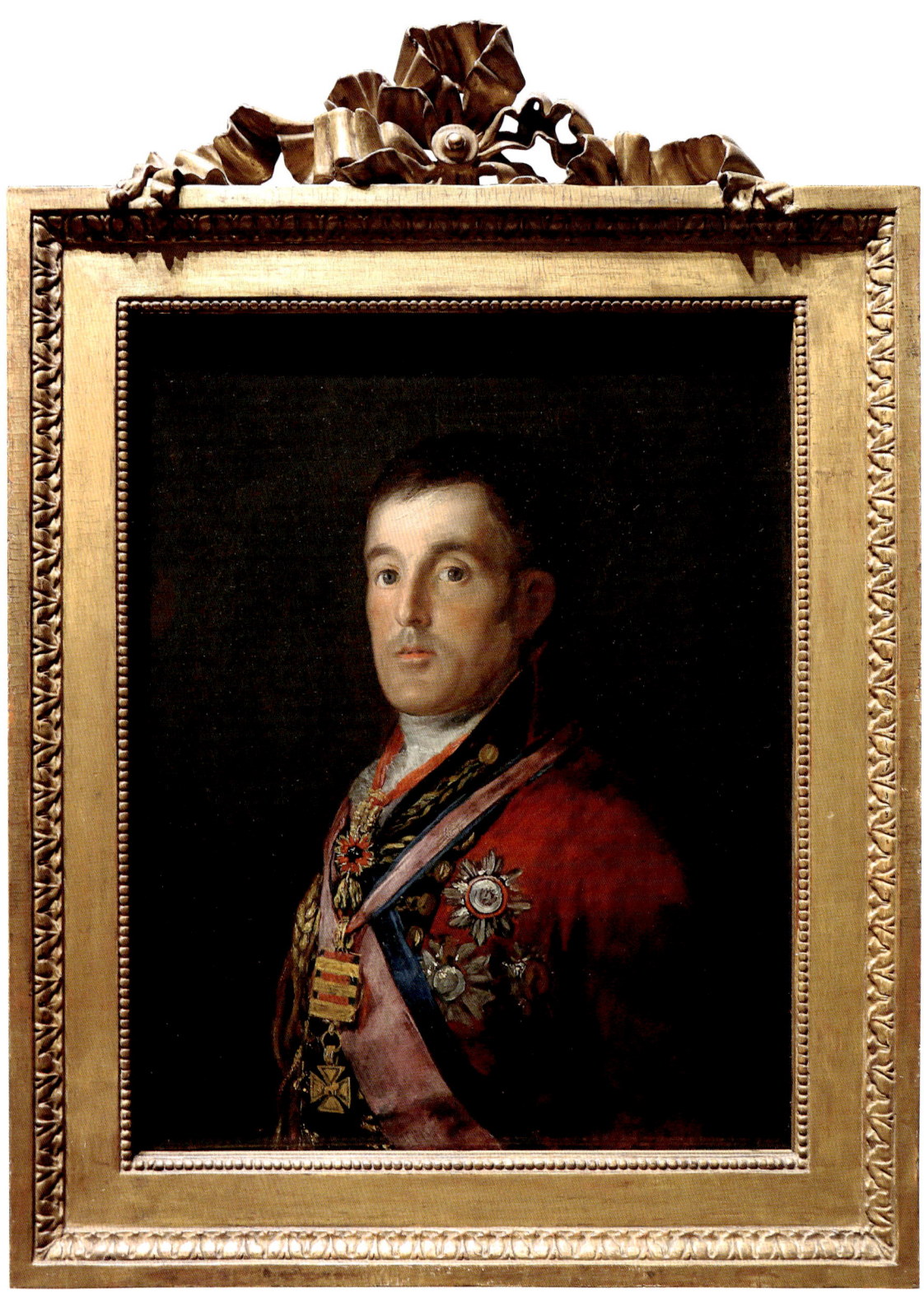

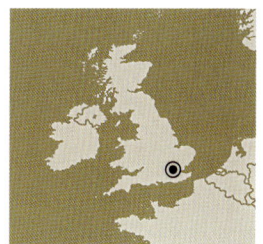

When: August 21, 1961

Where: National Gallery in London

What: Theft of Francisco de Goya's *The Duke of Wellington* (c. 1812–14)

STEALING ART FOR FREE TV

August 21 is an auspicious day for art theft. On this day in 1911, the *Mona Lisa* was stolen from the Louvre (p. 38). On the same day in 1961, Francisco de Goya's *The Duke of Wellington* was stolen from the National Gallery in London, an institution that had no recorded thefts in the previous 150 years. It is unclear if the Goya thief was aware of this parallel, but both thefts catapulted their purloined paintings into international consciousness.

Even before the theft, Goya's *The Duke of Wellington* was a newsworthy painting. The National Gallery prevented Charles Wrightsman, an American oil executive and art collector who had bought it, from taking it to the US. The British were against the portrait of such a prominent figure in British history leaving the United Kingdom, so the National Gallery bought the painting back from Wrightsman for the price he paid: £140,000.

The first Duke of Wellington was Arthur Wellesley, nicknamed the Iron Duke and famous for defeating Napoleon at Waterloo. Later, Wellesley became prime minister, which didn't go as well for him—he was rated the UK's worst nineteenth-century prime minister.

The painting was on display for only nineteen days before it was stolen. Police found the gallery locked and undamaged, but a small second-floor window in the men's toilet was ajar. It was just big enough for a person—and *The Duke of Wellington*—to fit through. Although the duke himself, as a man, was quite large, the painting was small, measuring 25 by 20 inches. Interestingly, it was stolen in its frame, which is unusual for art theft.

The thief communicated with police ten days later via the first of three notes, explaining that he was not trying to sell the painting but ransom it: he wanted £140,000 to be given to charity to buy television licenses for old and poor people.

Opposite: Though Francisco de Goya's painting of the Duke of Wellington took the headlines in 1961, it was actually the painting's frame that would inspire a change to British law in 1968.

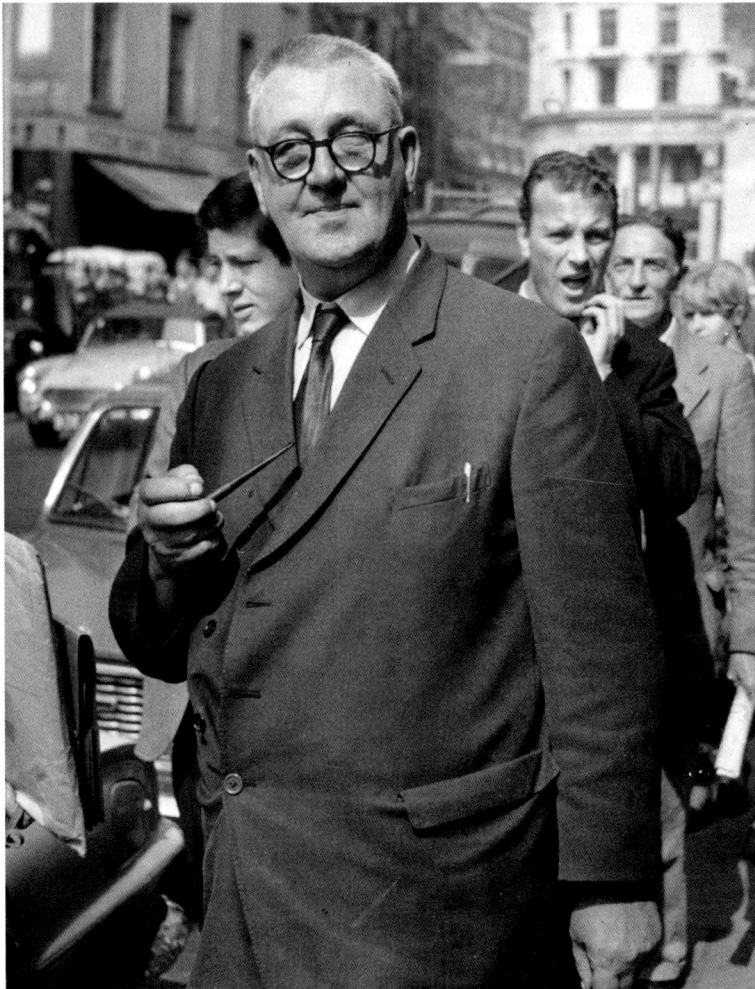

The thief was a crusader—a modern day Robin Hood for free television.

Years went by before the thief reached out again in 1963, sending police a label of authenticity, again demanding £140,000 for the TV license charity and immunity from prosecution. He urged them to "assert thyself and get the damn thing on view again. I am offering three pennyworth of old Spanish firewood, in exchange for £140,000 of human happiness." Clearly, the thief had a sense of humor. Goya was Spanish and had painted *The Duke* on wood, thus the reference to "old Spanish firewood"—a pretty good burn. Pun intended.

The last note, which came in March 1965, proposed a new idea: that the painting be anonymously returned and the National Gallery hold a ticketed exhibition, in which visitors would pay five shillings to view it. At closing, the collected entrance money would go to a television license charity. The thief wrote, as Napoleon might have to the duke himself: "I know now that I am in the wrong, but I have gone too far to retreat."

Finally, in May 1965, police received a left-luggage ticket for New Street Station, where they retrieved *The Duke of Wellington*. The painting was in good condition but frameless. Almost four years after being stolen, the painting went back on public display, where it remains.

So, who was the Robin Hood–style thief? For years, he eluded police until he turned himself in months after *The Duke of Wellington* was recovered. Kempton Bunton, a fifty-seven-year-old unemployed taxi driver, waltzed into a police station and confessed that he had stolen the painting to prod the government to provide free television licenses.

The case against Bunton went to court, where he was represented by Jeremy Hutchinson, the lawyer who had successfully defended D. H. Lawrence, the author of *Lady Chatterley's Lover*, from obscenity charges in 1960. Hutchinson made a compelling case for Bunton, whom he painted as sympathetic and who only *borrowed The Duke* to help society. He argued that since Bunton had given it back—albeit after several years—he could not be prosecuted for stealing it. Instead, he was prosecuted for stealing the frame, which he did not return, receiving three months in prison. Ironically, Bunton had been imprisoned once before for thirteen days. The crime? Repeatedly refusing to pay his television license fee.

Bunton's escapade inspired lawmakers to supplement the British Theft Act of 1968 with an important clause, making it illegal to "remove without authority any object displayed or kept for display to the public in a building to which the public have access."

Even though Bunton confessed, police had always questioned his claim of responsibility for the theft. As the police report recorded, Bunton was a disabled, heavy, tall man who didn't have the agility to scale the museum's outer wall and climb in and out the second-floor window, as the evidence suggested.

A closed national archive file, opened in the 2000s, revealed that Bunton had not stolen *The Duke* as claimed. Rather, his son, John, who was twenty years old at the time and in good physical shape, was the real culprit. In 1969, John was fingerprinted in Leeds in connection with a stolen car. Thinking his fingerprints would connect him to the theft of the painting, he confessed to stealing the Goya. His description of the crime scene convinced police, but they chose not to prosecute John, who said his intentions were always to give it to his father for his TV license campaign.

In 2000, Bunton's dream came true. The UK government funded free television licenses for people seventy-five and older but phased them out again in 2020. Though Bunton's legacy did not secure free television for all, his theft does live in infamy in the 1962 James Bond film *Dr. No*, in theaters a year after the Goya was stolen. When Bond sees *The Duke of Wellington* displayed in Dr. No's underwater lair, he does a double take, clearly recognizing the stolen painting. Bunton may not have been a *Dr. No* character in real life, but he was beloved by the public—hailed as an underdog, a champion for the people, and a "dreamer in a crumpled suit."

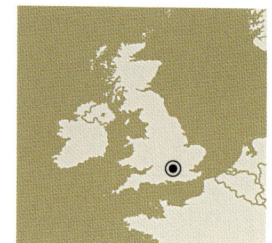

WHY2K?

On December 31, 1999, the eve of the dawn of a new millennium, everyone was thinking about Y2K. Would the millennium bug strike and cause global damage? Would life as we know it be completely upended? As people around the world fretted, time marched on and the new year was met with obligatory fireworks. In Oxford, England, as eyes and ears were focused on lights, pops, and crackles, thieves took advantage, using the Ashmolean Museum's construction-related scaffolding to scale its roof and break in via a skylight. Dropping a smoke bomb into the museum, they shimmied down a rope ladder and used a handheld fan to blow smoke around the gallery to obscure themselves from security cameras and guards. They cut Paul Cézanne's *View of Auvers-sur-Oise* out, broke the frame, and escaped the way they came.

There are various theories about what might have happened to the Cézanne. Alarms did go off when the thieves broke into the museum, but, because of the smoke bomb, guards thought there was a fire. They called police and the fire department, who discovered the reality: the bomb was a smoke-and-mirrors show to distract from the real crime. By the time authorities realized this, the thieves were long gone.

Because only the Cézanne was targeted (works by other luminaries like Toulouse-Lautrec, Rodin, and Renoir were nearby but remained unmolested), some suspect it was stolen to order by or for someone who wanted it particularly. This theory is compelling in the public imagination (perhaps the thieves were inspired by the 1999 movie *Entrapment*, which features an art theft on New Year's Eve), but it is more likely that the painting was stolen with the more mundane aim of sale on the black market.

Iain Pears, a world-renowned art historian and novelist who has written many fictional books about art crime, lived down the street from the Ashmolean on the fateful night when *View of Auvers-sur-Oise* was stolen. He told the *New York Times* about that evening: "We had a card game. The baby started crying, so there I was prowling up and down the street with a screaming baby in the pram. What a pity. If I had been there 10 minutes earlier, I could have helped them [the thieves] load it into the car."

Cézanne's *View of Auvers-sur-Oise* has not been seen since it was stolen in 1999. The theft

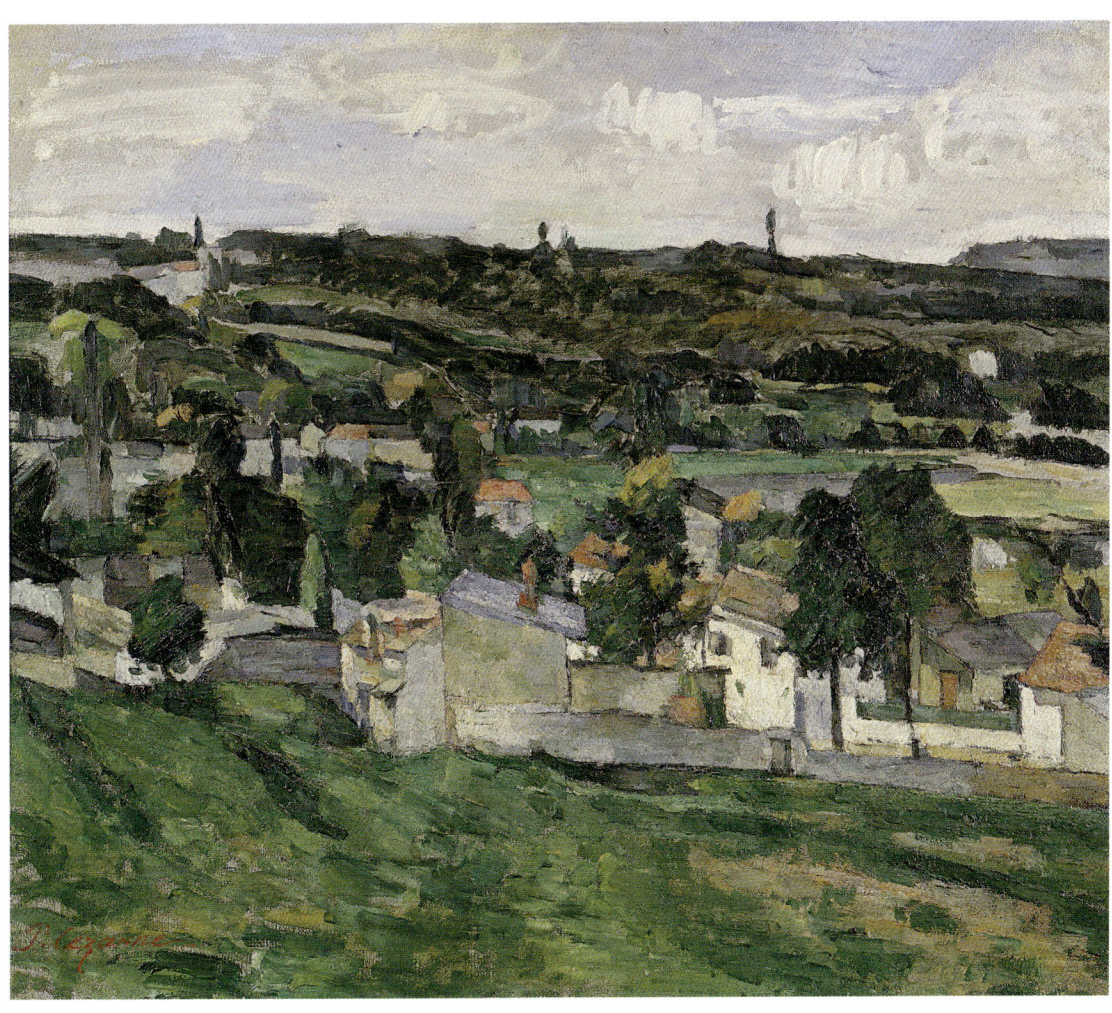

ranks in the FBI's list of Top 10 Art Crimes. Fears over the fallout of Y2K proved to be mostly overblown, but the Ashmolean entered the year 2000 with a glitch in their collection that continues to plague them to this day.

Above: Cézanne's *View of Auvers-sur-Oise* shows a small hamlet in northern France, but the exact location of the view has not been determined. Today, not only is the painting's setting undetermined, but also the painting's location.

When: April 26, 2003

Where: Whitworth Art Gallery at the University of Manchester

What: Theft of Vincent van Gogh's *The Fortification of Paris with Houses* (1887), Pablo Picasso's *Poverty* (1903), and Paul Gauguin's *Tahitian Landscape* (c. 1891–93)

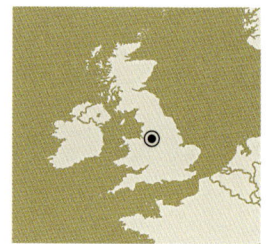

THE LOO-VRE CAPER

Sometime after closing on Saturday, April 26, 2003, a thief (or thieves) entered the Whitworth Art Gallery on the University of Manchester's campus. After smashing through doors at the rear of the museum that were "lightly" barricaded with steel, the burglars avoided security cameras and guards. They made off with a tidy haul of three works of art: Vincent van Gogh's *The Fortification of Paris with Houses*, Pablo Picasso's *Poverty*, and Paul Gauguin's *Tahitian Landscape.* The paintings were worth an estimated £4 million and were among the most prized objects at the Whitworth.

Staff returned to the museum the following day, which felt like a normal Sunday when they opened their doors at noon. Shortly thereafter, they discovered the three watercolor masterpieces were not where they should be. Police were called and the investigation began in earnest. Museum officials feared the worst—if the delicate and fragile watercolors were ever to be retrieved, their condition might be grave.

There was much speculation about who could have committed this crime. Some art-theft experts believed it was the work of an experienced gang who had spent hours studying the museum's security weaknesses. In the hours after the theft was committed, many suspected that the objects had already been smuggled out of the country and put up for sale on the black market or were being held for ransom.

We may never know the reality of who did what and how. But, if we are to believe the thief, we do know why. Police received an anonymous tip on the morning of Monday, April 28, 2003, that the missing paintings had been secreted in an unlikely place for world-class objects of art: a public toilet in Whitworth Park, where police found the three purloined pieces in a cardboard tube. As feared, the watercolors had suffered from exposure to damp. The Van Gogh had a small tear on one corner, but conservators were able to repair most of the damage over time.

Inside the cardboard tube was a note. In marker that was bleeding into the paper (affected, like the watercolors, by moisture), the thief wrote, "The intention was not to steal, only to highlight the woeful security." In this, the thief succeeded. The public toilet where the works of art spent some time became known as the Loo-vre. Admission is free.

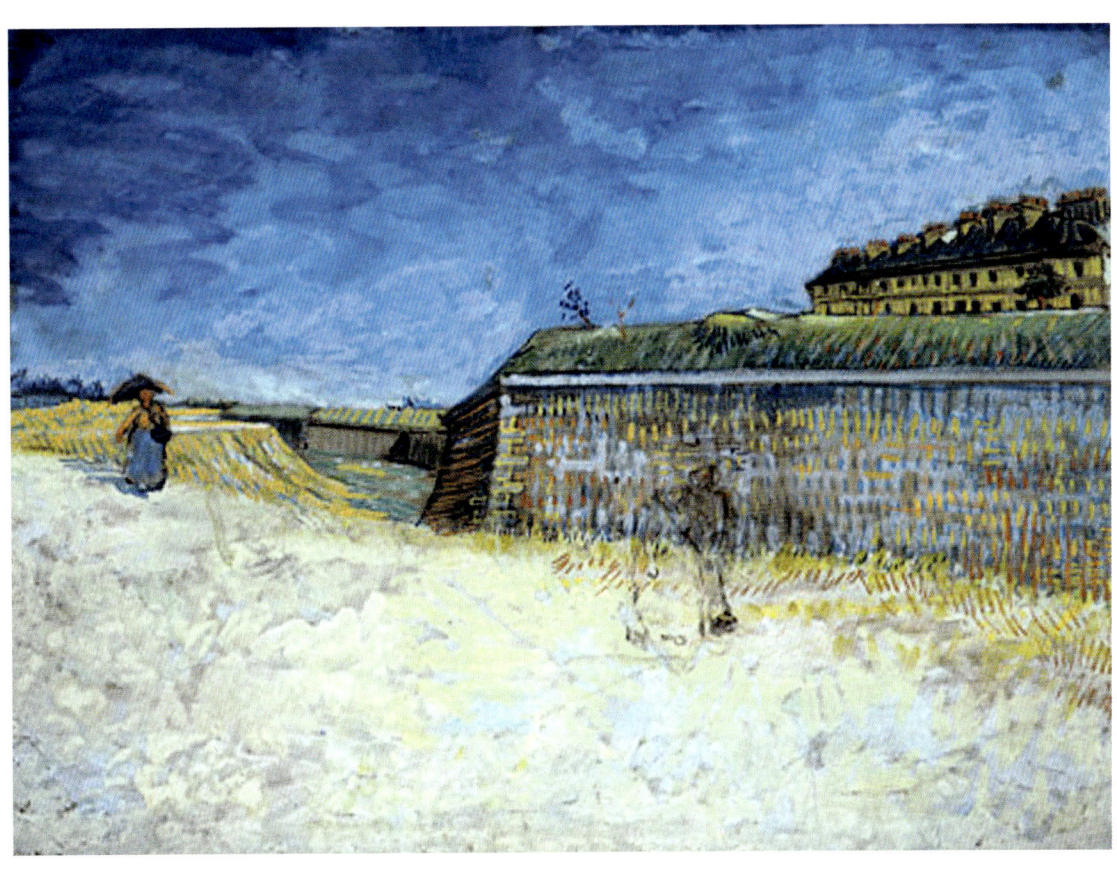

Above: Van Gogh's watercolor *The Fortification of Paris with Houses* depicts the defensive barricades around Paris. Those fortifications failed during the Franco-Prussian War in 1870–71, much like those at the Whitworth Art Gallery failed in 2003.

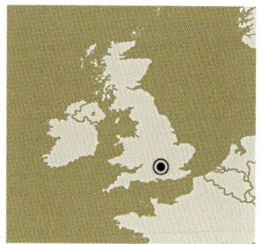

ROYAL FLUSH

Maurizio Cattelan is the court jester of the art world. Though entrenched in the complex and confounding landscape of contemporary art, he offers sarcastic, wry, and witty commentaries on art and life through his sculptures and installations. Oftentimes, the art world itself is the target of his jests, but truthfully, everything and everyone is a target for Cattelan. With his signature provocativeness, he has tackled religion, war, politics, loss, and many other challenging topics with tongue in cheek.

When a sculpture by Cattelan was stolen in 2019, the artist himself was suspected of staging the theft. After all, in 1996 he had broken into an art gallery in Amsterdam, then displayed the pilfered work as his own at a rival gallery in the city. In this heist, Cattelan also stole the gallery's office equipment. Cattelan titled the installation of purloined art and gear *Another Fucking Readymade*. Under threat of arrest by the police, Cattelan returned the stolen goods. So stealing his own work seemed like the sort of thing that this prankster artist might have done.

But Cattelan swears he was not the thief. What was the stolen object? A toilet. And not just any toilet, but an 18-karat gold one. The gold toilet, cheekily titled *America*, was first exhibited in 2016 at the Solomon R. Guggenheim Museum in New York City. Cattelan, who co-founded an art magazine in 2010 named *Toiletpaper*, had the gold toilet installed in a bathroom at the museum. There, visitors (at least 100,000 of them) were able to use it after reserving their spot in advance. Each person was allowed three minutes of communing with *America*.

In 2017, President Trump asked to borrow a Van Gogh in the Guggenheim's collection for the White House. The Guggenheim declined and instead offered President Trump Cattelan's *America*. The White House did not comment on the proposed loan.

In September of 2019, Blenheim Palace—one of the largest and most stately houses in England, perhaps most notable as the birthplace and stomping grounds of Winston Churchill—hosted an exhibition of Cattelan's work. *America* was installed in a working bathroom in the palace. When Edward Spencer-Churchill, the founder of the Blenheim Art Foundation, was asked if he was worried about anyone stealing

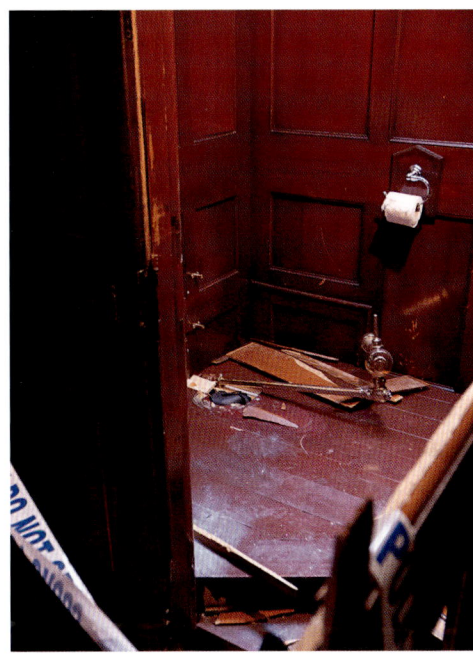

Above: The ripped pipework is all that remained of Maurizio Cattelan's golden throne *America* at Blenheim Palace. Fit for kings, queens, and commoners alike, use of the toilet was included with admission.

America, he told *The Sunday Times* that he was unconcerned because it would not be easy to spirit away. He added, "Firstly, it's plumbed in and secondly, a potential thief will have no idea who last used the toilet or what they ate. So no, I don't plan to be guarding it."

Famous last words. At around 5:00 a.m. on the day after the exhibition's opening event, thieves broke into Blenheim Palace and ripped the toilet out of the bathroom, causing significant damage and flooding. *America*, which could be worth as much as $6 million, has not been seen since. Though seven individuals have been arrested in connection with the theft, only four have been charged with burglary and conspiring to transfer criminal property. The four men were still awaiting sentencing from Oxford magistrates in late 2023. Regardless of

the outcome of the legal proceedings, art-crime experts suspect the worst: that *America* was melted down within twenty-four hours of the theft and sold.

After the theft of Cattelan's *America* in Woodstock, the town nearest to Blenheim Palace, locals had fun with the publicity and created their own versions of *America* by spray-painting mock toilets gold and placing them in prime positions in their pubs and fish-and-chips shops.

Cattelan, however, remains more optimistic about the fate of his sculpture, calling the thieves "great performers," and told the *New York Times*, "I want to be positive and think the robbery is a kind of Robin Hood inspired action." Maybe Cattelan was thinking about other art thefts that had a purpose other than financial gain behind them, such as Kempton Bunton's theft of Goya's *Duke of Wellington* (p. 20) or Mario Roymans's theft of Vermeer's *The Love Letter* (p. 48)—and hoping the same was true of *America*. If the thief were not Robin Hood, then Cattelan suggested that the stately Blenheim Palace might be a good setting for a game of *Clue* and inferred that "the major suspects" in the theft of *America* could be "the butler, the chef, and the house owner."

After suggesting that the toilet thieves might be the real artists, Cattelan wrote in a statement after the theft, "I always liked heist movies and, finally, I'm in one of them." The artist then asked the thieves to let him know if they liked the toilet and how it felt to pee on gold.

Perhaps *Comedian* (first exhibited in December 2019) was created in response to the theft of *America* (stolen in November 2019). Replacing a banana is a lot easier and less expensive than replacing an 18-karat gold toilet (p. 170). Either way, Cattelan is in on the joke.

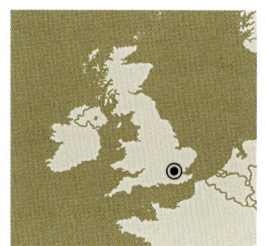

THE TAKEAWAY REMBRANDT

Rembrandt's early *Portrait of Jacob de Gheyn III*—the world's most stolen painting, according to *The Guinness Book of World Records*—has been stolen four times, earning it the nickname "The Takeaway Rembrandt."

Thieves first broke into a small back door of the Dulwich Picture Gallery early on December 31, 1966. Constrained by the size of the door, they targeted eight small paintings, including the Rembrandt, which, at about 11¾ by 9⅞ inches, is not much bigger than a sheet of letter paper. Within a few weeks, police arrested an unemployed ambulance driver, who was sentenced to five years in prison. The paintings were all recovered: some from bushes near the gallery by a man walking his dog, and the Rembrandt and others from underneath a cemetery bench.

The next theft was less ambitious, if not more humorous. In 1973, a man simply walked up to the painting, stuffed it under his shirt, and walked out of the gallery unnoticed. Police tracked him down almost immediately; he escaped by bicycle, carrying the painting in the basket. When police asked why he had stolen the portrait, he said it reminded him of his mother.

The portrait was stolen for a third time in August 1981 by a group of men, who were found a few weeks later with the painting in a taxi.

Finally, in 1983, thieves broke in through a gallery skylight. The museum had upgraded its security alarms and police responded within three minutes, but the Rembrandt and thieves were gone. Three years later, the painting was recovered at the left-luggage office at a train station in Münster, Germany.

The Rembrandt undoubtedly makes for easy pickings, fitting easily into a bike basket, under a shirt, and under a cemetery bench. However, it is extremely difficult to sell such a famous work of art, a common refrain among art thieves.

Opposite: Rembrandt painted *Portrait of Jacob de Gheyn III* and a portrait of de Gheyn's dear friend Maurits Huygens, on two boards cut from the same piece of wood.

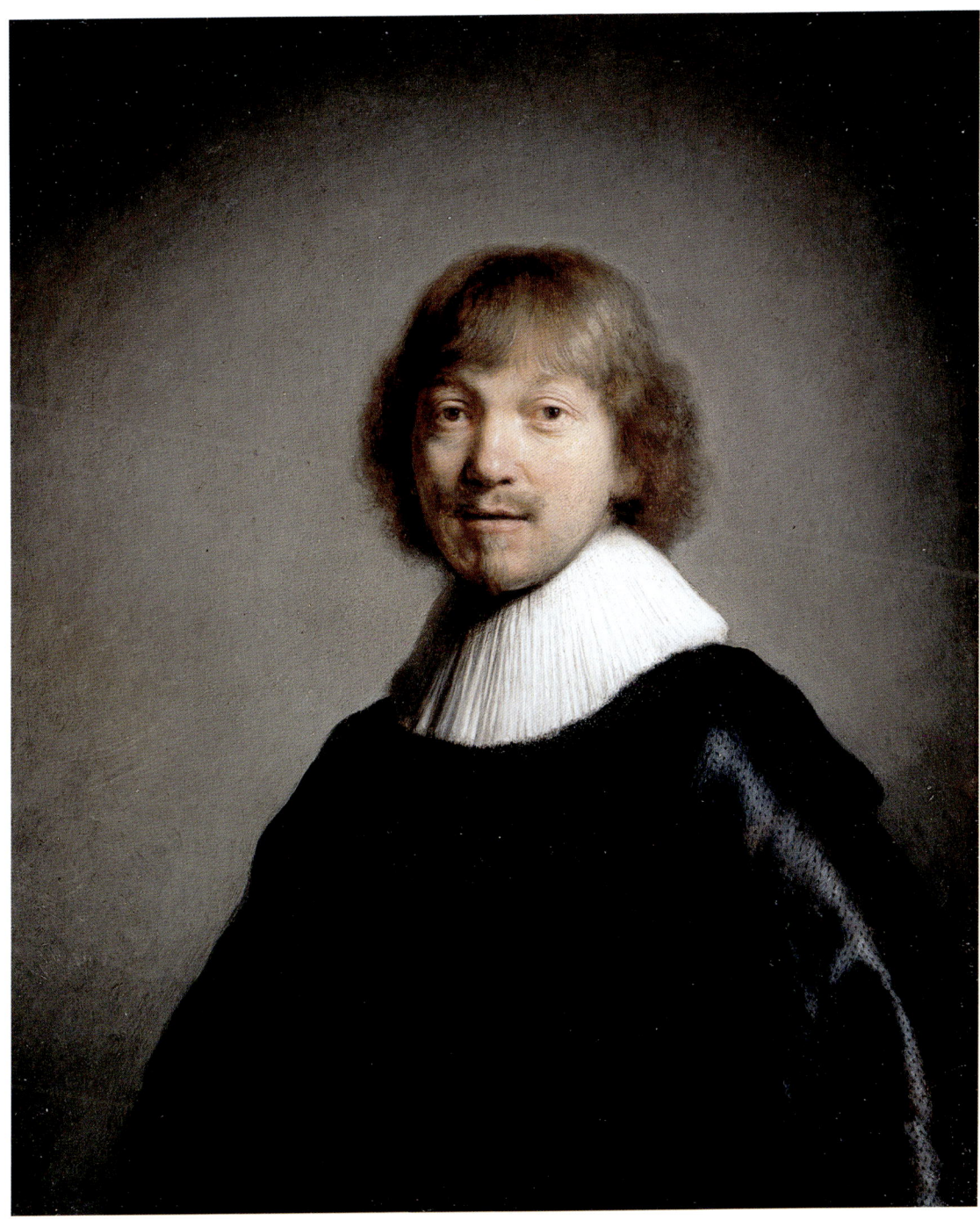

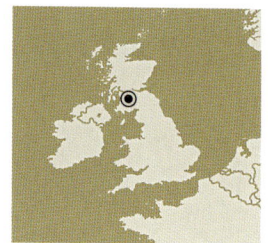

"THIS IS JUST PRACTICE"

Built between 1679 and 1689, Drumlanrig Castle, called the "Pink Palace" for its pink sandstone exterior, is famous for a number of reasons: hosting Bonnie Prince Charlie on December 22, 1745, as he made his way north to the Battle of Culloden; being featured in an episode of *Outlander*; and housing the most important private art collection in Scotland.

The Buccleuch Collection was started many, many generations before the current Duke and Duchess of Buccleuch and Queensberry took charge of Drumlanrig Castle. A star in the Buccleuch Collection is Leonardo da Vinci's *The Madonna of the Yarnwinder*, created around 1501, which entered the family's collection in 1767. In da Vinci's painting, a gigantic baby Jesus is seen playing with a yarnwinder, or spindle, of spun yarn. Significantly, the yarnwinder echoes the shape of the cross that Jesus would later be crucified upon. Baby Jesus looks at it with a sense of awareness, while his mother, Mary, carefully watches her son, her hand raised to steady him. Though art historians disagree about whether Leonardo had help creating the painting (the landscape was probably painted

by another artist), it was valued at around £37 million in 2007.

In 2003, thieves were aware of this jewel. While posing as tourists on a guided tour, they beelined for the painting. With a knife to their eighteen-year-old guide's throat and an axe, the two thieves warned other visitors and employees to stand back as they removed the painting from the wall. As they exited through a window, they told two visitors from New Zealand, "Don't worry love, we're the police. This is just practice." They escaped in a non-descript white Volkswagen Golf. CCTV footage recorded the whole escapade, as had other visitors. But even though the FBI placed the theft on its list of Top 10 Art Crimes, the thieves eluded capture.

In 2007, through an undercover sting operation that led to an extortion trial with many twists and turns, *The Madonna of the Yarnwinder* was returned to Drumlanrig Castle. Five men were arrested in connection with the crime, but all five were given a "not proven" verdict in a Scottish court. The 9th Duke of Buccleuch, who had been alive when *The Madonna of the Yarnwinder* was stolen in 2003, died just a month before its recovery and never

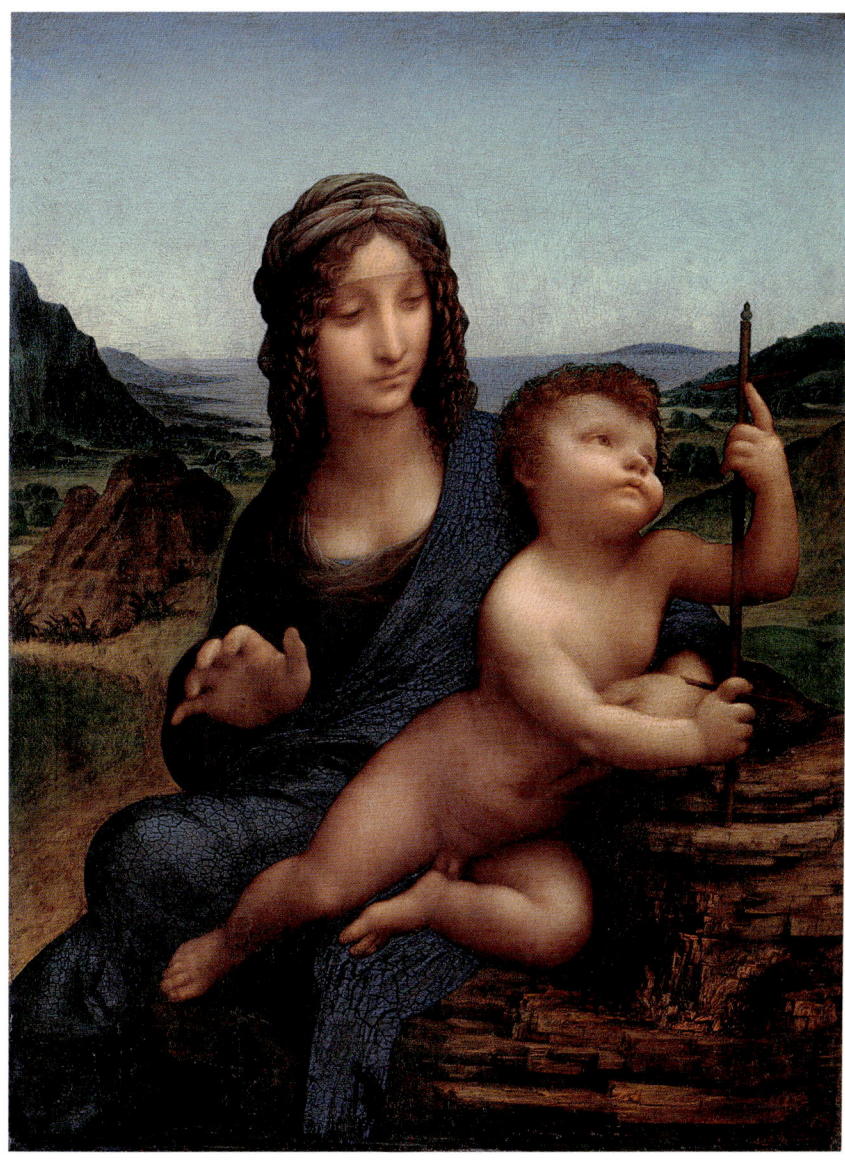

got to see it returned to his castle. In 2009, the 10th Duke of Buccleuch made the decision to loan the painting to the Scottish National Gallery in Edinburgh, where the work remains today. Museum security personnel attentively guard the painting in their care, much like Mary cautiously monitors her son in perpetuity in *The Madonna of the Yarnwinder*.

Above: Also known as *Madonna of the Spindles*, this painting depicts the baby Jesus gazing at a niddy-noddy, or a yarnwinder, a piece of spinning equipment used to wind yarn into a skein.

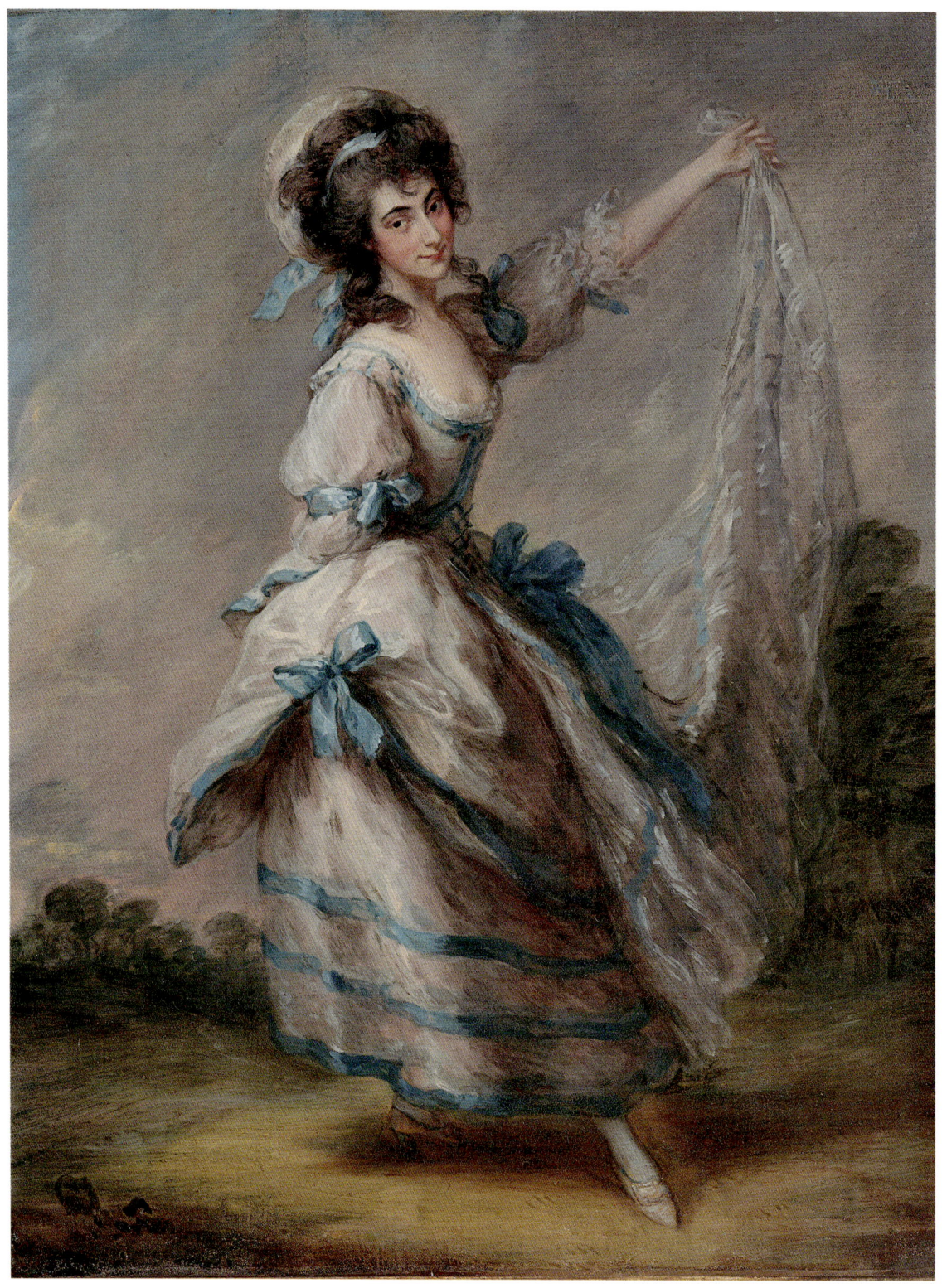

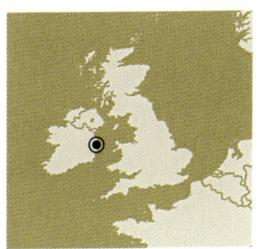

A WELCOME MAT FOR ART THIEVES

If "The Takeaway Rembrandt" (p. 30) was recognized by *The Guinness Book of World Records* for being the most stolen painting, Russborough House might be the home most burgled for its art. The stately County Wicklow home has been robbed on four separate occasions, and forty-four works of art have been stolen, two of which remain missing to this day. Russborough's impressive art collection coupled with a formerly paltry security system made it a compelling target.

Just before 9:00 p.m. on April 27, 1974, thirty-three-year-old British woman Rose Dugdale knocked on the front door, asking in a fake French accent for help with her car. She was followed inside by three male accomplices —a rogue unit of the Irish Republican Army (IRA)—and together they stole nineteen paintings, including a Vermeer, from the collection of Sir Alfred and Clementine Beit, a childless couple who had spent their marriage collecting artworks they called their "children."

Dugdale had been raised in Devon, England, on a similarly lavish estate, living a life of wealth and luxury. She studied at Oxford and earned a PhD in Economics but forsook her entitlements after an ideological awakening. She became a supporter of Irish liberation from the United Kingdom and orchestrated the Russborough theft in order to pressure the government into transferring four IRA prisoners back to Ireland. Dugdale promised that after the prisoners were transferred she would return five of the nineteen paintings. Though Dugdale had supposedly renounced capitalism, she demanded £500,000 to return the rest of the stolen goods.

The heist was the largest art theft at that time. Eight days later, the Irish Gardaí discovered Dugdale and all nineteen paintings in a rented cottage near Cork and sentenced her to nine years in prison. The media had a field day with headlines such as "Rich Girl Rebels," but the

Opposite: Thomas Gainsborough's portrait of the esteemed Venetian ballerina Giovanna Baccelli has been stolen on three separate occasions from Russborough House.

IRA renounced claims that she had stolen the paintings on their behalf.

Dugdale remains the only known female mastermind of an art heist. To this day she is unrepentant. Anthony Amore, author of *The Woman who Stole Vermeer*, reported that Dugdale, in her seventies at the time, was using *Lady Writing a Letter with Her Maid*—one of the paintings she had stolen in 1974—as her social media profile picture.

Dugdale's theft inspired Irish gangster Martin "The General" Cahill to steal from the same home in 1986. After the 1974 theft, the Beits installed a state-of-the-art security system, but it did not stop "The General." In the wee hours of May 1, Cahill and a team of thirteen men, notorious for exacting and calculated heists,

set off the Russborough House security system by removing a back window. One man entered the house, deactivated sensors to allow re-entry later, and then replaced the window on his way out. When police arrived and found nothing amiss, they called it a false alarm and left. Cahill and his cronies, who had been waiting half a mile away, then returned to the house, stealing eighteen paintings in six minutes. Again the Vermeer was taken, along with a Gainsborough (also first stolen by Dugdale), a Goya, and fifteen other paintings.

The day after the theft, seven of the stolen paintings were found by boys fishing nearby. In the ensuing years, one painting was found in Turkey, another three in London, four in Belgium, and one in a suburb of Dublin.

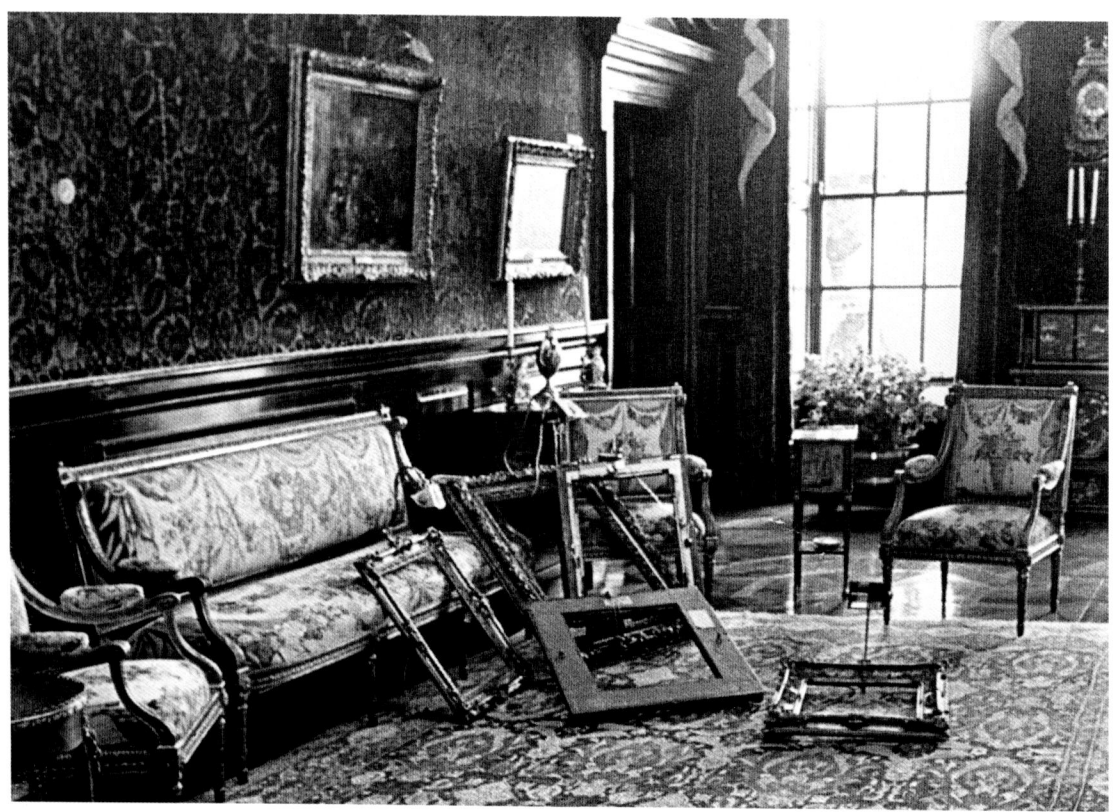

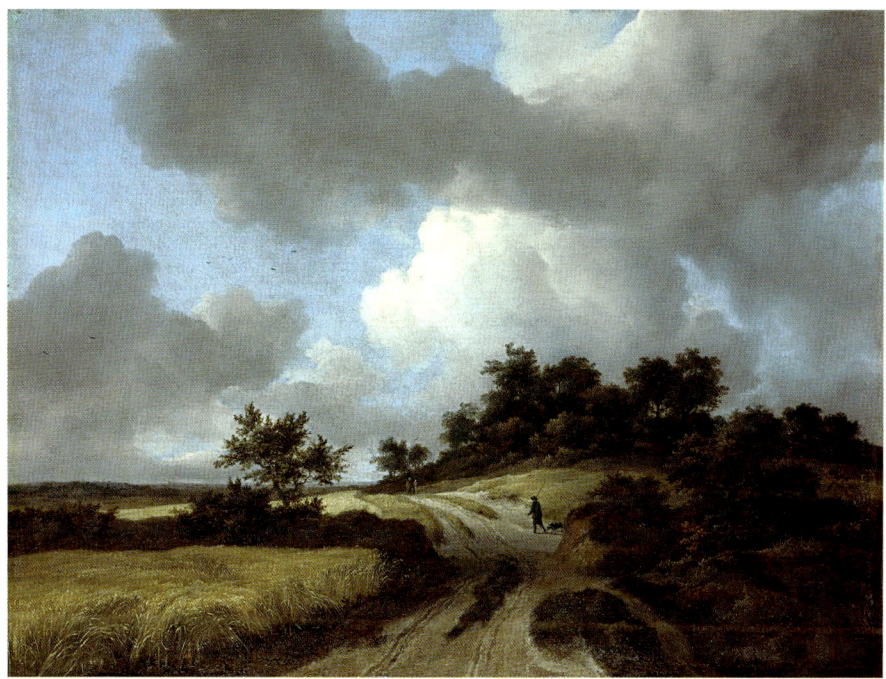

Opposite: Empty frames neatly rest on furniture at Russborough House after the 1974 theft of nineteen paintings by Rose Dugdale and company.

Above: After being stolen three times from Russborough House, Jacob van Ruisdael's *The Cornfield* was transferred to the Ulster Museum in Belfast, where it now resides.

Two eighteenth-century paintings of Venice by the Italian artist Francesco Guardi have not yet been recovered. Cahill, the mastermind of the theft, never served time for the Russborough heist; he was assassinated in 1994.

In 1987, the Beits donated seventeen of their most valuable paintings to the National Gallery of Ireland in Dublin, hoping that it would make Russborough House a less attractive target. It did not. In 2001, three people rammed through the front door of the Palladian-style stately home with a Jeep and stole two paintings: a scene of Florence by Bellotto and Gainsborough's portrait of the Venetian ballerina Madame Baccelli, which was taken for the third time, making it a close rival of "The Takeaway Rembrandt" for the most stolen painting. Both paintings were recovered a year later.

In 2002, Russborough was again broken into: a husband-and-wife team stole five paintings and hid them in clothing in their attic. Jacob van Ruisdael's *The Cornfield* was stolen for the third time, making the Gainsborough and the van Ruisdael tied for the most stolen works in the Beit Collection. All five paintings were recovered by the Gardaí within a few months.

In 2015, many more works of art were sold. After surviving four thefts and being stolen three times, Gainsborough's *Madame Baccelli* remains a fixture at Russborough, warily watching over the few remaining masterpieces as she gets ready to perform her ballet. The show must go on.

When: August 21, 1911

Where: Musée du Louvre in Paris

What: Theft of Leonardo da Vinci's *Mona Lisa* (c. 1503–19)

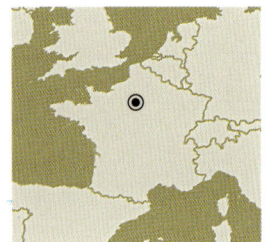

THE THEFT THAT MADE THE *MONA LISA*

The *Mona Lisa* is one of the most recognizable faces in the world with her enigmatic, puzzling smile. But she wasn't always as famous as she is today. In fact, she was mostly forgotten until she was catapulted into fame in the early 1900s—not because of her existence but her absence.

Who had the gall to steal the *Mona Lisa*? The mastermind of the scheme was Vincenzo Peruggia, a handyman for the Louvre who had built the portrait's behemoth 200-pound frame and case. Peruggia grew up outside of Milan and moved to Paris with his two brothers. The scrappy Italian aspired to more than construction work. Before the theft of the *Mona Lisa*, he had a few brushes with the law and was arrested for trying to fleece a prostitute and for bringing a gun to a fistfight. Even his brothers nicknamed him "the madman." His French fellow construction workers bullied him, called him "macaroni eater," and salted his wine during breaks.

One Sunday night, Peruggia and his two brothers, Lancelotti and Michele, snuck into the Louvre wearing white workmen's smocks. Sunday nights were big social nights in Paris, so most people were out drinking. And on Mondays they were all hungover and the museum was closed, which gave the thieves plenty of time to sneak out. From Sunday to Monday, they waited in a tiny storeroom. They stripped off the *Mona Lisa*'s heavy case and frame, wrapped the panel in a blanket, and hustled off to the train station, where they traveled home to the Parisian outskirts.

Twenty-eight hours later, the first person to notice the missing painting was a visiting artist who liked to paint in the gallery. He complained that he couldn't work without the *Mona Lisa* watching over him but wasn't worried that she was missing as a big project to photograph the entire collection was underway.

Opposite: With a face and smile known around the world, da Vinci's *Mona Lisa* needs little introduction.

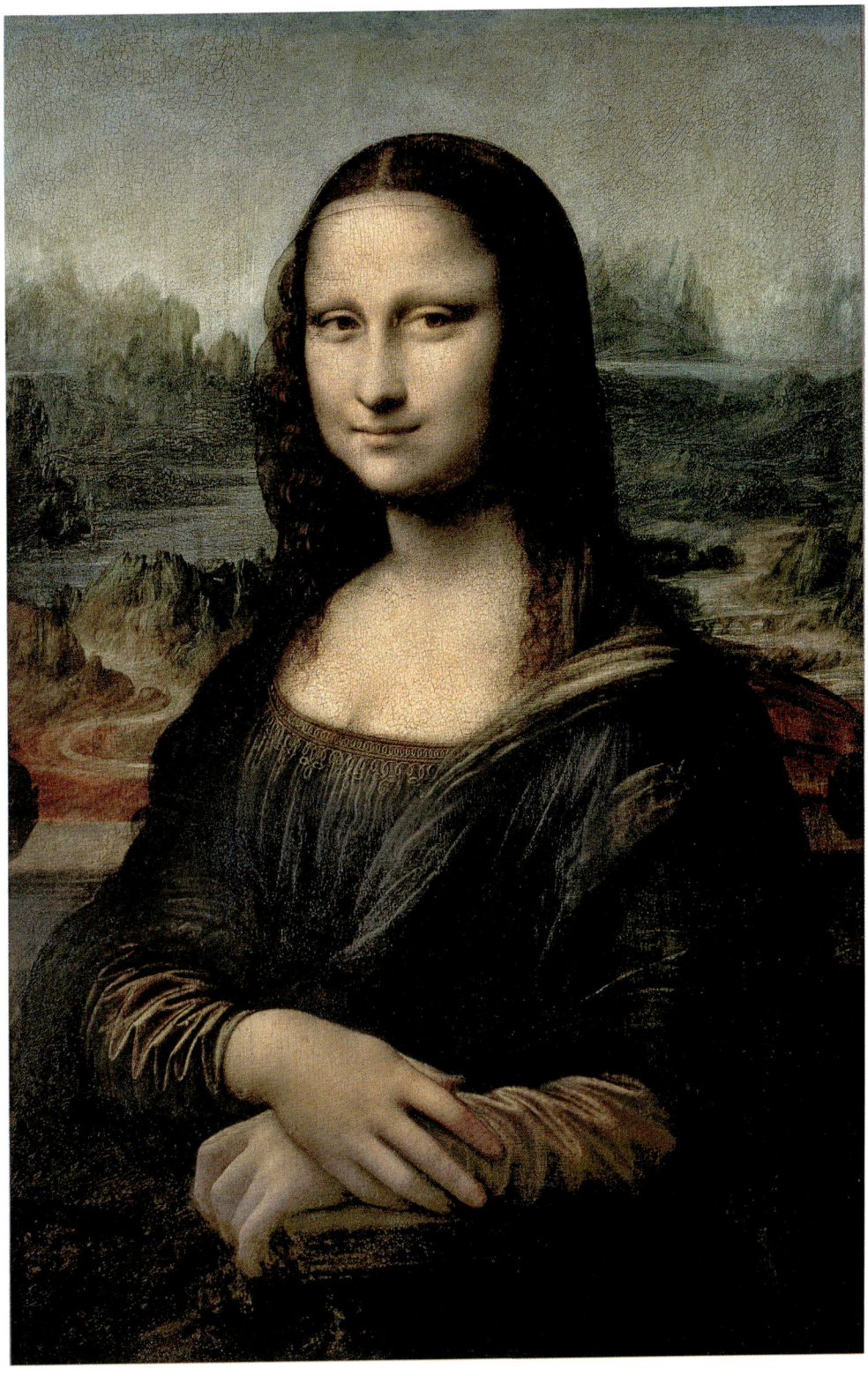

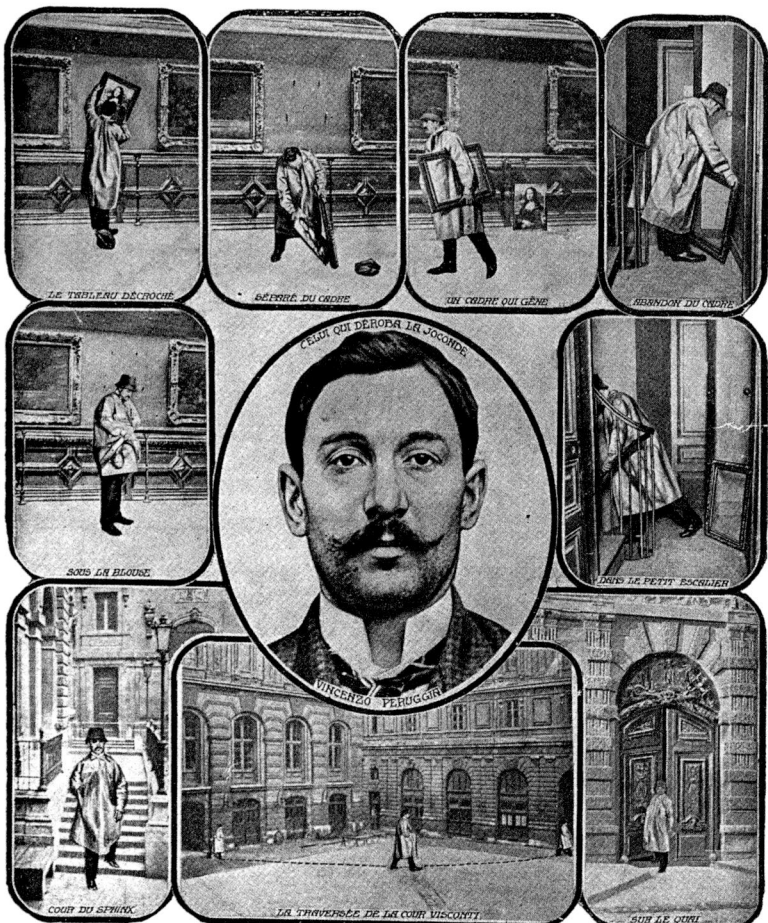

In 1911 photography was still relatively new, and artworks had to be taken to the roof to photograph them in natural light.

A guard went to the roof to find out how long the photographers would have the *Mona Lisa*. When she wasn't there, her disappearance launched her into international fame. The media jumped upon the theft and broadcast breathless updates. After closing for a week, the Louvre reopened to throngs of visitors wanting to see where the *Mona Lisa* had once been.

What was Vincenzo Peruggia up to while the swell of interest in the *Mona Lisa* ballooned? He could never have anticipated the attention: photos of the *Mona Lisa* all over Paris; Vaudeville shows mocking the theft; a short film produced; postcards sold; songs sung. Crowds waited outside police headquarters. The painting was now too famous to do anything with, and it remained in a false-bottomed trunk in Peruggia's boarding house. In November 1911, Peruggia was questioned along with other Louvre employees, but he proclaimed his innocence, saying he had been drunk on Sunday night and late to work on Monday because of a hangover.

Twenty-eight months after the theft, Peruggia left Paris on a train to Florence with the *Mona Lisa* tucked away in his trunk. At his hotel,

Peruggia made overtures to a Florentine art dealer, who became suspicious and consulted with the head of an Italian gallery. A stamp on the back of the painting proved it was the real *Mona Lisa*. The men congratulated Peruggia for his good work and asked him to leave the painting with them so they could prepare a reward. Half an hour later, police arrived at Peruggia's hotel to arrest him.

Peruggia believed that Napoleon had stolen the painting from Italy during the Napoleonic Wars. In court, Peruggia claimed that he was a patriot trying to return the painting to his homeland. Except Napoleon hadn't stolen anything: Leonardo had lived in France in his dying years and the painting had been acquired legally by King Francis I. Peruggia then claimed that he was in love with the *Mona Lisa* and had fallen victim to her smile. He was sentenced to eight months in prison.

The *Mona Lisa* was returned to the Louvre with much fanfare. In a book about the *Mona Lisa*, Dianne Hales wrote, "Something beyond the painting's wild popularity had changed. The *Mona Lisa* had left the Louvre a work of art; she returned as a public property, the first mass art icon." As we will see in the "Vandalism" chapter of this book (p. 134), being an art icon does not come without its own troubles. Regardless of what she has been subjected to, the *Mona Lisa* remains unfazed, smiling placidly from her frame.

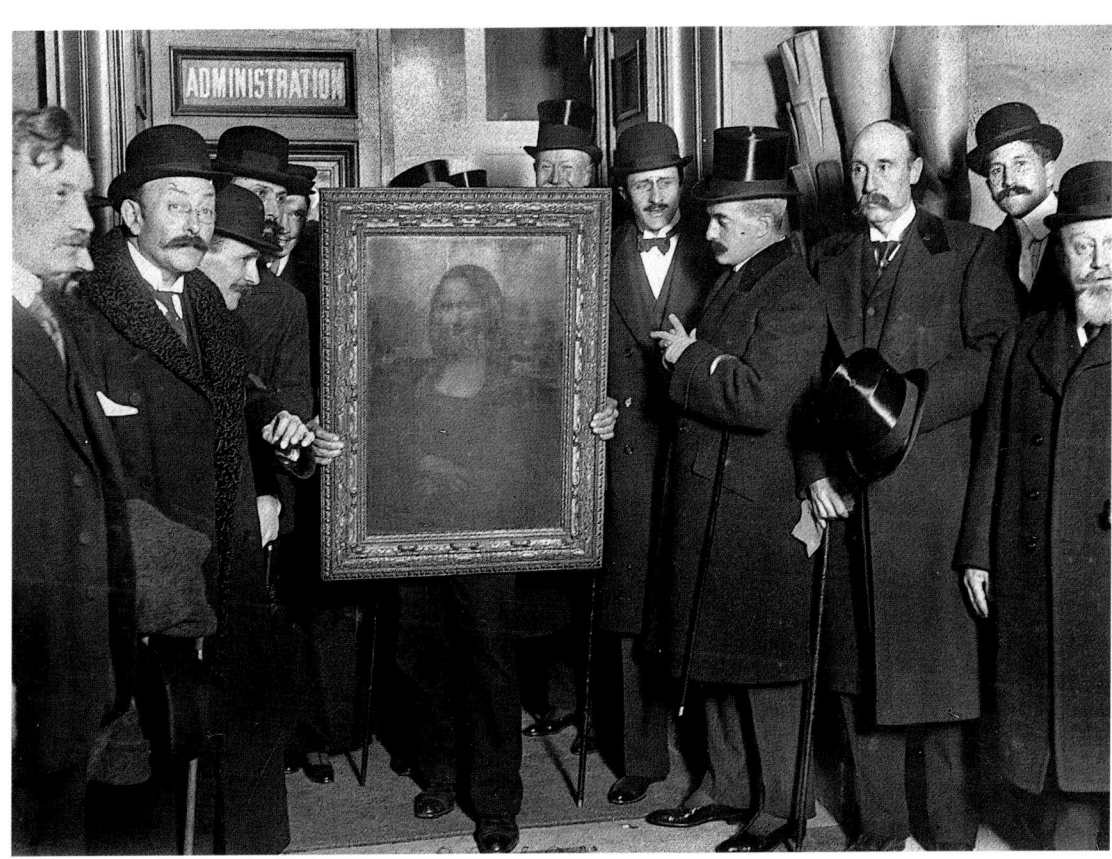

When: May 20, 2010

Where: Musée d'Art Moderne in Paris

What: Theft of Henri Matisse's *Pastoral* (1906), Georges Braque's *Olive Tree near l'Estaque* (1906), Pablo Picasso's *Dove with Green Peas* (1911), Fernand Léger's *Still Life with Candlestick* (1922), and Amedeo Modigliani's *Woman with Fan* (1919)

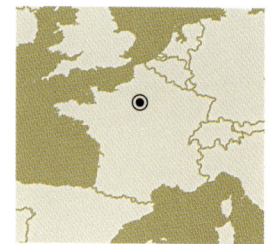

THE SPIDER-MAN THEFT

In 2011, when Vjeran Tomic was asked what his role was in the 2010 theft of five paintings from the Musée d'Art Moderne de Paris (MAM), he replied, "What role did I have? Arsène Lupin." Referencing the fictional character created by Maurice Leblanc in the early 1900s, Tomic aligned himself with the gentleman thief turned detective in Leblanc's stories. As a consummate cat burglar of wealthy Parisians' homes, there certainly seems to be some overlap.

As a born climber, Vjeran's burglary skills were exceptional. He would spend weeks breaking into the same apartment to sniff out the most expensive items before making off with his haul. After dreaming that he stole five paintings, Tomic made his dream come true by breaking into the MAM Paris. After some interior and exterior reconnaissance work, Tomic visited a business associate who ran a small gallery in Paris. For years, Jean Michel Corvez would launder and sell the gold, jewelry, and occasional painting that Tomic would bring him. When Tomic shared his vision, Corvez urged him on, even asking that Tomic steal a Fernand Léger for him for $40,000.

Tomic worked over six nights on May 14–20, 2010, to strip the screws from an exterior window of the museum. On the 20th, he successfully removed the window with suction cups and made his move, taking a Fernand Léger for Corvez, as well as a Matisse, a Modigliani, a Picasso, and a Braque. In two trips, Tomic carried his selections from the museum to his getaway car. He delivered the Léger to Corvez, who agreed to store the paintings. Paris was in a panic over the five lost masterpieces, worth at the time more than $70 million.

A witness provided a description of the suspect, Tomic, whom police surveilled for many months, watching as he bought gear to break into the Centre Pompidou, Paris (though he eventually decided against the job). Police also tapped Tomic's phone and even tried calling him; his voicemail instructed, "If you want to buy paintings or works of art, or exceptional jewelry, do not hesitate to contact me. Among the many paintings, there are five that are extremely expensive."

Armed with the evidence, police arrested Tomic and raided Corvez's gallery and the watch shop of a third man, Yonathan Birn, who had

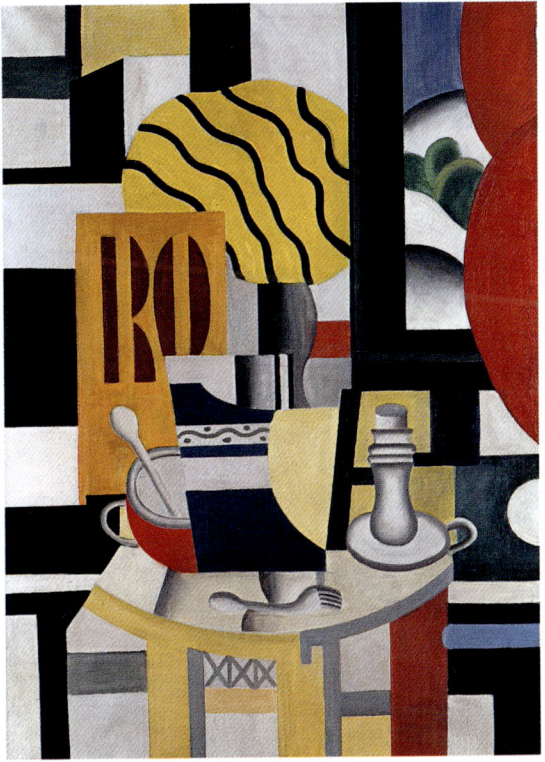

Above: Raised in a family of cattle farmers, Fernand Léger painted *Still Life with Candlestick* after fighting in the trenches of World War I. Léger wanted his modernist art to be accessible to his fellow soldiers.

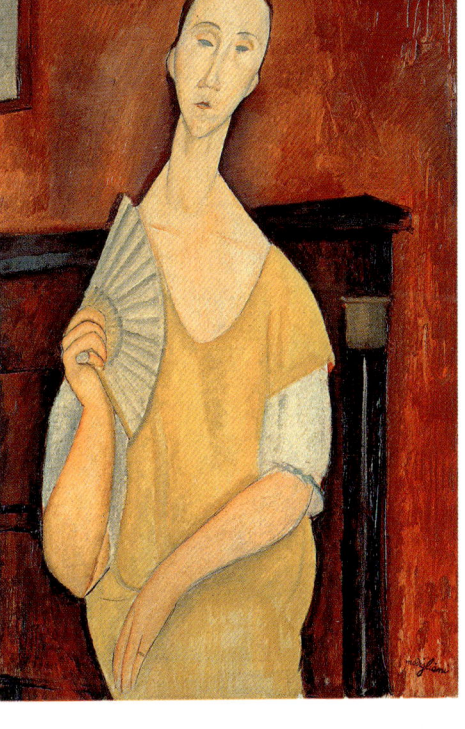

Above: Though Vjeran Tomic was drawn to another Modigliani, *Woman with Blue Eyes*, he instead stole *Woman with a Fan*, after feeling that the first painting would bring him bad luck. So much for instinct.

been pulled in by Corvez to help sell the stolen paintings. Birn claims that, after the raid, he tore up the hidden paintings and threw the pieces in the garbage.

Nicknamed "Spider-Man" by the French press, Tomic was sentenced to eight years in prison, Corvez to seven, and Birn to six. As for the five stolen paintings, they remain missing, though not everyone buys Birn's claim that he destroyed them. Many believe he had already sold the paintings or hidden them before he was arrested, meaning that the paintings might still be out there in the world, waiting to be found. Where is Arsène Lupin when you really need him?

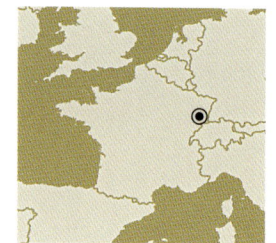

THE PATHOLOGICAL THIEF

Stéphane Breitwieser appeared to many to be an unassuming-looking waiter from France. But under the surface of banality bubbled Stéphane's secret: he was an art thief of grandiose proportions. Breitwieser has admitted to stealing almost 240 objects from nearly 180 different museums throughout Europe between 1995 and 2001, averaging a theft every fifteen days. After his hidden identity as a wildly successful art thief was exposed, his clandestine hobby earned him titles such as "the world's greatest" (*GQ*), "the world's most successful" (*Hyperallergic*), "the world's most prolific" (*Observer*), and "the world's most consistent" (*Guardian*) art thief.

With a cache estimated at $1.4 billion, Breitwieser appears to be an art thief who is unmotivated by profit. He never tried to sell any of his ill-gotten objects before 2001, keeping them in his always-locked bedroom at his mother's home. Instead of money, Breitwieser was driven by a compulsion to possess objects that were beautiful and captivating to him. In a 2019 *GQ* article, Breitwieser explained, "The pleasure of having is stronger than the fear of stealing."

With the help of his girlfriend, Anne-Catherine Kleinklauss, who acted as his lookout, Breitwieser targeted small museums with limited security. In broad daylight and using a variety of tools and techniques, Breitwieser would cart away objects of different sizes and mediums, but usually all were created before the Industrial Revolution. The most valuable piece in Breitwieser's collection was a sixteenth-century double wedding portrait of a bride and groom by Lucas Cranach the Younger.

On a hot streak in 2001, Breitwieser, seemingly untouchable, stole a sixteenth-century bugle from the Richard Wagner Museum in Lucerne, Switzerland. Kleinklauss slipped away after the theft, but Breitwieser was nabbed by police. They initially suspected he was just a petty criminal, though soon realized they had a pathological thief on their hands. French and Swiss police searched the home of Breitwieser's mother, Mireille, in Mulhouse, France, but found nothing except the braided cord of the Wagner bugle.

Meanwhile, someone strolling along the Rhône-Rhine Canal, which runs through Mulhouse, noticed a shiny object in the water

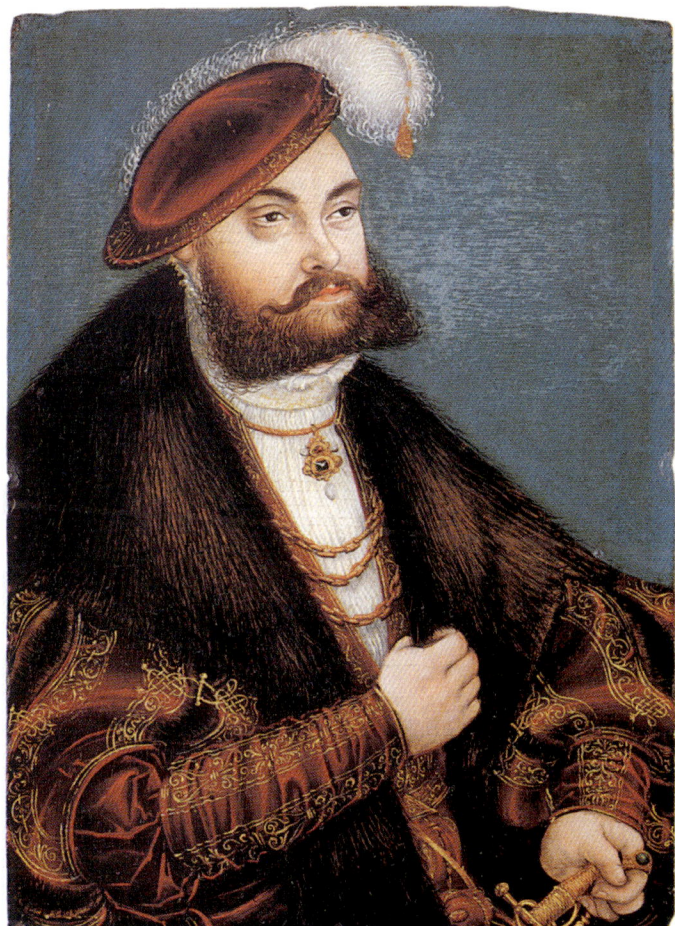

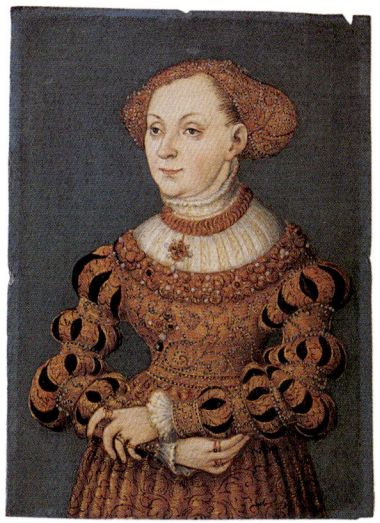

Left and Above: Painted in the sixteenth century by Lucas Cranach the Younger, these portraits show Johann Friedrich, elector of Saxony, and his wife, Sibylle of Cleves. Sibylle's younger sister, Anne, would become the fourth wife of King Henry VIII. A painting of Anne by the famed painter Hans Holbein the Younger hangs in the Louvre. The portrait of Sibylle was stolen during a Sotheby's auction preview in Baden-Baden, Germany.

and fished out a gold chalice, pieces of silver, and a jeweled dagger before telling the police. The police dredged the canal and found a cornucopia of objects, all stolen by Breitwieser. After hearing from Kleinklauss that her son was in prison for stealing from museums, Mireille had pre-empted the police raid. In a fit of rage and fear, she had thrown her son's beloved objects in the canal and claimed that she destroyed his paintings in the garbage disposal or burned them in a bonfire. In prison, when Breitwieser heard the fate of his treasures, he was so devastated that he was medicated and placed on suicide watch.

In 2005, Breitwieser was sentenced to three years in prison, as was his mother for destroying evidence. Out of jail, it didn't take long for Breitwieser to succumb to his compulsions to possess art. In 2011, he was jailed for another three years after police raided his home and found thirty new stolen objects. Breitwieser was arrested again in 2019 for the same reason. Old habits die hard. In Breitwieser's case, you can take the art away from the thief, but you can't keep the thief away from the art.

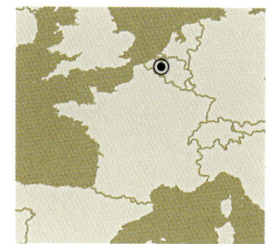

When: April 10, 1934

Where: Saint Bavo's Cathedral in Ghent

What: Theft of a panel from Hubert and Jan van Eyck's *Ghent Altarpiece*, or *Adoration of the Mystic Lamb* (c. 1432)

THE LOST SHEEP

The *Ghent Altarpiece*, or *Adoration of the Mystic Lamb*, by Hubert and Jan van Eyck, has been coveted and stolen by many, including Napoleon and Hitler—two of the most rapacious art thieves in history. The altarpiece has also suffered additional humiliations in its nearly six hundred years: it was almost destroyed in a fire (twice), censored, taken apart, sold by the Diocese of Ghent, stolen by German troops in World War I, and forged.

The twelve-panel altarpiece weathered these storms with the equanimity and grace of the Biblical characters it depicts. Except for one incident. On April 10, 1934, a thief broke into Saint Bavo's Cathedral and stole one of the panels from the lower left of the altarpiece—*The Just Judges*, which depicted Saint John the Baptist on one side and a number of figures of the 1400s on the other (possibly including a portrait of the two artists).

The thief sent twelve ransom notes. The first was mailed to the Bishop of Ghent, asking for one million Belgian francs. When this demand was refused, the second note was sent to the Belgian government, which took over negotiations. To show their seriousness, the thief divided the stolen panel in half vertically and left the Saint John the Baptist side at the Ghent train station's luggage claim. By October 1934, ten more ransom notes were sent, with no progress made.

In November 1934, a stockbroker named Arsène Goedertier confessed on his deathbed that he had stolen *The Just Judges*. With his last breaths, he told his lawyer to look in his desk drawer, which contained carbon copies of the ransom notes and a draft of a new ransom note. The unsent ransom note read, "*The Just Judges* is in a place where neither I nor anyone else can take it without drawing the public's attention."

And then Goedertier died.

One hundred years later, *The Just Judges* has still not been found, but not for lack of trying. During World War II, Joseph Goebbels wanted to find the panel and gift it to his Führer, sending a Nazi detective to investigate. The detective wrote a 180-page report on his unsuccessful attempts. In a less thorough but more mystical approach in 1995, an amateur gumshoe dug up Goedertier's skull and held a séance, hoping Goedertier's ghost would finish his deathbed confession. Detectives have realized that

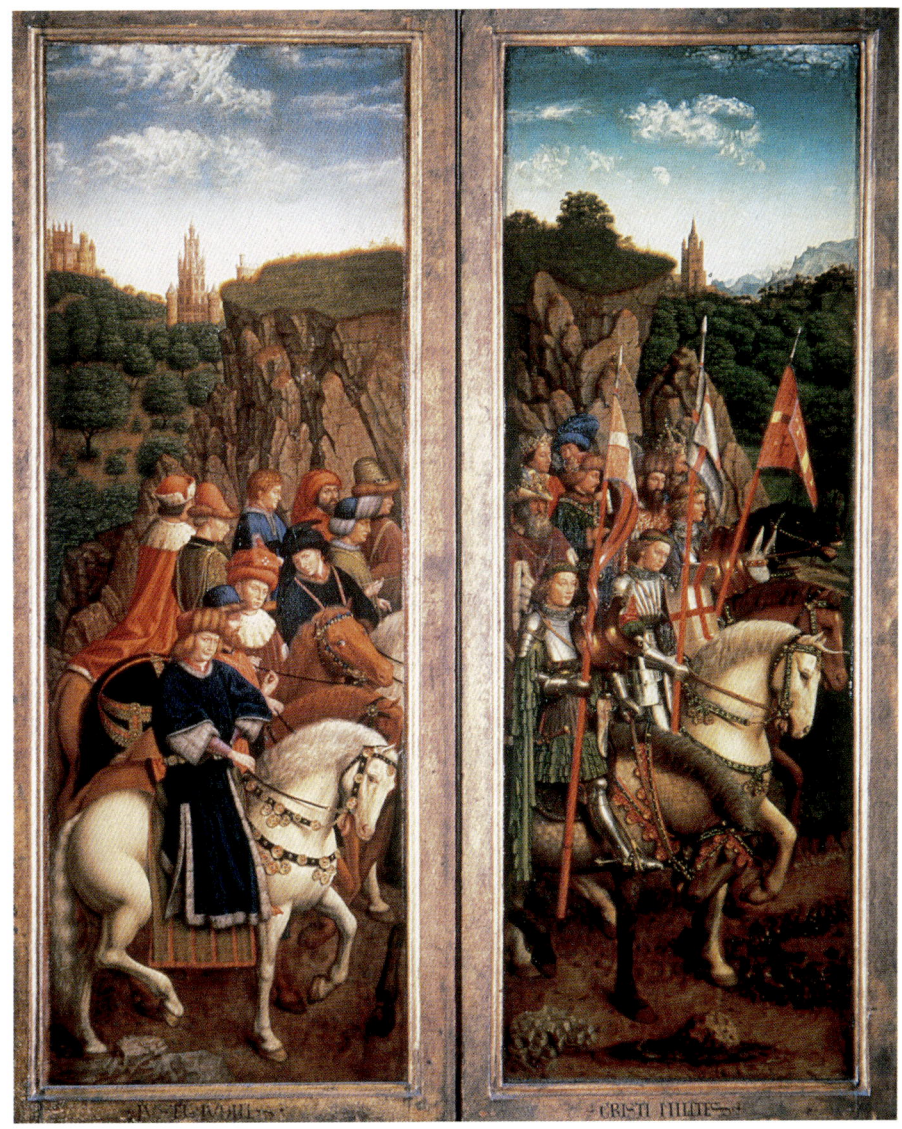

Goedertier couldn't have acted alone in the theft due to an eye condition and because the height of the altarpiece would have required more than one thief. Who, then, were the other thieves?

The Ghent police have received hundreds of tips about the panel, but it remains hidden. To this day, a detective of the Ghent police force continues to work on the case, trying to bring the *Adoration of the Mystic Lamb* back to its flock.

Above: During World War II, the Belgian art restorer (and sometimes art forger) Jef Van der Veken was tasked with creating a copy of *The Just Judges* panel after it was stolen.

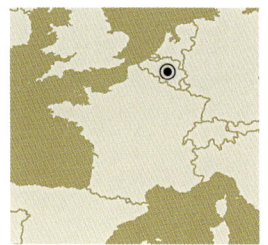

THE BELGIAN ROBIN HOOD OF ART CRIME

In 1971, a twenty-one-year-old Belgian man named Mario Pierre Roymans was distraught while watching and reading the news. He struggled to comprehend the images on television and in newspapers of the Bangladesh Liberation War. While the world watched the horrific treatment of Bengali refugees in what was then East Pakistan, George Harrison and Ravi Shankar held a concert on August 1, along with other all-star performers like Bob Dylan and Eric Clapton, to raise awareness of and provide funds to the Bangladeshi refugees. Perhaps moved by this arts-led charity concert, Roymans hit upon another art-motivated idea to raise money to help the Bangladeshis' plight. Inspired by the folk hero Robin Hood, Roymans decided he needed to steal from the rich to help the poor.

To do this, on September 23, Roymans locked himself inside an electrical cabinet at the Centre for Fine Arts (BOZAR) in Brussels. He waited until the museum was closed before popping out to steal Johannes Vermeer's *The Love Letter*, a treasure on loan from the Rijksmuseum in Amsterdam. The Vermeer was part of an exhibition on the Dutch Masters of the seventeenth century, *Rembrandt and His Age*, which included 136 works by the likes of Rembrandt, Frans Hals, Pieter de Hooch, and Jan Steen. Foiled by the small size of the window he had planned to escape from and the unexpectedly large frame of the Vermeer, Roymans used a linoleum knife to roughly cut the painting out of its frame. He rolled the canvas up, slipped it under the waistband of his pants, and hopped out of the window. Roymans managed to elude the four unarmed guards who were on duty at the museum at the time and took a taxi home.

Like Stéphane Breitwieser (p. 44), the prolific art thief who paid his bills by working as a hotel waiter, Roymans worked as a server at the Soete-Way Hotel in nearby Heusden-Zolder. After the theft, Roymans returned to his room at the hotel and hid the painting there. Worried about being caught with the painting that the media was reporting to be worth two million francs, Roymans buried the Vermeer in nearby

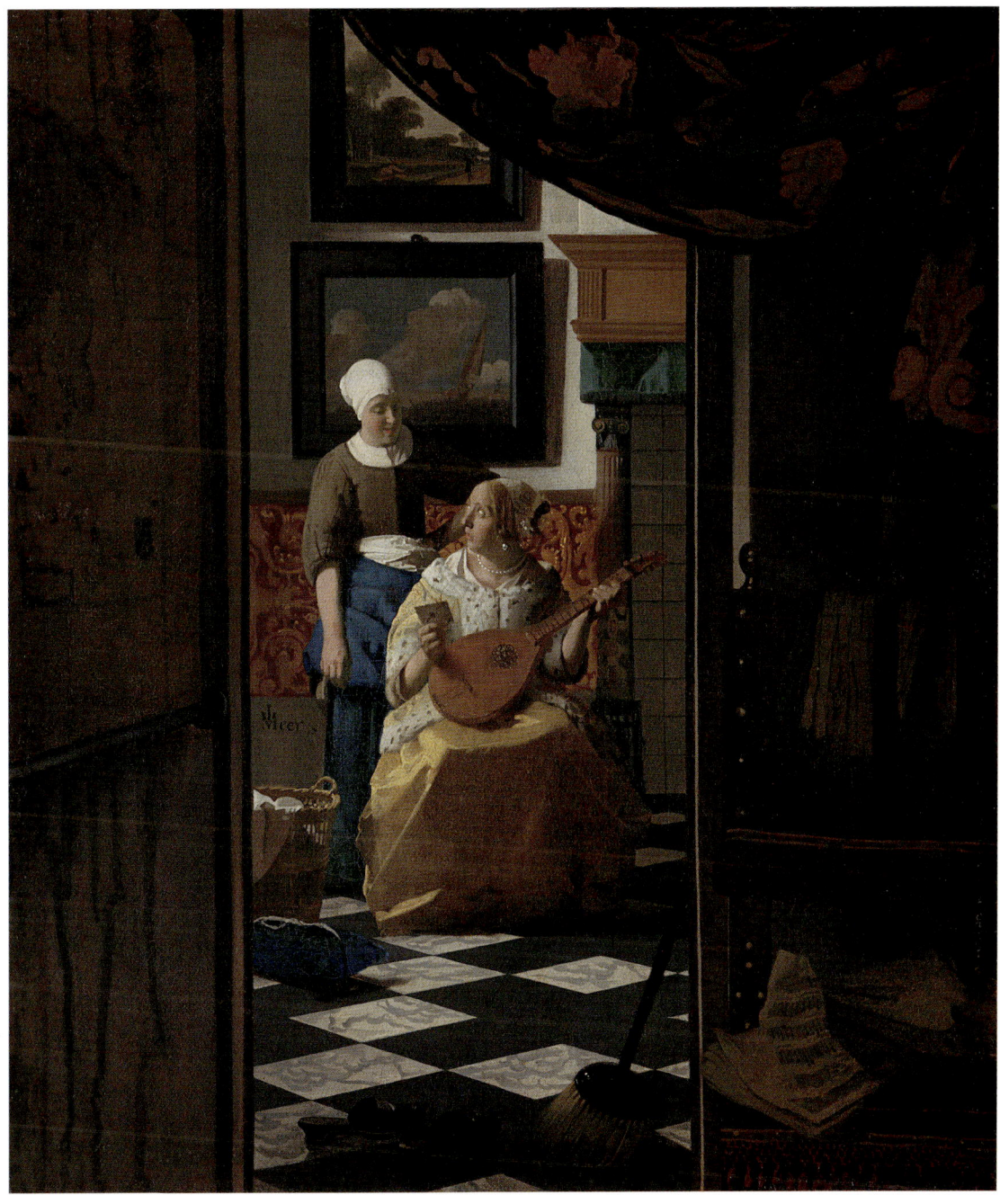

Above: In Vermeer's *The Love Letter*, a mistress holds a note while exchanging expectant looks about what it could contain with her maidservant. Perhaps it was a warning of the painting's future theft in 1971.

woods. When it started raining, Roymans went back to the woods to fetch the painting, which he put into his pillowcase and hid underneath his mattress.

On October 3, Roymans messaged the Belgian newspaper *Le Soir* to make his demands, using the name "Tijl van Limburg," an amalgamation of the Flemish folk hero Tijl Uilenspiegel and Limburg, the Belgian province where Roymans lived.

Roymans asked for a *Le Soir* reporter to meet him at a nearby church. After meeting there, Roymans blindfolded the reporter and drove him into the woods, where Roymans revealed the stolen Vermeer and let the reporter take photos of the painting in the car's headlights. He told the reporter that although he loved art, he loved humanity more, and he asked *Le Soir* to publish his demands for the return of the Vermeer: 200 million francs to be sent to the Bengali refugees suffering in East Pakistan. He also asked that the Centre for Fine Arts in Brussels and the Rijksmuseum in Amsterdam start campaigns to fight world hunger. The newspaper published his demands and launched Tijl van Limburg into the national consciousness. Roymans's campaign was met by the public with sympathy and encouragement. Roymans, perhaps enjoying the showmanship, upped the ante by phoning another Belgian newspaper, *Het Volk*, and threatening that if his ransom demands were not agreed to during a live TV broadcast, he would sell the Vermeer to a hungry American collector.

POTTY TALK

....

Roymans's idealistic art theft puts him in league with other Robin Hood-like characters who committed art crimes for larger, social justice-related purposes, such as Kempton Bunton (p. 23), Rose Dugdale (p. 35), Mary Richardson (p. 136), and Tom Keating (p. 182). Roymans tied himself to the legendary Belgian hero Tijl Uilenspiegel, a fictional character from European folklore, dating back to 1510. In Belgium, Tijl Uilenspiegel is often depicted as a symbol of Belgian resistance, freedom, and independence. A master of disguise and deception, he was known for his practical jokes and sharp wit. He is often portrayed as a trickster who uses his cunning to expose the hypocrisy and corruption of the world around him. Uilenspiegel is a wry social critic who, with humor, challenges the status quo.

Scatological stories abound in Uilenspiegel's exploits and even in his name, which might be a pun that translates as "wipe-arse" from Low German. Scholars have speculated that Uilenspiegel's bathroom humor is a way to shock people into thinking about the world differently. Though Roymans might have related to Uilenspiegel in trying to expose hypocrisy and corruption, there is also a scatological connection between the two. When hiding from police at Herkenrode Abbey, various reports suggest that Roymans buried himself in a pile of manure in an attempt to mask his own smell from the investigators' sniffer dogs. Though it didn't work (Roymans was still apprehended), both Uilenspiegel and the artist Maurizio Cattelan (p. 28) would, no doubt, approve of the effort.

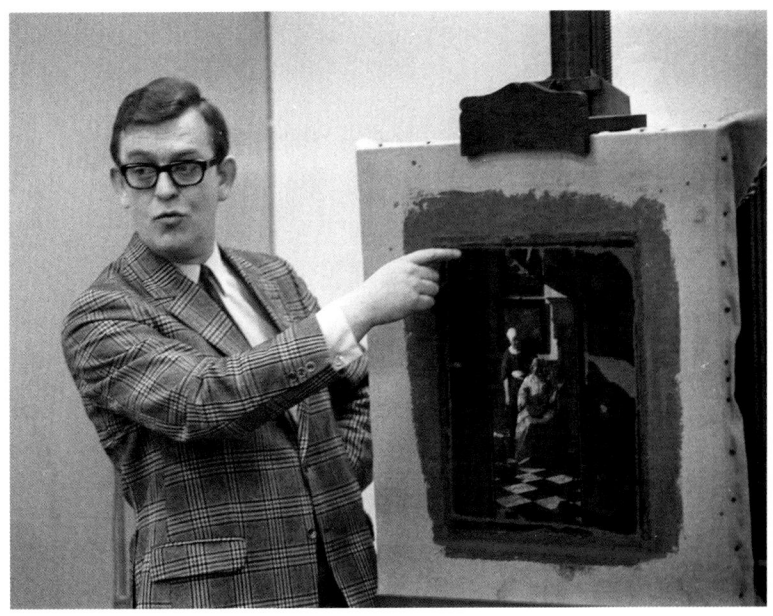

Right: An art restorer gestures to the considerable damage inflicted on *The Love Letter* due to Mario Roymans's theft. It would take a global panel of experts over a year to repair the painting.

Three days later, Roymans called a radio news program from a gas station and was broadcast live to share his demands and his concerns about the Bengali genocide and about combatting famine around the world. An employee at the gas station overheard Roymans's rant and called the police. Roymans gave police a run for their money, in a chase that involved hiding under the straw and between two cows in a nearby stable at Herkenrode Abbey. But he was eventually arrested. The Vermeer was discovered under his mattress.

While awaiting trial, Roymans became, much like Robin Hood so many years before him, a folk hero of sorts. Petitions were circulated for his release, songs were sung about his bravery and idealism, T-shirts were made, and graffiti decried that Tijl van Limburg should be set free. The gas station where Roymans was ratted out supposedly didn't have a customer for months. When his trial arrived, the courthouse received bomb threats from Roymans's legions of supporters.

At his trial, Roymans received a slap on the wrist—two years in prison (of which he served only six months). *The Love Letter*, on the other hand, needed more than six months for its rehabilitation. The damage from Roymans's knife and his manhandling of the painting took over a year to repair, with guidance from an international committee of conservators. On September 28, 1972, *The Love Letter* was put back on display at the Rijksmuseum.

After serving his sentence, Roymans married and had a child. He fell into a deep depression, divorced, and started living in his car. In 1979, at the age of twenty-eight, Roymans was found in his car with internal bleeding. He died ten days later.

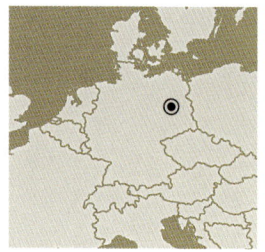

When: December 12, 1976, and September 3, 1989

Where: Neue Nationalgalerie (1976) and Schloss Charlottenburg (1989) in Berlin

What: Thefts of Carl Spitzweg's *The Poor Poet* (1839)

THERE IS A CRIMINAL TOUCH TO ART THEFT

Carl Spitzweg's painting *The Poor Poet* has been stolen twice: once in December 1976 as an act of art and once in September 1989, purely as an act of theft. *The Poor Poet*, of which there are three versions (two are nearly identical while the third, held in a private collection, has slight variations), is beloved in Germany. Carl Spitzweg never struggled financially like the poet in his painting, who is a caricature of the "starving artist." The poet, who works on a mattress on the floor, is so poor that he can stay warm only by burning the pages of his books or poems. An umbrella hangs above the poet's head to keep the melting snow from dripping on him.

Spitzweg started his career as a pharmacist, but when his father passed away, he used his inheritance to transition into his true love—art—and became a painter at the age of twenty-five. He was successful during his lifetime and became one of the leaders in the Biedermeier art movement, which celebrated domestic bliss and common sensibilities as the middle class grew in Central Europe between 1815 and 1848.

Spitzweg has remained one of the most beloved artists in Germany. Rose-Marie and Rainer Hagen write in their book *What Great Paintings Say* that Germans voted *The Poor Poet* their second-favorite painting. First place went to Leonardo da Vinci's *Mona Lisa*, which has also been subject to a theft (p. 38), and third place went to another German work, Albrecht Dürer's *Hare*. Interestingly, *The Poor Poet* has also been cited as one of Hitler's favorite works.

Perhaps because of its popularity, perhaps because of the irony of an image of a suffering artist being worth millions and millions of dollars, or perhaps because it was the only picture printed in color in his school textbook from the 1940s, the German artist Frank Uwe Laysiepen (known as Ulay) decided to steal the painting in 1976. Before this, Ulay and his then partner, Marina Abramović, had earned some renown as performance artists. Shortly before Ulay's staged theft, the pair had performed in Amsterdam in a piece titled *Talking about Similarity*. In front of an audience on their shared November 30 birthday, Ulay sewed

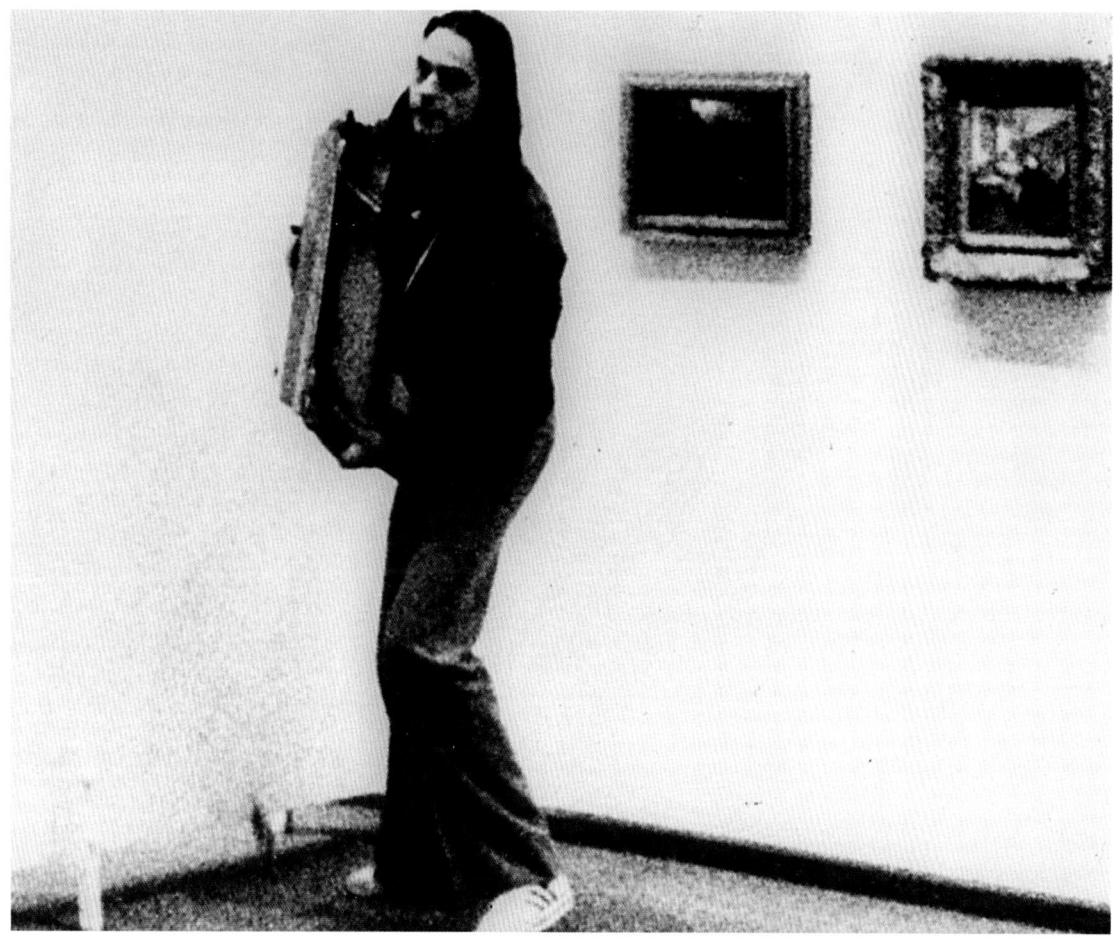

Above: A master of reinvention, the performance artist known as Ulay died in 2020, but not before orchestrating artistic hijinks around the world. Here he executes a work of art/theft at the Neue Nationalgalerie in 1976.

his own mouth shut. Afterwards, Abramović answered any questions and spoke for him. This is just one of the tamer examples from their oeuvre that shows that Ulay and Abramović were willing to take great risks for their art.

Ulay further proved this on December 12, 1976, with a new piece of performance art. He walked into Berlin's Neue Nationalgalerie, plucked *The Poor Poet* off the wall, and dashed

out of the museum's emergency exit and into the falling snow. It is likely that Abramović recorded the in-museum antics while another collaborator, German cinematographer Jörg Schmidt-Reitwein, who had worked with the filmmaker Werner Herzog, was ready with a video recorder outside of the museum.

With the painting barely wrapped in a felt blanket (the poor poet remained badly insulated

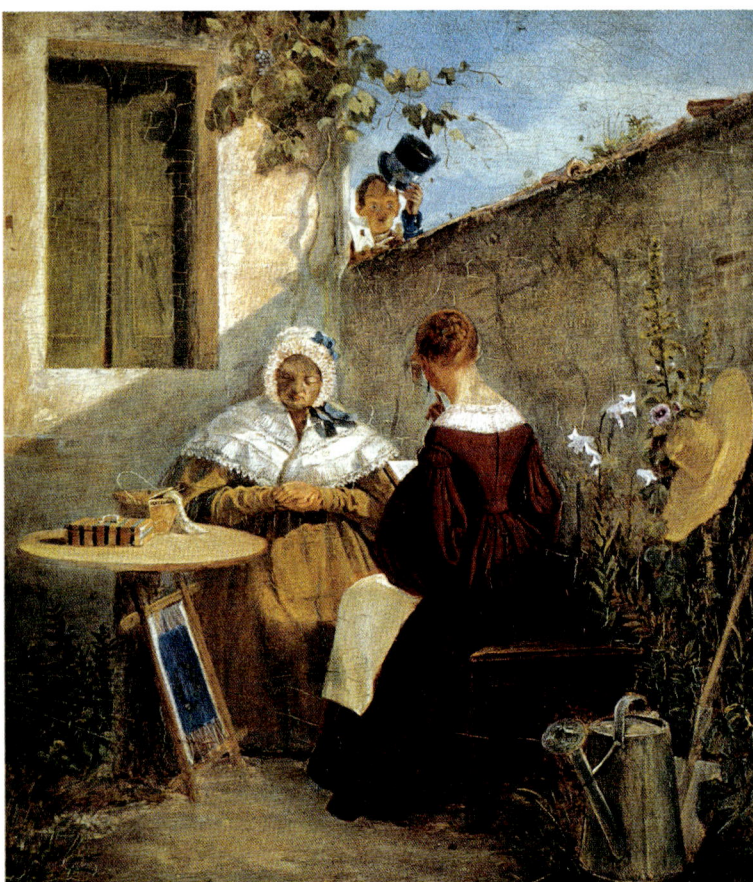

Left: Carl Spitzweg, the beloved German painter of the Biedermeier movement, painted *The Love Letter* in 1846. It was stolen from the Schloss Charlottenburg in 1989 and has not been seen since.

Opposite: *The Poor Poet* has won numerous popularity contests in Germany, but it wasn't always that way. Purportedly, when Carl Spitzweg first submitted it to the esteemed Munich Art Association exhibition in the 1830s, it was rejected.

and chilled during his adventure outside of the museum) and security guards rushing after him, Ulay drove off in the black getaway van that doubled as his and Abramović's home. Perhaps Ulay and Abramović could more than relate to the struggles of Spitzweg's poet in their cramped, wheeled home. Ulay ditched the van to walk to the Kreuzberg neighborhood in Berlin, which would have had many residents living in difficult conditions. On the way to a preselected Turkish immigrant family's apartment, Ulay stopped at a pay phone to call the police to ask the director of the museum if he would like to see *The Poor Poet* hung in its new home. Ulay

then carted the painting up to the apartment, where the Turkish family thought he would be filming a documentary. They didn't know that Ulay would be replacing their own painting on the wall behind their sofa with a stolen one to bring attention to the mistreatment of Turkish immigrants in Germany.

After recording the stolen painting in its new surroundings, Ulay chain-smoked in front of the Turkish family's home for an hour, waiting for the museum director to arrive. Meanwhile, police were busy sealing off the block. The director arrived, the painting was returned unharmed, and Ulay was arrested. He later

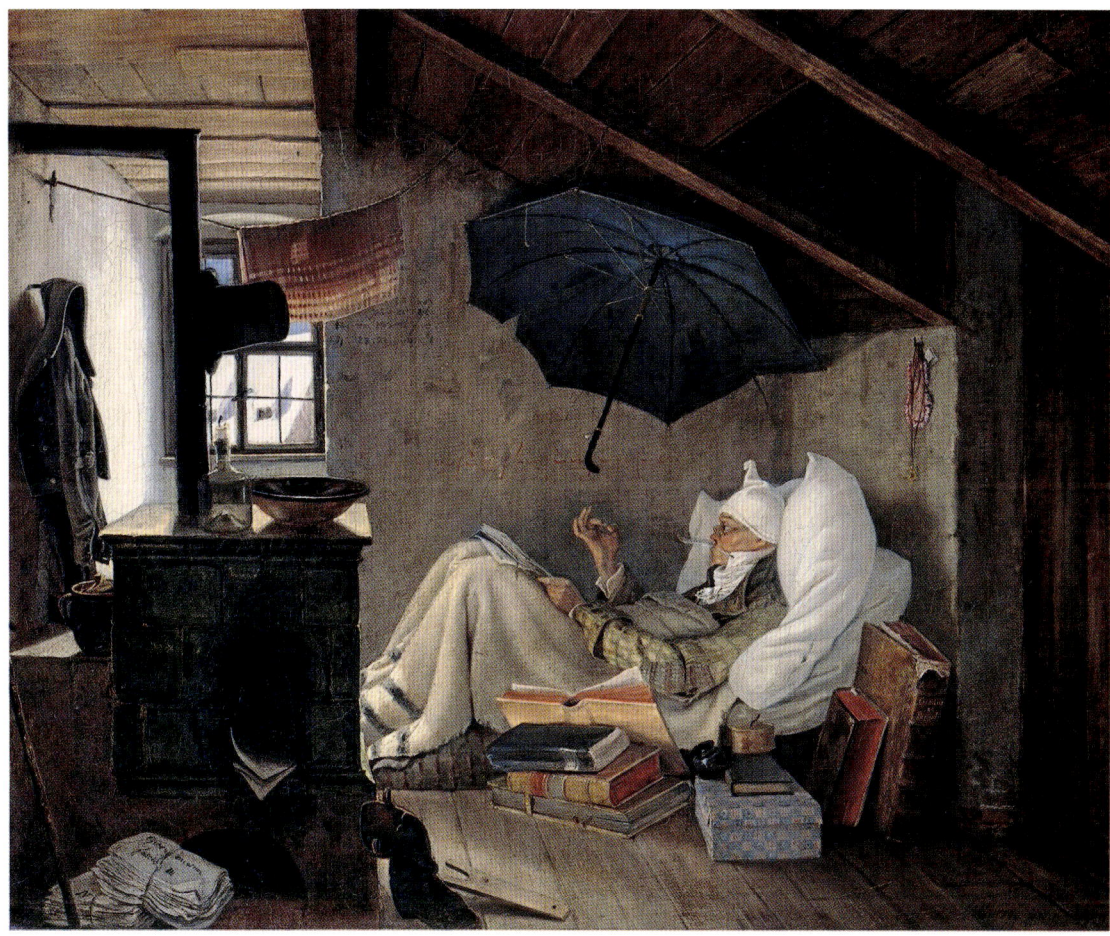

had to pay a fine and spend about two weeks in jail. But, as he had hoped, his theft brought him a lot of attention (and perhaps some attention to the plight of Turkish immigrants). Newspapers and the media decried "the madman's" antics and the theft further cemented *The Poor Poet*'s place in the hearts of Germans. Ulay would go on to name his performance piece *There Is a Criminal Touch to Art*.

No doubt its continued status as a beloved painting of Germany—after Ulay helped to make it even more of an "identity icon"—led to *The Poor Poet*'s second theft in 1989. The painting had been moved from the Neue Nationalgalerie

to Schloss Charlottenburg, also in Berlin. Its new home didn't keep it safe from a pair of thieves during the museum's open hours on September 3, 1989. Using a wheelchair as a prop, one of the thieves pushed the other up to *The Poor Poet* and another Spitzweg painting, *The Love Letter*. The two men clipped the hanging wires and ran out with the paintings, leaving the wheelchair behind at the scene of the crime. Neither painting has been seen since.

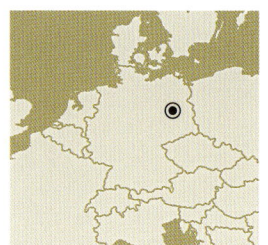

When: May 27, 1988

Where: Neue Nationalgalerie in Berlin

What: Theft of Lucian Freud's *Francis Bacon* (1952)

WANTED

Lucian Freud's exhibition at the Neue Nationalgalerie was his first major retrospective outside of the United Kingdom, but the achievement was marred by theft. On May 27, 1988, nearly eight hundred people visited the exhibition. As of that morning, Freud's portrait of his friend Francis Bacon, painted on copper and measuring 7 by 5 feet, had been screwed to the wall; a camera crew photographed the retrospective around 11:30 a.m. By 3 p.m., the 1952 painting, on loan from the Tate, was missing. The museum had no alarms or cameras.

In 2001, the Tate organized a retrospective of Freud's work in London and made one more effort to find the missing portrait, which they still technically owned. The statute of limitations in Germany for such crimes was twelve years, so now that thirteen years had passed they thought the thief might come forward, knowing they could not be prosecuted.

After the theft in 1988, Freud allowed the painting to be reproduced only in black and white. In monochromatic tones, the portrait looked like a wanted poster. Freud added "Wanted" in bold, red letters, and underneath, in German, "A reward of up to 300,000 Deutschmarks is offered for clues leading to the recovery of this small painting" and a phone number. He assured thieves that their calls would be confidential. Freud also asked: "Would the person who holds the painting kindly consider allowing me to show it in my exhibition next June?"

Two thousand five hundred copies of the wanted poster were distributed throughout Berlin. Despite the reward and the expired statute of limitations, *Francis Bacon* was not returned. Freud hung a copy of the wanted poster outside of his London studio. When Freud died in 2011, the portrait was still missing; its whereabouts remain unknown. The Tate simply lists the portrait as "not on display," and the phone number on Freud's wanted sign yields a busy signal.

Opposite: The artist Lucian Freud created this wanted sign in the hope he could persuade the thief to return his portrait of Francis Bacon. It didn't work.

WANTED

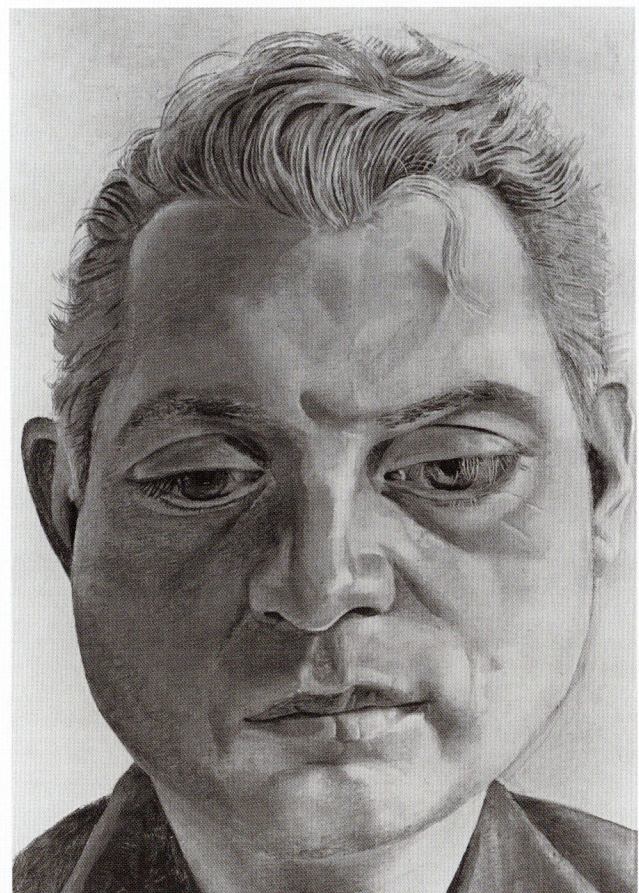

Für Hinweise, die zur Wiedererlangung dieses kleinen Gemäldes führen, ist eine Belohnung von bis zu

DM 300.000,–

ausgesetzt. Mitteilungen, die auf Wunsch absolut vertraulich behandelt werden, bitte unter

Telefon (030) 31 10 99 40

If calling from outside Germany please dial + 49 30 31 10 99 40

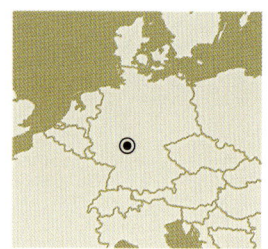

When: July 28, 1994

Where: Schirn Kunsthalle in Frankfurt

What: Theft of J. M. W. Turner's *Shade and Darkness: The Evening of the Deluge* (1843) and *Light and Colour (Goethe's Theory): The Morning after the Deluge* (1843) and Caspar David Friedrich's *Nebelschwaden* (1820)

REWARD, RANSOM, OR FEE FOR INFORMATION?

On July 28, 1994, two paintings by J. M. W. Turner—*Shade and Darkness: The Evening of the Deluge* (1843) and *Light and Colour (Goethe's Theory): The Morning after the Deluge* (1843)—and one by Caspar David Friedrich, *Nebelschwaden* (1820), were stolen from the Schirn Kunsthalle in Frankfurt. The three thieves hid in the museum until 10:00 p.m., when they surprised a security guard who was just about to turn on the museum's security system. They shoved the guard into a broom closet and systematically unscrewed the frames of their three chosen paintings from the wall and left through the back entrance.

The Turners were on loan from the Tate Britain in London and the Friedrich was loaned from the Hamburger Kunsthalle in Hamburg. When the Tate loaned its two Turner paintings to the Schirn Kunsthalle in 1994, each was insured for £12 million.

Three men were arrested quickly after the theft, and two other men accused of giving museum keys to the thieves were acquitted. None would squeal on anyone else who was involved or reveal where the paintings were. The thieves were represented by a lawyer, Edgar Liebrucks, known for being legal counsel to members of organized crime in the past.

After several years without word on the paintings, Lloyd's, the insurer of the Turners, paid £24 million to the Tate in 1996. In a risky move, the Tate decided to buy back the title to their two Turners for £8 million in 1998. If the paintings were ever successfully recovered, the museum would own them, rather than the insurance company.

Then things got interesting. Edgar Liebrucks, who had represented the thieves at the trial, suggested to the Tate that he might be willing to provide information on behalf of his clients regarding the location of the paintings . . . for a fee. The fee? 3.1 million euros. The High Court of England gave the Tate permission to use part of their insurance payout to help get their Turners back. Operation Cobalt, named by the Tate, was in motion. Through the negotiating of Sandy Nairne, then program director at the Tate, the paintings were returned and announced

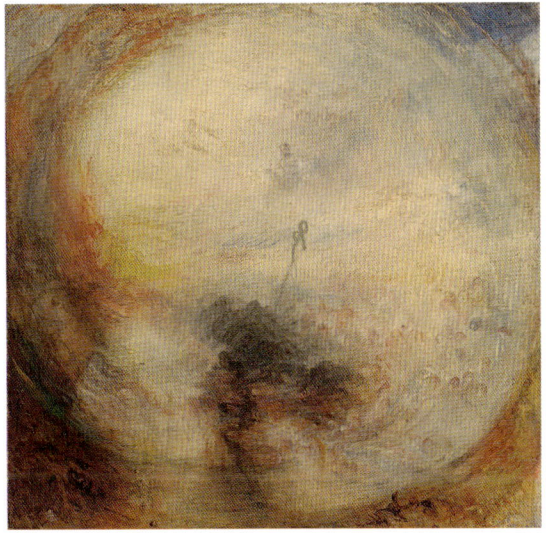

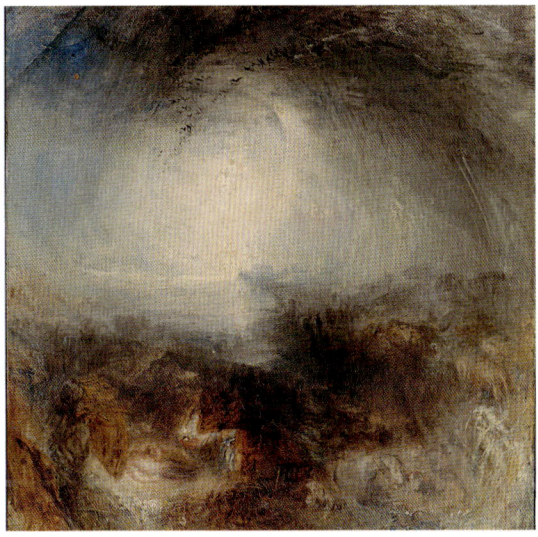

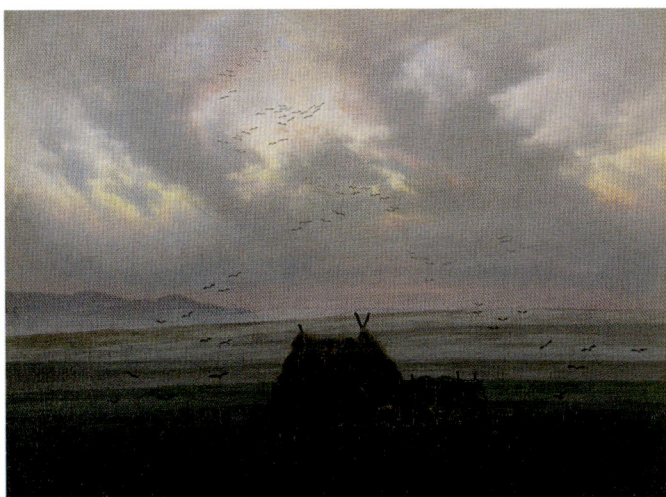

Above: Turner intended *Light and Colour (Goethe's Theory): The Morning after the Deluge* to be paired with *Shade and Darkness: The Evening of the Deluge.* As in life, so in theft: they were stolen together.

Left: Friedrich's *Nebelschwaden*, which translates to English as "wisps of mist," seemed to disappear into the fog when it was stolen along with the two Turners in 1994.

as being back in the Tate's custodianship as of Christmas 2002.

Still missing was the Friedrich owned by the Hamburger Kunsthalle. When Liebrucks contacted the Hamburg museum to offer information on their painting in exchange for 1.5 million euros, the museum offered 250,000. The painting was returned in August of 2003.

The Tate maintains that they never paid a reward or ransom. The only money they paid was a fee for information, which is common in cases of missing art. The case raises important and complicated questions about rewards, ransoms, and art theft. Should either museum have paid money to get back their paintings? On the one hand, the money got the paintings back into museums' collections and available to the world again. On the other hand, it could encourage more thefts if thieves realize they can make a pretty penny from "sharing information" for a fee.

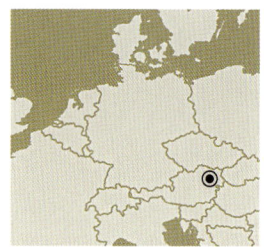

STEALING THE "*MONA LISA* OF SCULPTURE"

n 2003, Vienna's Kunsthistorisches Museum was undergoing a reconstruction project and its exterior was covered in scaffolding. In the early morning hours of May 11, a thief took advantage of this scaffolding to climb to the second floor, where he entered the museum and made off with Benvenuto Cellini's Italian Mannerist masterpiece, a not-so-simple salt cellar referred to by the museum's director as "The Mona Lisa of sculpture." The robber was in and out of the museum in fifty-six seconds.

Robert Mang, the thief, was, at the time, a fifty-year-old security engineer. One rainy day in Vienna, he decided to go to the Kunsthistorisches Museum and joined a public tour. Inside the museum, with his experience as a security specialist he took note of the scaffolding, outdated security scanners, and glass cases that hadn't been properly reinforced.

A few weeks later, Mang, a resident of Vienna, found himself at a dance club near the museum. He left the party in the early hours of the morning and claimed that he wanted to test the museum's poor security system. It wasn't

until 8:20 a.m. that the broken glass and empty vitrine housing the saliera were discovered by cleaning staff at the museum. Meanwhile, Mang had taken the saliera home and hidden it in a box under his bed.

Once the saliera was discovered missing, the museum offered a reward of tens of thousands of euros for information leading to the arrest of the thief and the return of the saliera. For two years, the saliera remained missing. Mang continued his work as a security engineer.

Things changed for reasons still unknown in October of 2005 when Mang contacted the company that insured the saliera for the Kunsthistorisches Museum. Mang finally got up the courage to ask for a five-million-euro ransom and provided Neptune's trident (a removable part of the saliera) as evidence that he had the work in his possession. One week later, he contacted the insurance company again and upped the ransom to ten million euros, perhaps after learning through the ensuing media frenzy that the saliera was valued at more than fifty million euros.

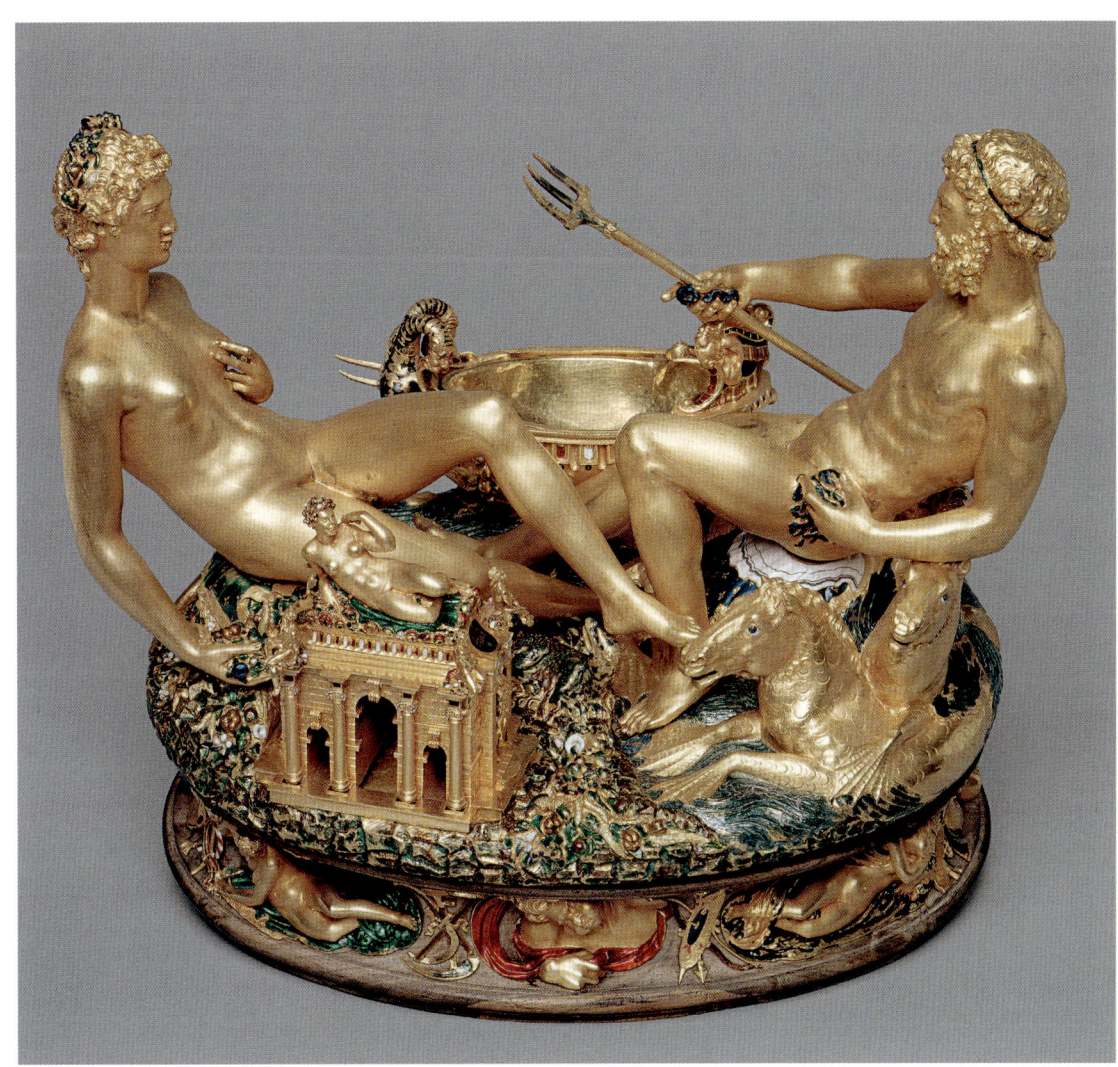

Above: Created in 1543 for Francis I of France, Benvenuto Cellini's opulent saliera is fit for a king's table but could also fit in your hands: it measures just 10 inches by 13¼ inches.

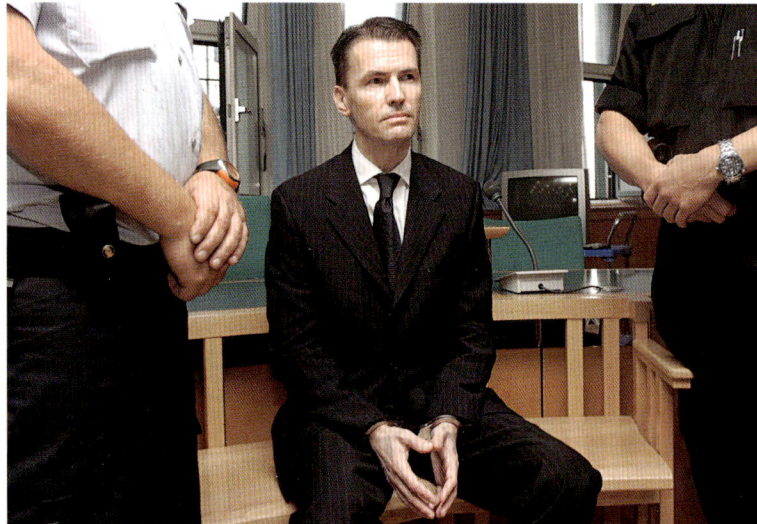

Mang started texting the insurance company and sent instructions for how the ten-million-euro ransom should be handled and directions for where the money should be dropped. He was careful to use each disposable cellphone only once, so as not to be traced. At one point, Mang thought he noticed unmarked police cars on the route to the money drop, which angered him. In his fury and haste, Mang reused a cellphone. When he sent a text from that cellphone, police were able to trace the phone back to the shop Mang had bought it from and, consequently, use the shop's hidden cameras to identify Mang.

The police made public the images of Mang, who contacted the police to identify himself, but also to express his innocence. Police searched his apartment and found evidence of notes pointing to his involvement but no saliera. Later, with his lawyer, Mang confessed to the crime. Mang led police to a forest about an hour north of Vienna where he had moved the saliera as things heated up. He had wrapped the saliera in linen and plastic, put it into a waterproof box, and buried it.

Mang was convicted and sentenced to four years in prison. To this day, Mang has maintained that his theft of the saliera was a practical joke with personal significance. Mang had collected sculpture as a youth, and, as a security specialist, he saw a challenge in removing the saliera. Perhaps he should have been satisfied with a souvenir instead. At the Kunsthistorisches Museum's gift shop, you can buy your own mini saliera. Though 695 euros is very expensive for a salt container, it is a lot cheaper than four years in prison.

A TOUR OF "THE MONA LISA OF SCULPTURE"

Cellini's saliera is a prime example of Mannerism, an art movement characterized by wildly exaggerated bodily proportions and embellished colors. The sculpture portrays Neptune, god of the sea, with Tellus, Roman goddess of the earth, and symbolizes their harmony, which is necessary to create salt. Tellus and Neptune's legs are intertwined, just like earth and sea are intertwined. The saliera would have held salt (in the open ship by Neptune's trident) and pepper (in the temple). The saliera is only about ten inches in length and thirteen inches in width. It was commissioned for the table of Francis I of France, who is remembered for, among other things, kicking off the French Renaissance. The female figure (Tellus, the earth goddess) has her right fingers resting on a horn of plenty, which has connections to nature and abundance. With her left hand, she squeezes her nipple, a gesture meant to suggest fertility and wealth. Tellus is surrounded by animals and flowers, and she leans back on an enameled, green hill draped with cloth displaying fleurs-de-lis, one of France's national symbols. She lounges on top of an elephant. Because pepper was imported from India during this time, Cellini might have included the elephant for its connections to the origin of the spice. Neptune is surrounded by hippocampi, mythological sea monsters that are half horse, half fish. Hidden on the saliera is a salamander, the personal emblem of Francis I.

The saliera was not cast but hand-formed by Cellini. It is made of hand-rolled gold with an ebony base and ivory rollers. Francis asked for the saliera to be made of gold after seeing a model Cellini had made of wax. After the commission was ordered by the king, Cellini wrote in his autobiography about how he single-handedly fended off several armed thieves as he walked home with a basket filled with gold from the king's treasurer to make the saliera. Can we believe this? Who knows. We should probably take these sorts of accounts from Cellini with, ahem, a grain of salt.

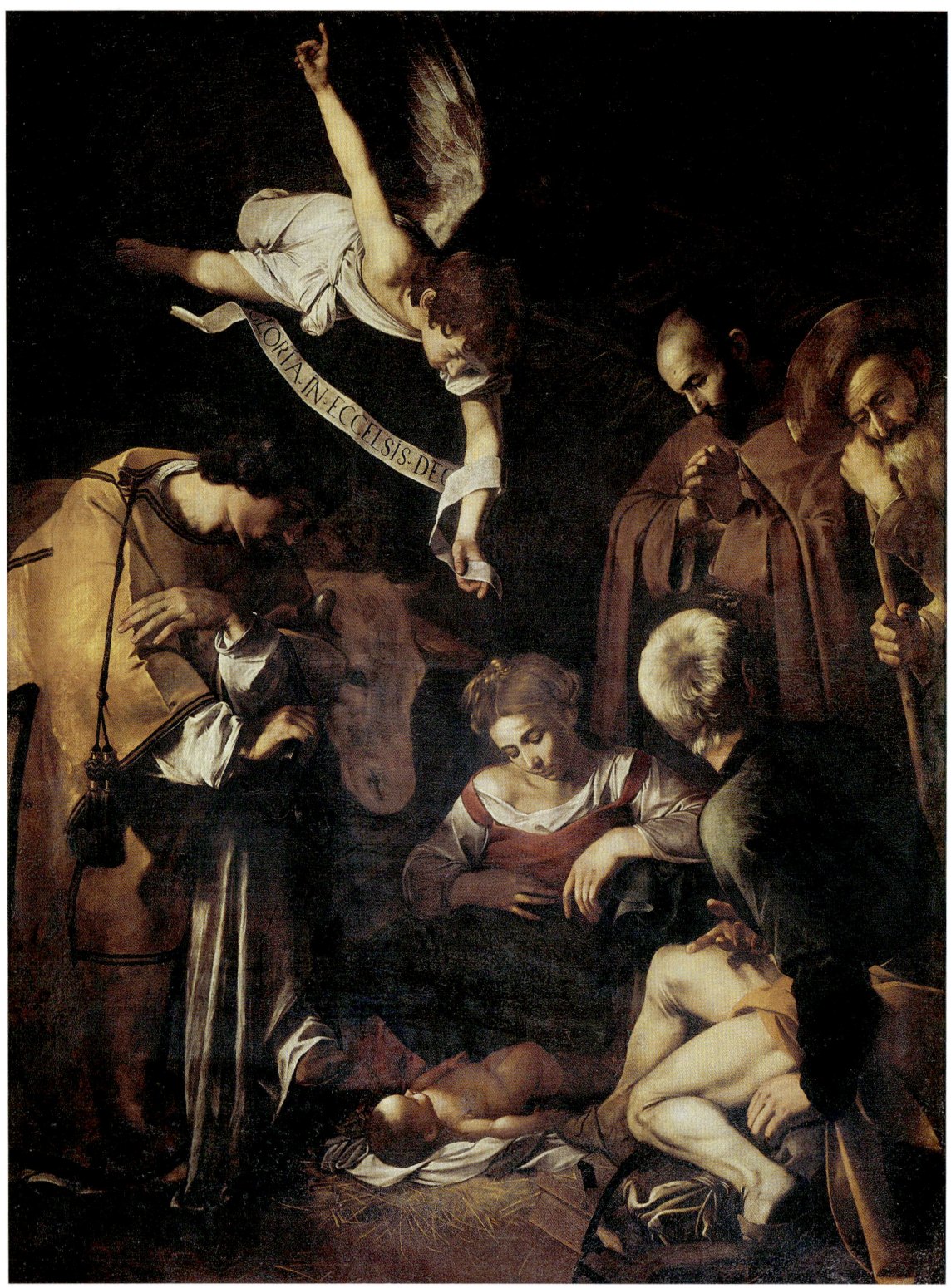

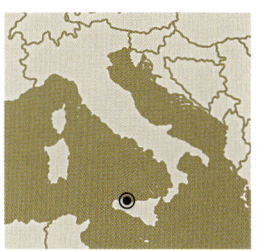

PRAYING FOR A CARAVAGGIO'S RETURN

On October 17, 1969, it was a rainy night in Palermo, Sicily, at the toe of Italy's boot. The day before, Caravaggio's altarpiece *Nativity with Saint Francis and Saint Lawrence* had been featured on an Italian television show about forgotten pieces of art in Italy. It did, indeed, seem to be a bit forgotten.

The painting hung in the Oratorio di San Lorenzo, where it had been on display since the early 1600s. The mother of the priest of the church remembered several men coming by the church before the theft, asking to see the work. She had requested permission from the Vatican to reinforce the windows of the room and secure the entry. The Vatican declined, stating that the painting had been there for hundreds of years with no trouble.

Thieves pried open one of those unreinforced windows and spent an hour cutting the painting out of its frame with razorblades. At 9 x 6½ feet, it was too big to carry out intact. The thieves also took a carpet, and must have used it to roll up and carry the painting. The stolen altarpiece was one of only seventy paintings by Caravaggio, worth approximately $25 million today. The following morning, two of the church's custodians noticed that the front door was open. The painting has not been seen since.

Over fifty years later, the theft of Caravaggio's altarpiece from Palermo is still on the FBI's list of Top 10 Art Crimes. Every so often, there is new energy in the case. The latest lead came in 2019 when a Mafia informant, perhaps seeking to trade information in exchange for a lighter sentence for another crime, claimed that the painting was in Switzerland. Police are looking into that but, so far, no news.

Opposite: We will probably never know the full story but, over the ensuing half century, there have been many theories about what happened to the stolen Caravaggio, with one similar theme: La Cosa Nostra (the Sicilian Mafia).

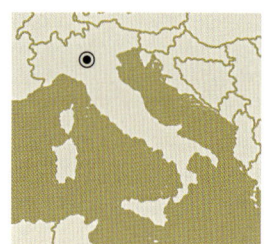

HIDDEN PICTURES

With her parted lips and intense gaze, Gustav Klimt's lady looks like she may have a secret—indeed, she has many. Her first secret: She has more than one identity. In 1996, a local high schooler, Claudia Maga, realized that the Ricci Oddi's Klimt looked similar to another portrait she had seen in a catalogue raisonné of Klimt's work. A photograph of *Portrait of a Young Woman* was included in the catalogue, but the painting had not been seen since 1912. Maga traced the Ricci Oddi's Klimt over the missing image. The women had different hair, clothes, and accoutrements, but both had the same penetrating gaze over the left shoulder, the same partial smile, and the same beauty mark under the left eye. After Maga took her findings to the director of the Ricci Oddi, the gallery had the painting X-rayed at a local hospital. The scan confirmed that the Ricci Oddi Klimt had a twin: the missing *Portrait of a Young Woman* lay beneath *Portrait of a Lady*. Maga and art historians pieced together what had happened. Klimt was in love with the young woman in the hidden portrait. When she died suddenly, Klimt was heartbroken. He tried to dull his pain by painting over her, but he couldn't bring himself to obscure her face. The result is a double painting, the only one known in Klimt's oeuvre.

The Ricci Oddi and all of Piacenza were delighted by this revelation, and the museum made plans to display the painting at a special exhibition. Maybe the excitement and the resulting increased value piqued the interest of thieves because the painting vanished from the museum on February 22, 1997. The clues were confounding, and red herrings abounded. The frame was found next to a skylight on the museum's roof, but it was too big to fit through. A few months after the theft, police seized a fake that they thought was the painting. And almost two decades later, a local art thief shared a tall tale with an Italian police investigator, claiming that he had stolen the Klimt and replaced it with a copy in November 1996. He supposedly then stole the copy in February 1997 because he feared it would immediately be detected as a fake when it became the centerpiece of the museum's special exhibition. He claimed no knowledge of the whereabouts of the painting, saying that he had sold it immediately for cocaine and money.

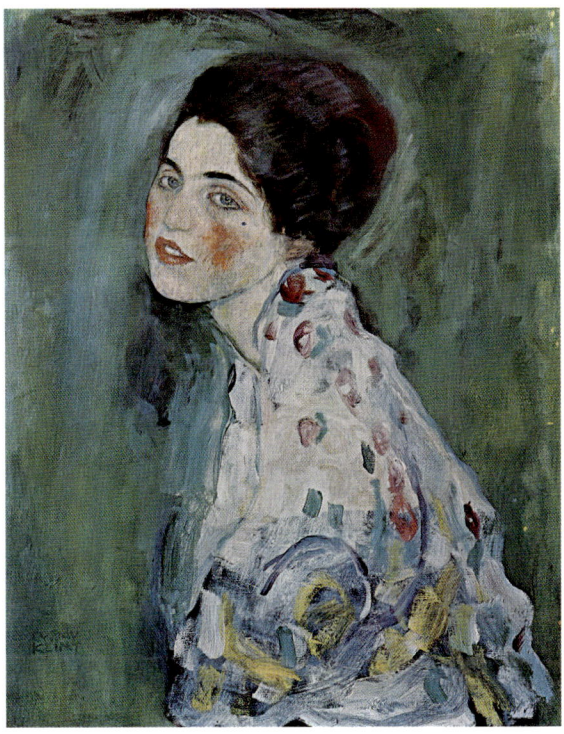
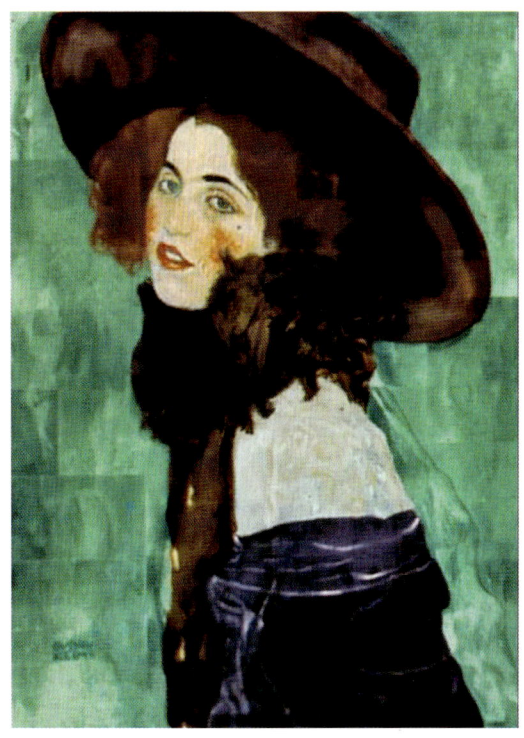

Above: The lady with two faces: Klimt painted *Portrait of a Lady* (left) between 1916 and 1917, and it was bought by Giuseppe Ricci Oddi in 1925. It became a hallmark of his collection and, later, his museum. Almost eighty years would pass before a high school student realized that the lady had a twin, the young woman on the right.

In December 2019, twenty-two years after it was stolen, Klimt's *Portrait of a Lady* was unceremoniously found by a gardener clearing away ivy from an exterior wall of the museum. Under the ivy was a small metal door with a black plastic bag inside. In the bag was the Klimt. Had the painting been there for all those years?

If so, it was in remarkably good condition. Had it been placed there recently? Only the two painted women with their beguiling secrets who were witnesses to the robbery know, and they're not talking.

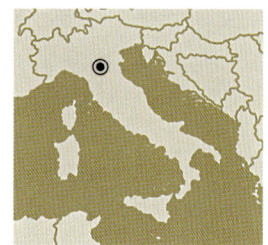

THE RESURRECTION OF A STOLEN ALTARPIECE

I n 1630, Duke Alfonso III d'Este commissioned the popular Bolognese painter Giovanni Francesco Barbieri to create a large, six-by-ten-foot altarpiece painting to hang in the Chiesa di San Vincenzo, one of the most important churches in Modena in the 1600s. Barbieri was known as Guercino, "squinter," due to his strabismus—he had a lazy right eye and a pronounced squint, making his masterful ability to depict depth in his paintings even more impressive. Guercino was not alone in his affliction; other all-star artists may have had the same condition, including Leonardo da Vinci, Dürer, Rembrandt, and Degas. Regardless of challenges with his vision, Guercino was a much sought-after artist during his lifetime.

Guercino's altarpiece, *Madonna with the Saints John the Evangelist and Gregory the Wonderworker*, hung in San Vincenzo from the 1600s onward, surviving World War II and the destruction of part of the presbytery and choir by a bomb in 1944. In spite of its hundreds of years of existence through peacetime and war, the

painting seemed like it might not survive its most recent humiliation. In 2014, it was stolen from San Vincenzo. Because there was no sign of forced entry, police believe thieves hid in the church after Sunday mass. They cut the canvas from its frame and rolled it up—disastrous treatment for a five-hundred-year-old painting. The painting was not insured, and alarm systems were not operational; both were too expensive for the church to maintain. The painting was estimated to be worth between five and six million euros.

When the painting was found three years later in Casablanca, Morocco, it was crumpled up and nearly unrecognizable. After being rolled up and transported, the altarpiece had lost nearly one-third of its paint. Three men were arrested after trying to sell it to a collector for ten million dirhams (nearly $1,000,000). The collector recognized the stolen Modena painting and alerted authorities. Italy's Carabinieri art crime squad brought the Guercino back to Italy. After undergoing emergency conservation work in Rome, it was ready to be returned to Modena

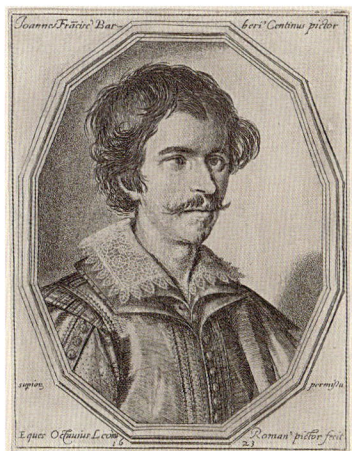

Above: The artist Giovanni Francesco Barbieri was known in Italian as il Guercino, or "the squinter," because he was cross-eyed.

Right: Self-taught, Guercino was an in-demand painter in the 1600s and was praised by his fellow artists, such as Ludovico Carracci, who wrote of Guercino's talent that "even the top painters are awestruck."

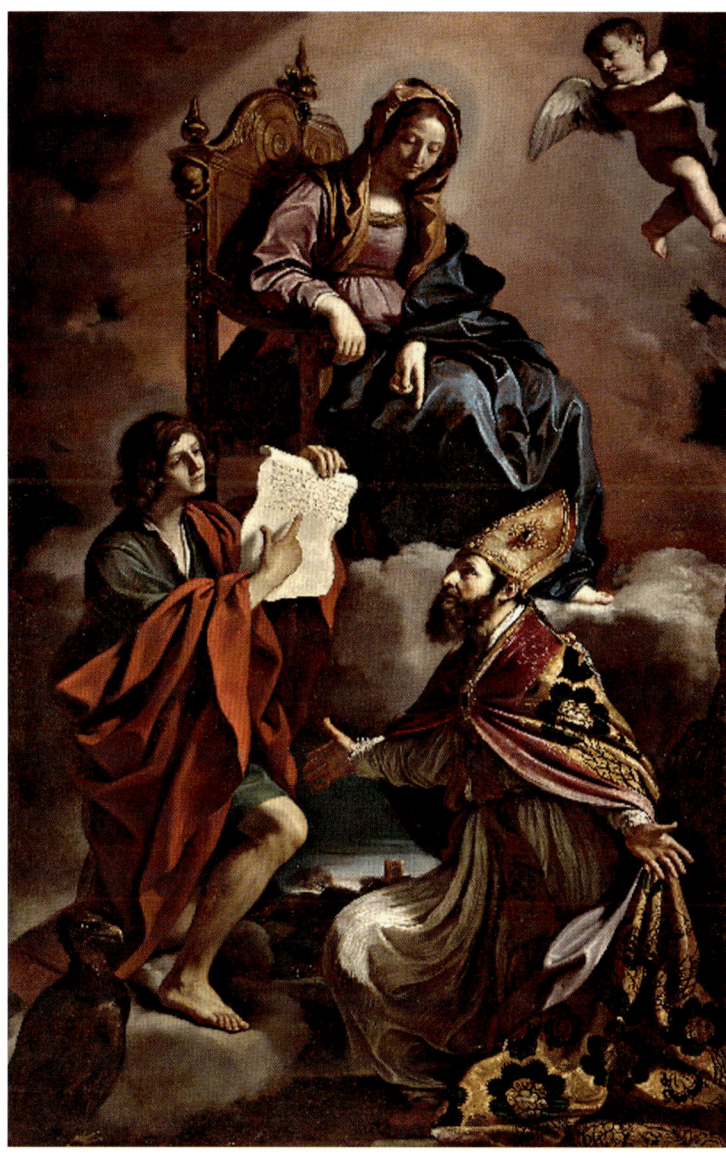

in 2019. Meanwhile, one thief (though there may have been more conspirators) was given a two-year sentence.

Gregory the Wonderworker, one of the saints depicted in the Guercino altarpiece, is the patron saint of earthquakes, floods, and desperate, forgotten, impossible, and lost causes. After the theft in 2014, it certainly seemed

that the Guercino painting was a lost cause. Perhaps Gregory, along with a little help from the Carabinieri and the conservators on the case, worked his wonders to give hope to the impossible cause of the Guercino altarpiece and bring it home to San Vincenzo where it belongs.

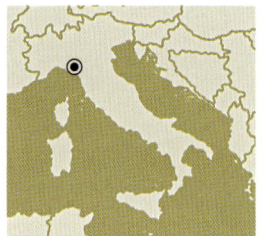

IN GOD'S IMAGE

"Thou shalt not steal." Though it is one of the Bible's Ten Commandments, thieves in Italy were not concerned with sinning when they broke into the Chiesa di Santa Maria Maddalena in Castelnuovo Magra on March 13, 2019. Once inside, the robbers stole the church's crown jewel: Pieter Brueghel the Younger's *Crucifixion*. The painting was valued at around three million euros at the time.

The theft took place at lunchtime, when thieves knew the priest, Reverend Alessandro Chiantaretto, would be away from the church. During lunch, the reverend often administered communion to members of his congregation who were unable to come to the church in person. He believes the thieves knew this and took advantage of his compassionate routine.

The thieves made quick work of their mission. With a hammer, they smashed through the glass covering the painting and fled in their getaway car. Though the church had security cameras and an alarm, a local was the first to notice something was wrong when they saw a white Peugeot speeding through town and noticed that the church's door was open. The town's mayor, Daniele Montebello, was bereft,

expressing the small town's heartbreak over the theft. For Castelnuovo Magra, this was some déjà vu. The same painting had been stolen once before in 1981. At the time, the Carabinieri were able to recover the painting a few months after it was pilfered.

The Catholic church in Castelnuovo Magra was built in the seventeenth century, and the *Crucifixion* was created by the Flemish master painter Pieter Brueghel the Younger in the early 1600s in Belgium. Brueghel the Younger, sometimes referred to as "de helse Brueghel" (Hell Brueghel) because of his paintings of fiery and surreal images, was inspired by his father, Pieter Bruegel the Elder, who had painted a similar crucifixion scene (though Bruegel the Elder's version has been lost to history). A very similar version to the one in the Chiesa di Santa Maria Maddalena is in the Philadelphia Museum of Art. The Castelnuovo Magra version was donated to the church by a wealthy family and protected during World War II from bombing and looting.

In early 2019, unbeknownst to the thieves, the Carabinieri received a tip that the *Crucifixion* might be stolen. Weeks before the March theft,

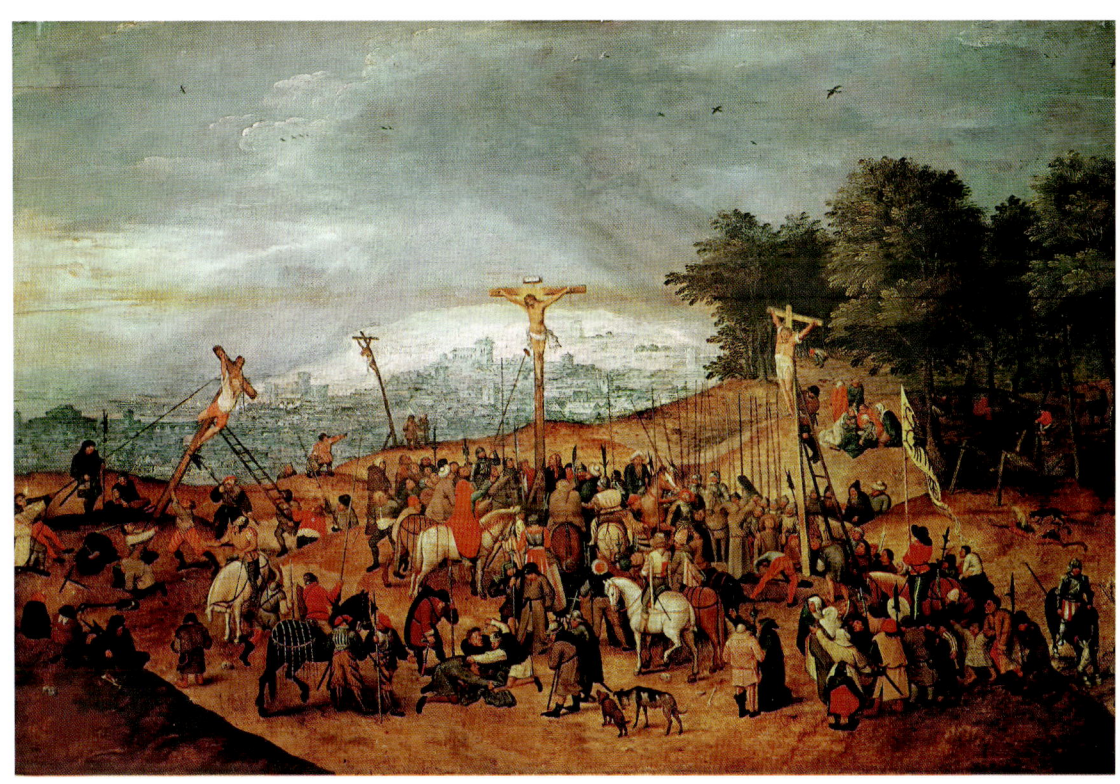

Above: In an act of divine justice, thieves stole a well-made copy of Pieter Brueghel the Younger's *Crucifixion* in 2019, while the real thing remained safe and hidden.

the Carabinieri swapped the real painting with a copy. Only a few citizens of Castelnuovo Magra knew about the plan. The mayor, the reverend, and a few eagle-eyed congregation members who spotted the copy were the only ones in on the switch. When the fake painting was stolen, those in the know gave award-worthy performances to the media until their plot was revealed.

The real painting has been kept in a secret, safe location until the thieves are apprehended using the CCTV footage from the theft. Meanwhile, if any of the thieves would like to confess, both the Carabinieri and the priest at the Chiesa di Santa Maria Maddalena are equipped to listen to their confession, though with very different results.

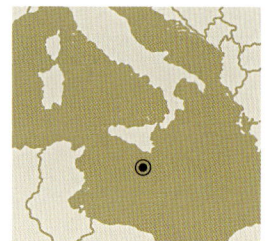

WORK IN PROGRESS

On New Year's Day in 1984, three men dressed in coveralls hung a "Work in Progress" sign at the front of Saint John's Co-Cathedral in Valletta to prevent anyone from entering the church. Inside the cathedral are a breathtaking array of ornate decorative elements: intricate carvings, stunning paintings, and a whole lot of bling. Two of the church's crown jewels are paintings by Caravaggio: the dramatic masterpiece *The Beheading of Saint John the Baptist* (1608) and the quiet study *Saint Jerome Writing* (c. 1607–8).

After hanging their "Work in Progress" sign, the thieves did just that: they got to work. They proceeded to lower one of the cathedral's two Caravaggios—*Saint Jerome Writing*—from its place on the wall and cut the painting from its frame.

An American tourist found a priest to complain that the cathedral wasn't open during the hours listed in his guidebook. The priest was perplexed as the church was supposed to be open, and this is how it was discovered that Saint Jerome had been artnapped.

The thieves smuggled Saint Jerome up to Florence but couldn't find a buyer; nor could they find an auction house to sell the painting on their behalf. Of course, no one wanted to touch this painting that was stratospherically famous and also known to be stolen. When the thieves couldn't sell it, they tried to ransom it back to Saint John's. The priest of the church at the time was Father Marius J. Zerafa. He was a great art lover with several art history degrees from prestigious universities. At the time of the theft, he was also the director of the Maltese National Museums.

Eventually, Father Zerafa was approached by a man with an envelope and a cassette tape who said he had been sent by Joe Borg, which is a common name in Malta—so common, in fact, that Joe Borg was the name of Zerafa's cousin, and Zerafa assumed his cousin had sent him the envelope and tape. Much to his surprise, Zerafa opened the envelope to find a polaroid of Caravaggio's *Saint Jerome* cut out of its frame. On the cassette were instructions not to go to the police. The thieves said they would know if Zerafa went to the police. Rather, they asked him to prepare a ransom of half a million Maltese lire. Fearing that the thieves had police contacts, Zerafa tried to negotiate with them

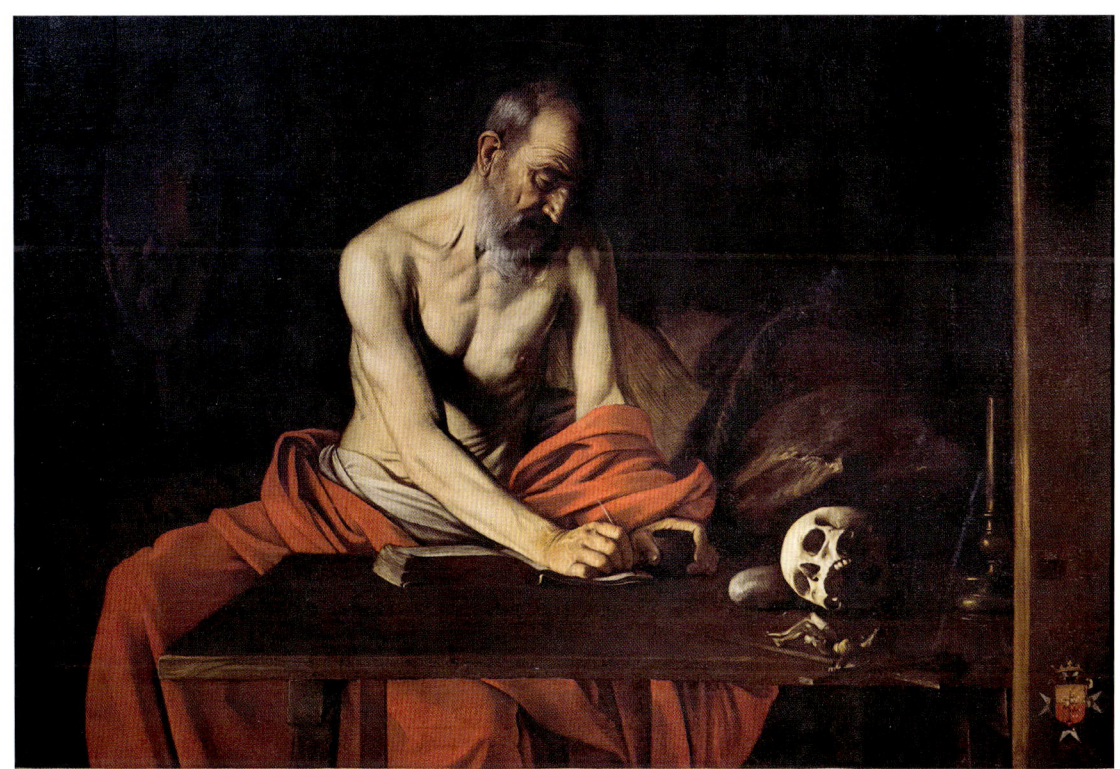

Above: Caravaggio created two paintings of Saint Jerome writing. One, made pre-murder, is at the Galleria Borghese in Rome. The one above, made post-murder, is in Valletta.

on his own for nine months. As the thieves got more and more frustrated, they started cutting off strips of the masterpiece and sending them to the church.

Wily Father Zerafa started working with an anonymous young man with a penchant for technology. They managed to tap the phone line of the thieves and trace the calls Zerafa

was receiving to a shoe factory in Malta. After narrowing down the thieves' location, they decided to involve the police and coordinated a sting operation that involved a helicopter. Unfortunately, the helicopter completely ruined the element of surprise—the thieves heard it coming and ran. (Maybe Father Zerafa and the local police had seen too many art-heist films

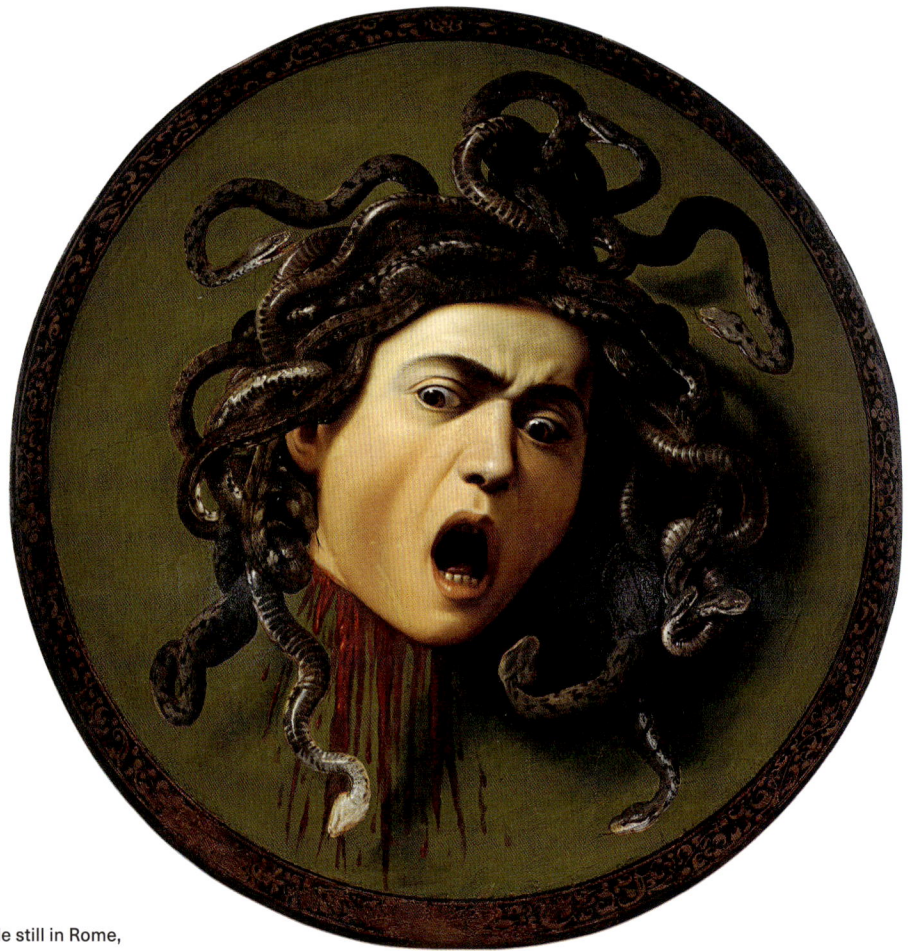

Above: While still in Rome, Caravaggio painted this gruesome head of Medusa after she had been slayed by Perseus. Medusa's face is Caravaggio's face: the painting is a self-portrait.

when they made the regrettable decision to use a helicopter.) In spite of this misstep, two of the thieves were caught in the sting. A third escaped. It later emerged that the thieves had been planning to kidnap Father Zerafa to add leverage to their ransom.

In a surprise twist, the thieves employed the services of a really good lawyer who started a case for the two men, based on the fact that Father Zerafa's homemade phone tapping was, technically, unconstitutional. The case dragged on for years, and both thieves died—one of "natural causes" and one of a drug overdose. The painting was returned badly damaged, but thanks to the heroic efforts of a team of conservators it is back on display in the cathedral in Valletta.

Sadly, Father Zerafa passed away in 2022. Before his death, a reporter asked him what the secret to his vitality was, to which he replied, "I drink and smoke a lot." Father Zerafa and Caravaggio could have had some fun together.

CARAVAGGIO'S DRAMATIC LIFE

Saint John's Co-Cathedral in Valletta acquired two of Caravaggio's sixty-eight known paintings when Caravaggio spent time in Malta after fleeing a bounty on his head. According to the *New York Times*, Caravaggio "had every possible defect of character," and had moved to Rome from Milan at the age of twenty-one. In Rome, he accelerated to rock-star status as an artist after patrons from the church and society bought and commissioned his work. Caravaggio's bad behavior didn't keep patrons away, though it did keep him in jail for crimes ranging from throwing a plate of artichokes in a waiter's face to smearing excrement on his landlady's door. Caravaggio really crossed the line when he killed a rival and was sentenced to beheading. He fled to Naples, where, in an attempt to avoid his sentence, he tried to become a Knight of Malta, an order of military men who were literally above the law,

having their own legal code. Surprisingly, his plan worked, and he lived in Malta, painting portraits of other knights and the great pieces in Saint John's Co-Cathedral.

Things went well for Caravaggio in Malta until his hot-headed nature saw him self-imploding again. He was part of an attack that wounded one of the most important knights in the order. Never one to accept his fate, he escaped prison by breaking out onto the rocky cliffs and scaling down a two-hundred-foot precipice into the sea, where he met a boat that smuggled him over the ocean to Sicily. He was never tried for this crime, though the knights ritually defrocked an effigy of Caravaggio at his altarpiece. In total, Caravaggio lasted only six months as a Knight of Malta.

The rest of Caravaggio's tale is sad and dark. It involves more violence and eventually death at a seaport north of Rome at the age of only thirty-nine. His paintings are his legacy.

EUROPE: THE NETHERLANDS

When: April 14, 1991, and December 7, 2002

Where: Van Gogh Museum in Amsterdam

What: Thefts of twenty paintings by Van Gogh in 1991 and two paintings—
Van Gogh's *View of the Sea at Scheveningen* (1882) and *Congregation
Leaving the Reformed Church in Nuenen* (1884–85)—in 2002

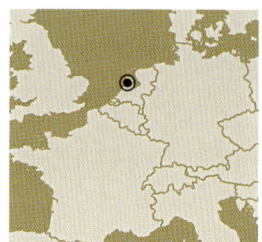

HOLLAND'S MOST STOLEN ARTIST

Though all have since been recovered, between 1991 and 2020, twenty-nine paintings by Vincent Van Gogh were stolen in the Netherlands, making him the country's most popular artist to steal. Two of the highest-profile Van Gogh thefts were from his namesake museum in Amsterdam. The first theft happened on April 14, 1991, around 3:00 a.m. After hiding in a museum bathroom for hours after closing, the thief snuck up on the two security guards on duty, stuffing one in a closet while the other, who was in on the theft, turned off the security system. The thief then let in another accomplice. After a leisurely forty-five minutes or so, the thieves packed twenty paintings into two expandable garment bags and drove off in a Volkswagen Passat. Among the stolen paintings were some of Van Gogh's most famous works: *The Potato Eaters* (1885), *Sunflowers* (1889), and *The Bedroom* (1888).

The theft was notable for two main reasons. First, it was the largest theft from a museum in the Netherlands. And second, it had the shortest recovery time: thirty-five minutes. The museum guards had called the police at 4:48 a.m., and by 5:23 a.m., the paintings had been found in the thieves' getaway car, which was parked at a train station in Amsterdam. The thieves had planned to rendezvous with a second getaway car, but got a flat tire en route. Panicking, they fled and abandoned their haul. Four men were eventually arrested for the theft and sentenced to prison.

In another robbery that took place on December 7, 2002, Octave Durham, who calls himself "a born burglar," along with a partner, stole two paintings from the Van Gogh Museum after entering through a skylight. The police eventually nabbed the thieves, but not the paintings. Fourteen years later, the two missing paintings were recovered, wrapped in cloth, from a farmhouse north of Naples, Italy, belonging to the mother of a Mafia boss, and were back on display by 2017.

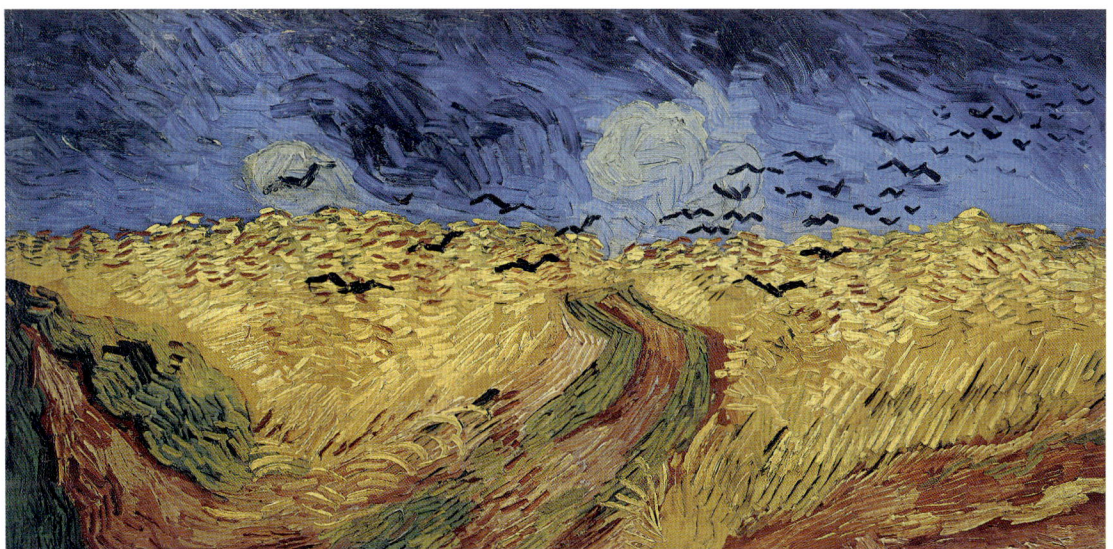

Above: One of twenty paintings stolen from the Van Gogh Museum in 1991, *Wheatfield with Crows* is an iconic image. Some think it was Van Gogh's last painting, a foreshadowing of his tragic death.

Right: Van Gogh's *Irises*, painted while the artist was convalescing at a psychiatric hospital in Saint-Rémy, is another of the paintings stolen in 1991.

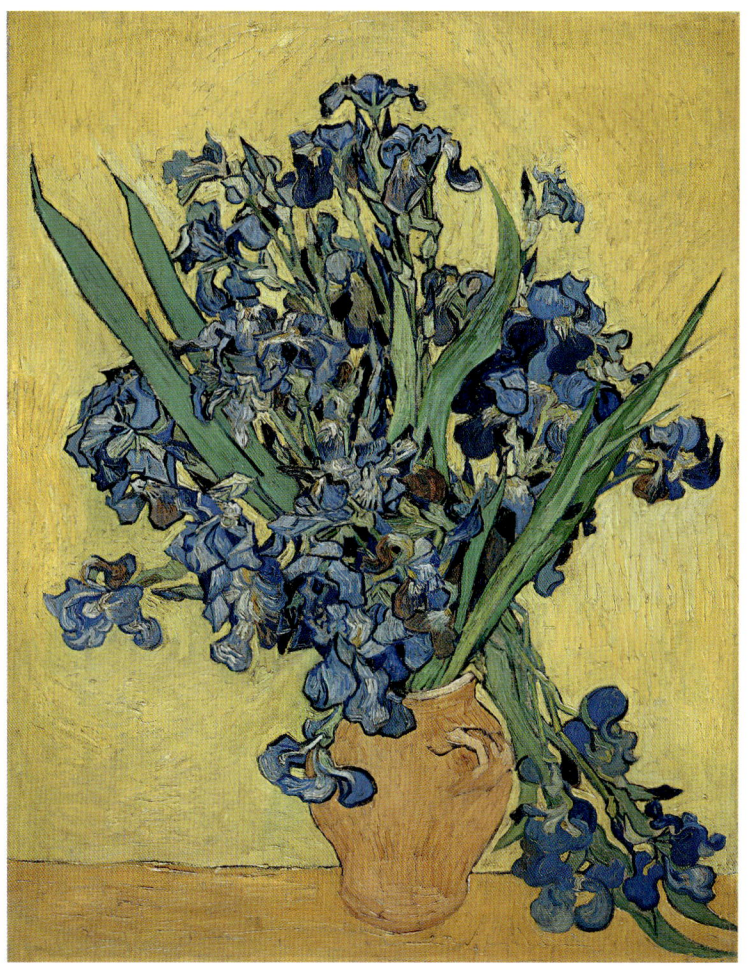

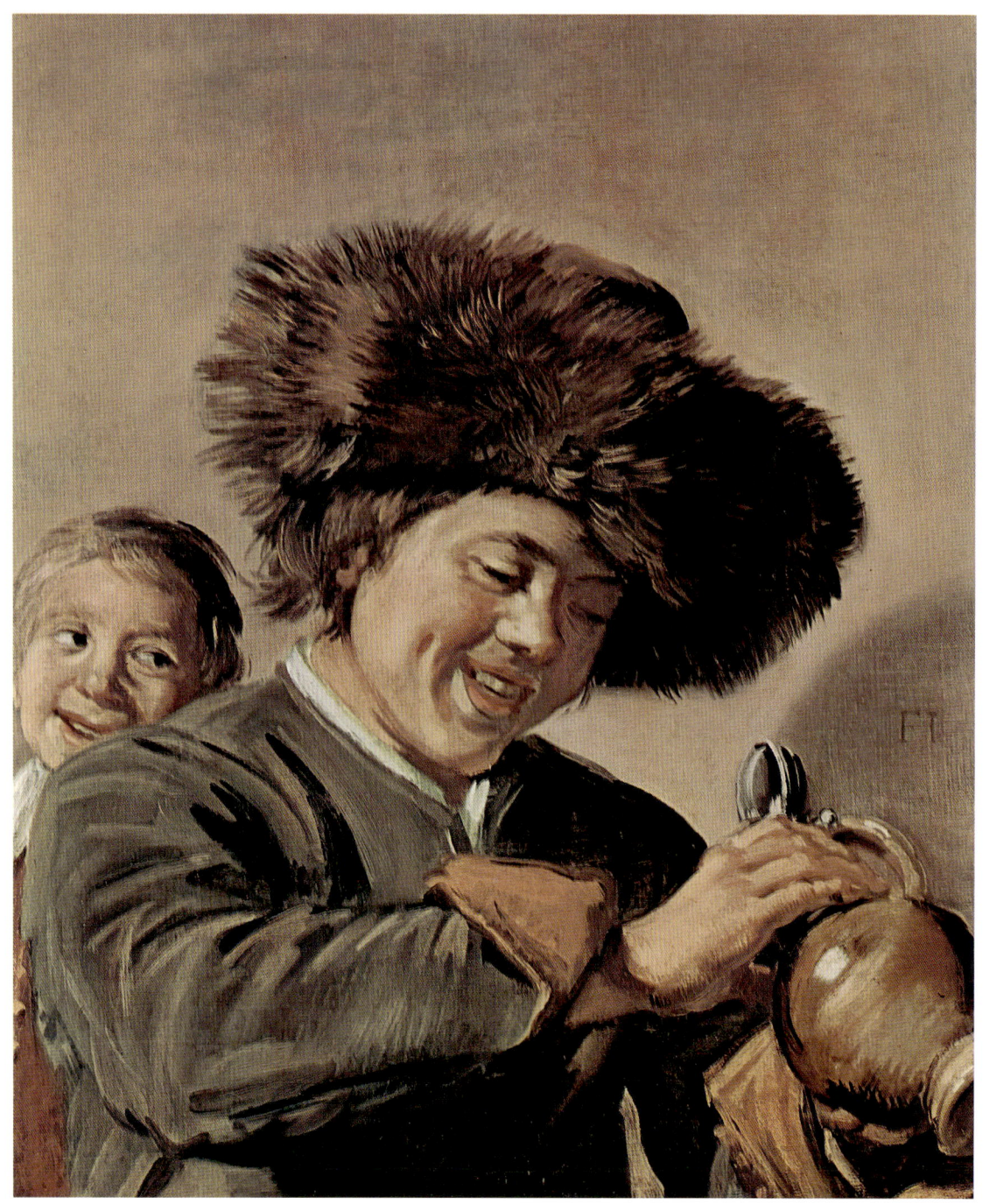

Above: This Hals painting was stolen from the Hofje van Mevrouw van Aerden on three occasions. Even today, the museum doubles as a traditional *hofje* or almshouse, which offers lodgings to unmarried women, a Netherlandish tradition going back to the Middle Ages.

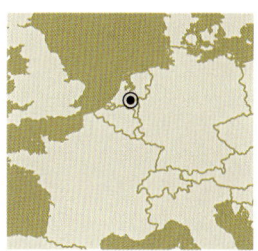

THIRD TIME'S THE CHARM?

Frans Hals's *Two Laughing Boys and a Mug of Beer* contains a moral message about gluttony—*Kannekijker* (mug-looker) being an old Dutch word for a greedy person. Thieves seem to have ignored this message, however, as the painting has been stolen three times.

In 1988, thieves broke into the Hofje van Mevrouw van Aerden in Leerdam through a window, taking the facility manager's wife hostage and forcing her husband, at gunpoint, to disarm the security system. He sounded the alarm, but not before the thieves snatched the Hals painting along with another seventeenth-century piece, *Forest View with Flowering Elderberry* by Jacob van Ruisdael.

The painting was returned three years later, after the insurance company paid 500,000 guilders to the bodyguard of an infamous Dutch criminal, Klaas Bruinsma. After Bruinsma's 1991 murder, the bodyguard leveraged his knowledge and ransomed the paintings. A year after their return, the thieves' getaway driver developed a conscience and two people were arrested.

In the early hours of April 27, 2011, the Hals was stolen again. The frame was found in a bush outside the museum, which was contacted by parties demanding a "recovery fee." Four men were busted five months later by undercover police pretending to be insurance agents. The four refused to tattle on the real thief, who eluded prosecution.

Early on August 27, 2020, security cameras captured two men puttering up to the museum on a scooter. The alarm sounded at 3:30 a.m., and video shows the two men driving away again, carrying a painting-shaped item.

In 2021, police arrested the thief, who had already had a busy year: Not only had he committed the Hals theft, but he had also stolen Van Gogh's *The Parsonage Garden at Nuenen* (1884) from the Singer Laren (p. 213). The thief claims he doesn't know what happened to either painting, and art crime experts believe him; the paintings probably disappeared into the criminal underworld. The thief was sentenced to a maximum of eight years in prison. Both paintings remain missing.

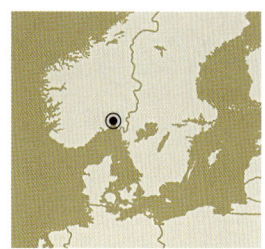

When: May 7, 1994, and August 22, 2004

Where: National Museum and Munch Museum in Oslo

What: Theft of Edvard Munch's *The Scream* (1893) from the National Museum in 1994 and Munch's *The Scream* (1910) and *Madonna* (1894) from the Munch Museum in 2004

SOMETHING(S) TO SCREAM ABOUT

Edvard Munch's *The Scream* exists in four different versions—two in paint (dated 1893 and 1910) and two in pastel (dated 1893 and 1895). The two painted versions have endured two very different thefts from two different museums in Oslo.

At around 11:10 a.m. on August 22, 2004, armed men shrouded in balaclavas stormed the Munch Museum. Brandishing guns and threatening terrified museumgoers and guards, they ordered everyone to the ground, then ripped off the walls two works by Norway's beloved artist Edvard Munch: the 1910 version of *The Scream* and his 1894 *Madonna*. An eyewitness photographed the robbers casually walking to an ordinary hatchback car with the paintings.

The two paintings were valued at around $100 million at the time. Police found the frames of both paintings, along with the thieves' stolen getaway car, but had no further leads. It was feared that the paintings had been destroyed or seriously damaged. *The Scream* was made on cardboard, making it extremely fragile.

Police waited for a ransom demand, as such an iconic work would be impossible to sell, even underground. Because of Norwegian privacy laws, we know very little about what happened next except that the stolen Munchs were not recovered, even after arrests had been made. In 2006, six people faced trial for the crime. Half were convicted and sentenced to four to eight years in prison and required to pay the city of Oslo for the art, which the court calculated to be worth $117 million.

Later in 2006, almost two years after the pieces were stolen, Norwegian authorities proudly announced the return of the Munch works. Police have not revealed specifics as to how the paintings were found, but no reward or ransom was paid, nor did those convicted of the

Opposite: The 1893 version of *The Scream* has a message from Munch, scrawled in light pencil. It reads, "Kan kun være malet af en gal Mand!" In English: "Could only have been painted by a madman!"

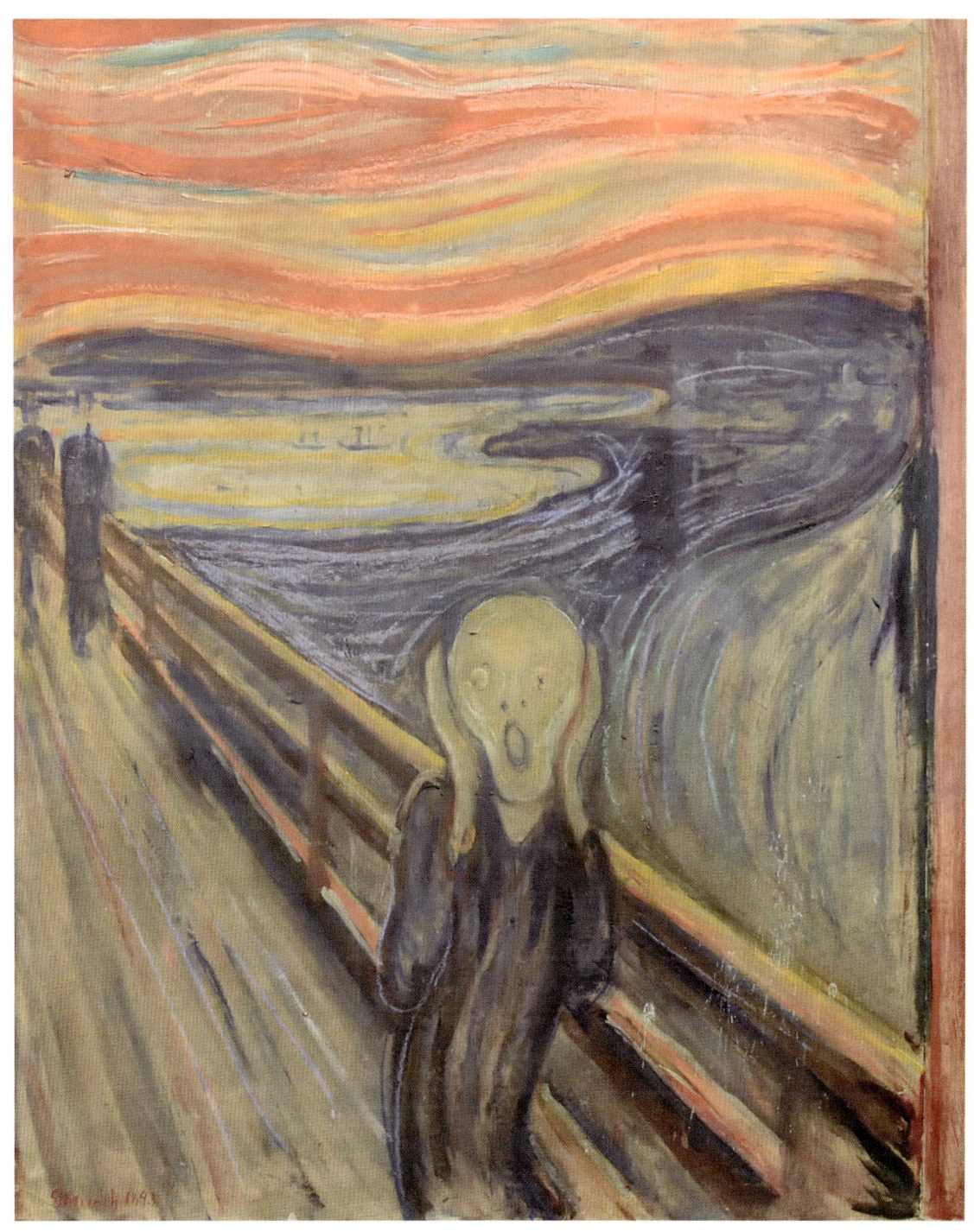

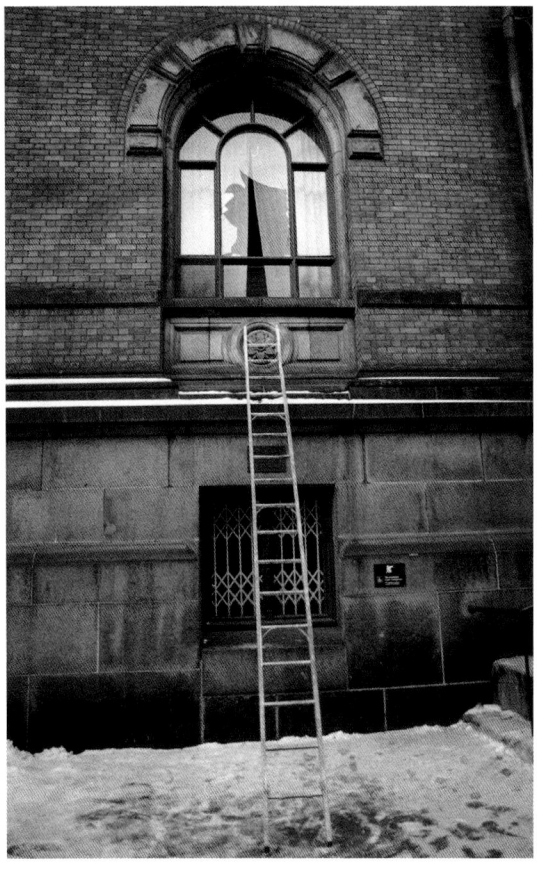

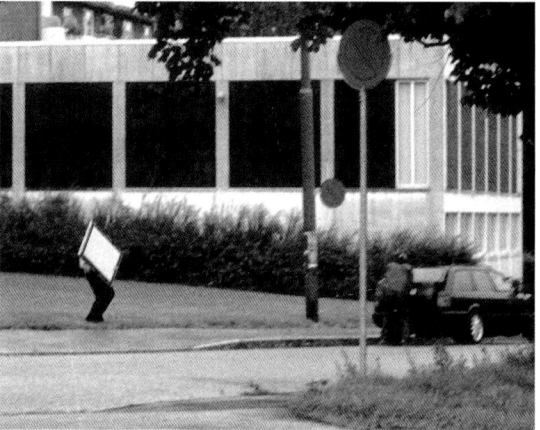

Left: The infamous ladder from the 1994 theft at the National Museum of Norway. In the heat of the robbery and the chase, one of the thieves and a police officer both fell off this ladder.

Above: In the 2004 theft from the Munch Museum, a bystander snapped a photo of the thieves walking their haul out to their hatchback car.

theft help in the recovery operation. Fortunately, the works suffered only minor damage that conservators were able to repair.

The National Gallery of Norway was the site of a second theft in 1994. Norway was eager to put its best forward as the hosts of the 1994 Olympic Winter Games. The museum wanted to show off *The Scream*, so they moved it to the second floor for easier access; however, they placed the work near a window that did not have reinforced glass or metal grates over it.

At 7:00 a.m. on the day of the Olympic opening ceremony, the thieves parked their stolen car and placed the ladder they had stashed near the museum at the window. Security cameras recorded them, but the museum's night guard, who was at the end of his shift, was not paying attention. The first thief got to the top of the ladder and promptly fell off but clambered back to the top and smashed the window with a hammer, setting off a security alarm. The guard simply turned it off without checking.

In less than a minute, the thief had removed *The Scream*, leaned out the window, and dropped it down to his accomplice below.

Another alarm was tripped about ten minutes later when a motion sensor reacted to wind blowing through the window. Finally, the guard called a supervisor, who advised them to call the police.

A squad car that was already driving around the area saw the ladder and the broken window, and the police quickly raced in to assess the situation. One officer climbed up the ladder and, like the thief, promptly fell off. Backup was called so that the officer could be taken to the hospital. Ladders in Norwegian winters must be treacherous.

Smartly, the other officers took the stairs, finding two things: a pair of wire cutters and a postcard. The postcard depicted a painting of three men, laughing heartily in a cheery style. On the back, the thieves had scrawled "Thanks for the poor security."

Museum officials were flabbergasted and faced with a public relations nightmare as the Winter Olympics began. They framed a poster of *The Scream* from the gift shop and hand-wrote "Stolen" on it.

Security-camera footage was too grainy to identify the thieves and there were no eyewitnesses. Norwegian authorities looked at many false leads. Through a series of events, the art crime unit of the United Kingdom's Scotland Yard was brought in as part of the operation, led by experienced British-American art detective, Charlie Hill. They developed a nuanced sting operation in which Hill would play a character named Christopher Charles Roberts, who represented the J. Paul Getty Museum, negotiating on behalf of the National Gallery. The basic premise was that the Getty would put up the ransom cash for the Norwegian National Gallery in exchange for a loan of *The Scream*. The plan worked, and Hill, who had entered the country as Roberts, was able to recover *The Scream*, miraculously unharmed.

Two years later, a former professional soccer player turned thief was convicted of masterminding the theft and sentenced to six years in prison. Three other accomplices received sentences ranging from three to five years in prison. All four men appealed; shockingly, all but the mastermind were set free on the grounds that the Scotland Yard detectives' testimonies were inadmissible because they had entered the country under false names, making prosecution of the thieves unlawful. Upon this news, the detectives may have put their hands to their cheeks, opened their mouths, and screamed.

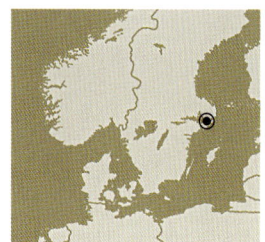

When: December 22, 2000

Where: Nationalmuseum in Stockholm

What: Theft of Pierre-Auguste Renoir's *Young Parisian* (c. 1875) and *Conversation* (1878) and Rembrandt van Rijn's *Self-Portrait* (1630)

SLASH AND DASH IN SWEDEN

On December 22, 2000, five minutes before the closing of the Nationalmuseum in Stockholm, a man walked into the lobby, pointed a submachine gun at the guard, and ordered everyone to the ground. Two other men, already inside the museum, brandished their handguns and removed three small paintings—two Renoirs and a Rembrandt—from the walls. The three men dashed out of the museum and into their getaway … boat! Stockholm is set across fourteen islands and the Nationalmuseum is right on the water, so the thieves made their escape by speedboat. While the men were robbing the museum, accomplices detonated two car bombs on opposite sides of the city, while other collaborators called the police to report the explosions. Police from all over the city rushed to the bomb sites, leaving the thieves to carry out their work uninterrupted. Just in case anyone tried to get to the museum, they threw nails on the road to hinder any vehicles.

Swedes were stunned and wounded by the theft. The three stolen artworks were worth around $45 million. The museum had not been allowed to set up security cameras because it was considered a violation of public privacy. This made it easy for would-be thieves to enter unhindered. (Future thieves beware: since the theft, the museum has been allowed to install security cameras.)

Shortly after the paintings disappeared, the museum received a ransom note for $3 million. Even though the paintings were worth more than ten times that, $3 million would have been a tidy amount for the thieves to quickly and easily get their hands on. Within a month, police had arrested ten people for their involvement in the heist, which included an international mix of Russians, Iraqis, a Gambian, and Swedes, along with two lawyers who had acted as middlemen during the ransom demands. But though arrests were made, there was no sign of the paintings.

A few months later, the first painting was recovered when police were least expecting it. They discovered Renoir's *Conversation* during a drug raid, which goes to show that drugs and art are strange bedfellows. Perhaps surprisingly,

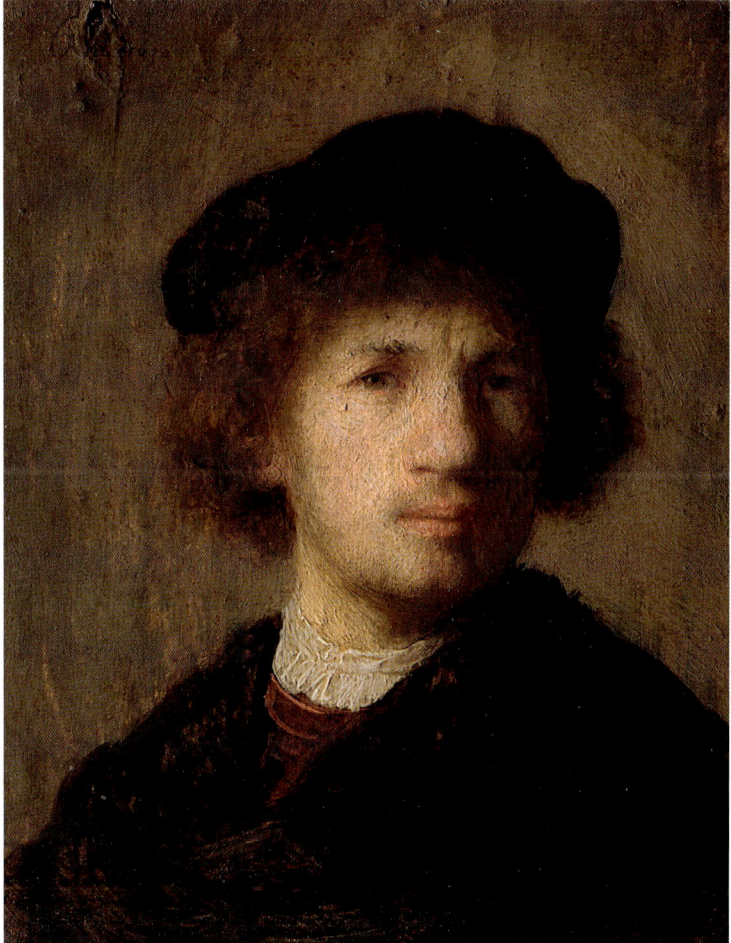

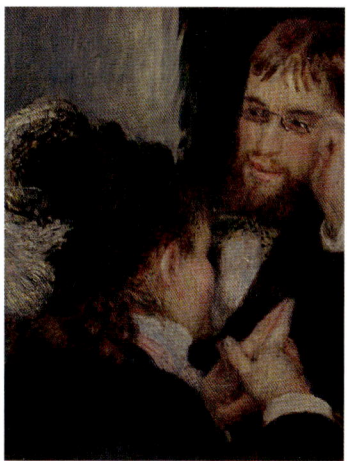

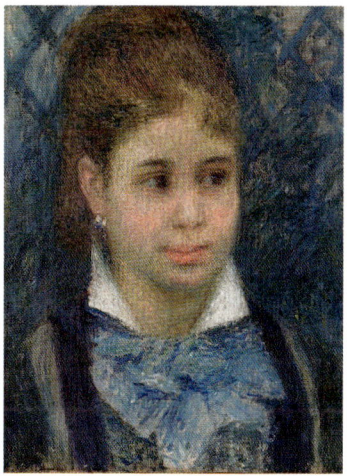

Above: One of Rembrandt's many self-portraits, this one from 1630 was one of three paintings stolen in 2000 from the Nationalmuseum in Sweden. It was the last of the stolen works to be recovered in 2005 thanks to a sting operation led by the FBI in Copenhagen.

Top right: *Conversation* (1878), by Renoir, was found during an unrelated drug raid. The police report at the time read, "We weren't looking for the painting so it was a bonus when we found it."

Above: Renoir's *Young Parisien* (c. 1875) was recovered with help from the FBI.

art crime is the third-highest-grossing illicit trade after drugs and arms. When a work of art can't be sold or thieves don't get the ransom they expect, they may use the art as a form of currency in exchange for guns and drugs. Only 5–10 percent of stolen art is ever recovered, so the Stockholm police were not optimistic that the other two paintings would be found. But,

finally, five years after the heist, the second Renoir and the Rembrandt were returned to the Nationalmuseum. The paintings were recovered in separate sting operations; one involved an FBI agent posing as a member of the Russian mob and pretending that he wanted to buy Rembrandt's *Self-Portrait*, catching the thieves red-handed.

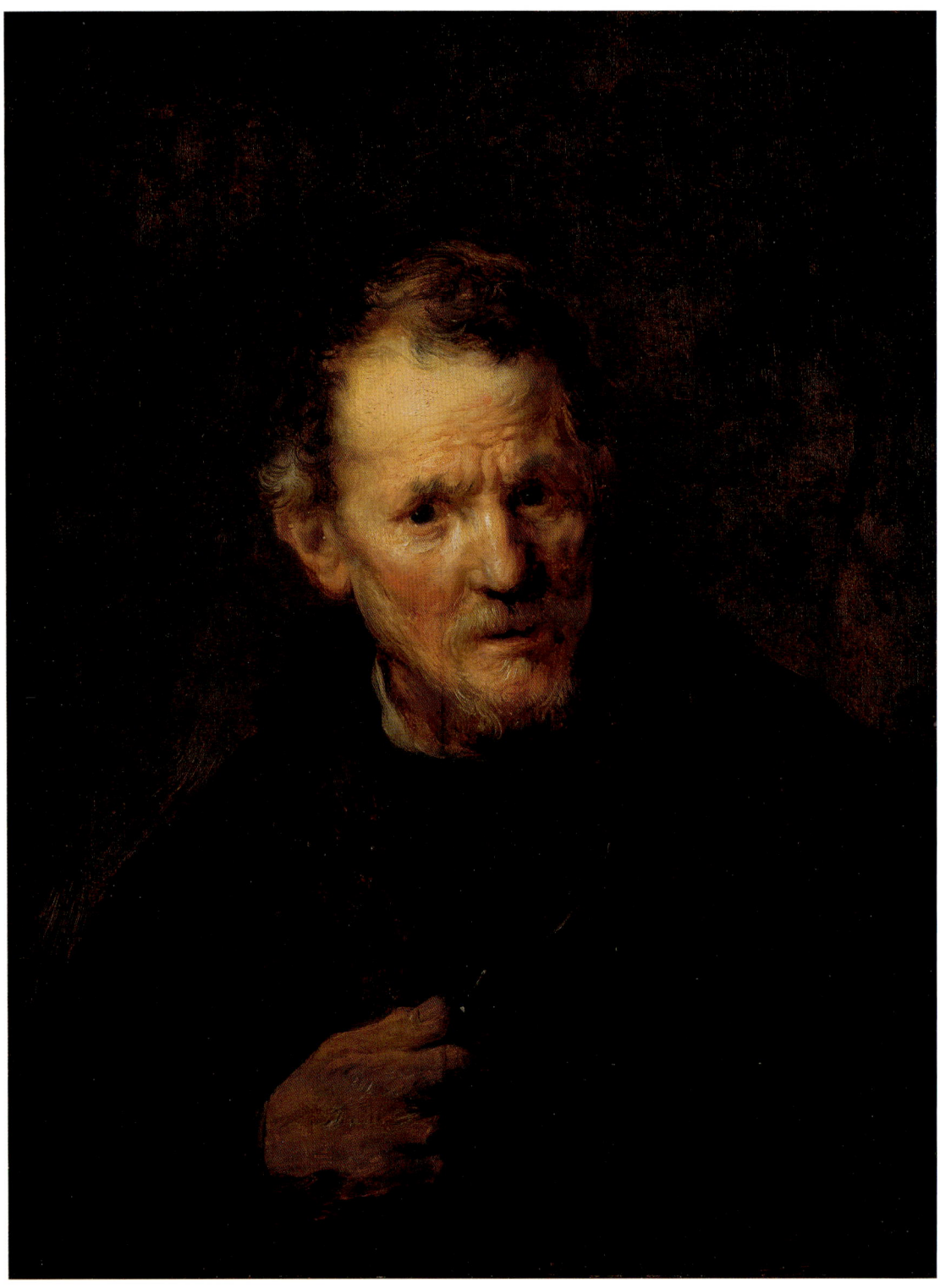

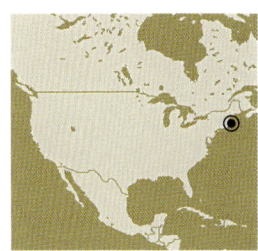

When: May 17, 1972

Where: Worcester Art Museum in Worcester, Massachusetts

What: Theft of Rembrandt van Rijn's *Saint Bartholomew* (1633), Paul Gauguin's *The Brooding Woman* (1891) and *Mademoiselle Manthey* (1884), and Pablo Picasso's *Mother and Child by a Fountain* (1901)

FIRST IMPRESSIONS

The 1972 theft of four artworks from the Worcester Art Museum in Worcester, Massachusetts, was a big deal for a few reasons. At the time, the Worcester Art Museum had a larger collection than both the Guggenheim and Whitney museums in New York; for a small city in Massachusetts, this was quite a coup. Also, at the time it was committed, the art heist was the second biggest in history. (In first place was the 1966 theft of eight paintings from the Dulwich Picture Gallery; p. 30). Least auspiciously, it was the first art theft at gunpoint.

In broad daylight on May 17, 1972, two thieves stole four treasures from the museum: Rembrandt's *Saint Bartholomew*, two Gauguins titled *The Brooding Woman* and *Mademoiselle Manthey* (the first Gauguins to enter an American museum collection), and Picasso's *Mother and Child by a Fountain*. The thieves made a strong impression on patrons and employees that day. Two teenagers completing a school assignment at the museum saw a man dart between the galleries with a painting. They investigated, and saw the man remove another painting from the wall and place it in a cloth bag. When the thief spotted the girls, he pulled his gun, ordered them to sit down in the gallery, and gravely told them that what they were witnessing was not a joke. They huddled under a table in the gallery while the thieves removed artwork from the walls.

The thieves were also painfully memorable to the unarmed guard posted at the doors of the museum. Suspicious of the men running through the lobby, with face masks on and carrying bulging bags, Philip Evans, who was fifty-seven at the time, grabbed the first thief's wrist. That thief hit Evans with a bag of art, but Evans was able to grab the second thief around the neck. As they struggled, Evans heard a gunshot, then felt a bullet strike his hip. The thieves hightailed it to the getaway car waiting outside. A patron, who happened to be a nurse, tended to Evans while the thieves escaped.

Opposite: Rembrandt depicted Saint Bartholomew with a knife, which, according to some accounts, was the instrument of his demise: he was flayed to death. Instead of a knife, thieves used a gun to steal this painting.

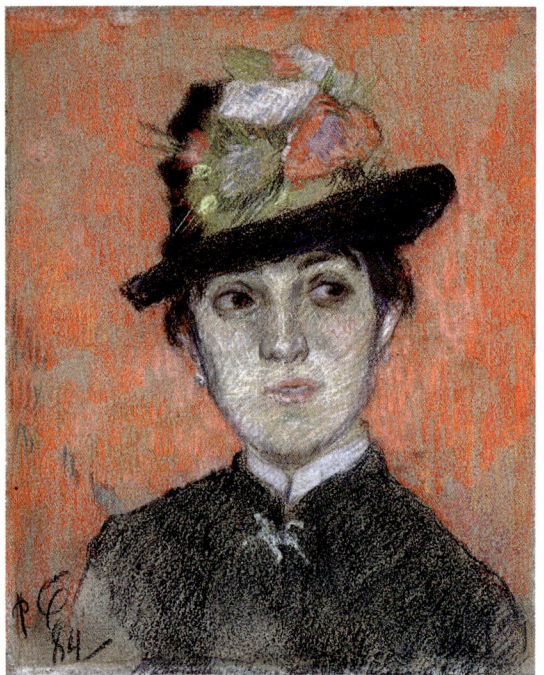

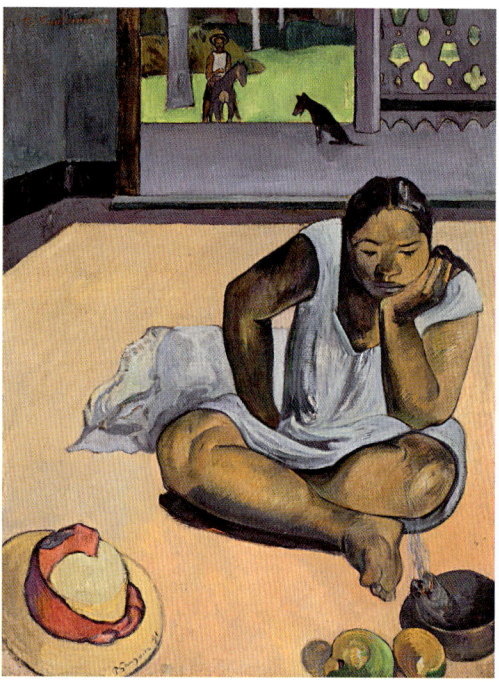

Above: A year after becoming a full-time artist, Gauguin created this oil pastel of Mademoiselle Manthey. Its theft was the first time in the history of art crime that art was stolen at gunpoint.

Above: Once a successful stockbroker, Gauguin left his family for the South Pacific, where he allegedly spread syphilis and took underage mistresses. This painting of a brooding Tahitian woman was stolen in the 1972 heist.

Two seventeen-year-old girls waiting outside in their car for their two friends who were completing their school assignment in the museum, had unwittingly parked right in front of the thieves' getaway car. Gobsmacked, they saw the two men furiously running out of the museum with giant pillowcases full of art, then hopping into the car parked behind them. The thieves threw one bag of art into the car and one onto the roof of the car. Realizing that they were boxed in by the girls, the thief with the gun ran up and pointed it in the driver's face, ordering her to move. She did, and a third accomplice, the getaway driver, peeled out of the museum's circular driveway, taking the thieves and their haul with him.

Though the two thieves wore ski masks (one blue, one orange), the many impressions they left during their time at the museum made it easy for witnesses to provide descriptions of their builds and clothing. Just two days after the theft, Worcester City Police and the FBI arrested three suspects—the two thieves, Stephen Thoren and William Carlson (who shot the guard), and a co-conspirator, Carol Naster (one of the few women involved in art theft throughout history). Two days later, David Aquafresca, the getaway driver, was arrested. Another man, Florian "Al" Monday, the mastermind behind the theft, eluded police for several years until he was arrested in Canada by the Royal Canadian Mounted Police in 1974. A former university art student who had

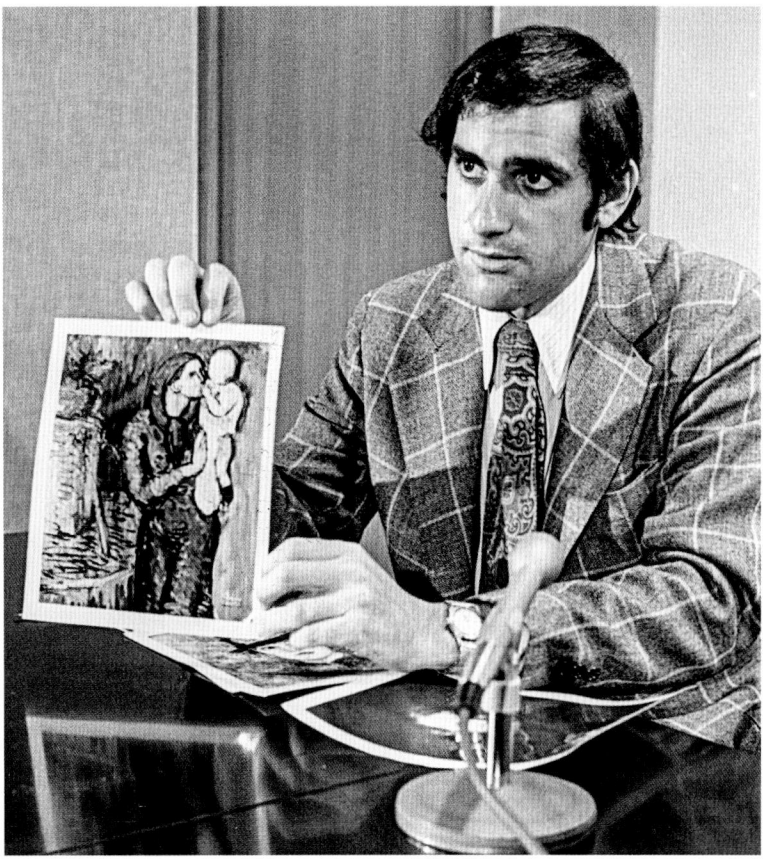

never graduated, Monday had an appreciation for art. Later, he would recount wistfully that he thought he had planned an infallible heist. He didn't account for the two thieves making themselves so visible and memorable. It also didn't help that, after the theft, they bragged about their heist in a bar. Though it took three and half years for all the suspects to be caught, they all served a prison sentence or probation for their crimes.

Due to his excellent art heist planning, Monday remained on the radar of police and the FBI, and, when the Isabella Stewart Gardner Museum was epically burgled in 1991 (p. 98), Monday was inevitably questioned and considered a suspect.

On June 12, almost a month after the Worcester theft, police announced that all the paintings had been recovered. Though two paintings were missing their frames, they were all in good shape, even after being hidden in a hayloft at a pig farm in Rhode Island. And, very happily, the guard who was shot made a full recovery and even returned to his work at the museum.

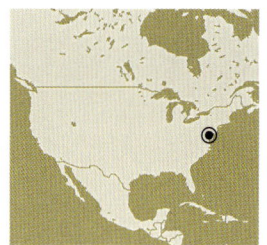

CHIP ON THE SHOULDER

In January 1983, the *Virgin of Alsace* was stolen from the Phillips Collection in Washington DC. Clocking in at over two feet high and weighing fifty pounds, the statue would not have been the easiest artwork to slip into a pocket or hide in an overcoat. In fact, it would be downright awkward to try to sneak a statue of that size and weight out of a museum unobserved. But that is exactly what a thief was able to do.

Émile-Antoine Bourdelle was a French sculptor, well known for his art deco and Beaux-Arts-inspired work. Bourdelle had been taught by the sculpture legend Auguste Rodin and would go on to teach rising superstars at the time, including Alberto Giacometti and Henri Matisse. The *Virgin of Alsace* was commissioned by Madame Vogt, an industrialist in Niederbrück, France, who swore she would erect a sculpture dedicated to the Virgin if her property was saved from destruction during World War I. Thankfully, her home was spared and, in 1919, Madame Vogt's son awarded the commission to Bourdelle, who created a twenty-foot-tall version of the *Virgin of Alsace* on the Vogt property in Niederbrück. Bourdelle used his wife, Cléopatre, and daughter, Rhodia, as the models for the statue. Cléopatre was also a sculptor. When working, she kept the dust out of her hair with a scarf, which is echoed in the Virgin's head covering in the statue. Bourdelle created several smaller versions of the *Virgin of Alsace* in varying sizes and materials. One of these happened to catch the attention of the Phillips Collection thief.

The day after the *Virgin of Alsace* was discovered missing from the Phillips Collection, the museum received a phone call from an anonymous woman who said that the statue could be recovered from an alley behind a gas station at 18th and S. Street N.W. When the director of the Phillips and other museum officials arrived on the scene, they found the *Virgin*, valued at around $35,000 at the time, in a green trash bag. Inside the bag was also a note written in block letters on a piece of yellow legal paper. The note read, "I have been a patron of your collection for some time. Recently I have been concerned about the laxness in security at the gallery."

As in some other art thefts—for example, the theft of three watercolors from the Whitworth

Gallery (p. 26) and the theft of the Cellini saliera from the Kunsthistoriches Museum in Vienna (p. 60)—here a vigilante thief claimed to have been protecting the art by pointing out weak links in a museum's security. Not everyone bought the Phillips Collection thief's rationalization. The director of the Phillips, Laughlin Phillips, scoffed, "I think the thief is just trying to put the best face on his action in case he or she is caught."

The thief was never caught, and the *Virgin of Alsace* was returned to the museum. She suffered a small bit of damage during her adventures in the alleys of DC—a small chip on her shoulder. Perhaps the thief had a chip on their shoulder, too.

Right: Created in 1920 and acquired by the Phillips Collection in 1925, Émile-Antoine Bourdelle's *Virgin of Alsace* was inspired by the artist's appreciation for French Gothic sculpture.

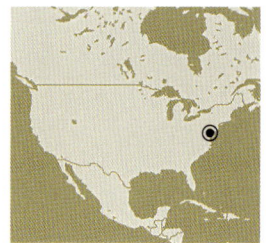

DAYLIGHT ROBBERY

As the story goes, Renoir created *On the Shore of the Seine* when he was dining and drinking beside the Seine with his mistress. He picked up a linen napkin from their table and dashed off a pretty little scene of the river and its surroundings for his lover.

Several decades later, in 1925, the pioneering art collector Saidie May bought the painting in France. May's biography shows the painting hanging in her New York apartment before she loaned it to the Baltimore Museum of Art in 1937. May would later donate it and many other valuable works when she passed in 1951.

After May's donation, the painting's provenance became even murkier than the river it depicts. Sometime between 4:00 p.m. on November 16 and 1:00 p.m. on November 17, 1951, the painting was stolen from the museum with no signs of forced entry. The painting is small enough—around the size of a piece of letter paper—that it would have been easy enough to slink away with. The museum noted its theft in their archives, but over time the theft was forgotten and never listed with any art-loss registries.

The river painting resurfaced in 2012 when Marcia "Martha" Fuqua claimed to have bought the Renoir at the Harpers Ferry Flea Market in West Virginia. Fuqua maintained that she had no idea what the $7 mystery junk box held when she bought it. After discovering the Renoir, she took it to an auction house, where it was expected to sell for more than $100,000. Everyone loves a story of a treasure fortuitously purchased on the cheap, so when it was taken up by the media, *Washington Post* journalist Ian Shapira decided to do more digging. Shapira knew that the previous owner, Saidie May, had been a significant donor to the Baltimore Museum of Art. Together, Shapira and the museum discovered not only that the Renoir belonged to the museum, but also that it had been stolen in 1951.

The waters continued to swirl. Martha's brother Matt told the press that he remembered the Renoir hanging in their mother's home for "probably 50 to 60 years." Other people also said they too remembered seeing the painting in the house. Martha and Matt's mother, Marcia, who was eighty-four at the time the painting reemerged, was an artist who had an affinity

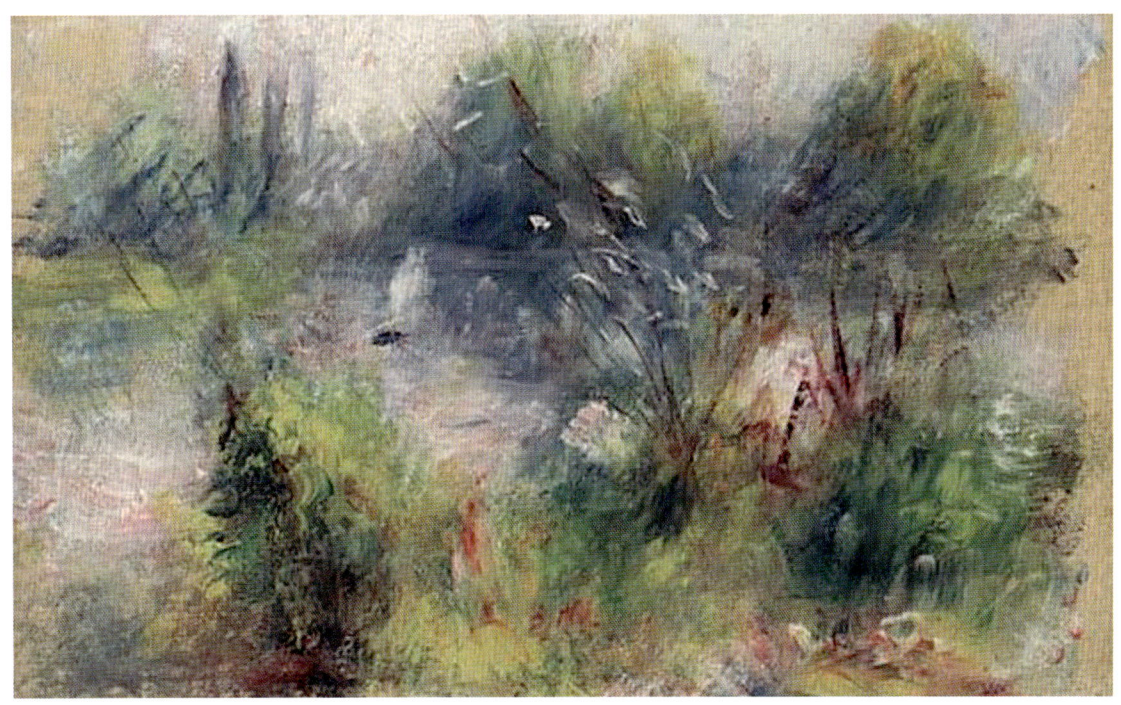

Above: Renoir could well have painted this scene on a napkin over lunch—he was known to work quickly. Over his lifetime, Renoir is believed to have produced somewhere between four and six thousand paintings.

for Renoir. She had written about Renoir in her 1957 master's thesis at the Maryland Institute College of Art, and, in her professional studio, she had specialized in recreating works by famous artists, including Renoir.

Marcia passed away from cancer in September 2013, never having been questioned by the FBI; they felt it was not "appropriate," considering her illness.

How Renoir's river scene ended up on the auction block may never be completely clear. Eventually, after a tangle of lawsuits, the Renoir was returned to the museum, where it was welcomed with exactly the sort of grand homecoming reserved for a painting the museum didn't even know was missing.

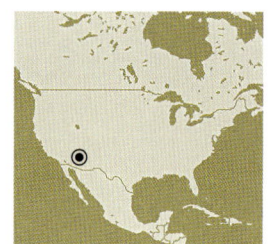

A COUPLE OF UNLIKELY THIEVES

Hollywood would like us to believe that art thieves are gorgeous, sleek, debonair cat burglars like Catherine Zeta-Jones in *Entrapment* or Cary Grant in *To Catch a Thief*. Rita and Jerry Alter of Cliff, New Mexico, belied these stereotypes. In 1985, the unassuming married couple were in their mid-fifties and looked like the speech pathologist and schoolteacher they were.

When the guard at the University of Arizona Museum of Art (UAMA) opened the doors to the museum on November 29, 1985, Rita and Jerry slipped in. While Rita chatted with the security guard, Jerry crept away to the Willem de Kooning painting, *Woman-Ochre*. Worth $400,000 at the time, *Woman-Ochre* is valued at $1.6 million today.

While Rita and the guard talked for nearly fifteen minutes, Jerry cut the painting out of the frame. But he hadn't anticipated that the canvas would be fixed to a supporting layer, making it hard to cut through. Jerry peeled the painted canvas away from the supporting layer, freeing the canvas but also causing damage. Rolling up the canvas and stuffing it into his clothing worsened its condition, though it did conceal the stolen work. The couple walked out into the November desert morning and drove off in a red sports car. The guard remembered Rita wearing a red jacket, and a composite sketch of the couple looks remarkably like photos of the two at the time. But there were no security cameras and no fingerprints at the museum to capture more evidence.

Woman-Ochre was not seen again for over thirty years, except by the Alters. They hung the painting behind a door in their bedroom. When the door was open, the painting was hidden. When the door was closed, the painting could only be seen from Jerry and Rita's bed. Before hanging it, the Alters amateurishly stapled the canvas onto a tacky frame and varnished the

Opposite: Antiques dealer David Van Auker helped to discover the stolen de Kooning. He didn't ask for a reward, only that he be allowed to keep the painting's frame, proudly displayed in his New Mexico shop.

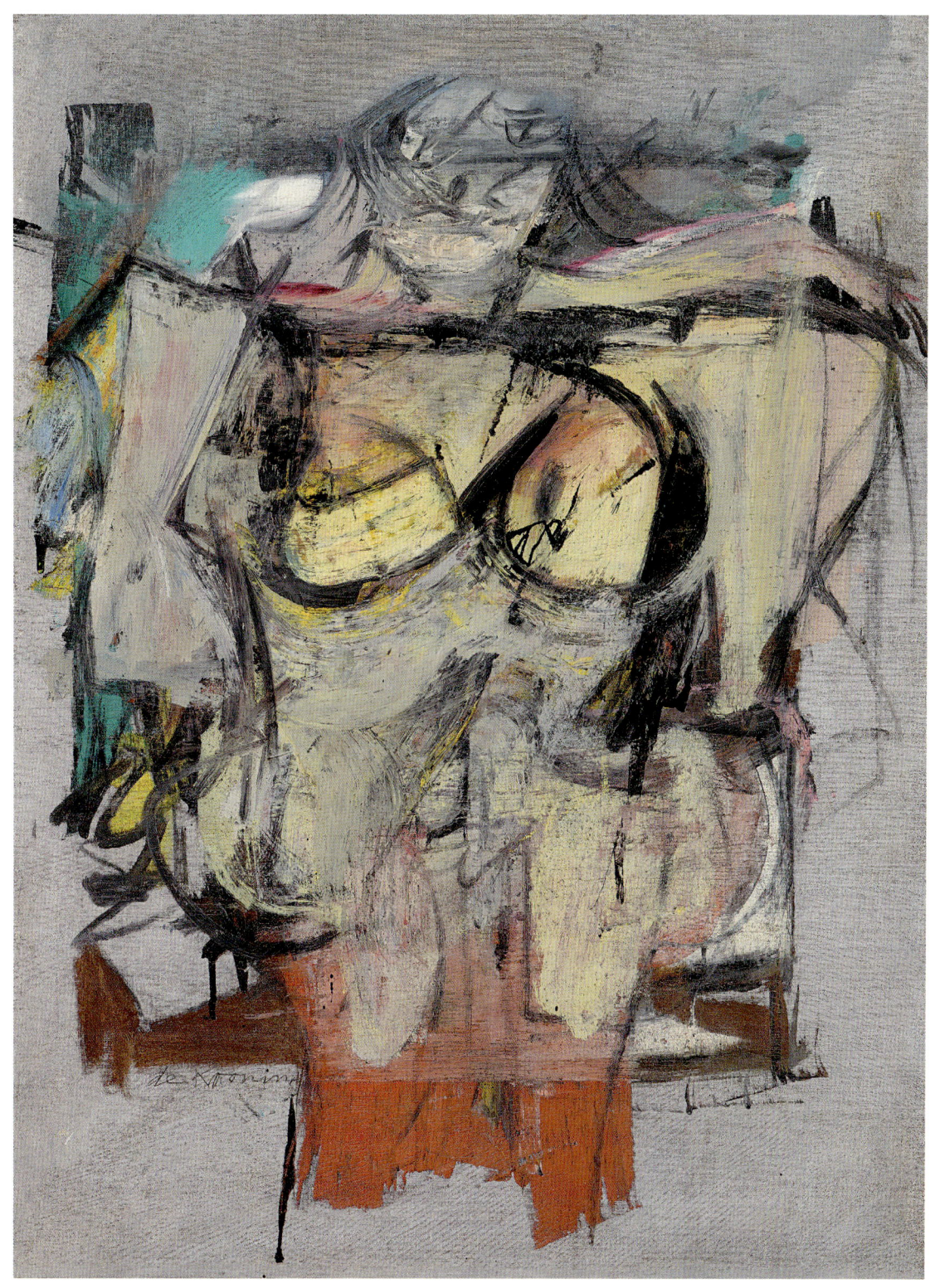

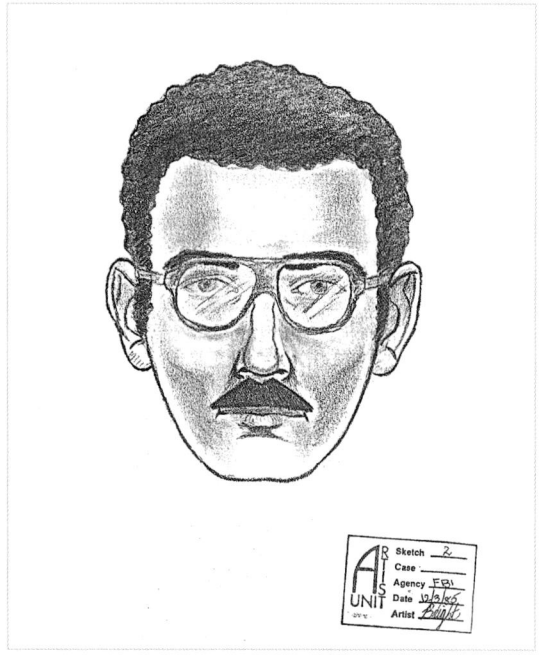

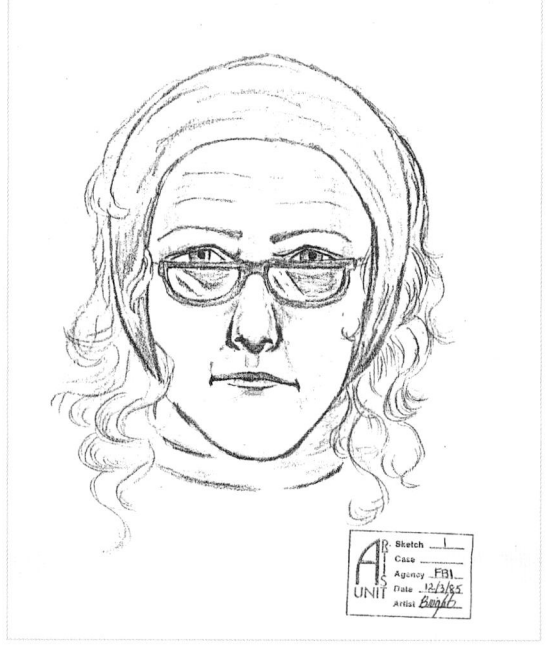

Above: A police sketch of the thief, Jerry Alter, a music teacher, who stole Willem de Kooning's *Woman-Ochre* from the University of Arizona Museum of Art in 1985.

Above: A police sketch of Jerry Alter's accomplice, Rita Alter, a speech pathologist. She kept the guard busy with chit chat while her partner cut the painting out of its frame.

surface with the sort of glue you would buy at a grocery store. Between the damage done during the theft, the glue varnish, and the direct line of sight to the Alters' bed, *Woman-Ochre* endured many indignities.

In 2017, David Van Auker, an antiques dealer and estate buyer who co-owns Manzanita Ridge Furniture and Antiques in Silver City, New Mexico, was called by the estate agent for the Alter family. Rita Alter had passed away in 2017, Jerry in 2012. After walking through their home,

Van Auker bought the estate for $2,000. In his assessment of the Alters' property, he was struck by a painting behind the bedroom door. Van Auker liked it. He thought it must have been made by the homeowners.

Van Auker brought the contents of the estate from Cliff, New Mexico, to his store in Silver City, where he put the painting out in the shop. The first day it was on display, a customer remarked that it looked like a Willem de Kooning. Four other customers repeated that the new painting looked exactly like the work of the late abstract expressionist. It was enough to pique Van Auker's curiosity. After going through the first four pages of a Google search, Van Auker paused on an article about the theft of a de Kooning from the UAMA in 1985. When he saw that the stolen painting looked remarkably like the one in his shop, he telephoned the museum. A student staffing the front desk at the museum answered and connected Van Auker to a curator at the museum, Olivia Miller. Forty-eight hours later, a team from the museum, including Miller, drove from Tucson, Arizona, to Silver City, New Mexico. When Miller kneeled before the painting at Van Auker's antiques store, she cried.

Back in Arizona, the painting was analyzed by Dr. Nancy Odegaard, head of the Preservation Division at the UAMA, and one of her graduate students. Using the condition reports from before the painting was stolen, the two went over the painting inch by inch. When he had brutally cut the painting out of its frame in 1985, Jerry Alter left behind remnants of the canvas. When Dr. Odegaard fit the stolen painting into the remaining fragments, it was like fitting the last puzzle piece into a five-thousand-piece puzzle. The painting was home.

Though *Woman-Ochre* had been authenticated, it was in bad shape. When *Los Angeles Times* art critic Christopher Knight saw the painting, he called it a "corpse" and "as rumpled as last night's sheets." The painting wasn't home for long before it was sent to the art hospital at the Getty Conservation Institute. A team at the Getty spent years rehabilitating

the de Kooning, using an array of tools from the banal (dental tools) to the high-tech (macro X-ray fluorescence). After meticulous work, *Woman-Ochre* was returned to the UAMA. The conservationists at the Getty didn't want to completely erase the history of the painting. As such, *Woman-Ochre* still has visible scars in her canvas from when she was traumatically cut from her frame.

The Alters left behind many mysteries. Though they can never be tried for their crime, the evidence seems irrefutable. A photo from Thanksgiving of 1985 shows them at a turkey dinner in Tucson just before the painting was stolen. Jerry even wrote and published a short story called *The Eye of the Jaguar* about a grandmother and granddaughter who stole a priceless emerald from a museum after fooling the security guard stationed to watch over it. Life imitating art or art imitating life?

On the salaries of a schoolteacher and speech pathologist, they managed to travel to over 140 countries and had accumulated $1 million in their bank account when Rita died. Their house was full of art, leaving many to wonder if there are other art crimes that the Alters may have committed and hidden behind the doors of their mysterious lives.

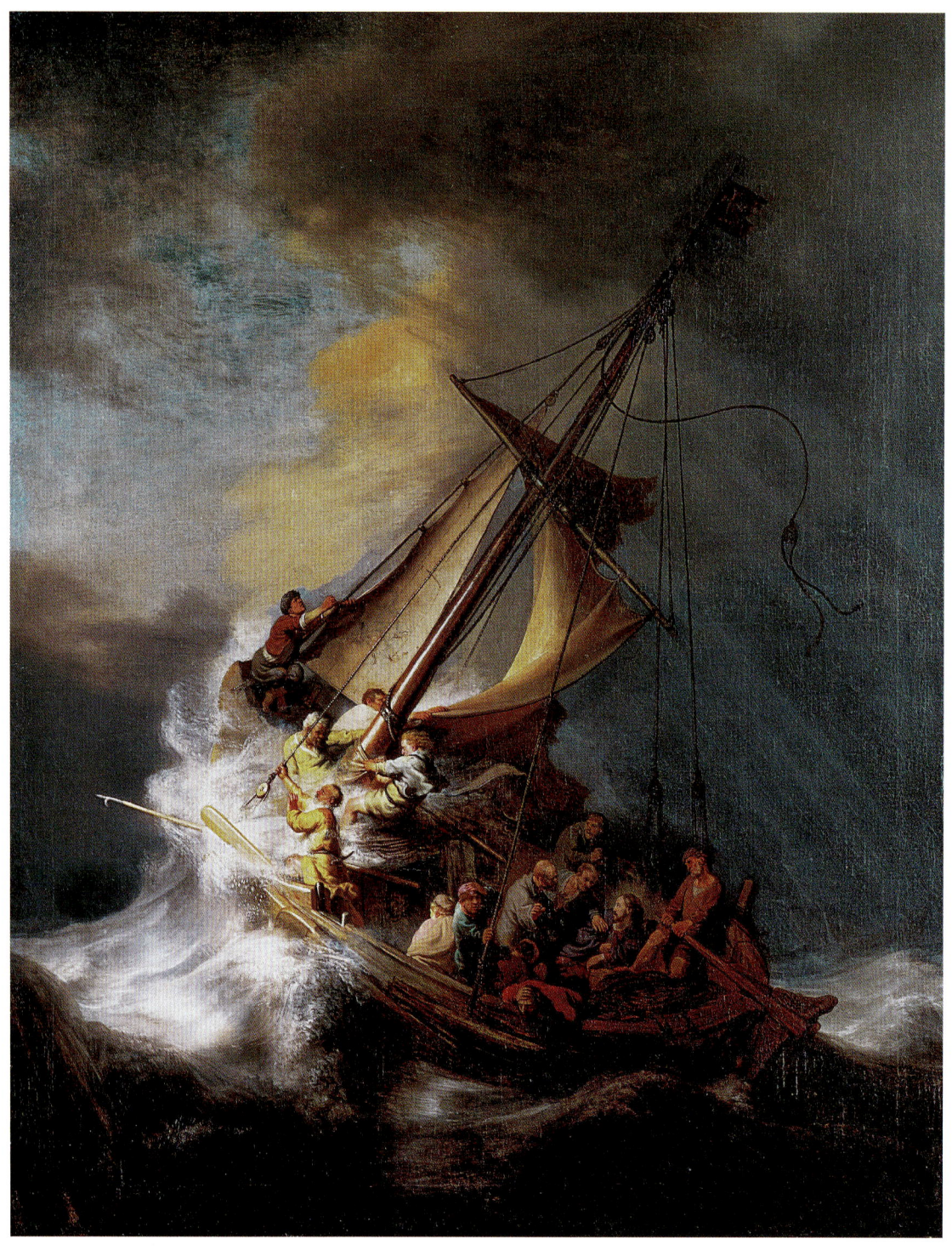

When: March 18, 1990

Where: Isabella Stewart Gardner Museum in Boston

What: Theft of Johannes Vermeer's *The Concert* (1663–66); Rembrandt van Rijn's *Christ in the Storm on the Sea of Galilee* (1633), *A Lady and Gentleman in Black* (1633), and *Portrait of the Artist as a Young Man* (c. 1633); Govaert Flinck's *Landscape with an Obelisk* (1638); Édouard Manet's *Chez Tortoni* (c. 1875), five works on paper (1857–88) by Edgar Degas, a bronze eagle finial (1813–14), and an ancient Chinese gu (1200–1100 BCE)

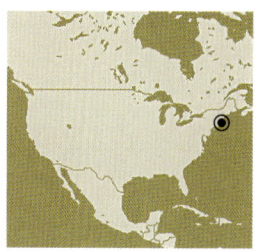

AN UNCLAIMED $10 MILLION REWARD

Boston, a largely Irish city, is known to celebrate March 17—St. Patrick's Day—with great enthusiasm. Two thieves were no doubt aware that most of Boston would be sleeping off well-deserved hangovers on the morning of March 18 and planned their robbery of the Isabella Stewart Gardner Museum accordingly. The heist remains the largest unsolved art theft of all time.

Isabella Stewart Gardner was a woman ahead of her time. Born in 1840, she had a reputation for being eclectic and passionate, and she was a friend to many artists of the time. The novelist Henry James once wrote that Isabella was "not a woman, she is a locomotive—with a Pullman car attached." She was known for driving fast, smoking cigarettes, and, purportedly, walking lions on leashes down Boylston Street in Boston. She dressed to the nines and said that she had never caught a cold in a ballgown, which is why she wore them so frequently.

The Isabella Stewart Gardner Museum, which opened in 1903, houses an incredible collection in a building designed to mimic a Renaissance-era Venetian palazzo. Isabella built the museum to house what she called "the picture-habit (which I seem to have), [which is] as bad as the morphine or whiskey one." In her will, she stipulated that nothing in the museum should be sold, bought, or changed upon her death.

The thieves, dressed in Boston police uniforms and phony mustaches, arrived at the museum at 1:20 a.m. on March 18, 1990. They rang the side-door buzzer and told the night guards that they were there to investigate a disturbance. Once inside, the thieves revealed the robbery and in less than fifteen minutes, the two guards' heads were duct-taped and their arms were handcuffed to a pipe and a bench in the basement. The thieves told the guards that they would receive a big reward in about a year if they didn't tattle on them to investigators.

Opposite: Rembrandt's *Christ in the Storm on the Sea of Galilee* depicts Jesus (remaining calm on the right) and his disciples (one ready to puke over the side of the boat) riding out a tempest.

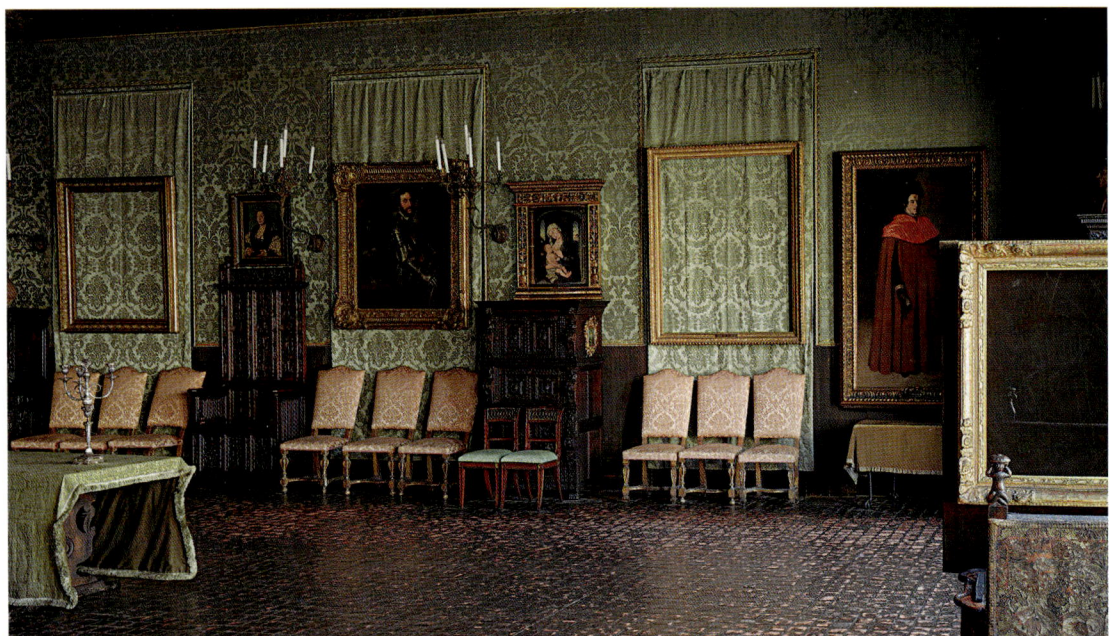

After disabling the security cameras, the thieves then spent eighty-one minutes wandering through the museum, their movements captured by infrared motion detectors. In no apparent rush, they strolled through the galleries, choosing works and cutting them from their frames. They took two of the museum's most valuable and rare pieces: *The Concert* by Vermeer (one of only a few dozen Vermeers in the world) and *Christ in the Storm on the Sea of Galilee*, Rembrandt's only seascape. They also took two other Rembrandts, a Manet, five works on paper by Edgar Degas, and a landscape by Govaert Flinck.

Though they seemed to know which works of art were worth the most, they also perplexingly passed over one of the museum's most valuable pieces, Titian's *The Rape of Europa*, and other paintings by all-star artists like Michelangelo, Raphael, and Botticelli. They also took two pieces that didn't seem to fit with their other choices (oil paintings): a Napoleon-era bronze

eagle that would have topped a flagpole (after trying to steal a silk flag from Napoleon's Imperial Guard but giving up on that particular item) and an ancient Chinese gu, a ritual beaker used to serve wine during the twelfth-century-BCE Shang dynasty.

The thieves stole a total of thirteen pieces, which they removed from the museum in two trips, stowing the priceless goods in their hatchback car parked out front. They left at 2:45 a.m. The fake police officers and the real, priceless works of art have never been seen since. The items are conservatively estimated to be worth around $600 million.

The guards remained in the basement until their colleagues found them. They were heavily scrutinized because investigators believed the theft could only have been an inside job, but they were eventually cleared of any involvement.

In 2015, the FBI announced that they were fairly certain who had committed the 1990 robbery: Leonard DiMuzio and George

Reissfelder, two associates of mobster Carmello Merlino (all of whom are deceased) who resemble police sketches made from museum guards' descriptions. Though the FBI believe they have identified the thieves, they still have no clue where they might find the stolen art. The FBI determined that the works of art were trafficked into Connecticut and Philadelphia, but that is as far as the trail leads.

To this day, there remains a $10 million reward for tips that lead to recovery of the stolen works—the highest reward ever offered by a private institution. According to Ulrich Boser's 2009 book *The Gardner Heist: The True Story of the World's Largest Unsolved Art Theft*, the only other reward that has been higher than the Gardner's was the $25 million bounty for Osama bin Laden. A separate reward of $100,000 is offered for the safe return of the Napoleon-era bronze eagle finial.

Because Isabella Stewart Gardner stipulated in her will that nothing in her museum should be altered, the empty frames of the stolen works remain like gravestones, a haunting reminder of the devastation of art crimes that empty our shared visual history. When and if the paintings are returned, their spots on the walls are waiting for them.

Opposite: The frames of the missing paintings haunt the walls of the Isabella Stewart Gardner Museum.

Right: Isabella Stewart Gardner bought Vermeer's *The Concert* for a mere $5,000 at auction in 1892. Today, it is estimated to be worth more than $250 million.

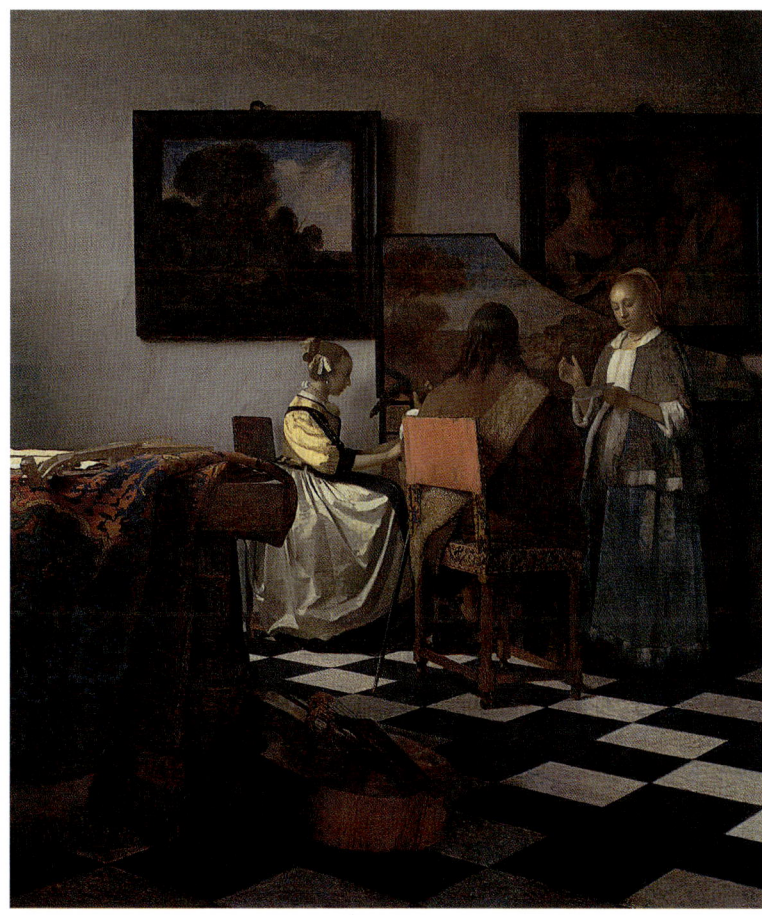

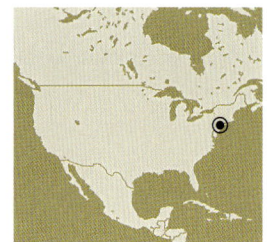

A DALÍ FEVER DREAM

I n 1965, Salvador Dalí was to teach a painting workshop for prisoners at Rikers Island, but he woke up with a 105-degree fever. Though too ill to conduct the workshop, Dalí quickly created an artwork and asked his business representative, Nico Yperifanos, to present it to the prison's warden. Dalí signed his name and wrote, "For the dinning room of the prisoners Rikers Ysland"—spelling mistakes (artistic choices?) included.

The *Christ on the Cross* painting would spend two decades in the prisoners' mess hall, but not all prisoners were fans of Dalí's work. In 1981, an inmate threw a metal mug at it, shattering its glass casing and adding a coffee stain. The painting took a circuitous route to its new resting place next to a vending machine in one of the prison's lobbies, where a plaque stated that it was estimated to be worth $1 million. If it seems odd that a prison would publicly advertise the worth of its art collection, it is. It also caught the attention of some enterprising crooks, who just happened to also be Rikers Island guards.

A fire drill at 1:00 a.m. on March 1, 2003, allowed the guards to swap out the real Dalí with a smaller, poor copy. The guards hadn't

bothered to buy a real wooden frame for it; they painted one directly on the canvas. The original Dalí had a mahogany frame and was made in ink on paper, while the copy was paint on canvas, proving their inexperience with art theft and forgery. They did manage to redirect one security camera so the theft was unseen.

A few days later, one of the guards came clean to the inspector general. He agreed to wear a wire; faced with the evidence, three guards confessed and received sentences ranging from nothing for the first guard, who was considered a cooperating witness, to three years in prison for some, and five years' probation for others. A fourth guard, the purported mastermind, Benny Nuzzo, would not confess. He hired high-profile attorney Joe Tacopina, who had represented the likes of Meek Mill and Jay-Z, to represent him, and was found not guilty.

The painting remains missing to this day. But the story of its theft is something that Dalí might have appreciated: the chaos of it all, his original painting with an added coffee stain, a bizarre copy of his work with a painted-on frame, and prison-guard thieves. It's so surreal, it's almost as if it came from Dalí's own imagination.

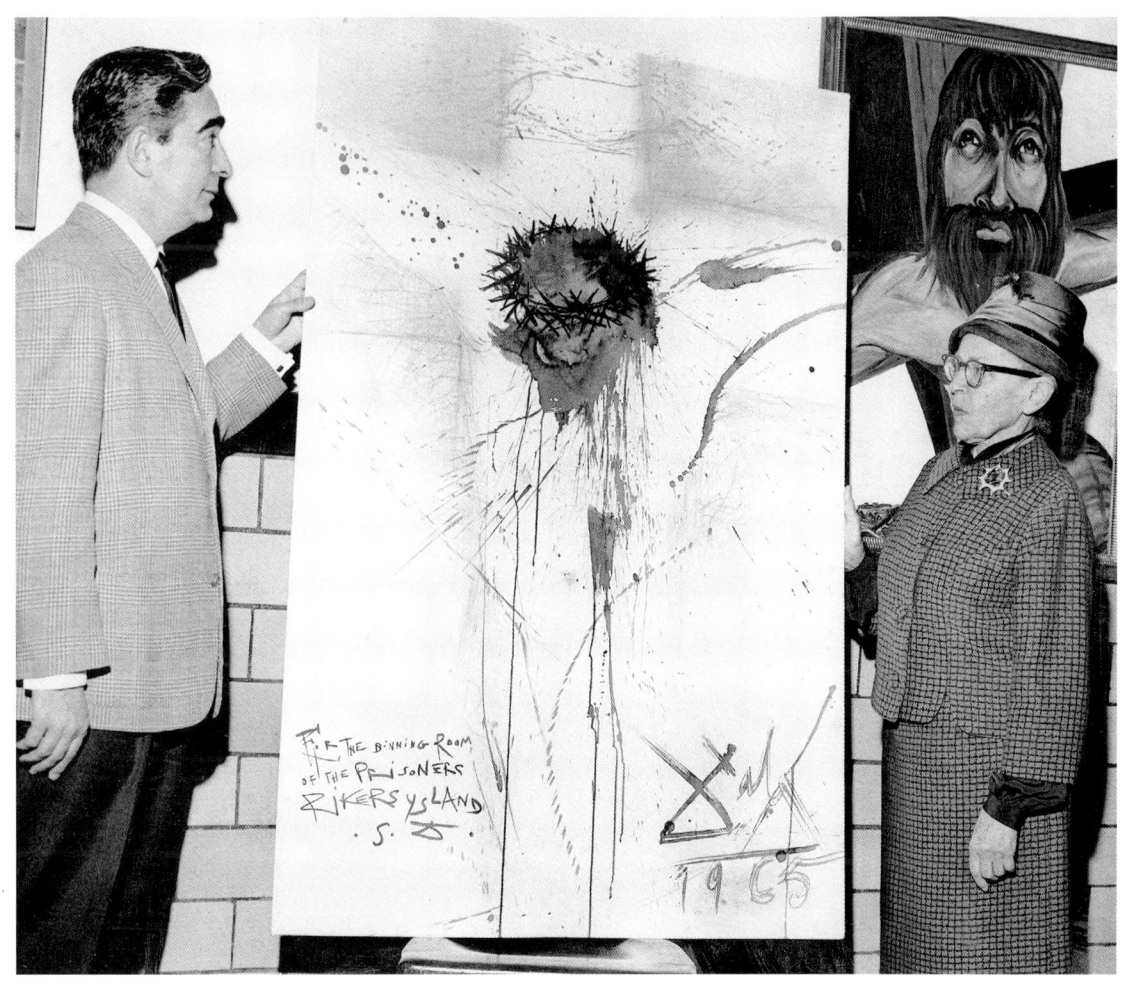

Above: Nico Yperifanos, Dalí's representative, hands Dalí's *Christ on the Cross* to the Rikers Island correction commissioner, Anna Kross, in 1965.

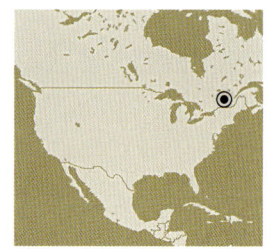

THE SKYLIGHT CAPER

"The Skylight Caper" sounds like a sequel to *The Great Muppet Caper* (an underrated 1981 movie that involves Miss Piggy crashing a motorcycle through a gallery's stained-glass window while the famed Fabulous Baseball Diamond is being stolen), but this 1972 theft of eighteen paintings and almost forty small figurines and jewelry from the Montreal Museum of Fine Arts (MMFA) remains one of the greatest unsolved (and overlooked) art thefts in history.

Early in the morning of Canada's Labour Day, September 4, one man wearing climbing shoes scaled a tree that grew over the museum roof. Workers had been repairing the roof and had left a ladder there, which the thief passed down to waiting accomplices. Wearing ski masks and carrying at least one gun, the trio of thieves, who spoke a mixture of French and English, used a nylon rope to rappel into the museum through the skylight. As they were gathering their haul, they were surprised by a roaming guard. One of the thieves fired his gun, which brought two other guards to the scene. The three guards were tied up, blindfolded, and gagged while one thief stood watch over them.

The other two attempted to lift their haul back up through the skylight using a pulley system. When that failed, they exited through a side door to get to a museum van they hoped to use as a getaway car. The side door was armed, and the sound sent the three thieves skedaddling down Sherbrooke Street with whatever they could carry in their arms and pockets (about fifty-seven objects in total), including small paintings by Jan Bruegel the Elder, Corot, Courbet, Delacroix, Gainsborough, Millet, Rubens, and Rembrandt. Left behind because of their size were fourteen paintings by the likes of Picasso, Goya, Renoir, El Greco, and Tintoretto. If their original plan with the pulley system had worked, the MMFA's collection would have been decimated.

The museum issued a statement titled "Attn: Stolen," which was picked up by some media

Opposite: Camille Corot's *The Dreamer at the Fountain* was one of fifty-seven pieces stolen from the Montreal Museum of Fine Arts in 1972, in the theft now known as the Skylight Caper.

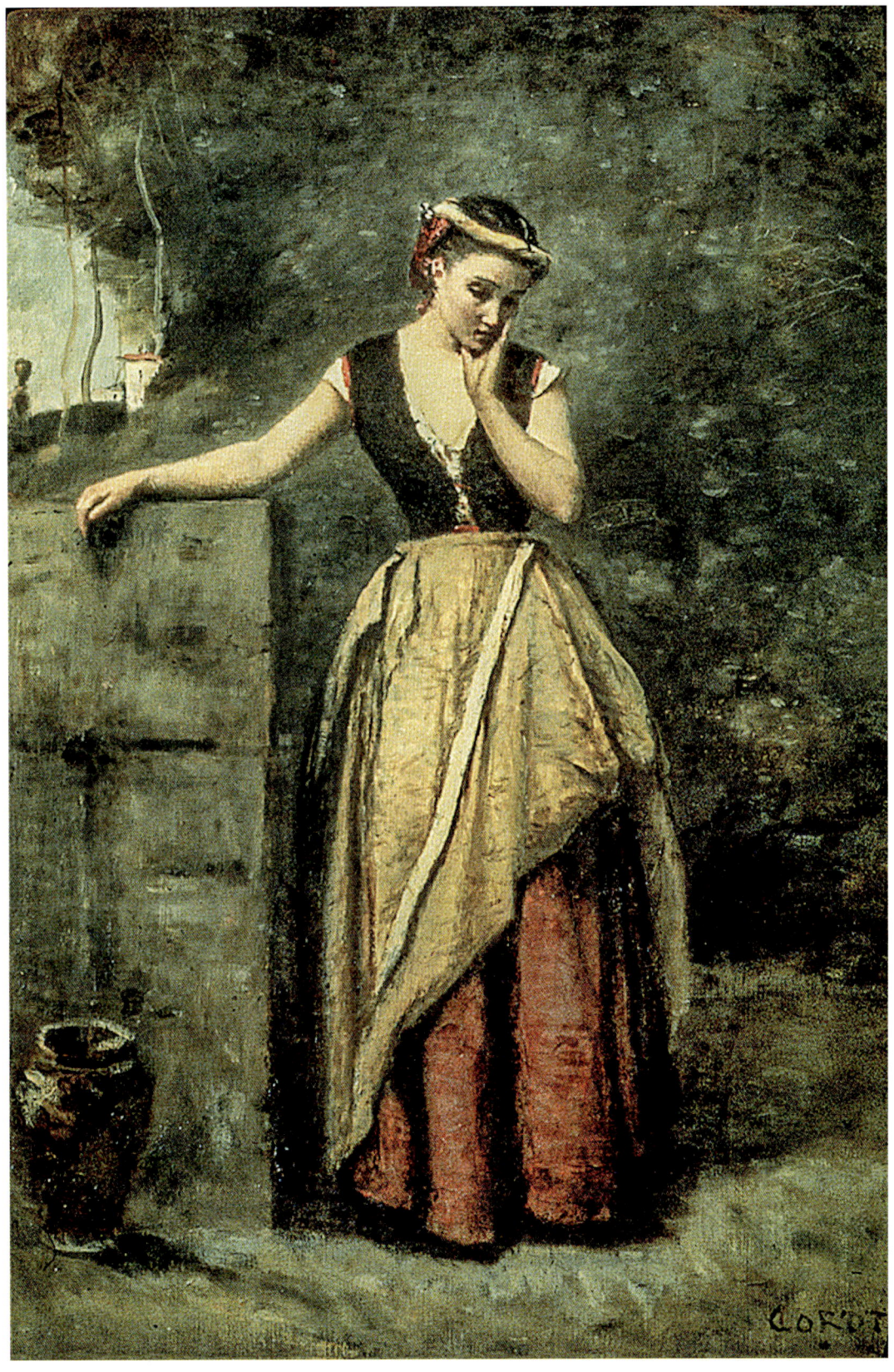

around the world, but much of the rest of the world was too enthralled by other events to notice. On the previous weekend, a massive fire at a Montreal nightclub had killed thirty-seven people and injured fifty-four. On September 5, the day after the theft, the world's attention was consumed by the hostage crisis at the Summer Olympics in Munich, during which one Israeli athlete and coach were killed and nine more Israeli athletes were held hostage by Palestine Liberation Organization terrorists.

Canadian border control, Interpol, the Art Loss Register, and the Art Dealers Association were alerted and given images of the stolen objects, and the company that insured the objects offered a $50,000 reward for information that would help track down the thieves or the stolen art. In spite of this, there were few clues and fewer leads. Museum employees told police that, while repairs were underway on the roof, they recalled seeing men smoking in folding chairs on the roof of a nearby building, watching the workers at the museum.

A few days after the theft, a ransom call asked for the museum to send an employee to a nearby phonebooth. The museum's director hustled there and was told to pick up an empty cigarette pack on the ground nearby. Inside was one of the museum's stolen pieces of jewelry, a pendant. On October 26, the museum received several photographs of the purloined objects, and the thieves requested half a million dollars for their return. Not very good at negotiating, they reduced their price to $250,000. The museum's director asked the thieves to relinquish one painting as a sign of good faith. The trio left one of the two Bruegel paintings, *Landscape with Vehicles and Cattle*, in a luggage locker at the city's central train station.

A second attempt at exchanging money for another painting was foiled when an off-duty police officer scared away the thieves, who

SANDPIT SWAG

The Skylight Caper wasn't the first theft from the MMFA. On April 17, 1933, a thief eluded the night watchman, hid inside the museum until after closing, and passed fourteen paintings by Canadian artists through a window in the women's restroom to an accomplice waiting outside.

Seemingly unrelated to the theft, Paul Thouin was arrested for shooting a police officer while breaking into a train. However, under questioning, he admitted to the museum theft and told police he would lead them to the paintings, but only if he were allowed to go home and change his clothes first. Police agreed; Thouin changed, then brought them to a sandpit where he had buried the paintings. They were wrapped in newspaper and tarpaulin and in good condition.

Back in prison, Thouin, facing a murder sentence, was found dead the next morning. When he changed his clothes, he had put on a pair of shoes with a false heel where he had hidden a dose of strychnine, which he used to poison himself.

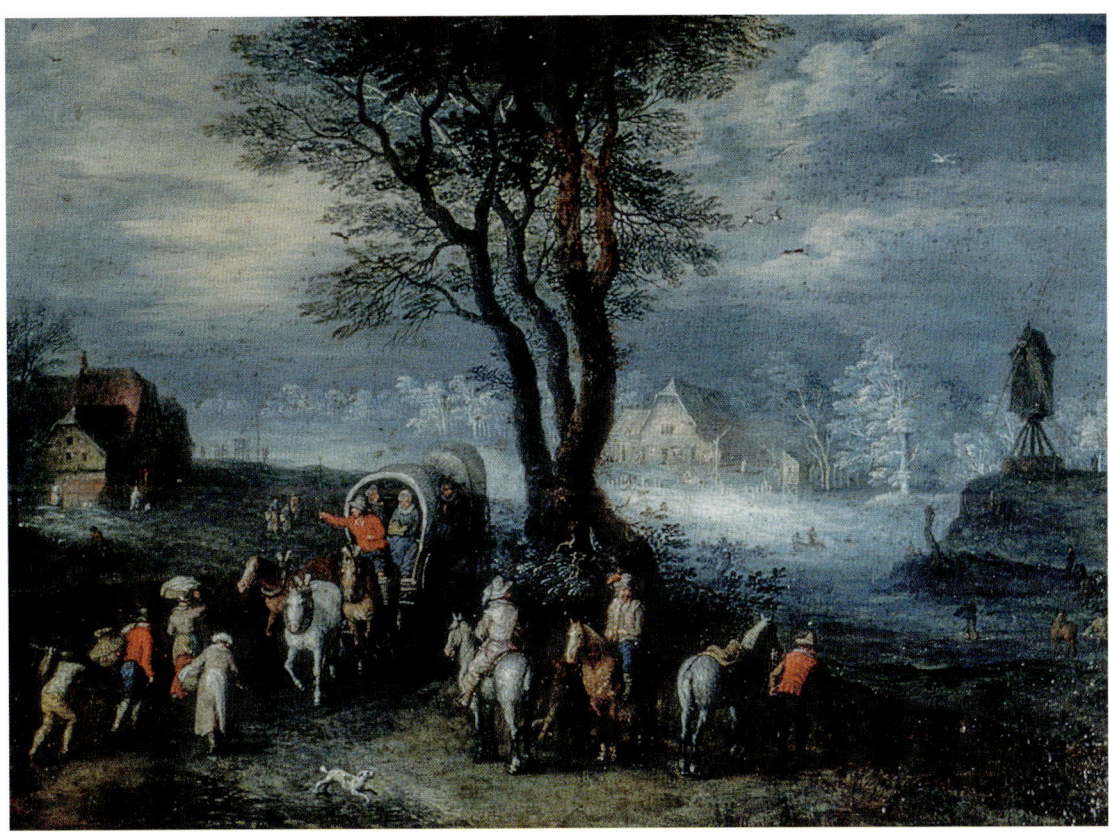

Above: *Landscape with Vehicles and Cattle*, another of the works stolen from the Montreal Museum of Fine Arts, was believed to be by Jan Bruegel the Elder but was later reattributed to his students.

thought they were being set up. The trio went underground, not emerging until the summer of 1973 when they led police on a wild goose chase. Communications with the thieves dissolved, and besides the two items already returned, none of the other objects stolen during the Skylight Caper have been seen since 1972.

To make matters worse, in 1975 the MMFA used most of its $1,945,300 insurance payout from the stolen works to buy a big, beautiful Rubens painting entitled *The Leopards*. Twenty years after the Skylight Caper, the Rubens was quietly removed from the museum's walls. It turns out it wasn't really a Rubens. It had been misattributed and had been made by Rubens' assistants, not the master himself. It has not been exhibited since.

Most of the people involved in the Skylight Caper have passed on, making recovery of the works increasingly unlikely. Regardless, Miss Piggy remains on the suspect list.

When: Sometime between December 25, 2021, and January 6, 2022

Where: Fairmont Château Laurier in Ottawa

What: Theft of Yousuf Karsh's photograph of Winston Churchill, *The Roaring Lion* (1941)

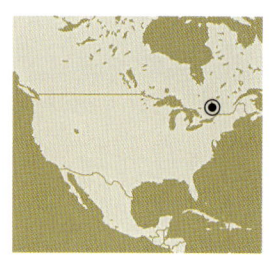

ROARING LION ESCAPED

When Armenian-Canadian artist Yousuf Karsh was tasked with photographing Winston Churchill in 1941, he was worried that Churchill's infamous cigar smoke would obscure the prime minister's visage. In the two minutes Karsh had to capture his subject, he courageously said to Churchill, "Forgive me," and plucked the cigar out of Churchill's mouth, snapping the photograph. The result is *The Roaring Lion*, one of the most iconic images of Winston Churchill. In it, Churchill scowls, defiantly looking at the camera (or, perhaps, at who was behind it). After the photo session, Churchill said to Karsh, "You can even make a roaring lion stand still to be photographed."

For twenty years, Karsh and his second wife split their time between Manhattan and a suite in Ottawa's Fairmont Château Laurier hotel. As a token of his appreciation, Karsh signed a copy of *The Roaring Lion* and installed it in the hotel's reading room. The photograph hung there from 1998 to sometime between December 25, 2021, and January 6, 2022. During this span of twelve days, *The Roaring Lion* was replaced by a copy with a forged signature.

It took until August 2022 for a hotel maintenance worker to notice the switcheroo. Police narrowed down the time of the theft from guests' selfies with the original photograph taken up until Christmas Day 2021. By January 6, 2022, the selfies showed a copy in a cheap frame. To add to the mystery, the hotel was in lockdown during these two weeks as the COVID-19 pandemic had struck many of the hotel's employees, leaving only a skeleton staff and a perfect set-up for an inside job.

The photograph remains missing. It might be that, between the time the original was removed and the copy discovered, the thief was able to sell the image before the heat was turned up. According to Canadian police, the case remains active. Meanwhile, Churchill appears, by his gruff demeanor, ready to wait it out.

Opposite: Yousuf Karsh, who made this photograph of Winston Churchill, *The Roaring Lion*, said that Churchill "looked so belligerent, he could have devoured me."

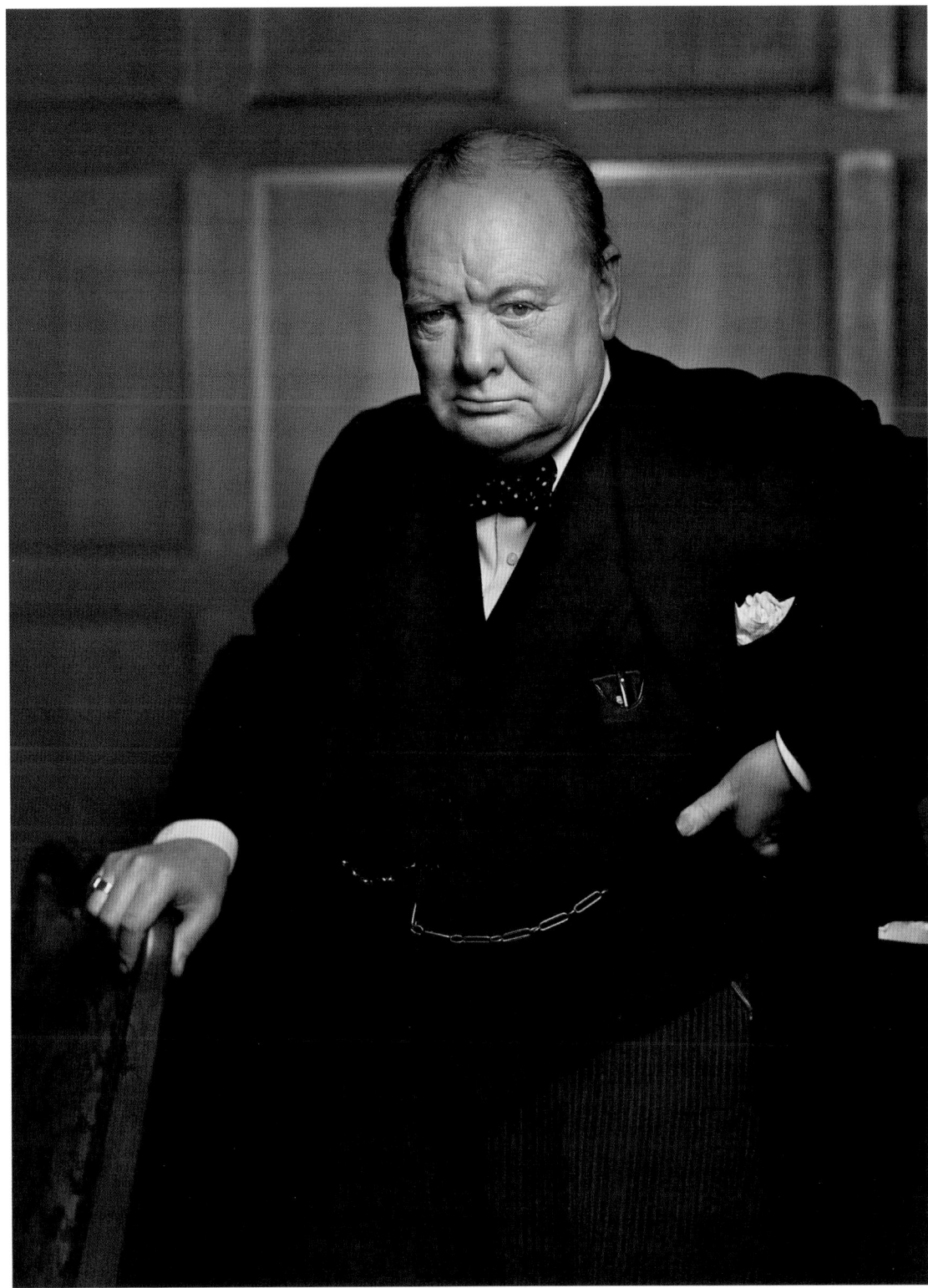

When: Before February 16, 1975

Where: National Museum of Bermuda (previously the Bermuda Maritime Museum)

What: Theft of Tucker's Cross, an emerald and gold cross salvaged from the *San Pedro*, shipwrecked off Bermuda in 1594

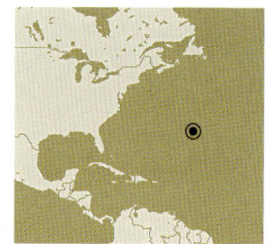

BERMUDA'S LOST CROWN JEWELS

Edward "Teddy" Bolton Tucker—intrepid shipwreck explorer, inspiration for the character of Quint in *Jaws* and the real-life story behind the film *The Deep*—was born in Bermuda in 1925, the son of a prominent architect. Tucker was sent to several prestigious private schools in the United States but was promptly kicked out of all of them and returned to Bermuda for his education. He constantly sought out adventure and experiences. He was always drawn to the sea, and his first job was at the Bermuda Aquarium.

At the age of sixteen, Tucker joined the Royal Navy and was put forward for special training as an underwater demolitions expert, during which time he discovered a way to make Bermuda millions of dollars. Tucker realized that he could salvage all kinds of scrap metal from the countless shipwrecks surrounding the island. The money Tucker was able to generate from his salvage work was worth more for Bermuda than all international businesses and tourism combined at that time; the work also funded his passion for treasure hunting.

Tucker was one of the founders of modern shipwreck treasure hunting. Local fishermen, aware of the shipwrecks that surrounded Bermuda, would find ballast and cannons in the water, but no one had really put in a determined effort to explore them.

Tucker changed all of that. In 1955, Tucker went to a site he had been tipped off to by local fishermen. The wreck was most likely the *San Pedro*, which had been lost at sea in 1594. The ship had started from Spain, with stops in Panama and Colombia. On the way home, it rounded Havana and headed for the Azores. The *San Pedro* had sailed out ahead of its armada and was probably taken slightly off course when it ran aground on the reefs of Bermuda with no witnesses.

Opposite: Teddy Tucker, the Bermudian shipwreck explorer, shows off some of the haul from his dives around the island. In the center, just below his left fingertips, is Tucker's Cross.

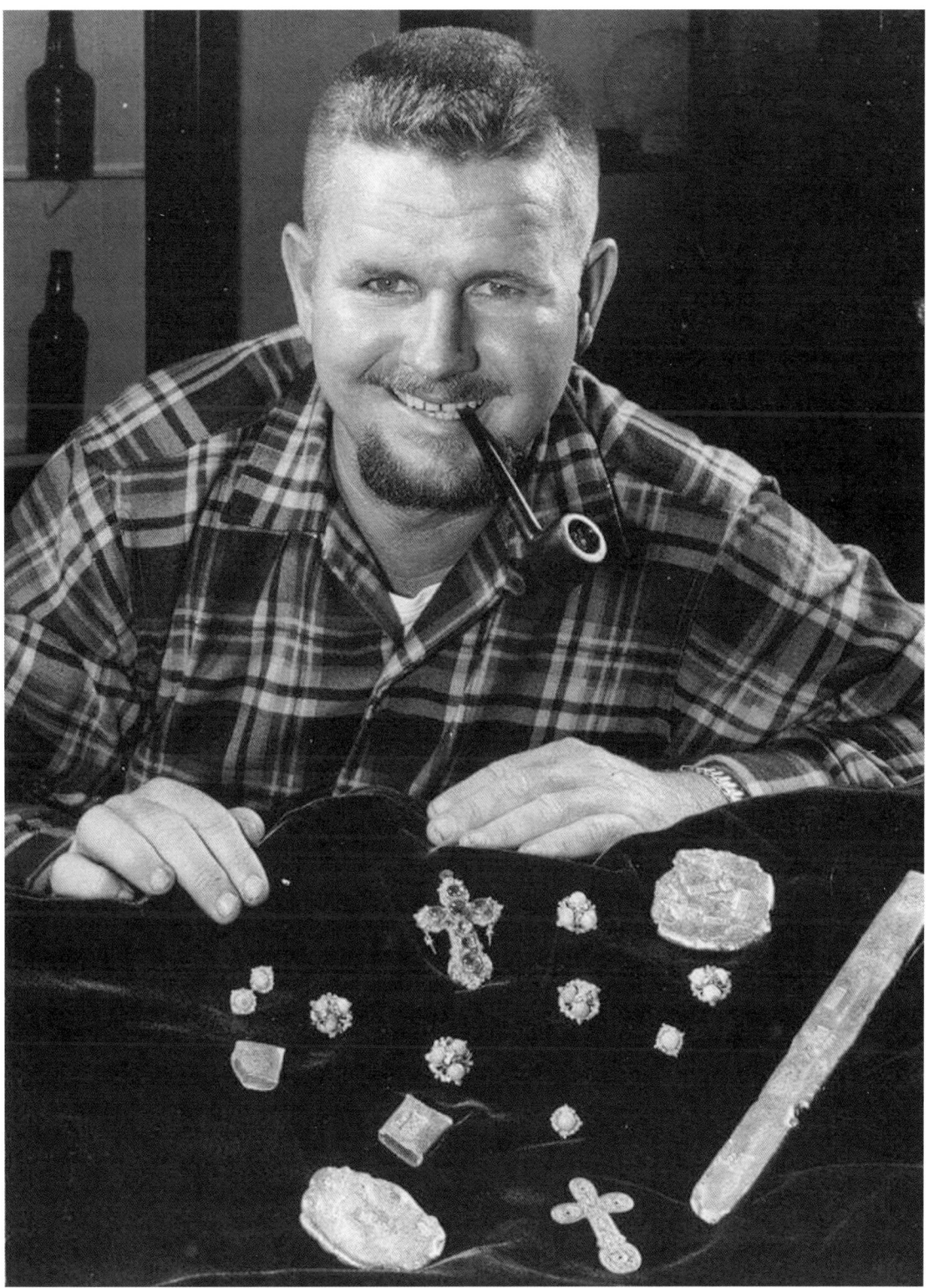

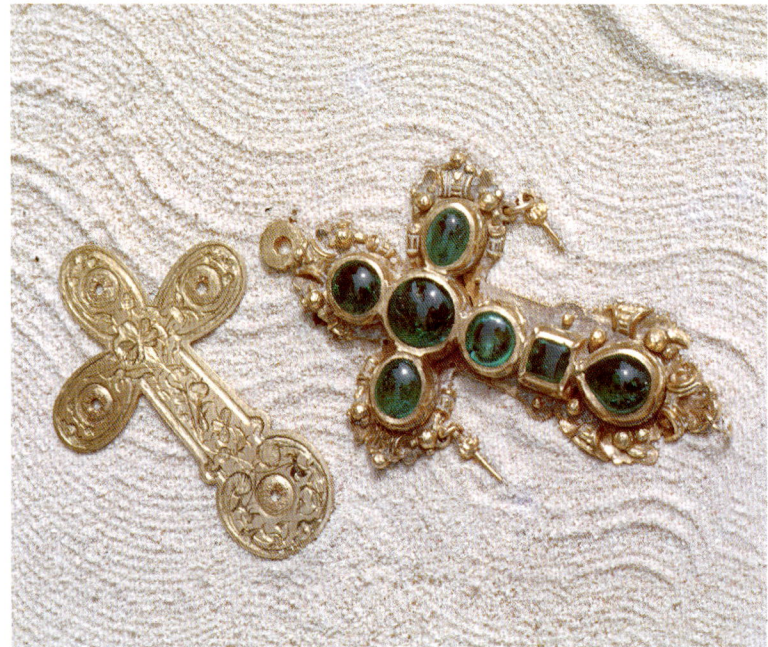

Underwater, Tucker used a technique called "fanning" to move the sand away. After finding a gold cube, Tucker said he knew he'd hit a big one. He went on to discover gold and pearl buttons, gold coins, and a gold bar weighing about thirty-six ounces. But all of that paled in comparison to the cross.

When he got it out of the water, Tucker's suspicions that the cross was the real thing were confirmed. Tucker's cross was made of 22-karat gold, with seven stunning emeralds, each about the size of a musket ball, though varying in shape. On the arms of the cross were small nails that were meant to symbolize the crucifixion of Jesus.

The cross was more than just a piece of jewelry: the back could be removed, revealing a space that may have been intended to hold a sacred relic. The cross and the ornate pearl buttons that Tucker found are believed to have been ceremonial adornments for a high-ranking bishop. The emeralds in the cross probably came from Muzo, Colombia; the *San Pedro* would have picked them up when it stopped in Cartagena before sailing back east from Panama.

After finding the emerald-studded cross, Tucker hid it in a closet at home for safekeeping and took his time reporting the find to the government of Bermuda. The government declared it their property, citing that the reef was part of their territorial seabed and therefore part of the British Crown Estate. Tucker said that if that was the case, he'd take what he had found to the reef and throw it back in the ocean for them to find for themselves. The government agreed to negotiate instead.

By this point, news of Tucker's treasures had spread around the world. Clare Boothe Luce was the US ambassador to Italy. She was also a recent convert to Catholicism, and she was intent on owning Tucker's cross. She offered Tucker $100,000 for the cross. Tucker refused. She offered $200,000. Again, Tucker refused. Luce upped her offer to "name your own price," but stubborn and loyal Tucker said that he didn't care about the money and thought the piece belonged in a museum. He called it, along with his other finds, "Bermuda's Crown Jewels," and agreed to sell it to the country of Bermuda for $35,000, much to the pleasure of Bermuda and much to the chagrin of the US ambassador to Italy.

In 1975, Tucker's Cross was in a maritime museum in Bermuda, carefully protected under a glass vitrine, and awaiting a very important guest: Queen Elizabeth II. As Tucker's daughter, Wendy, tells it, her father was arranging his shipwreck finds at the museum and picked up the cross to move it to a different spot in the display case. She watched as the blood drained out from her father's face as he held the cross. The cross was sticky, tacky, and wet with paint that had not yet dried. The exquisite gold cross was a cheap, fake, plastic replica that had been switched with the original. The authentic cross was nowhere to be seen.

Tucker quickly rearranged the remaining artifacts as Queen Elizabeth strolled into the gallery. He put on a brave face for the monarch, but inside he was reeling. After the queen left, police launched an investigation and discovered that many people at the museum had access to a key that unlocked the vitrine where the cross was kept and that many people had handled the cross in the preceding days. The Bermuda Police, Scotland Yard, Interpol, and the FBI all got involved in the case, suspecting that the theft was an inside job. Some people thought it must have been the work of an international art thief who wanted the cross for their own special collection (a seductive myth that is rarely found to be true in art crime). Others thought the cross would have been melted down and sold for its parts, which is a strong possibility because the emeralds and gold could have been sold separately without much risk. But no one was ever convicted, and the cross has not been seen since.

Tucker's Cross—hidden in the sands of the ocean for centuries, then brought to the surface—is hidden once again. Keep your eyes peeled when you go scuba diving or snorkeling. If you see a flash of gold and green, you may just have rediscovered a part of Bermuda's Crown Jewels and Teddy Tucker's legacy.

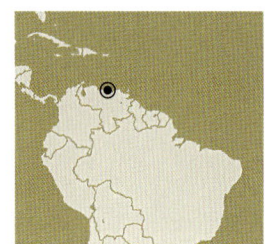

THE DECEPTION OF PAINT

In August 2012, more than a dozen topless women in red harem pants held empty gold painting frames outside the Museo de Arte Contemporáneo in Caracas. They were protesting the theft and delayed return of the museum's prized Henri Matisse painting, *Odalisque in Red Pants*. In it, a woman sits topless on her heels, dressed in brilliant red trousers.

This was the only Matisse in Venezuela, valued at $3 million; it had been stolen sometime between 1999 (when the painting was moved to protect it from potential flooding at the museum) and mid-2000. No one is entirely sure when or how the painting disappeared, but it was replaced with a disgracefully bad copy, made with acrylic paints rather than the oils of the original, and featuring a large brown stain in the middle, different shades of red in the trousers, and six green stripes in the lower right corner rather than seven.

As different as the copy was, no one at the museum seemed to notice or, more importantly, admit they were aware that the original had been swapped. In 2002, when Genaro Ambrosino, a Venezuelan-born, Miami-based gallery owner, heard that a fellow art dealer was discreetly trying to sell the Matisse, he was enraged that a part of the cultural landscape of Venezuela was being hawked. Several times, Ambrosino tried to contact the director of the Museo de Arte Contemporáneo but got no response. He then sounded the alarm and emailed over a hundred art dealers, museum professionals, and journalists in Venezuela, alerting them that the Matisse was up for sale on the black market. Though many scoffed at Ambrosino's claim, he finally got the attention of the director of the art museum. After examining the Matisse, he was shocked to find that Ambrosino was right.

The FBI took notice of Ambrosino's claim in Miami and set up an elaborate sting operation involving two agents posing as a dealer and a collector, through which they arrested a pair trying to sell the stolen painting. The two were sentenced to prison, but the FBI took its time returning the painting to Venezuela, inspiring the topless, red-pantsed women in Caracas to stage their protest.

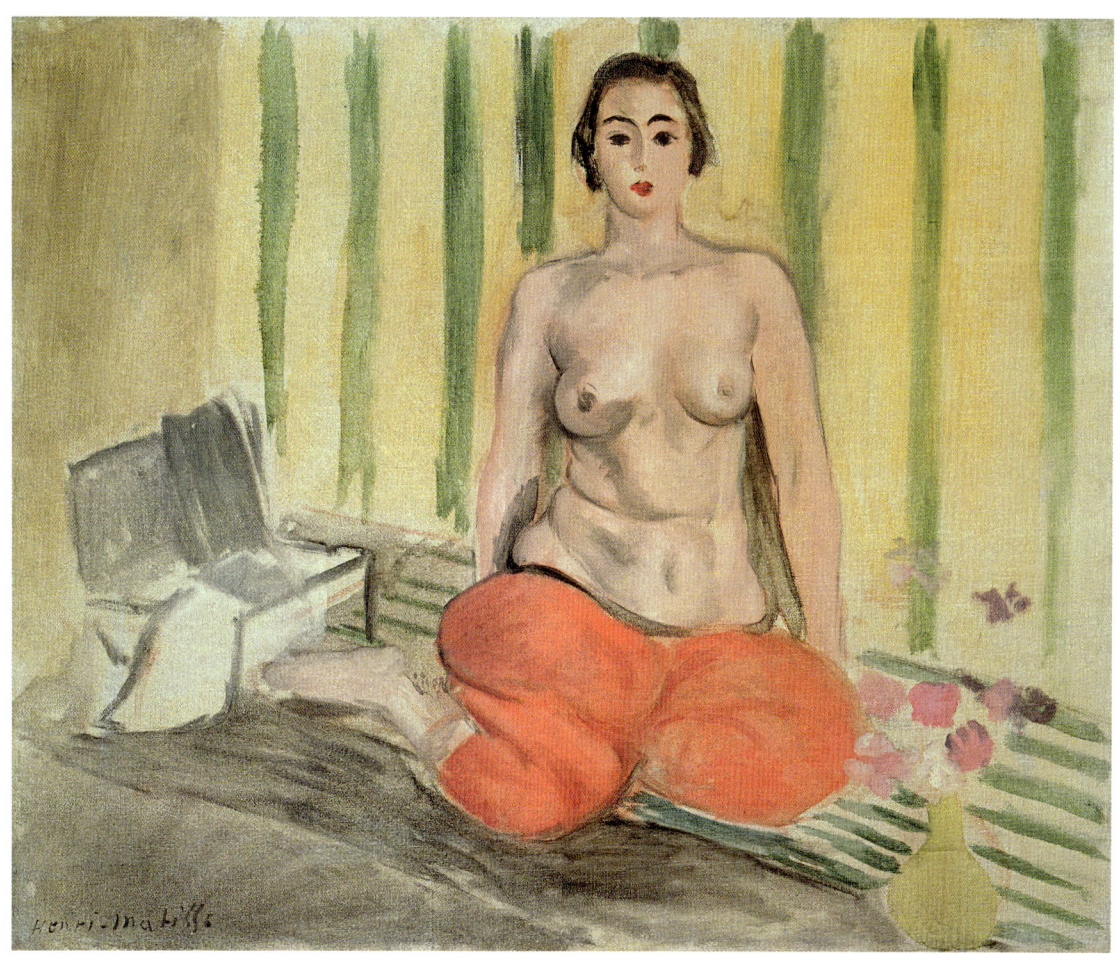

Finally, in 2014, eleven years after it was confirmed missing, the original *Odalisque in Red Pants* returned to the museum. She was hung next to the copy that had been her stand-in for too many years: deception and original, side by side.

Above: No one knows exactly when Matisse's original *Odalisque in Red Pants* was stolen from the contemporary art museum in Caracas. It was the only painting by Matisse in Venezuela.

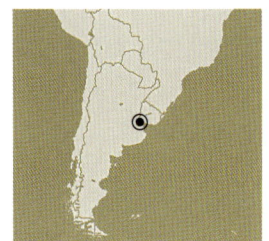

When: December 25, 1980

Where: Museo Nacional de Bellas Artes in Buenos Aires

What: Theft of sixteen paintings and seven ancient Chinese sculptures

STOLEN ART FOR CHRISTMAS

Early on Christmas Day, 1980, burglars broke into the Museo Nacional de Bellas Artes. Unlike Santa, they didn't use the chimney; they used ladders and gaps in the roof left by construction workers to squeeze inside. The robbers stole sixteen works by Degas, Gauguin, Cézanne, Matisse, Rodin, and Renoir as well as seven ancient Chinese sculptures. The twenty-three objects were valued at over $25 million, and the only thing left at the scene was a cheap whiskey bottle. The museum reported the loss to the Art Loss Register (ALR), the world's largest database of stolen art.

Two guards sleeping at the time of the robbery awoke to smoke-filled galleries. Argentina had been under a brutal and repressive dictatorship since a 1976 coup, and the guards were tortured for weeks by state police, though neither was charged. A few months later, a curator and museum photographer were also kidnapped and tortured. Both were released and resumed work. Rumors swirled that an Argentine army truck had been outside the museum in the early Christmas hours.

In 2001, Sotheby's auction house contacted the ALR—a Taiwanese arms dealer had asked them to appraise sixteen objects. The ALR determined the objects were from the 1980 theft. The seller reported to the ALR that the paintings could only be released with permission from the Taiwanese Ministry of Defense. There has since been speculation that the Argentinian military dictatorship stole the artworks to fund the Falklands War between Argentina and the United Kingdom in 1982.

In 2002, a pianist, whose uncle in Taiwan wanted to sell several Impressionist paintings, approached a gallery owner in Paris. He shared photographs and brought three paintings to the gallery. The gallerist requested a report from the ALR, which found that all three paintings had been stolen. The paintings—by Cézanne, Renoir, and Gauguin—were returned to Argentina and went back on display in November 2005.

As for the remaining thirteen paintings and drawings and seven Chinese artifacts, the trail has gone cold. The museum must hope that next Christmas, their stolen objects will be returned.

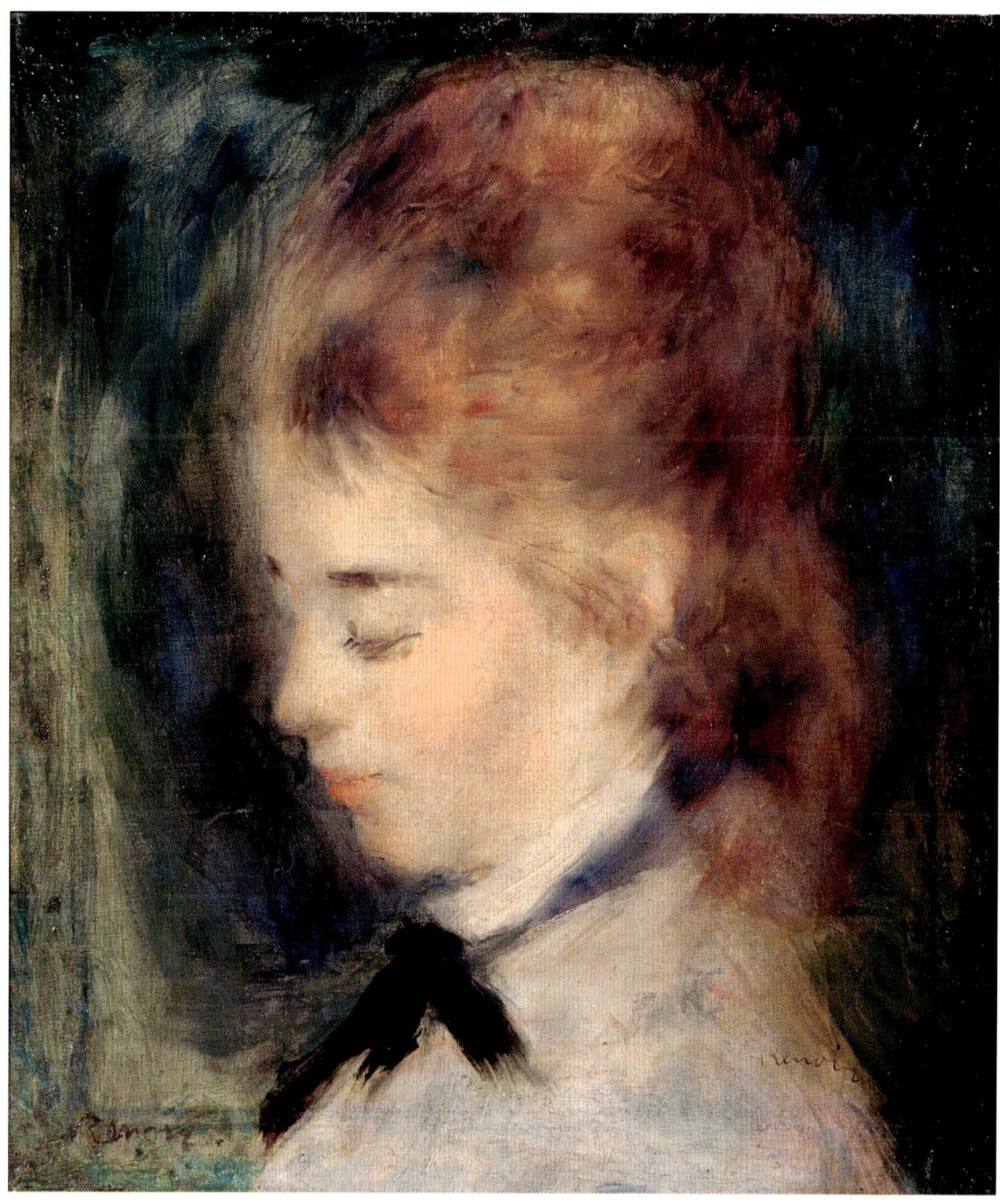

Above: Though the exact date of this portrait is unclear, Renoir developed severe arthritis by 1892 that forced him to dramatically change his technique. Renoir adapted, purportedly saying, "The pain passes, but the beauty remains."

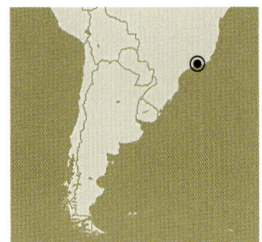

When: February 24, 2006

Where: Museu da Chácara do Céu in Rio de Janeiro

What: Theft of Claude Monet's *Marine* (1880), Pablo Picasso's *Dance* (1956), Henri Matisse's *Luxembourg Gardens* (1903), and Salvador Dalí's *Two Balconies* (1929)

THE CARNIVAL HEIST

Outside of the Museu da Chácara do Céu, the epic multi-day celebration that is Carnival had begun in Rio de Janeiro on February 24, 2006. Parties were already raging, and millions of people were dancing in the streets. The festivities were a welcome distraction to thieves, who took the opportunity to steal four paintings from the museum. Their timing was certainly not accidental. Carnival would ensure that not many people would be in the museum, the parties would mask any sounds of the robbery, and the crowds thronging the streets would make it impossible for the police to get to the museum.

Four armed men, one of whom was a teenager, took five minutes to overpower security guards (who did not carry weapons) and force them to turn off the museum's alarms and security cameras. The robbers spent a half hour picking out their four chosen works of art. They finally selected Claude Monet's *Marine*, Pablo Picasso's *Dance*, Henri Matisse's *Luxembourg Gardens*, and Salvador Dalí's *Two Balconies*. Though all noteworthy, *Two Balconies* was the only Dalí in a public collection in all of Latin America.

The guards, unarmed as they were, still tried to stop the thieves. One guard was whacked in the face, and another was smacked in the head with a gun after the guard tried to grab back the Picasso. Not content with the paintings, which were estimated to be worth around $10 million, the men also robbed five tourists unlucky enough to be in the museum at the time. The thieves, presumably, sambaed their way out of the museum and into the throngs of Carnival revelers, never to be seen again.

There is some speculation that the art may have been destroyed, as the passe-partouts from the paintings were found burned in a neighborhood on the outskirts of Rio. Local police were discouraged by this evidence and put the investigation on hold. Still, the theft remains active and on the FBI's Top Ten Art Crimes list.

Opposite: Though the gardens Matisse depicts in this painting, *Luxembourg Gardens*, are in Paris, the Museu da Chácara do Céu in Rio de Janeiro, which housed the painting, is similarly surrounded by lush gardens.

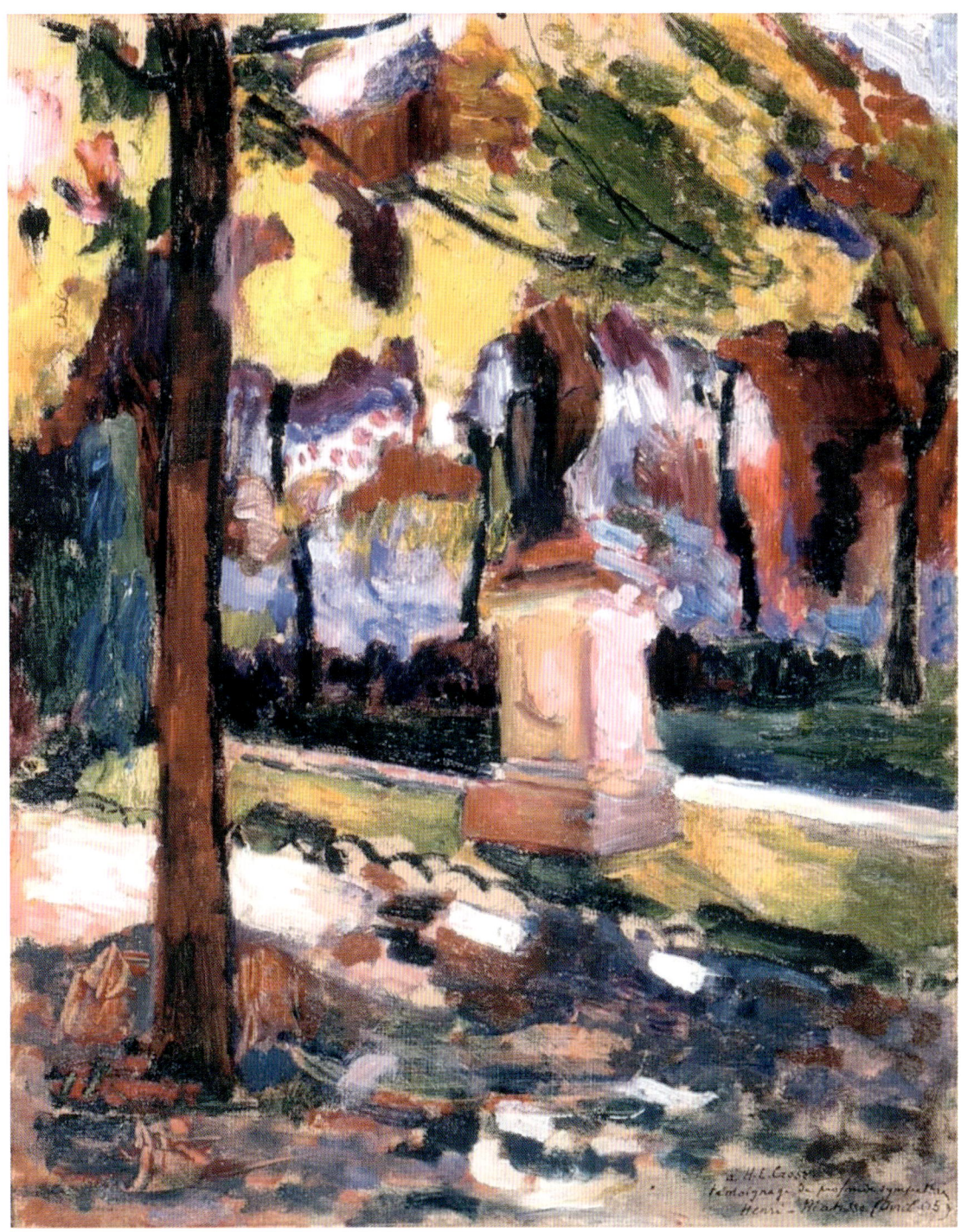

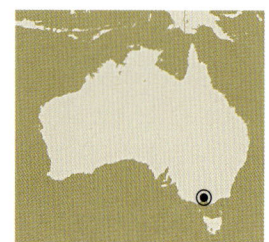

THE FACE THAT WOULD HAUNT MELBOURNE

Melbourne's National Gallery of Victoria (NGV) was properly chuffed when, in 1985, it acquired Picasso's *The Weeping Woman*, an unsettling, acidic green and purple Cubist rendering of a woman crying. At the time, it was the highest price Australia had ever paid for a work of art: 1.6 million Australian dollars.

When the National Gallery's director, Patrick McCaughey, unveiled the painting, he prophetically said, "This face is going to haunt Melbourne for the next 100 years." Though it hasn't yet been 100 years, the mystery of the theft of the painting on Saturday, August 2, 1986, has certainly perplexed and haunted the people of Melbourne.

Little is known about the theft, but some speculate that the thief or thieves hid out in the museum overnight before unscrewing the painting from the wall, removing its frame, stashing it in an alcove, and walking out one of the museum's doors. They left a card on the wall where the painting had hung, announcing that it had been moved to the Australian Capital Territory (ACT); thus, museum staff assumed the painting had been loaned to Canberra's National Gallery of Australia in the ACT.

No one noticed the theft until Monday, August 4, when the first in a series of notes arrived at newspapers and TV stations around Melbourne. Race Mathews, Victoria's minister for the arts, also received a letter; all the letters were addressed "ATTENTION: RANK MATHEWS." The letters stated, "We have stolen the Picasso from the National Gallery as a protest against the niggardly funding of the fine arts in this hick State and against the clumsy, unimaginative stupidity of the administration and distribution of that funding." They urged Mathews to meet two demands: 1) increase funding of the arts by 10 percent over the next three years, and

Opposite: *The Weeping Woman* was created by Picasso a few months after he finished his masterpiece mural *Guernica*. The woman in the painting resembles the grief-shattered mother who holds her dead child and wails in *Guernica*.

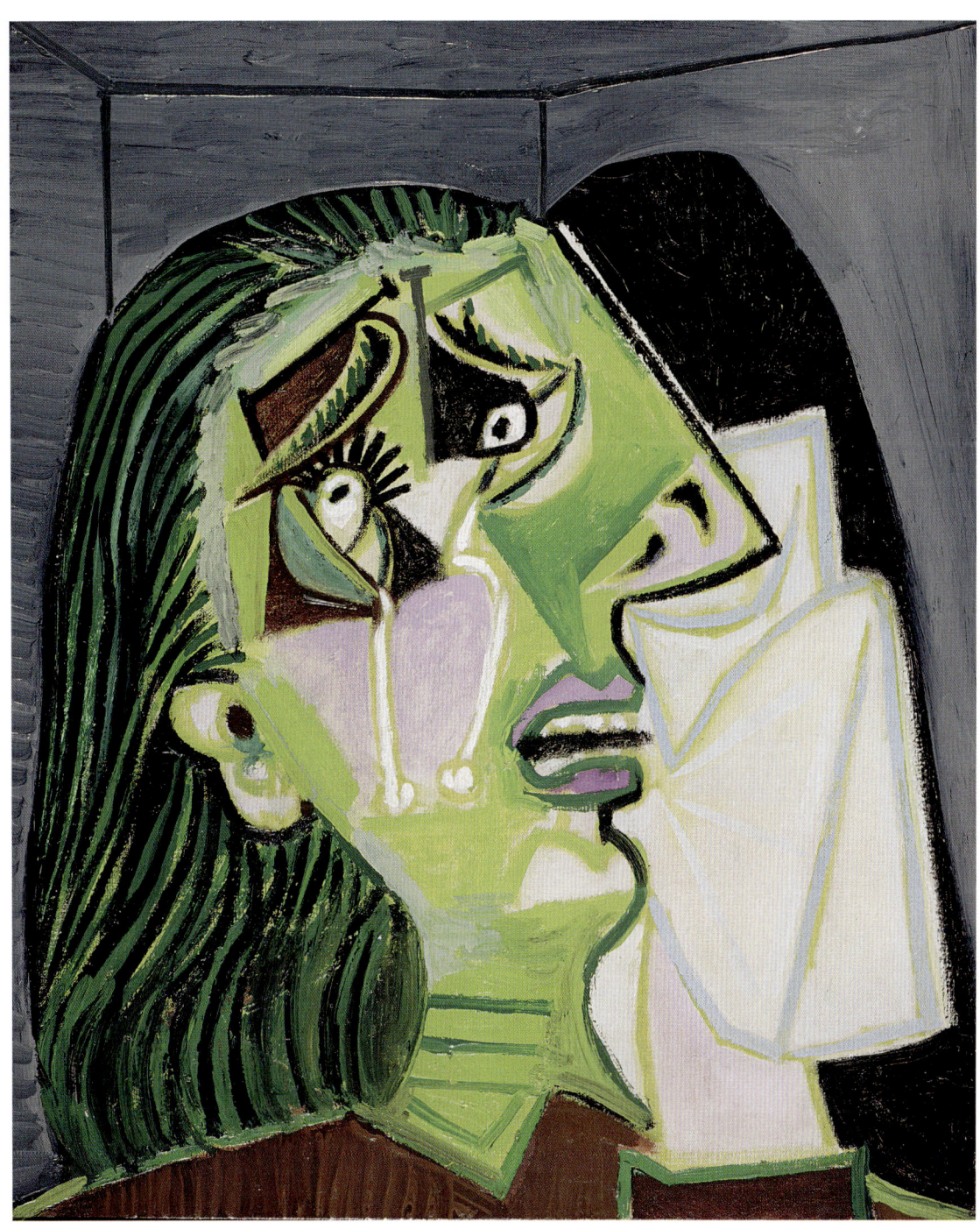

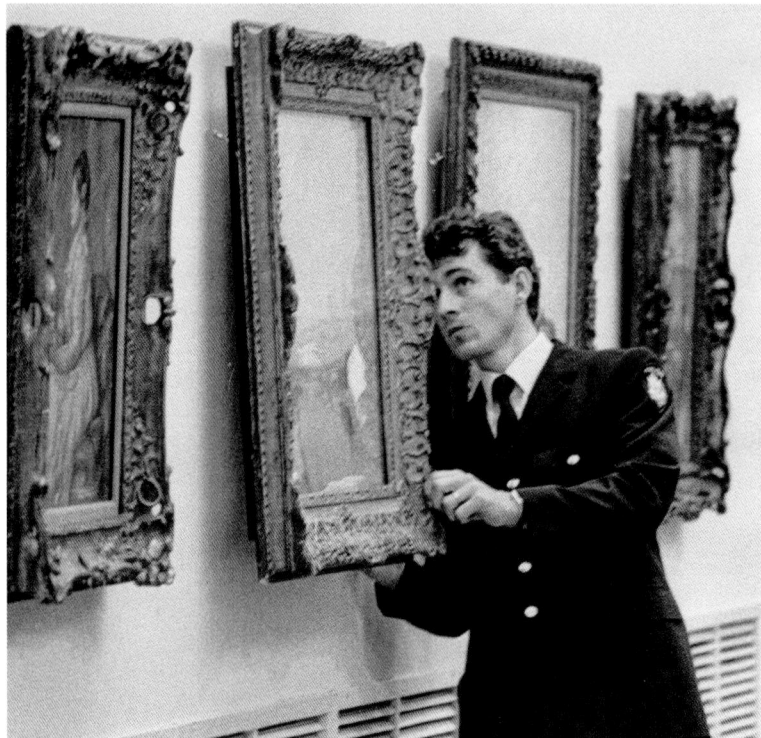

2) start an annual competition for artists under the age of thirty with five prizes of five thousand Australian dollars, to be called "The Picasso Ransom." The thieves signed the letter "Australian Cultural Terrorists" (also ACT). They gave Mathews "a sporting seven days" to meet their demands or they would destroy the painting.

It was clear that the thieves not only were vigilante supporters of contemporary arts, but also that they had a sense of humor. They sent more ransom notes after Mathews refused to meet their demands, calling Mathews a "tiresome bag of swamp gas," amongst other zingers.

Back at the NGV, the museum was in a tizzy. The painting was uninsured. The museum director pledged better security and banned chairs in the galleries so that guards would be more "attentive." Unimpressed, the guards went on strike for three days and the museum was closed until their chairs were returned. Meanwhile, in Melbourne, a cultural debate was raging about the monetary and aesthetic value of the Picasso and whether that money could have been better spent supporting contemporary artists in Australia, who were having a field day creating mocking tributes to the stolen Picasso. The ACT's act was having an impact.

A second letter from the ACT arrived, stating that *The Weeping Woman* would be burned on August 9 if their demands were not met. They wished Mathews "Good luck with your huffing and puffing, Minister, you pompous fathead." Two days later, they were back with another short letter in an envelope that contained a burnt match: "Thank you for your support. Phase two begins shortly."

It seemed that *The Weeping Woman* would soon have more to weep about. Most thought that after the last ACT letter, the Picasso must have disappeared in a blaze. So, when a tip on August 19 to check locker 227 at the Spencer Street railway station arrived, the NGV's director practically wept with relief to find the painting wrapped and tied in soft cloth and brown paper, in nearly perfect condition.

As the painting was victoriously returned to the NGV, the ACT sent one last letter, stating, "Our intention was always to bring to public the plight of a group which lacks any of the legitimate means of blackmailing governments." The ACT's demands follow precedent and harken back to other art thefts such as Kempton Bunton's theft of *The Duke of Wellington* (p. 20), Mario Roymans's theft of *The Love Letter* (p. 48), or Ulay's theft of *The Poor Poet* (p. 52).

The case was officially closed in 1989, but it remains unsolved. *The Weeping Woman* made headlines for her acquisition and her absence (in the week after her theft, the museum was flooded with gawkers who came to look at the blank wall where she once hung). Today, she is considered one of the most popular paintings in Australia and is worth approximately $100 million. She has inspired films, books, and countless political cartoons. Her tears—whether of joy or pain, loss or gain—are well earned.

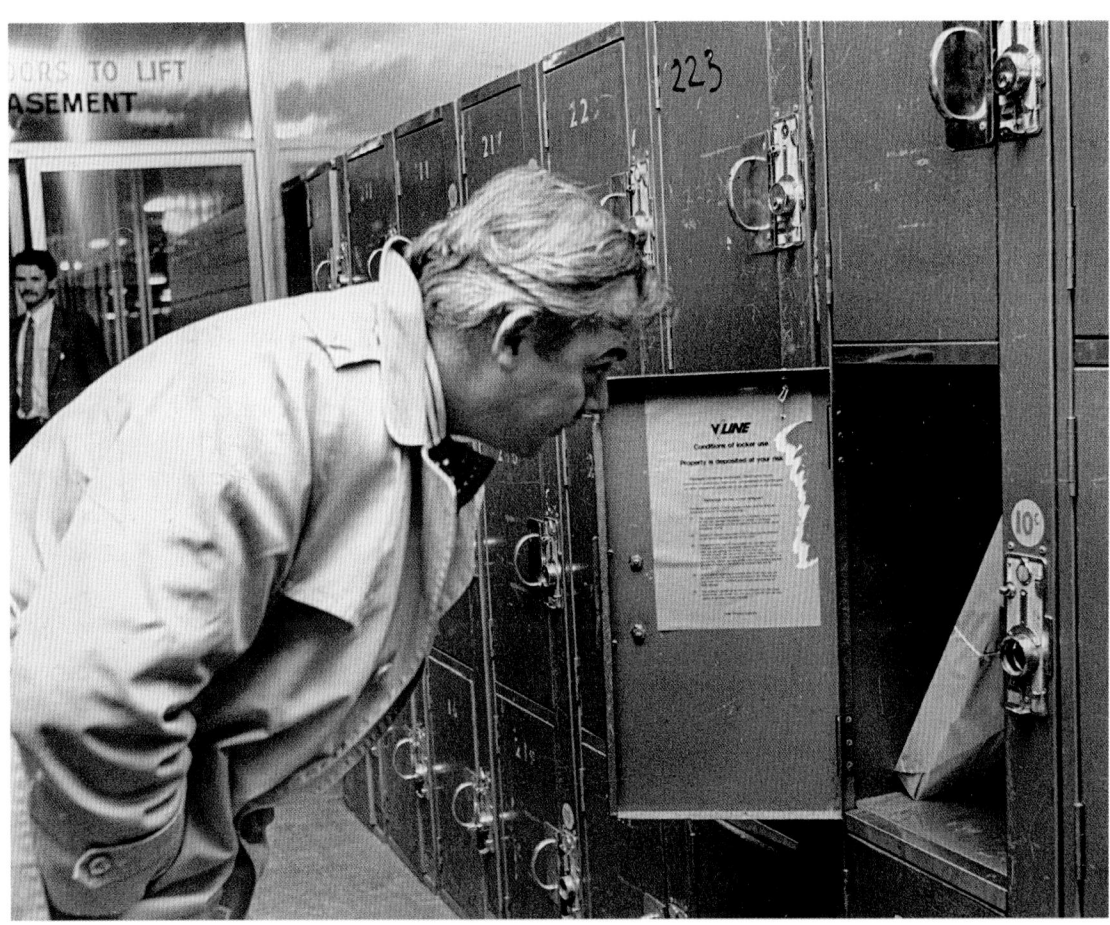

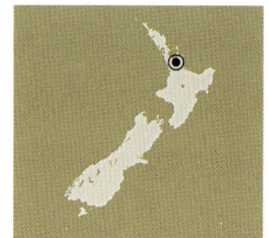

APRIL FOOL'S DAY DISASTER

April Fool's Day had dawned in New Zealand, but the state of things at the International Art Centre in Auckland was no laughing matter. At around 4:00 a.m., CCTV footage recorded a white sedan parking outside of the art auction house, a contemporary building with large glass windows through which a number of paintings were visible from the street. Two bandana-clad passengers emerged from the car. One used a blowtorch to the window, another stood watch, and the driver remained in the car. After the first passenger finished with the blowtorch, the second passenger threw a mysterious liquid from a bottle onto the window. The resulting white cloud led police to think it may have been liquid nitrogen, which can make glass easy to smash. The man with the blowtorch used the canister to attempt to shatter the window, but to no avail. The two passengers seemed to give up and drove away.

Eight minutes later, the white sedan reappeared with a red van (also stolen). The thieves were not to be fooled twice. They reversed and rammed the van into the windows. From the wrecked windows, the thieves plucked two Lindauer portraits and sped off.

Lindauer was a colonial-era Czech artist who immigrated to New Zealand in 1874 and became known for his detailed paintings of Māori people. The stolen paintings were of two Māori elders—Chief Ngātai-Raure and Chieftainess Ngātai-Raure—members of the Ngātai family from Tauranga. In 2017, they were valued around $1 million New Zealand dollars.

Leads never went anywhere. A year and a half after the theft, the portrait of Chief Ngātai-Raure appeared on the dark web, which stated, "Here you can bid on a TOP SECRET original painting from Bohemian painter Gottfried Lindauer that was stolen in New Zealand, Auckland 2017." Eager buyers had bid $400,000 in bitcoin, but police dismissed the auction as a scam though rumors about the paintings persisted.

Five and a half years later, Auckland police announced the return of the Lindauer portraits. They had been contacted by two gang members who, even though they were in jail, were able

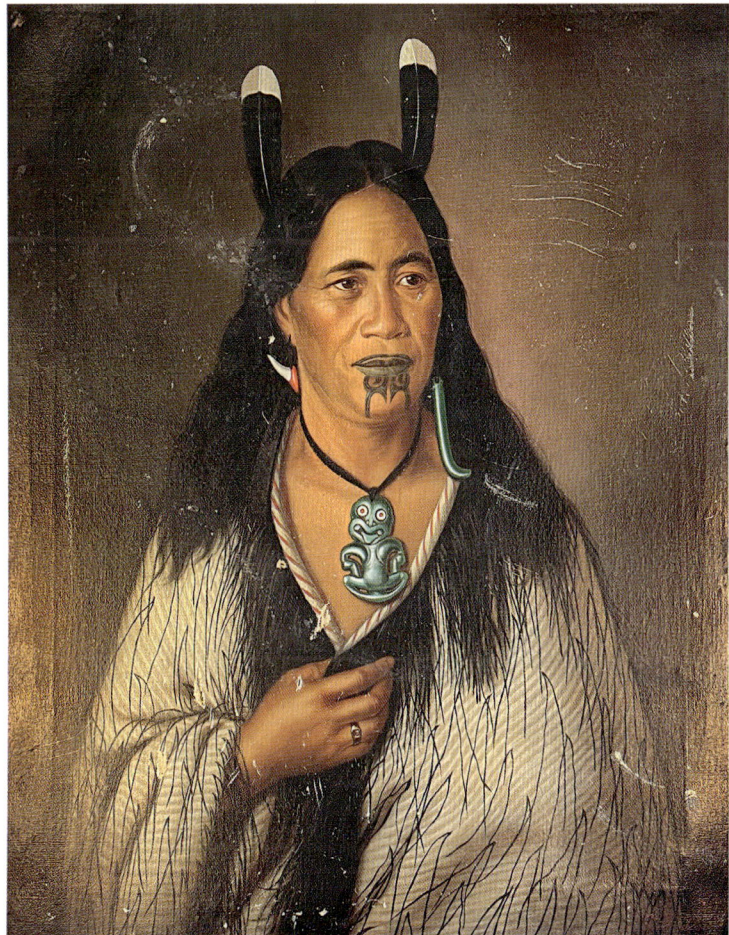

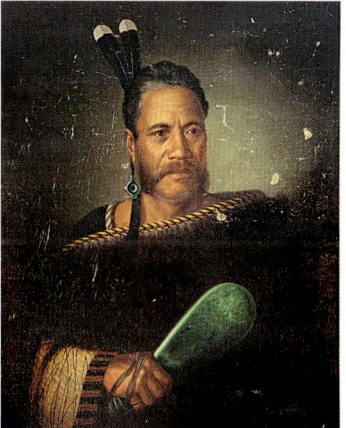

Above: It is believed that Gottfried Lindauer's portrait depicts Māori Chief Ngātai-Raure, a great-grandson of the esteemed warrior Hōri Ngātai of the Ngāi Te Rangi tribe from Tauranga, New Zealand.

Left: Chieftainess Ngātai-Raure wears a *taonga* (treasure) around her neck: a hei-tiki made of pounamu (greenstone).

to flush out and encourage the return of the paintings, which were in poor shape and needed conservation work. They were returned to their owner, a rich Auckland businessman with a large private art collection.

As the saying goes, "Fool me once, shame on you. Fool me twice, shame on me." Not to be fooled again, New Zealand police sent a message with the painting's return, saying, "No matter how much time passes we remain open to the fact we can hold a person, or people, to account for the burglary in 2017."

When: Between 2010 and 2019

Where: Museums throughout Europe with collections of Chinese art and artifacts

What: Thefts of objects looted from the Imperial Summer Palace in Beijing during the Second Opium War in the mid-1800s and the thefts of those objects again in the 2010s

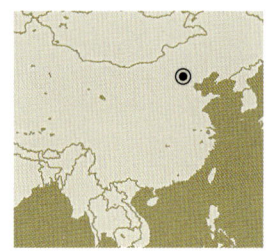

STEALING (BACK?) CHINESE ART FROM EUROPE?

Between 2010 and 2019, several European museums with significant collections of Chinese objects were the backdrops of cinematic heists: the Chinese Pavilion at Drottningholm Palace in Stockholm, Sweden, in 2010; the Musée Chinois at the Château de Fontainebleau outside of Paris (one in 2015 and another attempted in 2019); KODE art museum in Bergen, Norway (in 2010 and 2013); the Museum of East Asian Art in Bath, UK, in 2018, and many more.

Though geographically disparate, the thefts share some common themes. In most cases, the thieves resorted to Hollywood-level stunts—lighting cars on fire to distract local police from the scene, rappeling through ceilings, smashing through side doors, and even tunneling through brick walls and using smoke bombs and fire extinguishers to erase any evidence. But more importantly, in all cases the thieves almost exclusively stole art from China—specifically, art looted by European armies during the First and Second Opium Wars in China, otherwise known as the Century of Humiliation. In the mid-1800s,

during the Second Opium War, the French and British sent a delegation to work out terms to end the war. The delegates were taken hostage by the Chinese. Meanwhile, French and British troops captured the Imperial Summer Palace outside of Beijing, the residence of the Qing dynasty, a massive complex filled with incredible art and treasures.

When the British High Commissioner received news that the French and British delegation had been taken hostage and tortured, and nineteen members had been killed, he ordered the razing of the 860-acre palace. The complex was so extensive that it took four thousand men over three days to annihilate it. Countless invaluable objects were destroyed and even more were looted, ending up in at least forty-seven museums and innumerable private collections. It wasn't only objects that were taken out of the Summer Palace; soldiers also brought home five Pekingese dogs, specially bred for the Chinese royal family. One was given to Queen Victoria, who without any self-consciousness brazenly named the dog Looty.

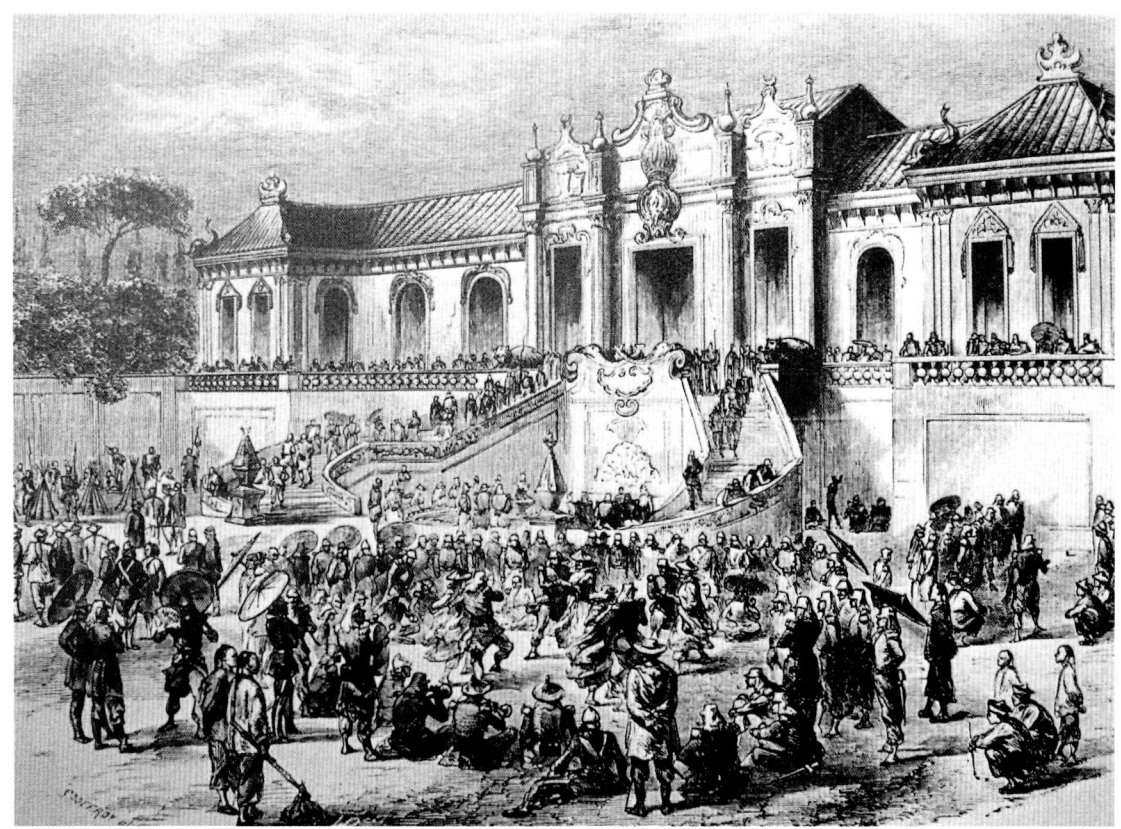

Above: This 1860 illustration by Godefroy Durand shows the looting of the Imperial Summer Palace by Anglo-French forces. Some of the stolen goods would end up being (re)stolen from European collections over 150 years later.

Who is carrying out the thefts of Chinese objects from European collections is the subject of much speculation. In a 2018 *GQ* article, Alex W. Palmer suggested two main suspects: one, the growing class of billionaires in China who might see returning the art as patriotic, helping to recover China's dignity after the Century of Humiliation. Palmer also suggested that the China Poly Group, one of the Chinese government's most powerful state-run conglomerates, could be behind the thefts. Other suspects include the Chinese mafia and enterprising thieves who are aware of the sky-rocketing prices of Chinese art, which has ballooned into almost 30 percent of the international art market. But, for now, who is ordering and executing these thefts and where the objects are going remains opaque.

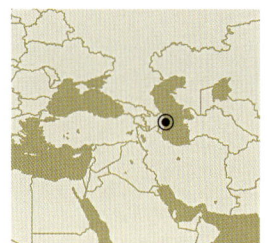

When: World War II and 1993

Where: Schloss Karnzow in Berlin and the Azerbaijan National Museum of Art in Baku, Azerbaijan

What: Theft of twelve drawings (originally from the Kunsthalle Bremen) from Schloss Karnzow during World War II and 180 objects from the Azerbaijan National Museum of Art in 1993

A MATRYOSHKA DOLL OF ART CRIME

Between 1820 and 1860, the Kunsthalle Bremen in Germany bought twelve Old Master drawings, including work by Rembrandt, Jacob van Ruisdael, and Jean-François Millet. The jewel of the group, *The Women's Bath* by Albrecht Dürer, was the first non-religious work of art to depict nude women.

During World War II, the precious drawings were moved to Schloss Karnzow, a castle north of Berlin, where 1,520 other art refugees were housed for their protection. As the Nazis retreated, the Soviet Army stormed the castle with its Trophy Brigades. The guardian of Schloss Karnzow did not stick around to witness the destruction of what he had kept safe during the war. With his mistress, he rowed out to the middle of the lake near the castle. There, they slashed their wrists, threw themselves into the lake, and drowned. The drawings, amongst other treasures, disappeared.

In 1993, the Azerbaijan National Museum of Art in Baku promoted an upcoming exhibition that included the stolen works from the

museum in Bremen. The drawings had been given to the Azerbaijani museum in 1947 by the KGB. The Kunsthalle Bremen protested and asked for the return of the drawings. Before any further action could be taken, the drawings, along with 180 other works of art from the museum in Baku, disappeared … again.

In 1995, a former wrestler named Masatsugu Koga showed up at the German Embassy in Tokyo with the twelve drawings. Koga, along with another former wrestler—an Azerbaijani Olympian named Aydin Ibrahimov—and his ex-wife, Natavan Aleskerova—a thirteen-year law enforcement veteran who held a position in Azerbaijan equivalent to a deputy attorney general—hatched a plan to ransom the drawings back to the Kunsthalle Bremen.

Opposite: Albrecht Dürer's *Sitting Mary with Child* (c. 1514) was one of the nearly two hundred objects stolen from the Azerbaijan National Museum of Art in Baku in 1993.

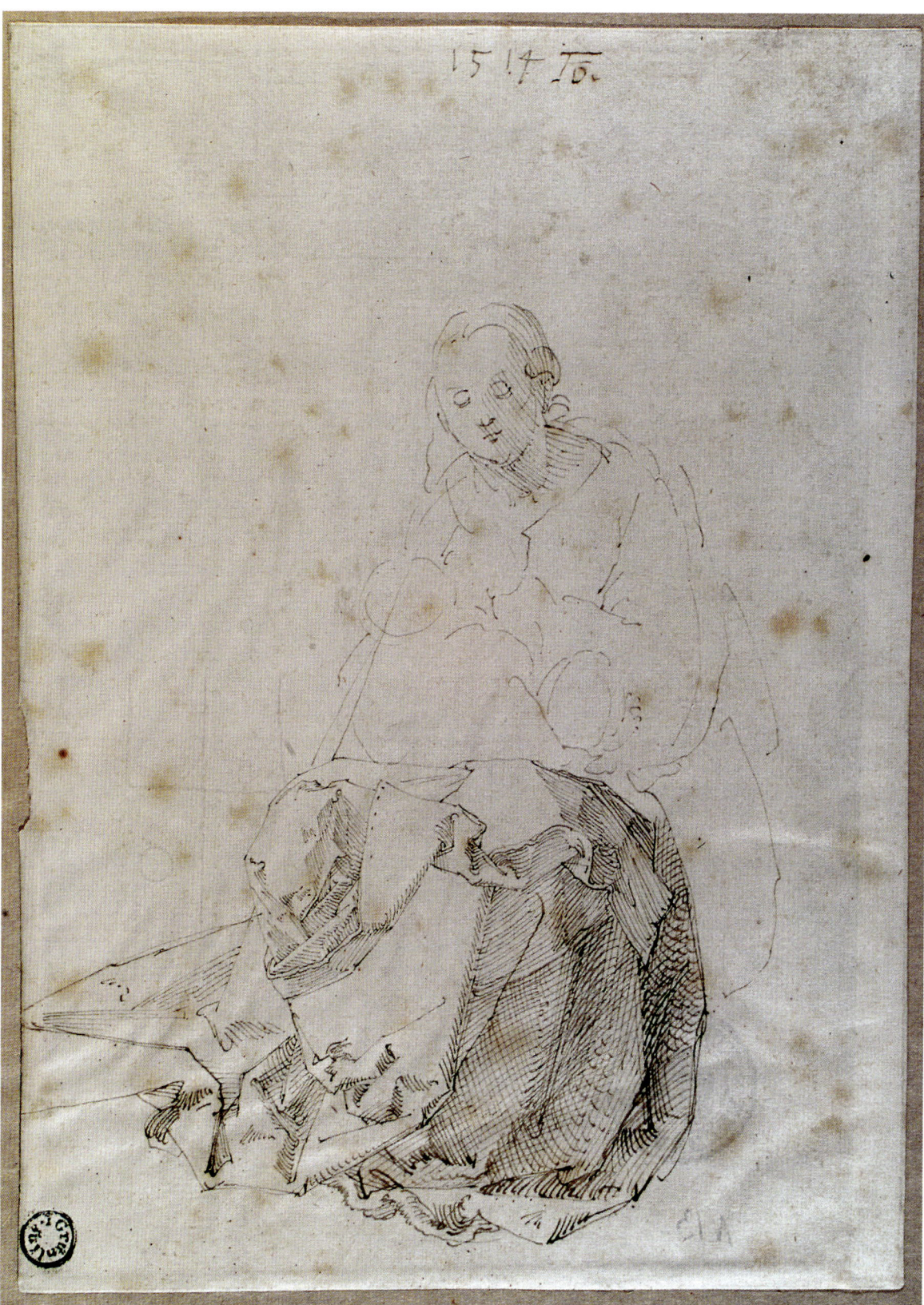

At the German Embassy, Koga, armed with photos of the drawings, asked for $12 million, claiming the artworks were family heirlooms. When informed by the embassy that the drawings had been stolen, Koga admitted to lying. He dropped his price to $6 million, saying he needed the money for a kidney transplant. The embassy declined and Koga left, but the drawings were on the international radar.

In 1997, Koga tried to sell the drawings again in New York, where he met with a curator from the Kunsthalle Bremen. Accompanying the curator was her "assistant," an undercover customs agent, who arrested Koga as soon as he pulled six of the Kunsthalle's drawings—including the Dürer and Rembrandt—out of a plain manila envelope. With Koga arrested, Aleskerova flew to New York, presumably to check on the fate of the remaining six Kunsthalle Bremen drawings and the 180 other pieces stolen from the museum in Baku. Aleskerova was also arrested. The stolen goods were found hidden under the bed and in a cupboard of a second Azerbaijani former wrestler (who was deemed innocent) in Brooklyn.

Aleskerova and Koga were tried separately for their crimes. Slapped with the same charges, Aleskerova pleaded not guilty and Koga pleaded guilty. In a surprise twist during Aleskerova's trial, Thomas Hoving, former director of the Metropolitan Museum of Art, was called in by the defense. Hoving—who called himself a "fakebuster"—took the stand to suggest that the stolen drawings were not by Dürer or Rembrandt. He believed they were bad forgeries or by lesser artists instead. Of the Rembrandt drawing, Hoving said, "I cannot imagine it being by the master whose ink drawings throb with energy. Its attribution is incorrect and does not fit Rembrandt's body of work." The Dürer Hoving dismissed as "very questionable."

Hoving's cries of fakery didn't change the verdict. In 1999, Aleskerova was given an eleven-

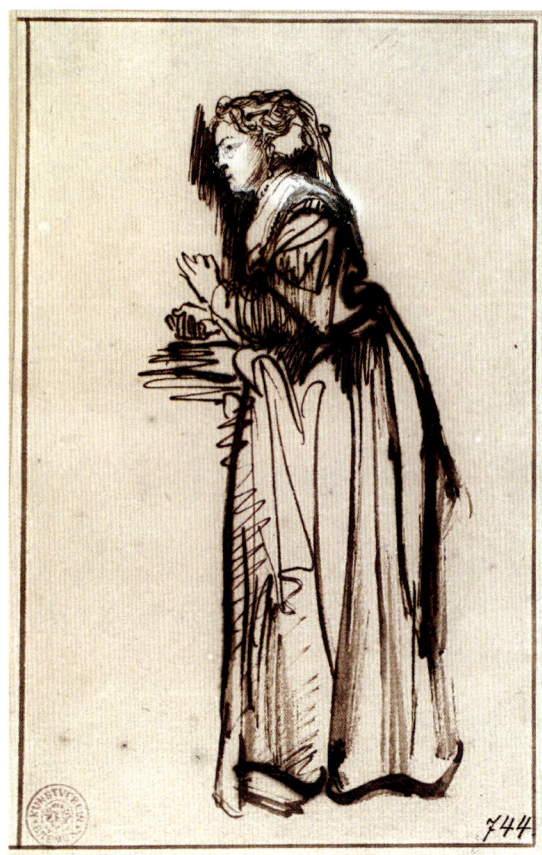

month sentence. Koga, who was not lying about needing a kidney transplant, died of renal failure in 1999. Ibrahimov, the former Azerbaijani Olympic wrestler, eluded authorities for many years, but finally turned himself in in 2006. He was given a seven-year suspended sentence.

The twelve drawings, originally stolen by the Red Army in World War II and again in Baku in 1993, were finally reunited with the Kunsthalle Bremen in 2001. And the 180 objects stolen from Baku were returned to the museum there too. If only we could hear what the women in the Dürer drawing might be talking about as they perform their ablutions. After their many adventures around the world, they must have a lot to share.

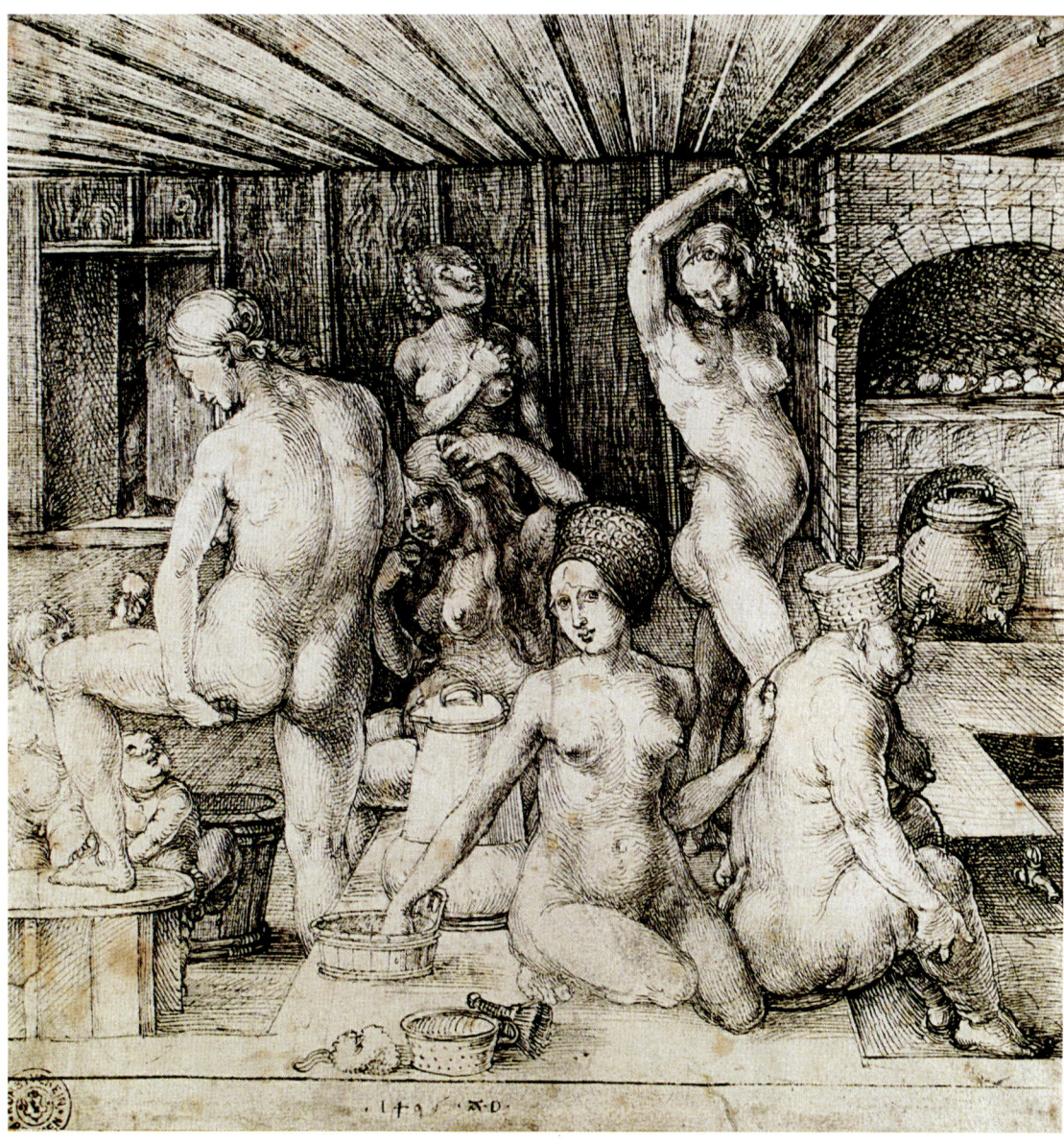

Opposite: Rembrandt's *Woman Standing with Raised Hands* was one of a dozen drawings that were returned to the Kunsthalle Bremen after being recovered by US Customs in 2001.

Above: In *The Women's Bath,* young Albrecht Dürer broke with tradition, choosing to show nude women outside of a religious context—one of the first known instances of this in art history.

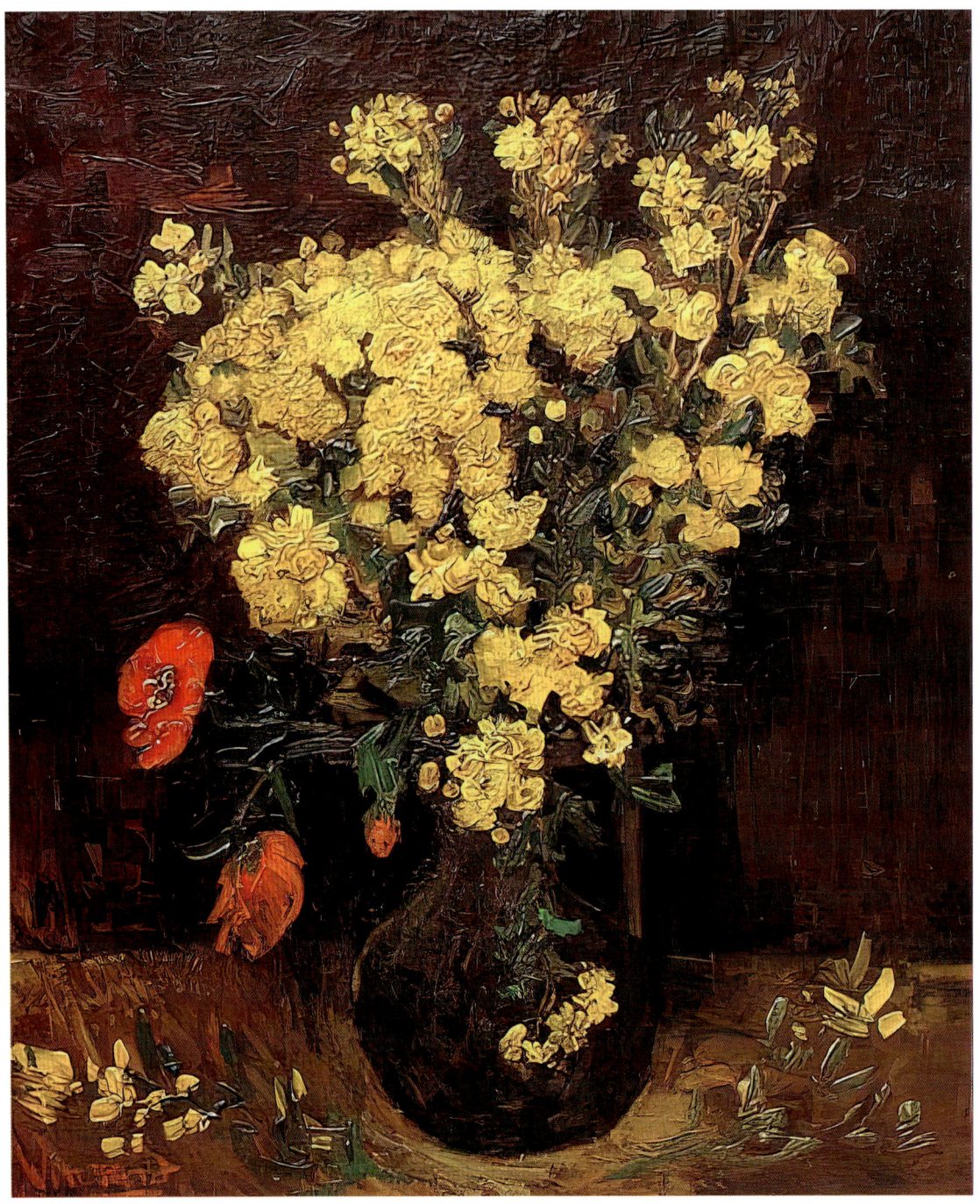

Above: Though often associated with the color red, poppies can be many colors—orange, blue, purple, white, and yellow, as in Van Gogh's *Poppy Flowers*. They can be diminutive or the size of a dinner plate.

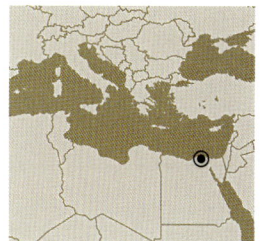

When: June 4, 1977, and August 2010

Where: Mohamed Mahmoud Khalil Museum in Cairo

What: Theft(s) of Vincent van Gogh's *Poppy Flowers* (1887)

DOUBLE INDIGNITIES

A treasure trove of Impressionist work collected by Mohammed Mahmoud Khalil and his wife, Emilienne Luce, sits in a palatial home on the Nile River. Khalil and Luce met in Paris and were at the cutting edge of collecting Impressionist art in the 1920s. The museum contains work by Monet, Renoir, Gauguin, Rodin, and, at one time, Van Gogh. *Poppy Flowers* may have been the first Van Gogh to be collected outside of Europe.

Its first disappearance from the museum in 1977 is shrouded in mystery, but the painting was recovered a decade later in Kuwait. Egyptian officials never released any further information.

After that, the painting was not allowed outside of Egypt, even when other paintings from the museum were loaned to exhibitions abroad. However, in August 2010, *Poppy Flowers* was stolen a second time. Police guess that the thief pushed a sofa against the wall to cut the painting out of the frame with a boxcutter. The painting was estimated to be worth $55 million.

Shortly after, Egyptian police detained and interrogated two Italian tourists at the Cairo International Airport. On the day of the theft, they had been visitors to the museum, along with eight other unrelated people. When the Italian tourists went to the bathroom and then left the museum in suspicious haste, police arrested them just before they boarded their flights. Hosni Mubarak, president of Egypt at the time, announced that *Poppy Flowers* had been recovered, but he later rescinded his pronouncement, claiming he had received bad information. The Italian tourists were released and will, no doubt, never think about visiting a museum bathroom again.

Some suspected an inside job. Several staff members were charged with negligence because of shabby security. Only seven of the museum's security cameras were working and none of the museum's fifty-four object alarms were operational. A number of culture ministry officials were charged with negligence and harming state property for ignoring the lax security, enabling the theft.

Despite a reward of one million Egyptian pounds offered by an Egyptian billionaire, *Poppy Flowers* remains missing to this day.

CHAPTER TWO
VANDALISM

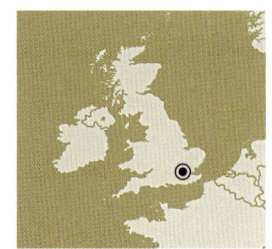

When: March 10, 1914

Where: National Gallery in London

What: Vandalism of Diego Velázquez's *The Toilet of Venus* ('*The Rokeby Venus*') (1647–51) with a meat cleaver

VOTES (AND VANDALISM) FOR WOMEN

Canadian-born Mary Richardson was a thirty-two-year-old suffragette when she entered the National Gallery on March 10, 1914, with a meat cleaver hidden up the sleeve of her jacket. Richardson's target was Diego Velázquez's painting *The Toilet of Venus*, known colloquially as '*The Rokeby Venus*' because it had once belonged to John Morritt of Rokeby Hall in Yorkshire. Morritt, who referred to the painting as his "fine picture of Venus's backside," had sold it to the gallery a decade earlier for a tremendous amount at the time: £45,000, the equivalent of around £3 million today. Even King Edward VII, then the ruling monarch, contributed to the purchase of Velázquez's Venus. The painting was considered a national treasure, an icon of art history, and, as the BBC once put it, "one of the most famous bottoms of all times."

Richardson managed to strike seven blows (or, as she would later call them, "lovely shots") with the cleaver, breaking the painting's glass case and lacerating Venus's shoulder blades, back, and famed bottom.

The guard on duty initially thought the sound of breaking glass was coming from one of the gallery's skylights. He slipped and fell on the freshly polished floor when he realized the sounds were coming from Richardson's blows, but she was eventually apprehended and marched out of the National Gallery. The gallery and other museums in London closed for two weeks after the incident, afraid of copycat attacks.

Dubbed "Slasher Mary" by the press, Richardson was part of the Women's Social and Political Union (WSPU), an organization that injected militancy into the women's voting rights movement. Women had been campaigning in the United Kingdom since 1860, but, when asking nicely failed to produce results, the WSPU was formed in 1903. The WSPU's rallying cry, "Deeds not words," encouraged women to use unconstitutional means—fighting, cutting telegraph lines, and destroying property, whether by stones, bricks, arson, or bombs, amongst other things—to achieve their goals. Richardson's was not the first vandalism of art on behalf of the WSPU, but her act was the most famous.

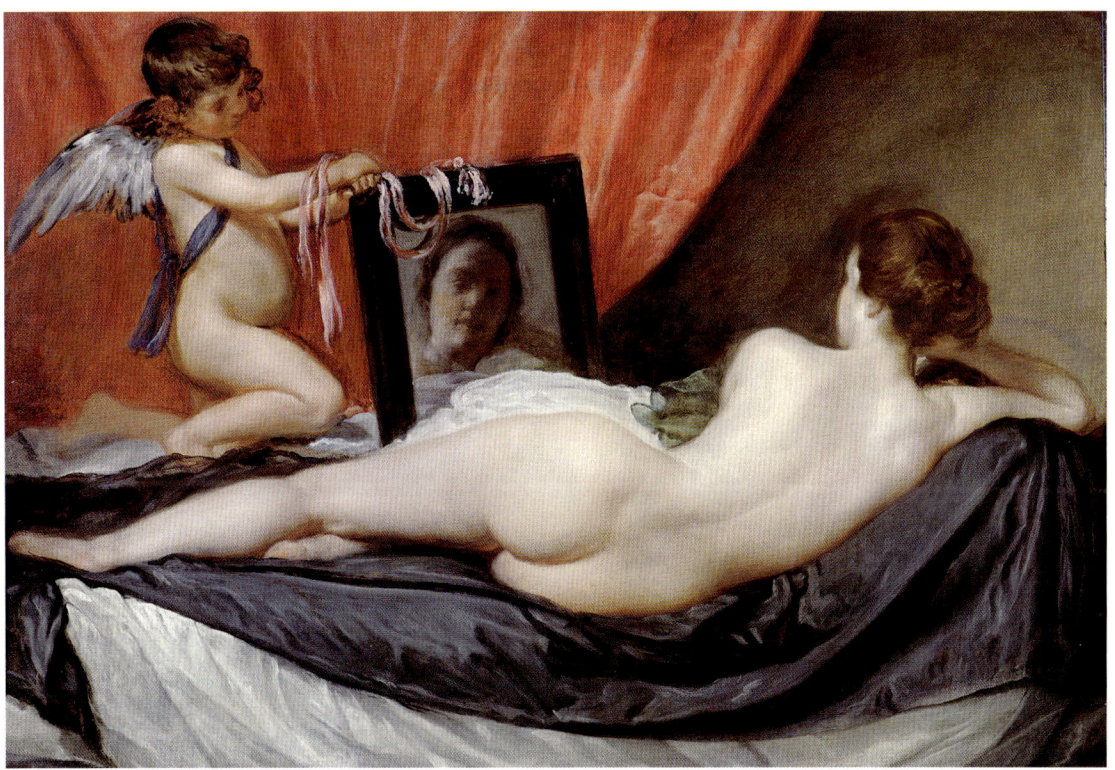

Above: "The Venus effect," coined from this painting, describes a perceptual phenomenon. We see Venus observing her own reflection, which is optically impossible, as we are not directly behind her. Venus should see us, the viewers, not herself.

Right: Evidence of the damage inflicted on *The Toilet of Venus* by Richardson's meat cleaver.

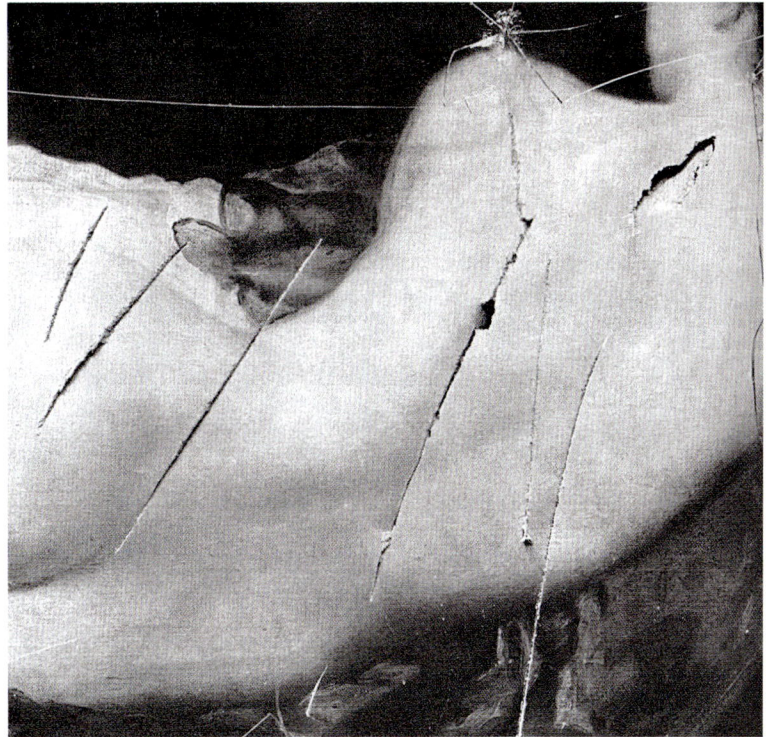

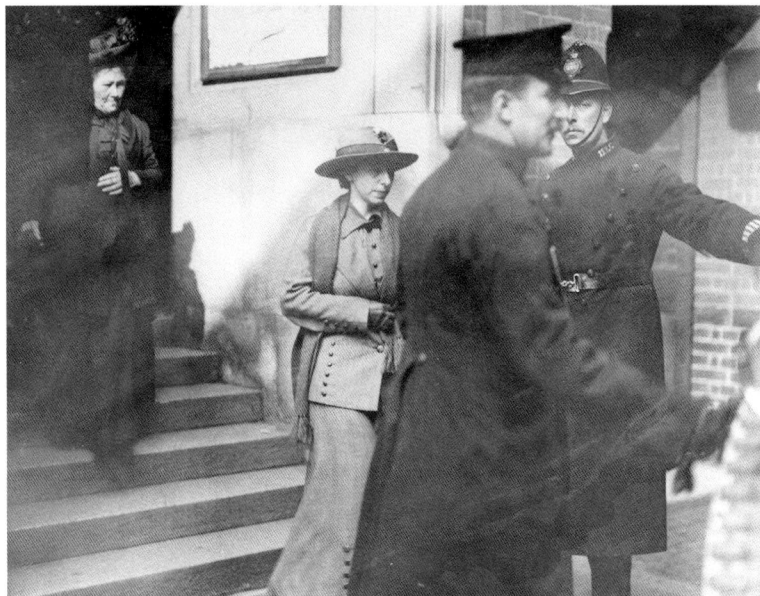

Richardson chose the Velázquez because she knew it would hit the government where it hurt: financially (the National Gallery estimated the attack reduced the painting's value by £15,000) and politically (by bringing attention to the women's movement). It was also a painting that Richardson felt embodied the stranglehold of the patriarchy. Almost forty years after the act, in a 1952 interview with the *Star*, Richardson said she had also chosen *The Toilet of Venus* because of "the way men visitors gaped at it all day long." Thus, Richardson's choice also was a social protest: women weren't objects to be ogled.

Richardson hadn't acted rashly. She had a plan, approved by the WSPU, and had even written an official statement for the WSPU press before she went to the National Gallery. At her trial, Richardson spoke about her reason for attacking the painting, referencing Emmeline Pankhurst, the founder of the WSPU, who had been arrested the day before. Richardson said, "I have tried to destroy the picture of the most beautiful woman in

mythological history as a protest against the Government destroying Mrs. Pankhurst, who is the most beautiful character in modern history. Justice is an element of beauty as much as color and outline on canvas." She continued, "You can get another picture, but you cannot get a life, as they are killing Mrs. Pankhurst."

Emmeline Pankhurst's health had been in sharp decline after protesting her own and other suffragettes' incarcerations by engaging in hunger and thirst strikes while in prison. After traumatic force-feedings in jail, where Pankhurst and others were fed with tubes shoved down their noses and throats, Richardson was concerned that another arrest and hunger strike would kill Pankhurst, who was arrested seven times during her years of campaigning. Pankhurst had been arrested so many times that she had taken to wearing disguises when out in public and was protected by an all-female, jujitsu-trained group called the Bodyguard.

In her defense, Richardson highlighted the hypocrisy of a painting of a woman being valued more than a woman's life. To Richardson, Pankhurst was a far more beautiful character than the two-dimensional painted Venus of Velázquez's canvas. Eventually, society would agree with Richardson's defense of Pankhurst, who was named one of *Time* magazine's 100 most important people of the twentieth century.

Richardson was sentenced for six months for malicious damage. This wasn't her first rodeo: she had been arrested nine times before for assault, arson, obstruction, and willful damage, and she had spent a total of three years in prison. The painting was nearly seamlessly restored and is still on display at the National Gallery today.

Richardson's vandalism catalyzed a frenzy of other acts of "suffragette iconoclasm." In the five months following, women vandalized at least fourteen other works of art in nine different attacks, with nine women arrested. In seven of the nine attacks, the works of art vandalized were of men or nude women. Today, there is some debate about whether Richardson's actions should be considered vandalism or iconoclasm (the destruction of images for political or religious reasons).

In 1918, women over the age of thirty who owned property with a value over £5 (or who had a husband who did) were allowed to vote. It took until 1928 for women, regardless of property status, to win the right to vote in the United Kingdom.

THE MORE THINGS CHANGE . . .

"Slasher Mary" isn't the only vandal of '*The Rokeby Venus*'. In 2023, almost 110 years after Mary Richardson's act, two members of the British environmental activist group Just Stop Oil added to Venus's history of vandalization. With five synchronized blows (or "lovely shots" as Richardson described them), the protestors used safety hammers to pound on the painting's covering, causing the glass to splinter. Citing the Women's Social and Political Union's motto, the activists stopped their hammering to pronounce, "Women did not get the vote by voting. It is time for deeds and not words. It is time to just stop oil . . . Politics is failing us. Politics failed women in 1914 . . . If we love history, if we love art, if we love our families, we must just stop oil."

They then sat down together in front of the painting and held hands.

In 1914, after Richardson's vandalization, many galleries in London closed to the public. Others stayed open with a rule of "No muffs, wrist-bags, or sticks." At the British Museum, women were allowed in but only if accompanied by a man who was responsible for them. An unaccompanied lady needed to have a letter of recommendation from an upstanding gentleman who could vouch for her good character and actions. In 2023, after the Just Stop Oil protests, it was business as usual at the National Gallery. The museum didn't miss a beat.

As to what Venus thought of this latest attack on her backside, like the *Mona Lisa* (p. 38), her expression remains unchanged.

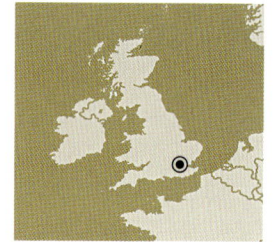

NOT WHAT HE SIGNED UP FOR

With a graffiti marker, Vladimir Umanets signed his name and the year, "12," in the lower right corner of Mark Rothko's painting *Black on Maroon*, then added "A potential piece of Yellowism." While the black ink dripped down Rothko's canvas, Umanets proceeded to hightail it for the Tate Modern's exit as onlookers gaped. It was around 3:25 in the afternoon of October 7, 2012.

If you are wondering what in the (art) world Yellowism is, you are not alone. Though this crime occurred over a decade ago, the concept of Yellowism remains impenetrable. Umanets, a self-described penniless activist and artist, described Yellowism as neither art nor art movement but also not anti-art. Making sense?

Twenty-six-year-old Umanets, who claimed he was not a vandal but an artist, later told the BBC that "art allows us to take what someone's done and put a new message on it." Shortly after the event, famed artist Anish Kapoor said at the opening of one of his exhibitions, "There is a big difference between being a radical and being a vandal and acts of vandalism are simply that … there is no symbolic value in it [Umanets's act] at all." Meanwhile, at the Tate, the graffiti marker had penetrated the layers of Rothko's paint and canvas. Umanets didn't see this as a problem, declaring, "With my signature this work will be much more valuable a work of art and also financially, because I changed the meaning. Someone who removes this signature will be an asshole."

There is little disagreement about who the asshole in this situation was. A team of conservators at the Tate removed Umanets's signature and became the heroes of this story. With the help of scientists from Dow Chemical Company, the team tested different solvents on the graffiti-pen ink. The conservators created a mock version of Rothko's painting, going so far as to artificially age it by fifty years so that it would more closely resemble the vandalized piece. They tested products until they found the right combinations. It took eighteen months for the painting to be put back on display, almost as long as Umanets's two-year jail sentence.

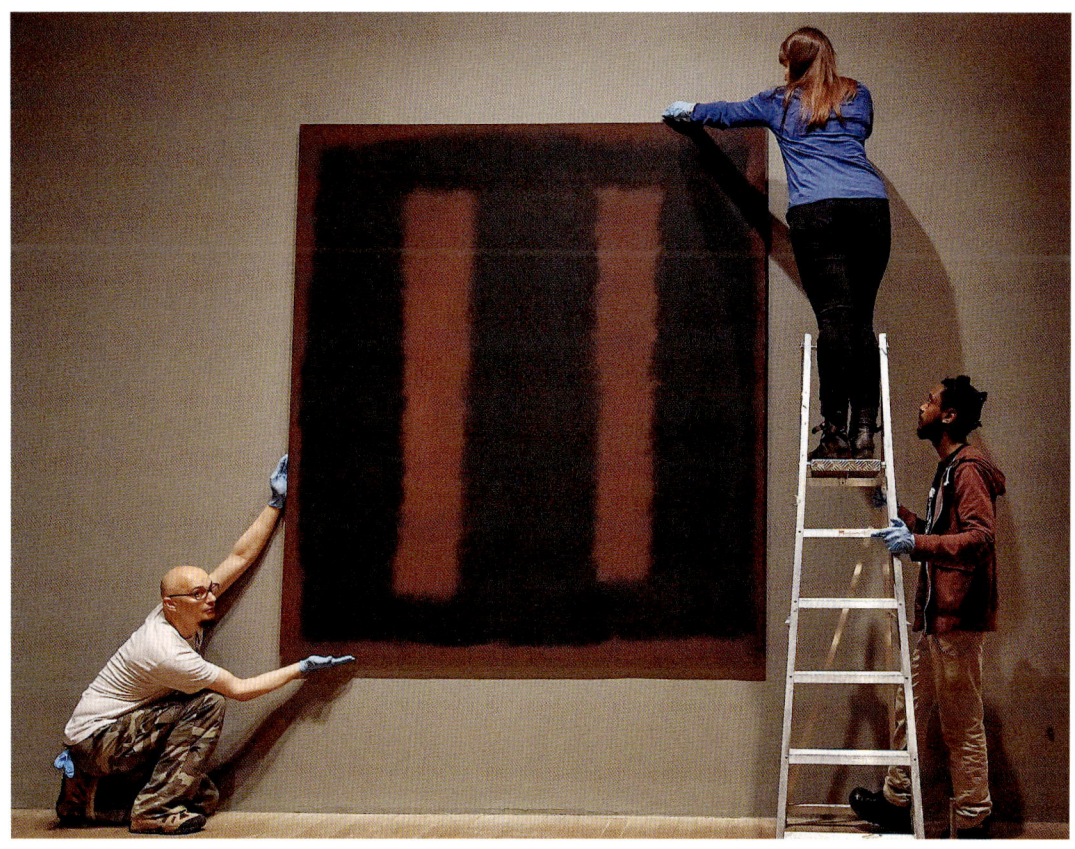

Mark Rothko, who died of suicide in 1970, had perhaps anticipated how such acts of vandalism could injure his images. He once wrote in the art journal *The Tiger's Eye* in 1947, "A picture lives by companionship ... It dies by the same token. It is therefore a risky act to send it out into the world. How often it must be impaired by the eyes of the unfeeling and the cruelty of the impotent who would extend their infliction universally."

Above: Rothko's *Black on Maroon* is rehung at the Tate Modern by gallery employees on May 13, 2014, returned to its former glory after 18 months of restoration work.

EUROPE: FRANCE

When: 1907

Where: Musée du Louvre in Paris

What: Vandalism of Jean-Auguste-Dominique Ingres's *Pope Pius VII Holding Chapel* (1800/1825) with a pair of scissors

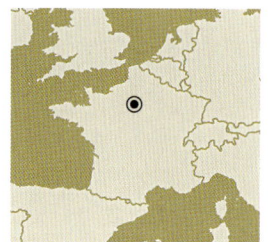

BEST CASE SCENARIO: A PRISON SENTENCE

"I have just spoiled a picture at the Louvre in order to be arrested." So began the statement that twenty-seven-year-old Valentine Contrel gave to police after turning herself in for gouging out the eyes and faces of several religious figures in Ingres's *Pope Pius VII Holding Chapel*. In 1907, armed with a pair of scissors, Contrel waited until the galleries were quiet. Around 4:30 p.m., she sliced through Ingres's early-nineteenth-century canvas. After her act of vandalism, she went to the Commissary of Police to turn herself in, telling police that she was tired of being poor and wanted to be locked up where she could enjoy three meals a day.

Contrel's story is a tragic one. Her parents had died a few years before, leaving her alone, penniless and destitute. She had worked as a governess in England (but didn't care for English life) and as a dressmaker in Paris, where she earned an appalling 13 cents a day for working from 4:00 a.m. to midnight. After not being able to make rent, she tried her luck at the Salvation Army. An officer remembered a conversation with Contrel in which he asked what she

intended to do for work. Contrel replied that she wanted to go to prison, that she was tired of working and being someone else's servant. "I want to eat and drink without working," Contrel said, concluding, "I'll have myself sent to prison for life."

In this, Contrel may have succeeded. Though records do not indicate the length of her sentence, Contrel was sent to prison for her scissor slashing at the Louvre, which she maintained was not an attack on religion despite the subject matter of the painting she chose. Instead, she eloquently said of her vandalism, "It is a shame to see so much money invested in dead things like those at the Louvre collections when so many poor devils like myself starve because they cannot find work."

Opposite: Pope Pius VII, depicted by Ingres sitting on his throne, was bullied by Napoleon and eventually taken prisoner by the dictator from 1809 to 1814. In 1907, he was bullied again by Valentine Contrel.

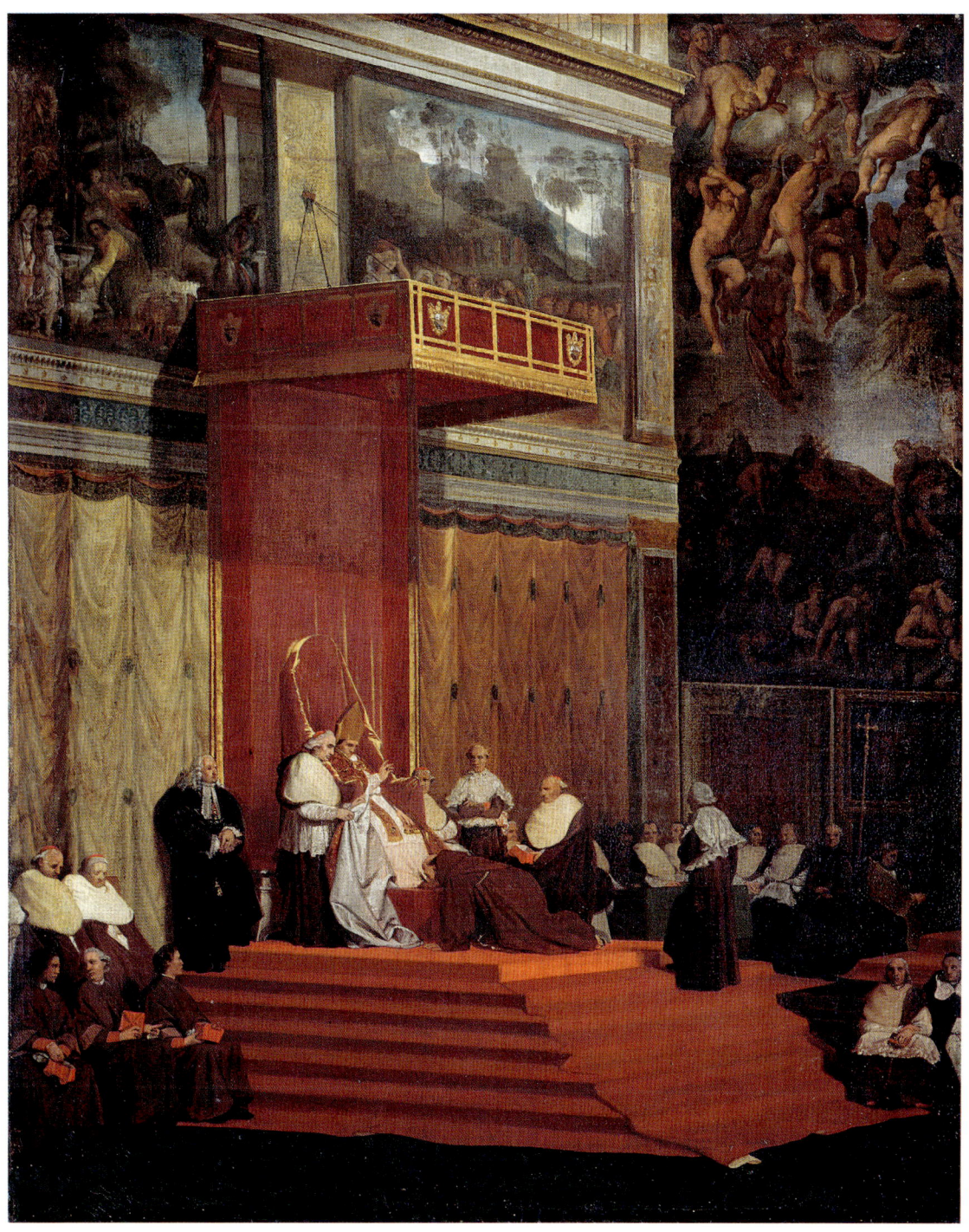

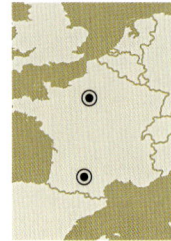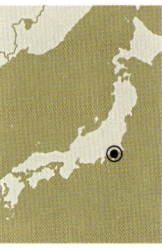

LET HER EAT CAKE

n 1963, Salvador Dalí wrote in an article for *Artnews*, "Why They Attack the *Mona Lisa*," that this "'simple portrait' … has had a power, unique in all art history, to provoke the most violent and different kinds of aggressions." At the time of Dalí's essay, the *Mona Lisa* had been attacked "only" twice (once with acid and once with a rock in 1956) and stolen once (p. 38). Four additional vandalisms, post-1963, prove Dalí's thesis.

In 1974, the painting traveled to Tokyo. A twenty-five-year-old Japanese woman was upset at the Tokyo National Museum's lack of accessibility for viewers with disabilities and expressed this by spraying the *Mona Lisa* with red paint. Though Tomoko Yonezu, who used a wheelchair herself, didn't seriously damage the painting, her act of vandalism did persuade the museum to set aside a day just for visitors with disabilities. Though this was a victory for Yonezu, she paid the price for her activism: a misdemeanor charge and a three-thousand-yen fine.

In 2009, a Russian woman who was refused French citizenship took out her frustration on the *Mona Lisa*, throwing a ceramic mug at the painting. The act achieved nothing; it didn't damage the painting and did not help the woman's citizenship case.

On May 29, 2022, a thirty-six-year-old man wearing a black wig rolled up to the painting in a wheelchair. The man took advantage of the close vantage point granted to visitors with disabilities as he stood from his wheelchair, smeared the glass case with a piece of pastry, threw red roses towards the shocked crowd, and proclaimed, "People are destroying the Earth … Artists tell you: think of the Earth. That's why I did this," as he walked away. He got some time to think about the planet himself, as the Paris Prosecutor's Office arrested and took him to a psychiatric unit.

On January 28, 2024, the *Mona Lisa* was served her second course; she was splashed with pumpkin soup by a pair of French climate activists. In spite of the spray paint, the mug, the cake, and the soup, Mona Lisa remained unscathed by every attempt to disrupt her placid, unperturbed smile.

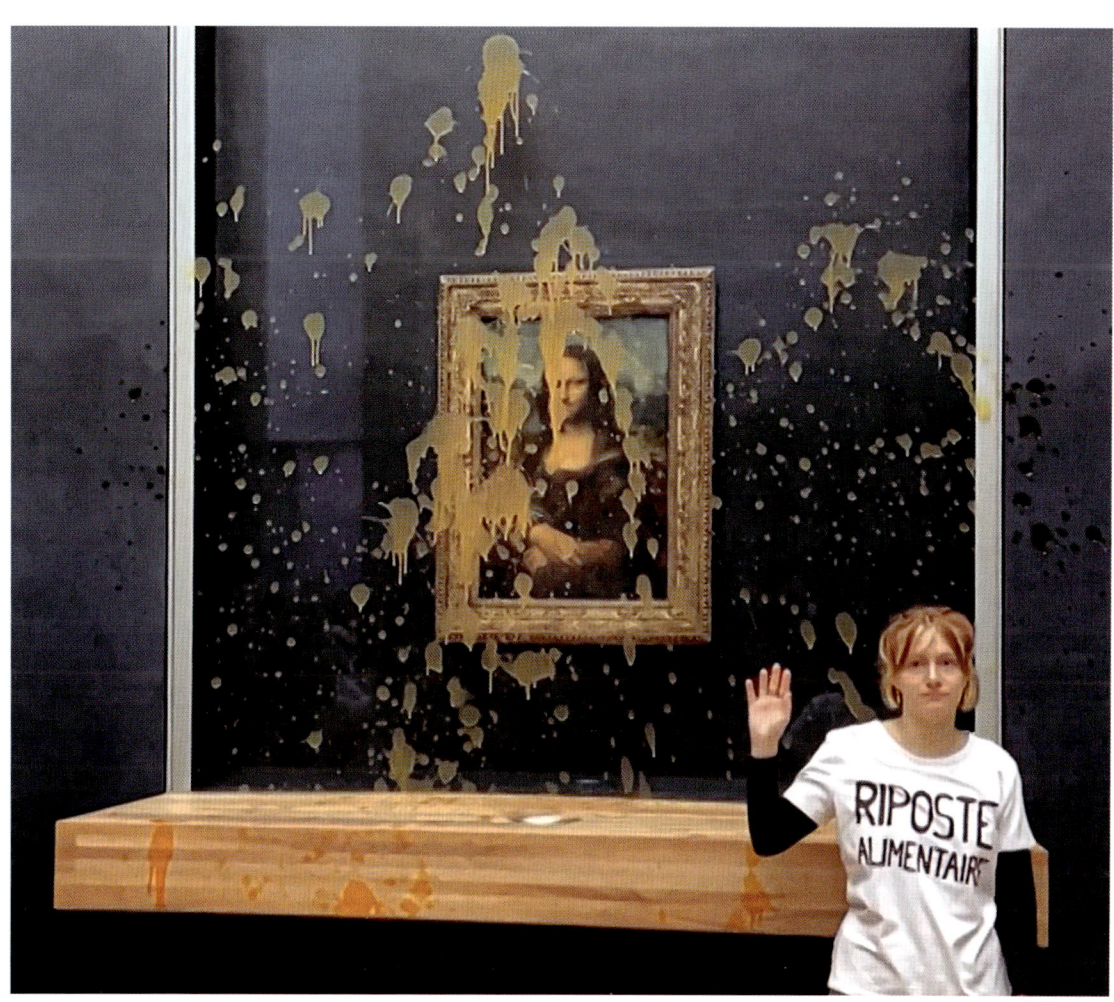

Above: Riposte Alimentaire (French for "food response" or "food retaliation") doused the *Mona Lisa* with soup to highlight the insecurity and instability of agricultural systems.

EUROPE: FRANCE

....

When: July 19, 2007

....

Where: Collection Lambert in Avignon

....

What: Vandalism of Cy Twombly's *Phaedrus* (1977) with a kiss

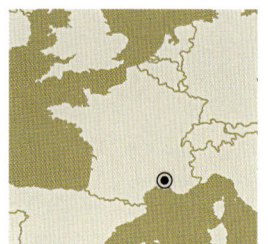

SEALED WITH A KISS

I n 2007, Rindy Sam, a thirty-year-old French-Cambodian painter, was wearing bright red lipstick when she encountered an all-white painting by the American artist Cy Twombly at the Collection Lambert in Avignon. The painting was part of a triptych titled *Phaedrus*. Later, Sam would say, "The artist left this white for me," which is why she decided to leave her own mark by kissing it with her red-stained mouth. After smooching the canvas, she reflected, "I stepped back. I found the painting even more beautiful."

Not everyone felt that way. The Collection Lambert had Sam arrested and she was taken to court. At her trial, Sam—wearing the same Bourjois Rouge lipstick with which she had vandalized *Phaedrus*—explained that she was "overcome with passion" when she saw the painting and explained that her kiss was an act of love. "I thought the artist would understand." Twombly, who was seventy-nine at the time of the vandalism, did not say if he understood Sam's act as one of love.

Perhaps the historical Phaedrus, known to be a friend of Socrates, would have been able to wax philosophical about Sam's act. In *Phaedrus*,

a dialogue in Plato's writings, Phaedrus recalls to Socrates a speech about love by the famous orator Lysias. The two men discuss love and madness, among other things. Socrates tells Phaedrus that mania, or divine madness, can be induced by love, and that in the state of divine madness inspired by love one can accomplish things that would be impossible in a normal state of mind. Perhaps Sam's mental separation from reality in the art museum was inspired by a manic love for *Phaedrus*, causing her to kiss the canvas. Socrates, Phaedrus, and Plato would surely have enjoyed having a philosophical debate about this very case on the steps of the Academy in Athens.

But in a courtroom in France, Agnes Tricoire, the prosecutor of Sam's case, vehemently disagreed with Sam's belief that her kiss was one of love, calling her action "a rape" and "a revolting bestial act of cruelty." Tricoire told the court, "I do not share the same vision of love. For me, love requires the consent of both sides."

The prosecutor called Sam's kiss "as aggressive as a punch," due to the invasiveness of the red pigment of her lipstick. Indeed, conservators tried nearly thirty different products to remove

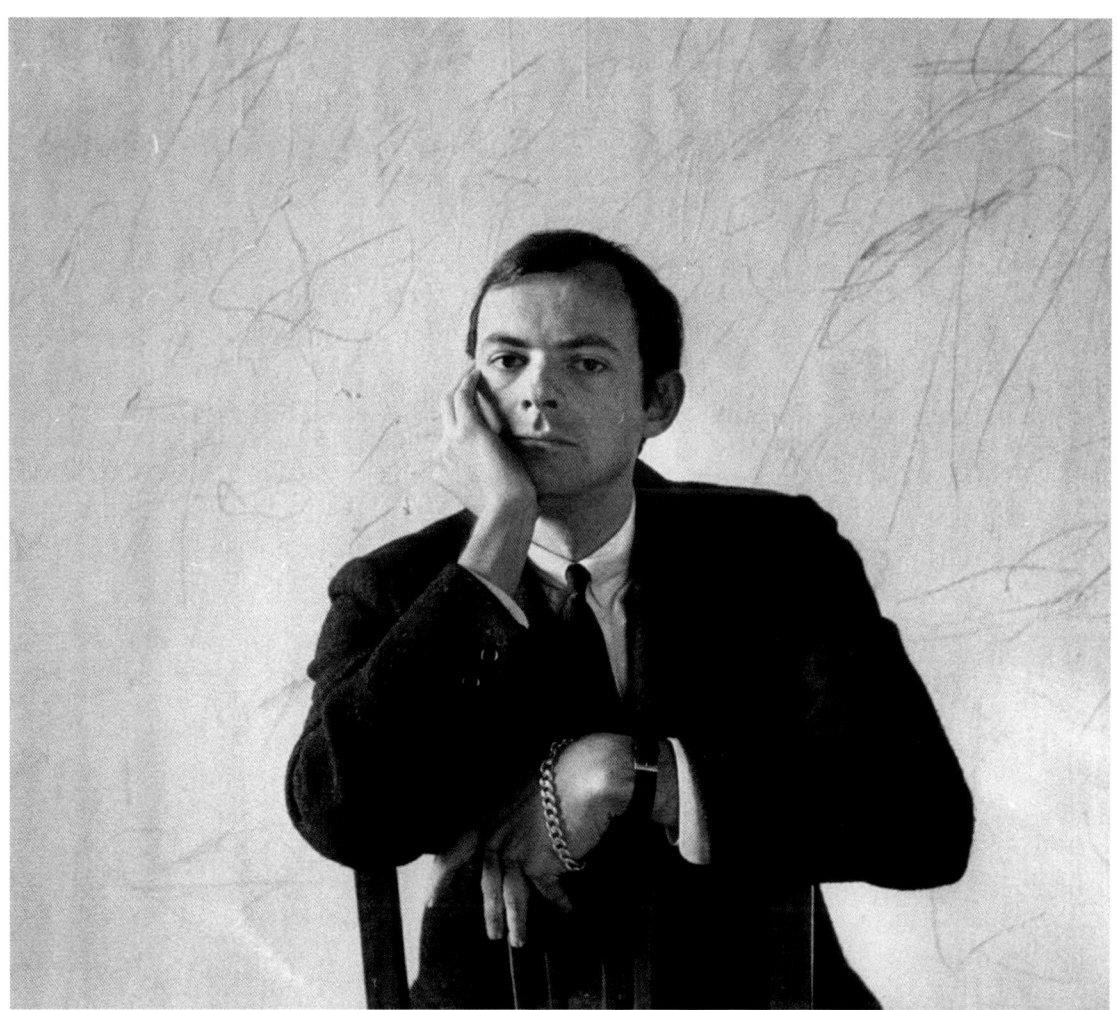

Above: Cy Twombly in black and white, no red in sight. Behind him, some of the gestures—scratches, scritches, scrawls, and scribbles—that became synonymous with his work.

the lipstick stain, but it persisted. NASA even contacted the gallery to offer to try to clean the painting using its atmospheric atomic oxygen cleansing protocol. However, the nine-by-six-foot all-white painting, which was once valued at $3 million, remains afflicted by Sam's act of passion. *Phaedrus* will never be completely white again.

Far from stealing kisses, Sam had to pay for hers: she was fined 1,500 euros (1,000 euros to the owner of *Phaedrus* and 500 euros to the gallery), and she was required to pay a symbolic one euro to the artist.

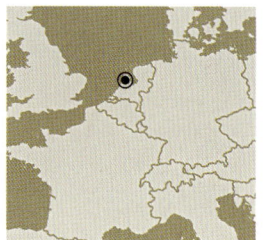

WILLFUL DAMAGE

Rembrandt's largest masterpiece, *The Night Watch*, measuring about twelve by fifteen feet, has been vandalized on three separate occasions. The first was in 1911 when a disgruntled former naval cook and shoemaker used a tool of his trade—a cobbler's knife—to attack the painting as a demonstration of his displeasure at being discharged from the Dutch Navy. Luckily, only the abundant varnish of the painting, which a journalist described as being "thick as a dime," was damaged during this first incident.

In spite of this attack, *The Night Watch* remained without a glass cover, which allowed another vandal to take a stab at it in 1975. A thirty-eight-year-old former schoolteacher stole a bread knife from a restaurant and, after fending off a museum guard, slashed the painting in more than a dozen places while shouting that he had been sent by the Lord. "I was ordered to do it," he later said. "I had to do it." He left the painting ragged with knife marks more than two feet long. A piece of canvas about 12 by 2.5 inches was completely ripped off.

The Rijksmuseum removed the painting and posted a notice which read: "We regret that Rembrandt's 'Night Watch' is not on display due to willful damage." It took a team of conservators four years to repair the damage that had been inflicted on the painting. Perhaps unsurprisingly, the vandal had a history of mental illness. A year after the incident, he committed suicide in a mental institution.

In 1990, a thirty-one-year-old unemployed Dutch man, described by police as "confused," sprayed *The Night Watch* with acid. A museum guard immediately applied a neutralizing agent, meaning the acid's damage was limited to the varnish layer. For the second time, the painting's varnish was a lifesaver. The vandal was remanded to psychiatric treatment.

The Night Watch, which depicts a militia company—an armed neighborhood watch of sorts—might just need to rouse its members to be on the lookout for future vandals.

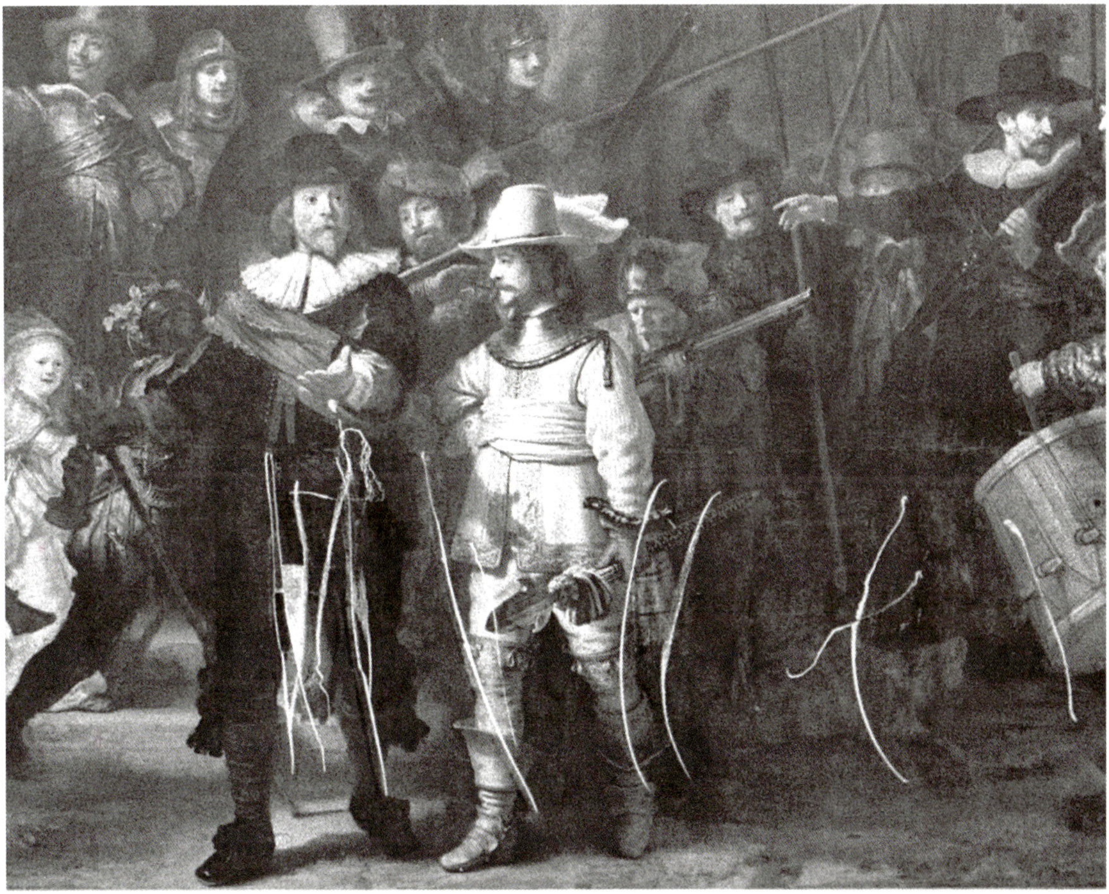

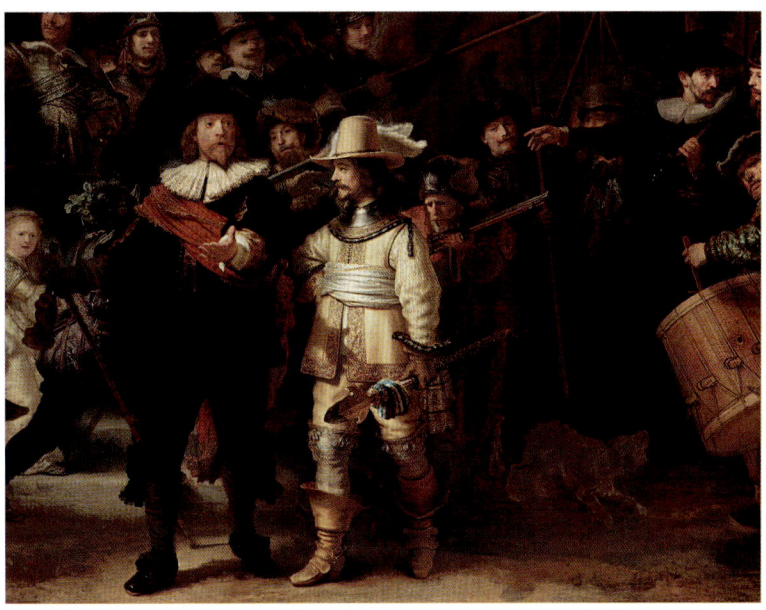

Above: A detail of *The Night Watch* after its 1975 brush with a stolen bread knife.

Right: A detail of the same spot as above after the damage was repaired. In 2019, the Rijksmuseum launched Operation Night Watch, a gigantic multi-year conservation and research project on the painting.

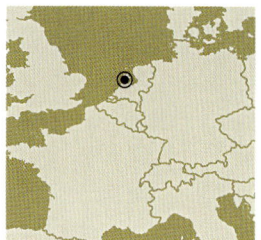

When: March 21, 1986, and November 21, 1997

Where: Stedelijk Museum in Amsterdam

What: Vandalisms of Barnett Newman's *Who's Afraid of Red, Yellow, and Blue III* (1967–68) and *Cathedra* (1951) with a knife and scissors

WHO'S AFRAID OF A REPEAT ART VANDAL?

Barnett Newman's *Who's Afraid of Red, Yellow, and Blue III* hadn't been embraced at the Stedelijk Museum in 1969. Amsterdam residents wrote how they hated it. But Gerard Jan van Bladeren, a struggling figurative painter who hated abstract art, voiced his displeasure in 1986 by attacking Newman's eight-by-eighteen-foot canvas in a series of slashes totaling more than fifty feet. After his murderous performance, Van Bladeren retired to a bench across from the painting to admire his work.

In court, Van Bladeren's lawyer argued that the painting and its title were a provocation, a question, that Van Bladeren felt called to answer in a participatory way. The public agreed and sent more letters to the Stedelijk, upholding Van Bladeren's actions and even suggesting that he be made director of the museum. Instead, he was jailed for five months.

Daniel Goldreyer, a New York-based conservator who had worked with Newman, promised to bring the painting back to 98 percent of its former glory. Four and a half years later, in 1991, the painting was unveiled at the Stedelijk to great horror. The slashes had been repaired and the painting was red, but Goldreyer's color was flat and dull, lacking the shimmering depth and nuance of Newman's juxtaposed magenta and sienna oil paints. There was such an outcry that the painting was sent to a forensic lab where they discovered acrylic paint (housepaint) and a paint roller (instead of a brush like Newman) had been used. To the art world, Goldreyer's work was more offensive than Van Bladeren's vandalism. Goldreyer sued the Stedelijk for reputational damage, and the Stedelijk counter-sued. The case was settled, with the proviso that the museum could never again discuss the botched restoration.

When Van Bladeren learned that his nemesis was back, he planned another attack, even calling the Stedelijk Museum's director to ask if he should cut up the painting again. In 1997, Van Bladeren slipped into the museum, but his archenemy was not on view. He settled for another giant Newman (this time blue)

titled *Cathedra* (1951). Using scissors, he slashed away. To much better result, Carol Mancusi-Ungaro restored the painting using orthodontic wire and surgical sutures.

    Cathedra is back on view at the museum, while *Who's Afraid of Red, Yellow, and Blue III* sits in storage, ruined by a vandal, destroyed by a conservator, and afraid of what the public might think.

Top: Barnett Newman called the thin blue and yellow vertical lines in *Who's Afraid of Red, Yellow, and Blue III* "zips." They became a hallmark of his style.

Above: To Newman, zips (shown here in white in *Cathedra*) were the essence of his work, creating contrast, tension, energy, and balance. A painter, Newman said in an interview, "creates a kind of dance of elements."

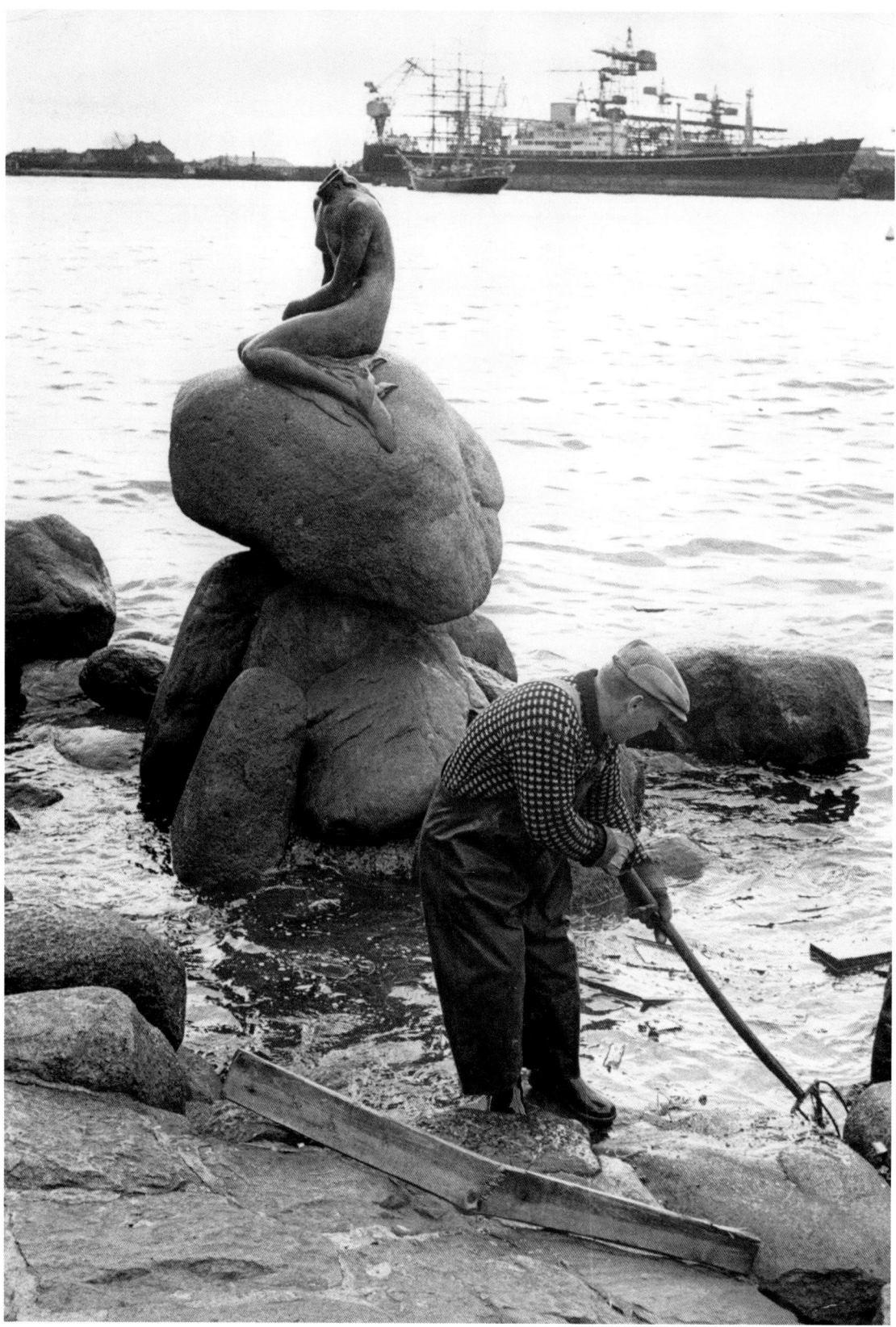

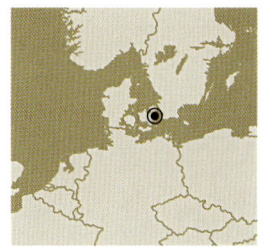

FLOTSAM AND JETSAM

Commissioned by the son of the founder of Carlsberg brewery, *The Little Mermaid*, based on the fairy tale of the same name by Danish author Hans Christian Andersen, was unveiled in 1913. The now iconic symbol of Denmark, captured in a moment of transformation from mermaid to human, perches on a rock overlooking the Langelinie promenade on Copenhagen's waterfront. Part human, part fish, with the head of a once famous ballerina, Ellen Price, and the naked body of the sculptor's wife, Eline Eriksen, *The Little Mermaid* is used to being part one thing and part another. Since 1964 the statue has also been a hodgepodge of various bronze parts as pieces of her body have been replaced due to willful damage.

The first known significant vandalism of the statue was in 1964 when *The Little Mermaid* was decapitated. Some thought the culprit was the Danish artist Jørgen Nash, along with other members of the politically motivated Scandinavian arts movement Bauhaus Situationniste, who were protesting consumerist society. Nash himself claimed the title of "mermaid murderer" in a 1997 memoir. But,

he said, he did it because he was mad at his two wives (yes, two wives). Regardless of motive, it has not been proven whether Nash was the vandal or if he merely chose to take credit for the deed, thereby increasing the visibility of his own name and art. The mermaid's original head has never been recovered.

The Little Mermaid remained unharmed for two decades after the 1964 incident. Since 1984, though, when her right arm was sawn off by two drunk Danes (and politely returned to police two days later when the vandals had sobered up), *The Little Mermaid* has not been able to catch a break.

Again, in 1998, *The Little Mermaid* was beheaded. A few days later, a group called the Radical Feminist Fraction left the head outside a Danish TV station with a message that the act was meant to symbolize the "sexually fixated and

Opposite: Known for losing her voice, *The Little Mermaid* has lost her head here. In 1964, a man pokes about in the rocks around the statue, searching for the fairy-tale character's missing noggin.

misogynist male dream of women as bodies without heads." The mermaid's head was reattached a month after it was removed.

Though the Copenhagen Police Homicide Squad led the investigations into the statue's (many) symbolic murders, there is some disagreement in several cases, including the one from 1998, over who the actual culprits were versus who was taking credit for the acts.

In 2003, the statue was blasted off her rock with explosives. No one is completely sure who to blame for *The Little Mermaid*'s first flight, but a group protesting Danish involvement in the Iraq War is suspected.

To dissuade would-be vandals, Danish officials have considered moving *The Little Mermaid*'s perch further out into the harbor, where she would be harder, though not impossible, to reach. It would just take more dedication (and a boat) from those who want to pick on her.

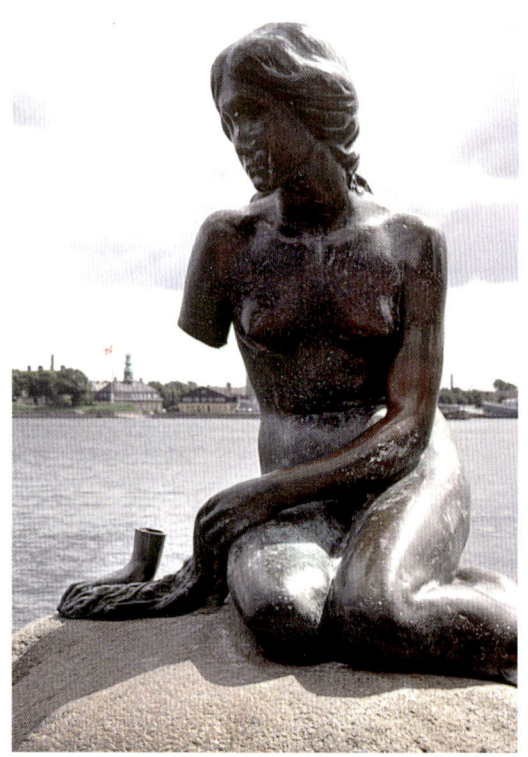

I SEE A MERMAID AND I WANT TO PAINT IT BLACK

Through the years, *The Little Mermaid* has been dressed in various sporting, symbolic, political, and religious garb. The dressing-up started in 1961 when she was seen wearing a bra and underwear, with painted red hair. She was put in a burqa in 2004 to protest Turkey's application to join the European Union.

The statue has been painted many times. In 2006, on International Women's Day, she was drenched in green paint and sexually liberated with a dildo attached to her hand, and "March 8," the date of the vandalism, written on her.

In May of 2017, she was painted blood red with the message "Danmark defend the whales of the Faroe Islands" written in protest in front of the statue. The Faroe Islands, an autonomous territory of the Kingdom of Denmark, have hunted long-finned pilot whales, which are not considered an endangered species, since the sixteenth century.

The statue's base was branded with the words "Racist Fish" in 2020 as protests over George Floyd's murder raged. Today, her body continues to be a painted battleground.

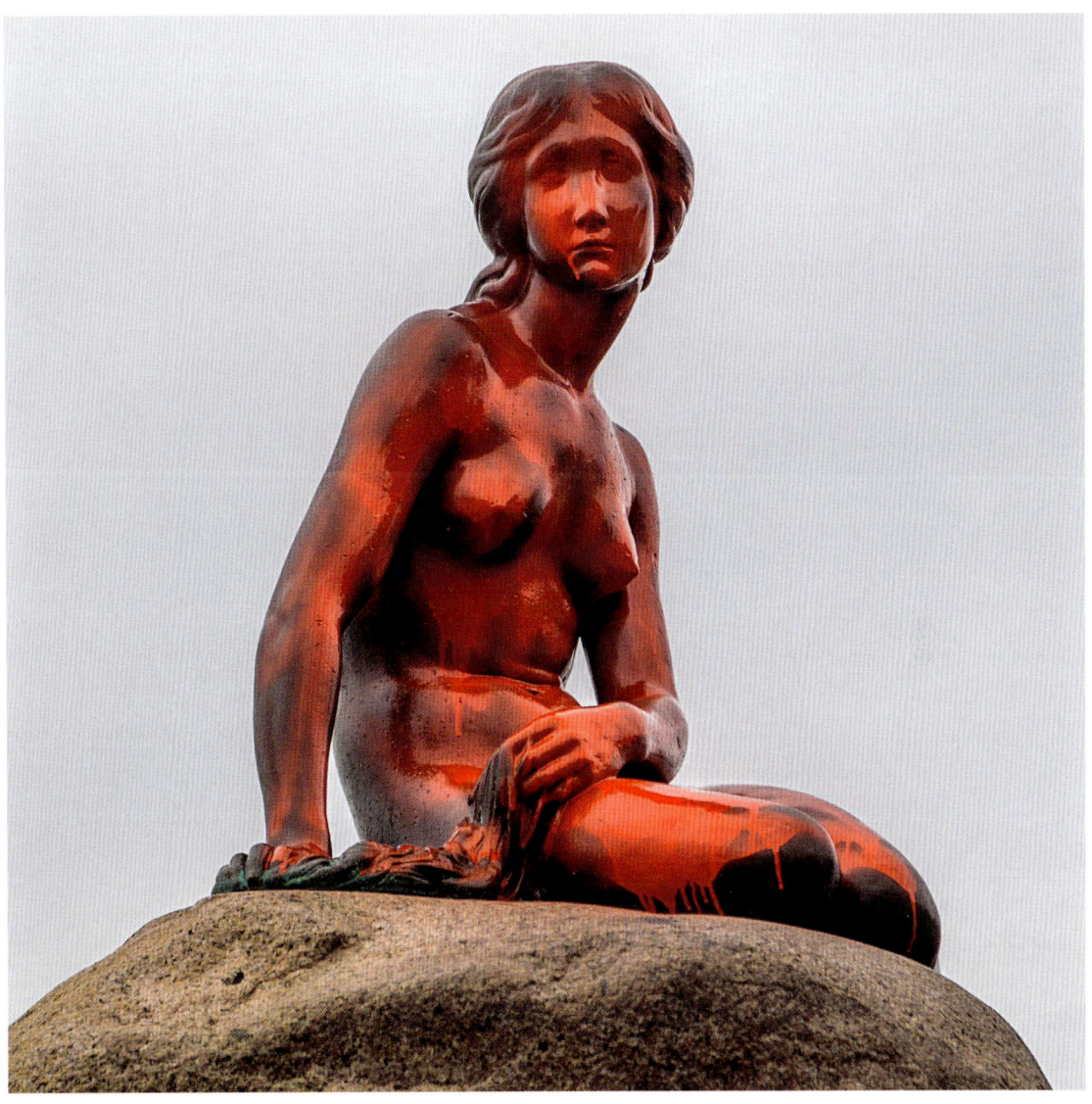

Perpetually trapped between the two worlds, *The Little Mermaid* may be glad not to have achieved full human status. A whole new world? Maybe not one she would willingly choose to inhabit after seeing how land people have acted towards her. Without her voice, *The Little Mermaid* continues to look mournfully out to sea, waiting for her next humiliation.

Opposite: *The Little Mermaid* lost another appendage—this time, most of her arm—in 1984. And yet, she persists.

Above: Over the years, *The Little Mermaid* has been painted a rainbow of colors. In 2017, she was doused in red paint, perhaps meant to symbolize blood, in an act of protest against whale hunting.

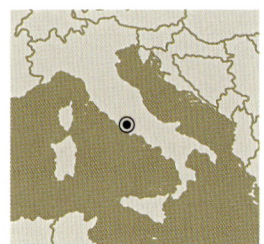

THE SEVEN MYSTERIES OF LASZLO TOTH

Michelangelo was only twenty-five years old when he carved *Our Lady of Piety*—known as *La Pietà* in Italian—out of a single piece of marble. After the vandal Laszlo Toth was through with it, the sculpture had been fractured into at least a hundred pieces, spread out across the floor of St. Peter's Basilica in Vatican City.

At the time of the attack, Toth was thirty-three years old, approximately the same age as Jesus when he was crucified. Toth had moved from Australia to Italy in 1971 with the express purpose of convincing the world that he was Jesus Christ reincarnated and had seven mysteries to reveal. He started with Pope Paul VI, to whom he sent many letters of introduction and whom he endeavored to meet on several occasions, though he was unsuccessful in his attempts.

Taking his plan to the next step, Toth went to St. Peter's on the day of Pentecost, May 21, where hundreds of other pilgrims had gathered to celebrate and pray. Unlike other worshippers,

Toth carried a geologist's hammer in his pocket. Toth, sporting a long red beard and a raincoat, clambered over the marble balustrade that kept congregants from communing with Michelangelo's fifteenth-century sculpture of Mary holding the lifeless body of her crucified son in her arms. Wielding his hammer, he yelled, "I am Jesus Christ, risen from the dead," while bringing the mallet down on Mary's body. He was able to get ten blows in before he was restrained by other visitors. Mary had been bludgeoned. Her left arm was shattered at the elbow, an eyelid was chipped, and her entire nose had been knocked clean off.

After Toth was hauled to the police station, the pope came to pray over the sculpture and left Mary red roses. Toth just missed his introduction.

After ten months of restoration, *La Pietà* was put back on display at St. Peter's—this time behind a thick, protective panel of bulletproof glass. The statue will never be the same; Mary's new nose came at some expense (the marble for her nose reconstruction came from her

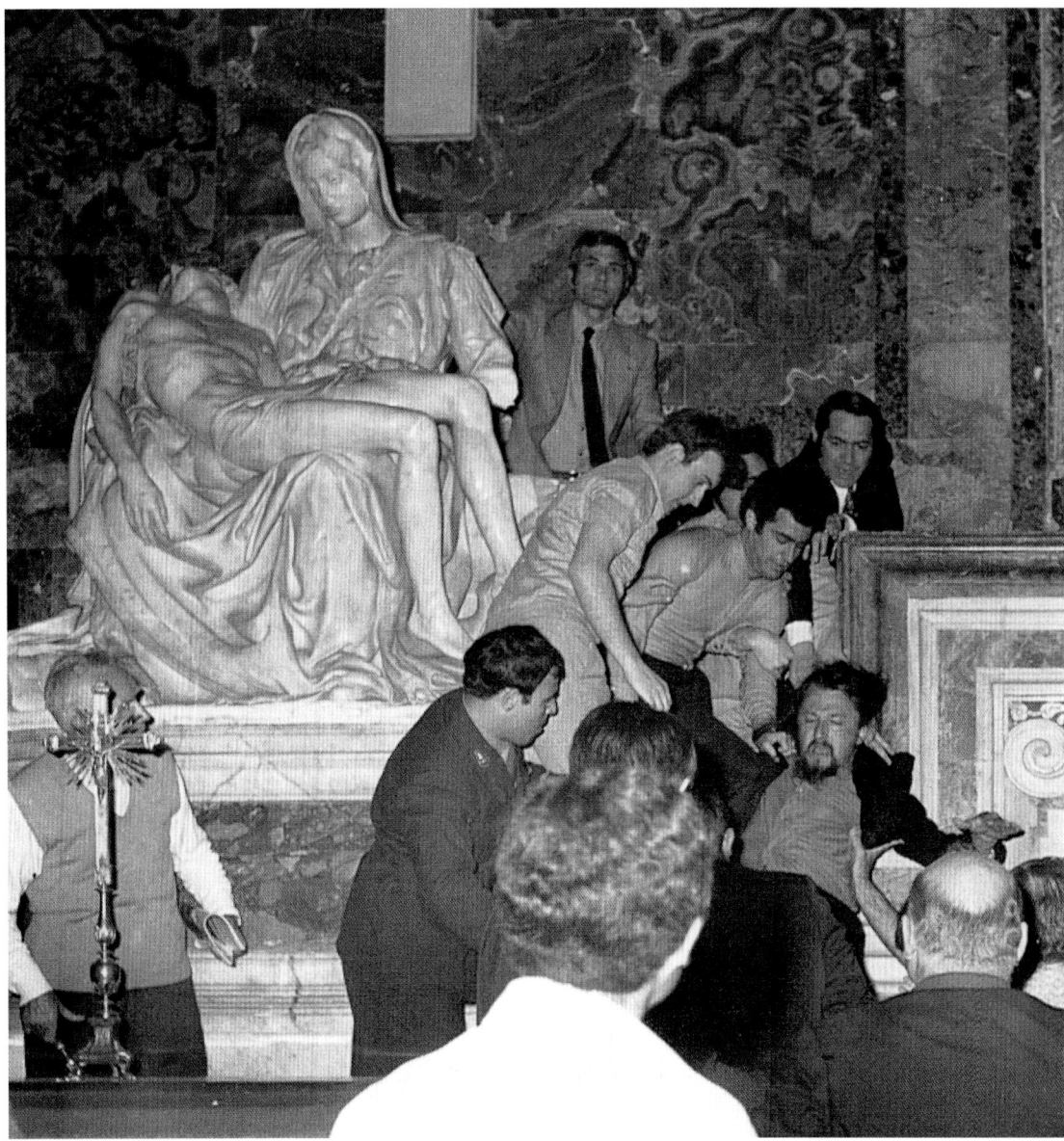

backside) and there are still other inconsistencies if you know where to look.

As for Toth, he was committed to a mental institution in Italy and then deported back to Australia in 1975, where he continues to live in obscurity. What his seven mysteries were, we may (thankfully) never know.

Above: Laszlo Toth, shown here with a beard, wreaked havoc in 1972, but his vandalism of *La Pietà* led to an important discovery: conservators repairing the statue discovered Michelangelo's initials carved in the creases of Mary's palm.

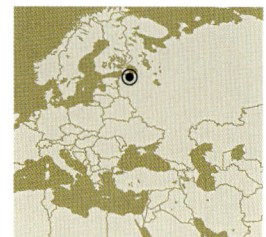

ACID RAIN

A Delphic Greek prophecy foretold that King Acrisius of Argos would be killed by his grandson. Not about to let that happen, Acrisius shuttered his daughter, Danaë, in a tower, to avoid a pregnancy. Sneaky Zeus, who lusted after Danaë, turned himself into golden rain and showered Danaë with his love, resulting in Danaë's pregnancy with a son, Perseus, who did eventually (if accidentally) kill his grandfather.

On June 15, 1985, *Danaë*, the stunning masterpiece by Rembrandt at the Hermitage in St. Petersburg, was showered not with golden rain but with acid. The vandal attacked Danaë's fleshy belly with a knife. Unsatisfied, he poured sulfuric acid on another quarter. The painting bubbled, burned, and smoldered. The attack happened on the weekend, so neither the conservation staff nor the museum director were in town. Two professors from the nearby technology institute arrived an hour afterward and recommended that the painting be kept upright to keep the acid from spreading and the affected area be washed with water.

The vandal, Bronius Maigys, a forty-eight-year-old Lithuanian man, was found to have explosives hidden in his pants and was arrested. He spent six years in a psychiatric hospital in the Kaliningrad region of Russia; after Lithuania's independence, he was transferred to another psychiatric hospital in Vilnius. He later wrote a three-hundred-page manifesto in which he claimed to have attacked *Danaë* for Lithuania's freedom.

Danaë, a woman to whom men have done much without her consent, was approached by conservators with great care. They took twelve years and used such unorthodox materials as "sturgeon glue melted with honey." The restored eight-by-ten-foot painting bought by Catherine the Great was not the same one that she brought to Russia in 1772. The Hermitage's director, Mikhail Piotrovsky, acknowledged that some parts of the painting remain Rembrandt's original work while others do not. Of the conservation work, Piotrovsky said, "The former *Danaë* does not exist any longer and we have to reconcile ourselves to the idea. What we have is disfigured, but yet preserved, beauty."

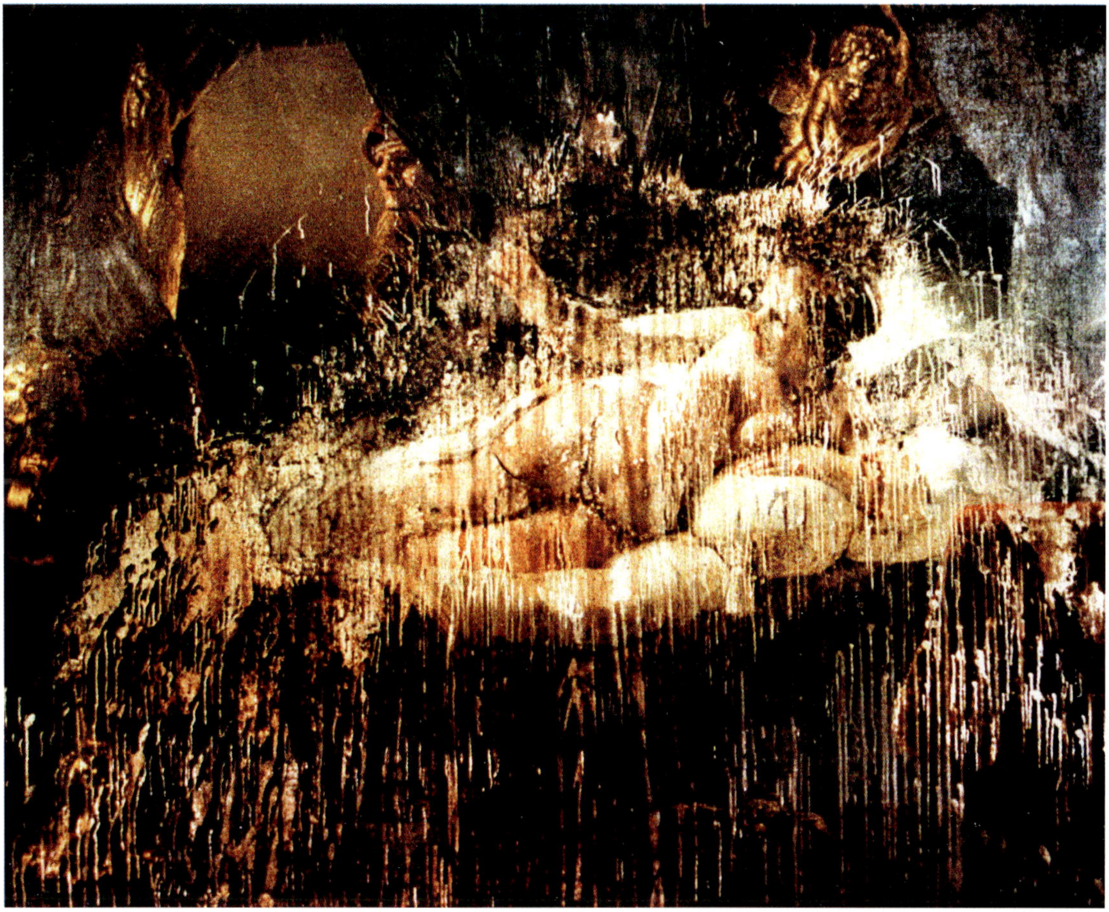

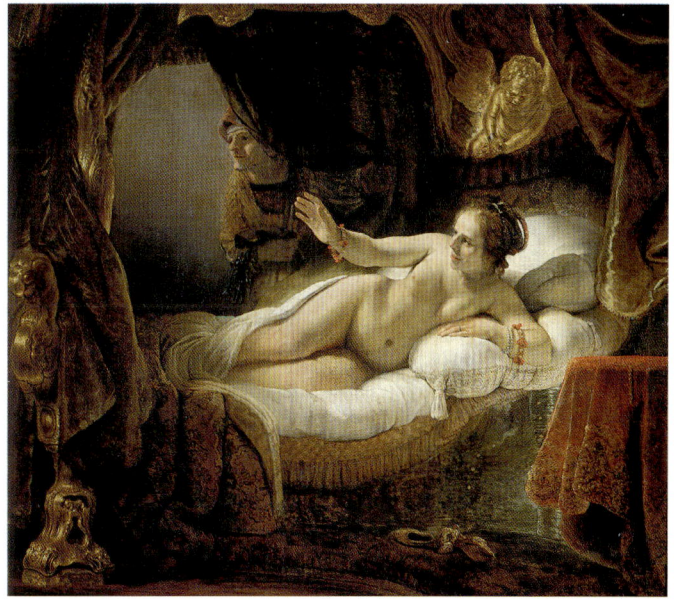

Above: Even before the 1985 vandalism shown here, *Danaë* was altered by Rembrandt himself. Rembrandt originally modeled Danaë on his wife, Saskia. After her death, Rembrandt changed the face to that of his new mistress, Geertje Dircx.

Right: *Danaë*, shown here after her repair, was one of Rembrandt's personal favorites. He kept it in his home and only sold it in 1656 when he declared bankruptcy and needed money to clear his debts.

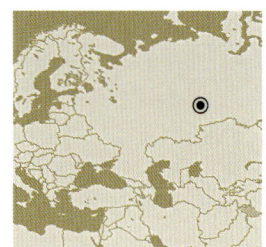

"NO EYES, NO MOUTH, NO BEAUTY"

It was Aleksandr Vasiliev's first day on his new job as a security guard at the Yeltsin Center. Vasiliev, a physically and psychologically injured, medaled veteran of the Afghan and Chechen wars, had found the job through the help of fellow veterans.

His first task was to guard an exhibition of abstract art on loan from the State Tretyakov Gallery in Moscow. He later admitted that he didn't particularly care for the work. In fact, he assumed that Anna Leporskaya's *Three Figures* had been made by children. Leporskaya, an avant-garde Soviet artist, painted *Three Figures* in the early 1930s. The painting was insured for $1.4 million.

As Vasiliev made his rounds, he saw teenagers tittering at the work, saying, "No eyes, no mouth, no beauty!" Vasiliev agreed with their art criticism. When one of the girls suggested he draw eyes on the figures because he worked there, Vasiliev, who still thought the work was by children, asked, "Are they your works?" "Yes," they said. Then, according to Vasiliev, the girls handed him a Yeltsin Center-branded ballpoint pen and he gave two of the three figures some perspective, drawing tiny dots for eyes.

It is not known exactly how long the faceless figures got to enjoy their new eyes. The vandalism was first noticed by visitors on December 7, 2021.

Though the damage was considered insignificant—the ballpoint pen had only slightly breached the titanium white of the figures' faces—and the State Tretyakov Gallery was able to fully restore the painting, sixty-three-year-old Vasiliev was charged with criminal vandalism and sentenced to up to three months in prison or one year of correctional labor, as well as a fine.

In an interview with the Russian news site *E1*, Vasiliev, genuinely repentant, asked, "What have I done? I'm a fool."

Opposite: Aleksandr Vasiliev's contribution to Anna Leporskaya's *Three Figures* can be seen in the eyes of the two background characters. Before Vasiliev, all three figures were sightless.

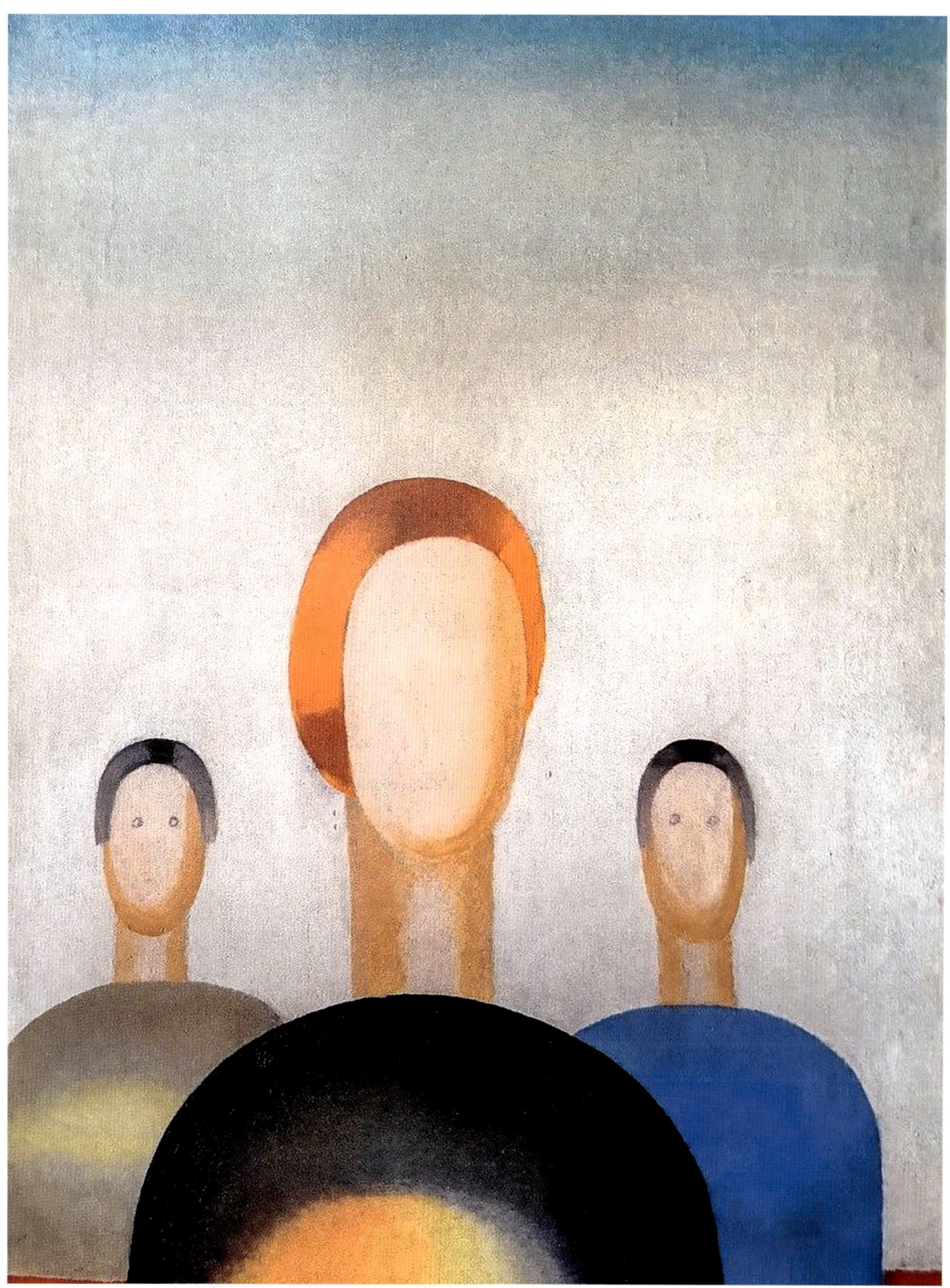

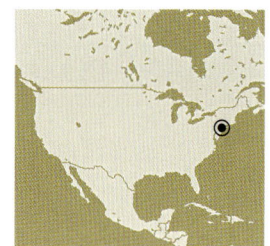

When: February 28, 1974

Where: Museum of Modern Art in New York

What: Vandalism of Pablo Picasso's *Guernica* (1937) with spray paint

NOW SHOWING: AMERICAN GRAFFITI

When Tony Shafrazi spray-painted Picasso's iconic *Guernica* with the foot-high, cherry-red words "KILL LIES ALL," the forty other Museum of Modern Art (MoMA) visitors were aghast. Shafrazi later said he intended the phrase to be read from left to right or right to left, in homage to James Joyce. As guards descended, the Iranian-American artist shouted "Call the curator! I am an artist!" and proceeded to spell his name as he was escorted out.

Interrogated in the museum's bathroom and later in the 54th Street precinct, Shafrazi claimed he defaced the painting because he was an artist and needed to tell the truth. What truth he was trying to tell is open to speculation. Though MoMA, fearing repeated vandalism, didn't want any publicity after the event, Shafrazi had called the Associated Press before his stunt, so his "artwork" was featured on the front page of the *Daily News* with the subheading "Now Showing, American Graffiti" (a good headline pun as *American Graffiti*, the film, had debuted the year before).

The twenty-five-by-eleven-foot painting was unharmed thanks to a thick layer of varnish. Conservators wiped away the spray paint with a solvent, and the few particles that stuck were picked off with surgical needles.

Shafrazi's premeditated act helped catapult him into the art world's elite. He went on to achieve great success (after serving five years' probation for "criminal mischief") as the owner of a gallery that specialized in the work of graffiti artists like Jean-Michel Basquiat and Keith Haring. Shafrazi continued to benefit from the *Guernica* scandal. In 2008, at an afterparty for one of his exhibitions, Shafrazi was presented with a cake that featured a reproduction of *Guernica* on top. With a tube of frosting, Shafrazi wrote in big red letters "I'M SORRY … NOT."

Opposite: Tony Shafrazi's antics were front-page news. In the image, conservators wipe spray paint—thankfully, easy to remove—from Picasso's *Guernica*.

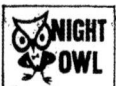 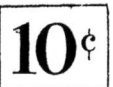

DAILY NEWS

NEW YORK'S PICTURE NEWSPAPER ®

10¢

Vol. 55. No. 212   Copr. 1974 New York News Inc.   New York, N.Y. 10017, Friday, March 1, 1974★   WEATHER: Partly cloudy, windy & cool.

VANDAL SPRAYS PICASSO MURAL

Priceless Work Attacked Here

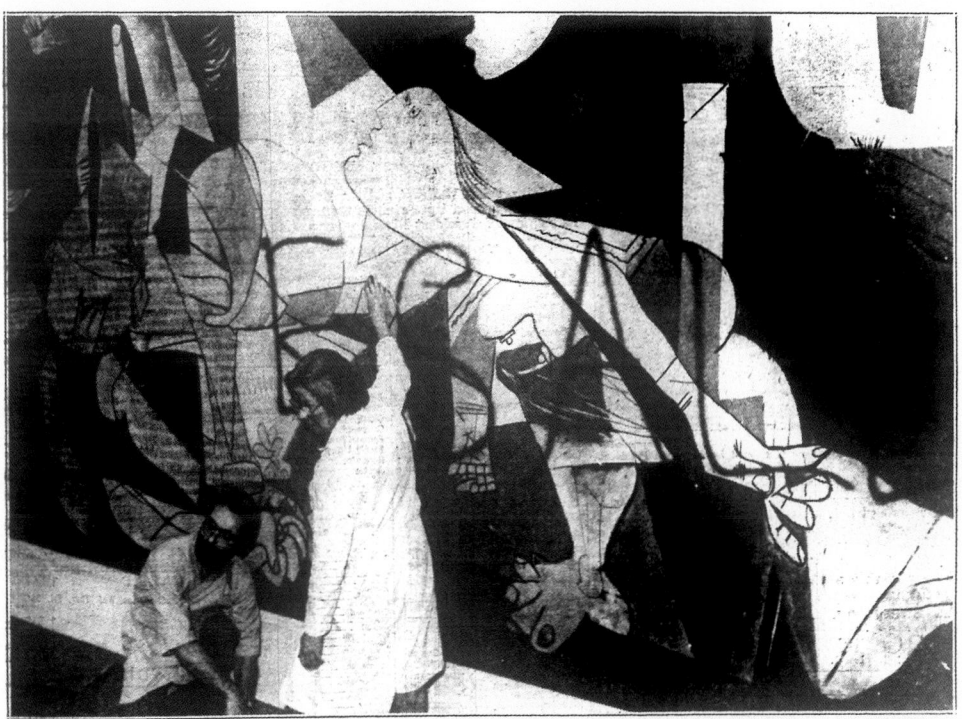

Now Showing, American Graffiti. Employes of Museum of Modern Art work fast to remove red letters sprayed on Picasso's "Guernica" yesterday. They were able to remove all traces in about an hour. Later, restaurant cook and artist Tony Shafrazi, who "did not like the painting," was arrested. —*Story p. 3*

Associated Press photo

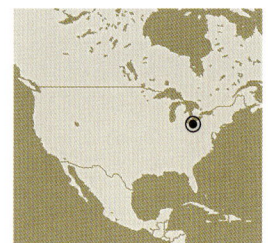

BOMBS AWAY

Around 1:00 a.m. on March 24, 1970, Auguste Rodin's iconic pensive statue *The Thinker* was blasted off its pedestal using a metal pipe bomb with a military-style fuse. The explosion, which had the force of three sticks of dynamite, catapulted the nine-hundred-pound bronze man into the air, landing on his face in the snow. To add insult to injury, the ever-naked philosopher lost his feet in the blast. Shrapnel from the explosion scattered over five hundred feet in every direction, breaking six windows, denting doors, and chipping the museum's marble columns.

The police had only two clues: 1) The bomb had a fuse that allowed the vandals seven and a half minutes to skedaddle after lighting it; and 2) A message that the rabblerousers had spray-painted a message onto the base: "Off the ruling class."

Over fifty years later, who committed the crime remains a mystery. No one has claimed responsibility for the attack. Though there were several protest groups active in Cleveland at the time, including Students for a Democratic Society, Cleveland Police suspect the bombing was the work of the Weathermen (later known as the Weather Underground), an ultra-far-left militant group. Categorized by the FBI as a domestic terrorist organization, their goal was to overthrow the U.S. government.

Over 1,200 people came to pay their respects to the fallen *Thinker*. Footless, mangled, and far from his pedestal-home, conservators at the museum wrestled with how to care for the statue. The CMA's sculpture was rare: it had been hand cast and patinated under Rodin's own direction. Fewer than ten casts of *The Thinker* were supervised by Rodin before his death in 1917.

They figured they had three options: 1) Use a replacement cast (though it would not have the same aura because Rodin wouldn't have selected it); 2) Mend the statue by casting new parts to replace the damaged bits; or 3) Do nothing. The museum chose option 3—with a twist. They remounted the injured *Thinker* on his pedestal but added a "before" photo of the statue in its prime and an explanation of why the present-day *Thinker* has seen better days.

The Thinker, originally named *Le Poète* (*The Poet*) by Rodin, may represent Dante Alighieri, the medieval Italian poet. The statue was the crowning element of a much larger sculptural

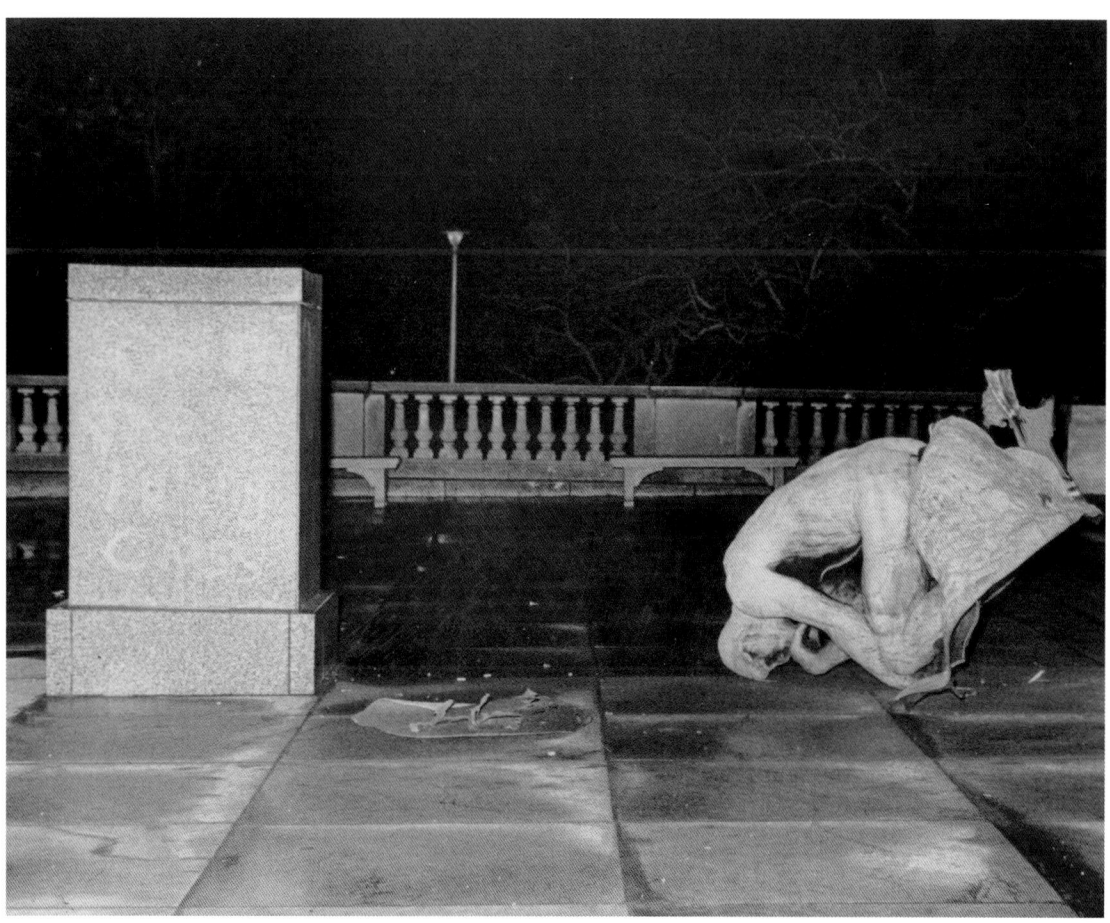

work meant to depict a scene from *Inferno*, the first section of Dante's famous work *The Divine Comedy*, in which the writer visits Hell. Such inspiration seems prescient for Cleveland's statue, its bombing, and its resurrection in its injured form. The poem reads, "Before me nothing but eternal things were made, and I endure eternally."

Above: No one was ever arrested for the 1970 vandalism of *The Thinker*. In 2017 an unidentified individual claimed to know who had done the deed, but the story could not be corroborated and the mystery remains unsolved.

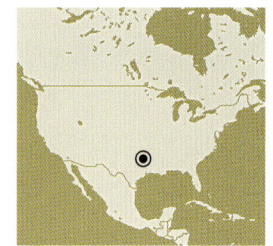

When: June 1, 2022

Where: Dallas Museum of Art in Dallas

What: Vandalism of three pieces of ancient Greek pottery, a Native American ceramic container, and a dozen other small pieces with a chair

HEARTBREAK ~~HOTEL~~ MUSEUM

Vandalism was in the air in the spring of 2022. Within a week between the end of May and the beginning of June, the *Mona Lisa* was "caked" at the Louvre (p. 144), and a young man broke into the Dallas Museum of Art, where he shattered three pieces of ancient Greek ceramics, a contemporary Native American container, and at least a dozen other small pieces … all because he was heartbroken. The museum guard who eventually apprehended the vandal, Brian Hernandez, told police that Hernandez "got mad at his girl so he broke in and started destroying property."

Perhaps mistaking the museum for a "rage room," Hernandez, then twenty-one years old, broke through the glass doors around 9:40 in the evening of June 1. Once inside, he went on a rampage, shattering a number of priceless ancient Greek vessels, including a sixth-century-BCE amphora, once used to hold oil or wine, which shows two warriors fighting while their mothers look on mournfully, anticipating the future tragic outcome of their sons' battles. He also destroyed a sixth-century-BCE kylix,

a kind of cup (most likely for wine), with scenes of Herakles (known to the Romans as Hercules) wrestling with the Nemean lion, one of his twelve seemingly impossible labors. Not limiting himself to ancient pottery, Hernandez damaged a contemporary Native American ceramic piece made to resemble a gar fish.

Hernandez, who called 911 on himself while in the museum, was also discovered by a guard after a motion sensor detected his movement through the museum's concourse. Police arrived around 10:10 p.m., about half an hour after Hernandez's temper tantrum had started.

Photos from the aftermath of the incident show Hernandez, dressed in a black polo shirt and jeans with the pockets turned inside out, in front of a squad car with lights flashing. As his photograph is being taken by a crime-scene analyst, he looks flatly at the camera, his hands cuffed behind his back. Hernandez was charged with criminal mischief: a felony. As for Hernandez's relationship with "his girl," the jury is still out.

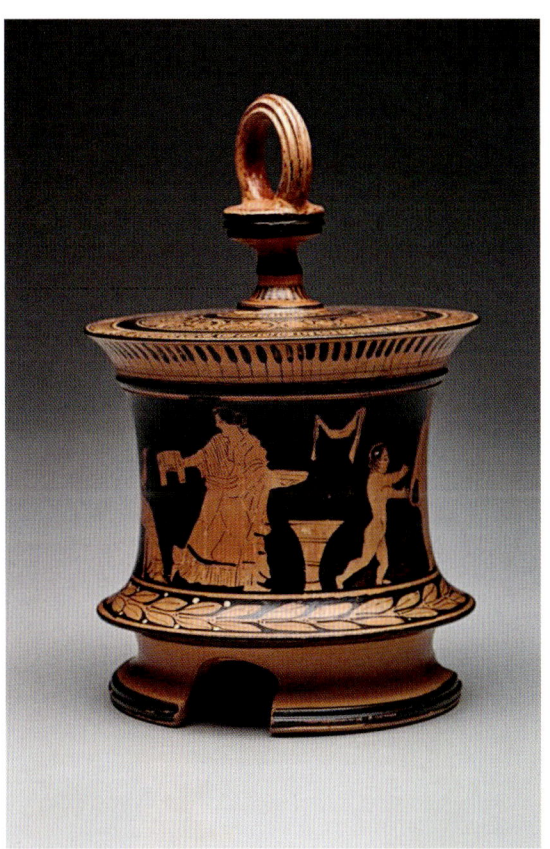

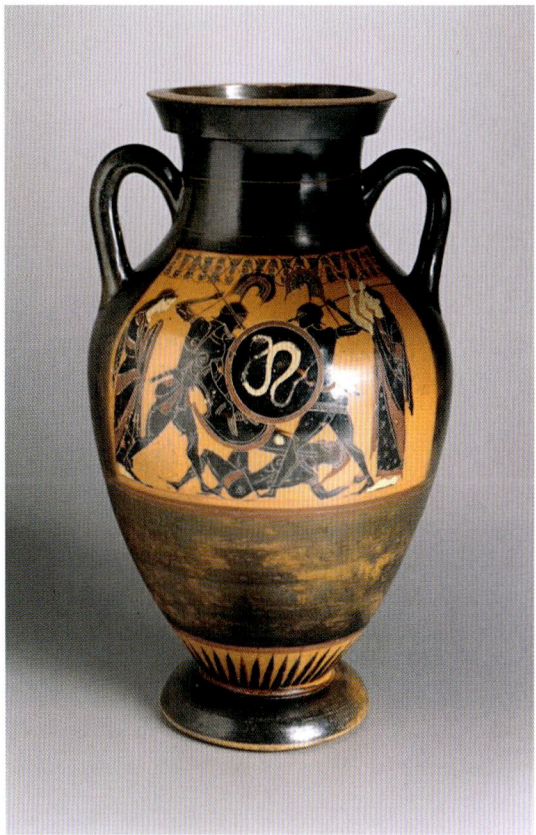

Above and Right: Brian Hernandez used a metal stool and a hand-sanitizer bottle to break into the glass cases of three ancient Greek objects (shown here) in 2022. The items had managed to survive for more than two thousand years before Hernandez's rampage. In a statement about the vandalism, Dallas Museum of Art Director Agustín Arteaga said, "The entire collection is invaluable in the shared experiences and inspiration it provides to our visitors."

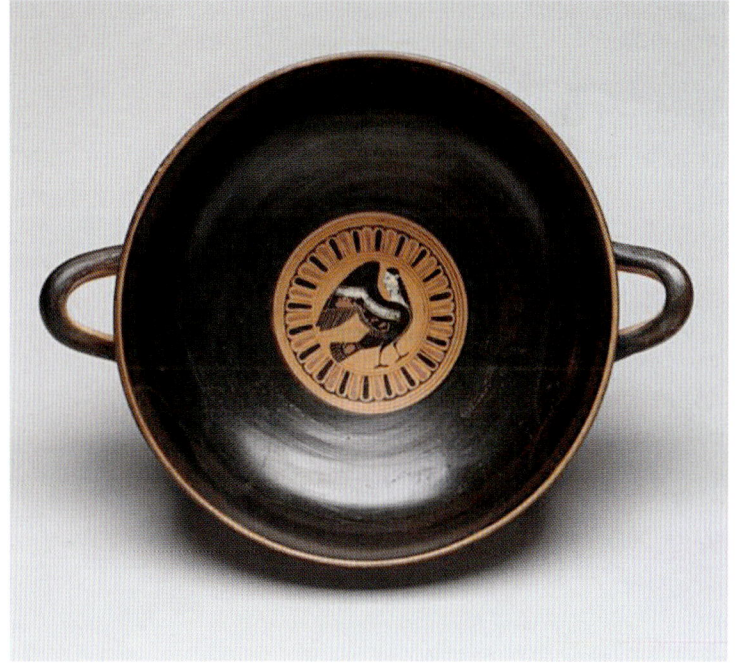

When: May 15, 1996, and November 2, 1996

Where: Art Gallery of Ontario in Toronto and Museum of Modern Art in New York

What: Vandalism of Raoul Dufy's *Harbor at Le Havre* (1905–6) and Piet Mondrian's *Composition in White, Black, and Red* (1936) with vomit

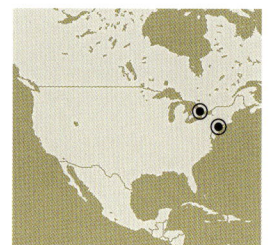

VANDALISM VIA VOMIT

Twenty-two-year-old Jubal Brown was a student at the Ontario College of Art and Design when he projectile-vomited on Raoul Dufy's painting *Harbor at Le Havre* at the Art Gallery of Ontario (AGO) in May 1996. The puke, a surprising shade of red, was quickly cleaned from the painting, leaving no lasting damage. The museum chalked it up to an unwell visitor.

A few months later, Brown, visiting the Museum of Modern Art in New York City, had another incident. This time, he vomited a brilliant stream of blue onto Piet Mondrian's *Composition in White, Black, and Red*. Much like the AGO, MoMA considered it a sick visitor's accident.

In December 1996, a month after the MoMA incident, Brown went public: his retching was intentional, not accidental. The episodes formed a piece of performance art he called *Responding to Art*—a trilogy of red, blue, and yellow projectile vomit on works of art he found uninspiring in places he found uninspiring (i.e., museums, which he called "stale, lifeless crusts"). In his artist statement, Brown said he hoped his performance would criticize the commodification and canonization of certain works of art that had been deemed sacred by the art world.

In an interview with the *New York Times*, Brown called Mondrian's painting "oppressively trite and painfully banal." As for why he chose the Dufy, Brown said that it was a boring painting and needed a dash of color.

To achieve maximum color saturation in his performance medium, Brown ingested red gelatin, pickled beets, and red icing. Before the Mondrian, Brown followed a similar diet: blue gelatin, blue icing, and blueberry yogurt. The third act of the performance remains unrealized. Maybe the Rothko vandal picked up where Brown left off with his theories of Yellowism (p. 140).

Brown insists that his projectile vomiting was induced by sheer banality of the art. But a classmate of Brown's provided more insight: Ipecac, an emetic syrup, had been used to catalyze Brown's heaving.

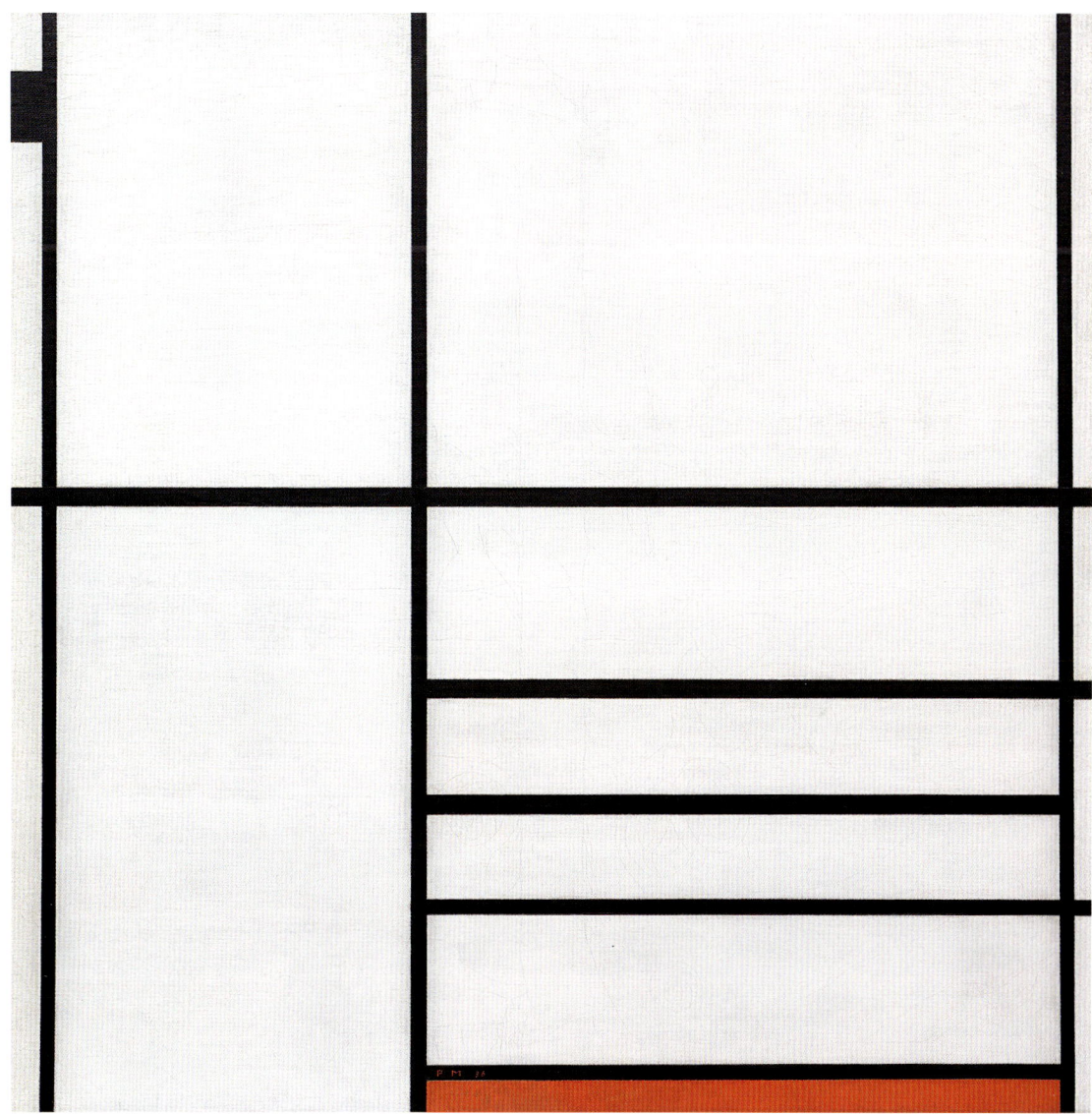

Above: Piet Mondrian believed that his pared-down arrangements, seen here in *Composition in White, Black, and Red*, could induce spiritual enlightenment. It did not have the intended effect on Jubal Brown.

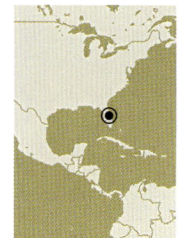
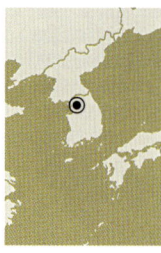

YES, WE HAVE NO BANANAS!

Maurizio Cattelan's *Comedian* debuted at Art Basel in Miami in December 2019 to great fanfare, indignation, and confusion. The banana duct-taped to Galerie Perrotin's white wall became an overnight global obsession. Cattelan had bought the bananas for *Comedian* for just thirty cents at a Miami grocery, but the first and second editions of the piece sold for $120,000.

Lest one think *Comedian* is *just* a banana taped to a wall, for $120,000, its new owners received a certificate of authenticity and an unexpectedly detailed fourteen-page instruction book, replete with diagrams, for how to install, display, and care for *Comedian*. Galerie Perrotin insisted that, while Cattelan was conceiving the idea, he traveled with a banana, hanging it in his hotel rooms, thoughtfully considering the perfect angle of display.

David Datuna, a Georgian-born American artist, had grander plans than just taking a selfie with a banana; he decided to make a new work he titled *Hungry Artist*, which entailed walking up to the banana, peeling it (with duct tape still attached), and eating it. As he was escorted away by security, Datuna cheerfully waved and said, "See you after jail, guys!"

Datuna, who claimed he didn't like the taste of bananas and only ate about one a year, later said at a press conference that the banana was "delicious" and "tasted like $120,000." Datuna insisted his act wasn't vandalism but performance art. He rationalized that he hadn't destroyed *Comedian* because Cattelan's *idea* was the work of art, telling *Vogue*, "Conceptually, I ate the concept of the banana." Cattelan agreed.

The gallery, who called Datuna's stunt "mundane," did not press charges against Datuna, who, far from going to jail, ended up inking a deal with Dole to sell fruit-centric NFTs to increase knowledge of food insecurity and malnutrition. Datuna, who passed away in 2022, died thinking he was the only hungry onlooker to ingest *Comedian*.

Noh Hyun-soo, an aesthetics and religion student at Seoul National University, felt that Cattelan's banana was meant to be eaten. And

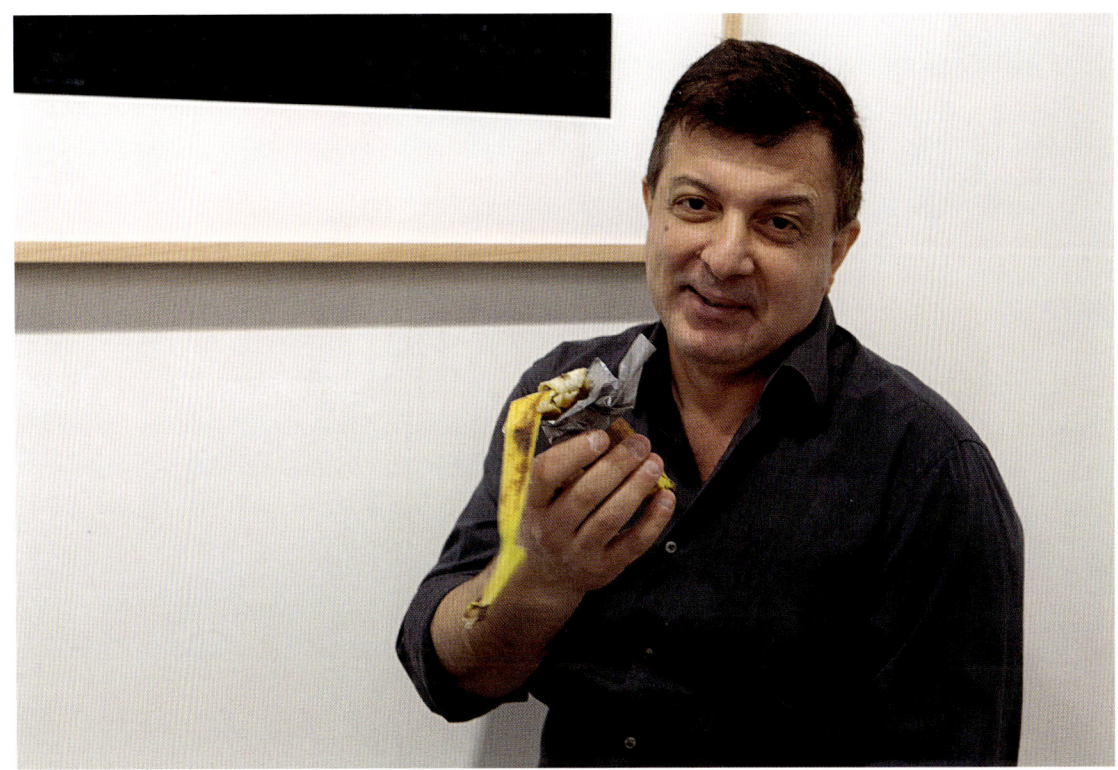

Above: The artist David Datuna performs his own work of art, *Hungry Artist*, by eating Maurizio Cattelan's *Comedian* at Art Basel in 2019. Thankfully, Datuna stopped before eating the duct tape.

he was hungry. Video footage from the Leeum Museum of Art (and a friend's cell phone) shows Hyun-soo yoinking the banana off the wall, eating it, and reattaching the peel with the duct tape. Hyun-soo says the nearby guard didn't attempt to restrain him and merely looked embarrassed. The missing banana was quickly replaced (within thirty minutes) and Hyun-soo

would get his fifteen minutes of fame. Hyun-soo opined in the *Guardian*, "Some people see my banana eating as simply vandalism. Others say it was done for publicity—and I agree. The act of damaging someone else's artwork has made me famous. I was an ordinary person, and now thanks to the 'comedy' of eating a banana, I'm in the *Guardian*."

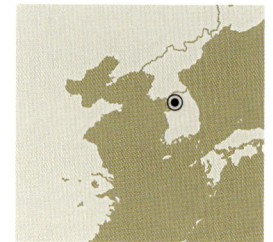

ACCIDENTAL VANDALS

When a young Korean couple saw paint cans, paint-splattered shoes, and brushes in front of a gigantic, colorful canvas at the *Street Noise* exhibition in the P/O/S/T gallery at Lotte World Mall in Seoul, they felt invited to participate in what they thought must be an interactive piece. Picking up a brush dipped in forest green paint, the couple each dabbed a smatter of brushstrokes onto the canvas. Their additions looked a bit like three flattened frogs in a sea of bright splotches of every other color imaginable. The new brushstrokes covered an area of about 35 by 11 inches in a painting the size of a large gallery wall. Their additions did not look out of place in the piece, a style of graffiti meets abstract expressionism that JonOne, the artist originally known as John Andrew Perello, aptly called "abstract expressionist graffiti." As one local Korean newspaper riffed, the couple's unintentional addition had created "graffitied graffiti."

The painting, part of an exhibition of about a dozen international graffiti artists, was the only one with paint brushes and paint cans in front of it. The additions were meant to symbolize the artist's process, which audience members saw firsthand when JonOne created the piece live in 2016. One of the exhibition organizers, Kang Wook, insists there were guidelines and notices to deter people from interacting with the art. The painting had previously been exhibited in the same manner without incident. The exhibition organizers called the police, who were able to track the (still nameless) couple down from security footage. The young couple pleaded their innocence and ignorance.

When JonOne, the then fifty-seven-year-old artist, heard about the accidental additions to his painting, he recalled his initial impulse while speaking with *Vice World News*: "What is this shit?!" After watching the security footage, he realized it was a misunderstanding. Meanwhile, the internet had gotten hold of the story and it soon became a topic of much interest online.

JonOne continued to revise his original interpretation of the vandalism in an email to *Vice*: "With just three brush strokes on my canvas, they [the vandals] have managed to cause a planetary buzz?!? There is strength in that." With JonOne's recognition on the world stage rising due to the vandalism, he admitted

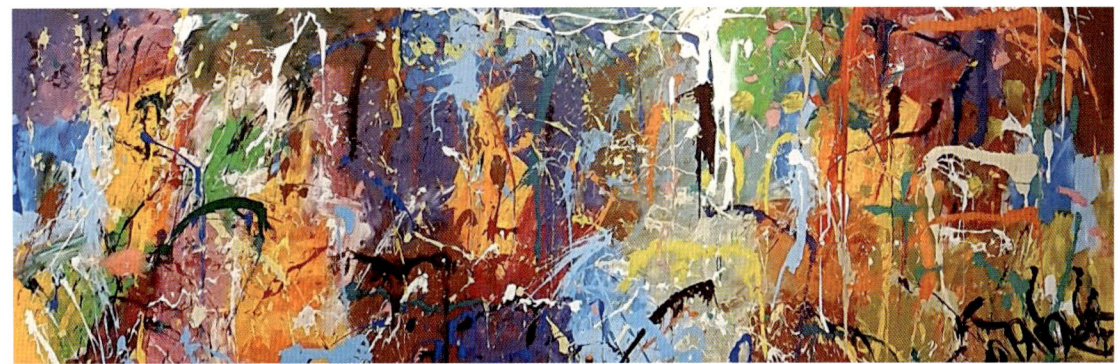

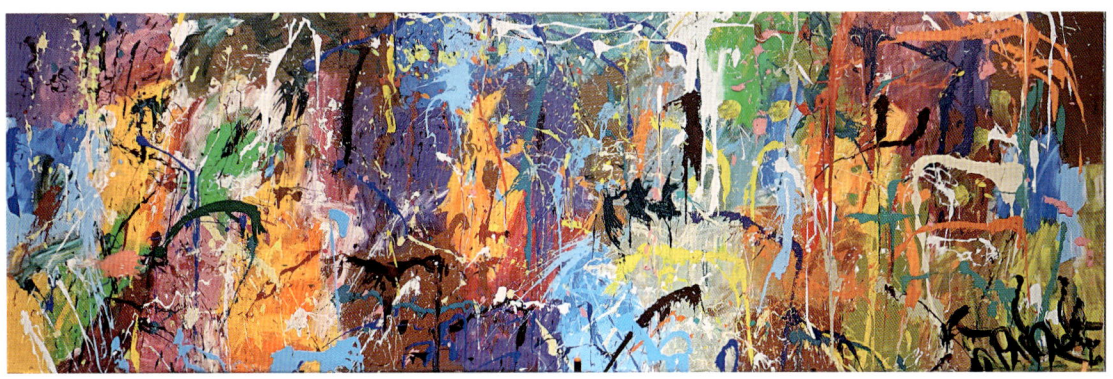

Top: *Untitled* is a riot of color created before a live audience by the artist JonOne in 2016. It would later star in *Street Noise* at P/O/S/T gallery at the Lotte World Mall in Seoul.

Above: The accidental vandals added the three dark-green splotches in the center right of the painting. According to *Korea JoongAng Daily*, the couple were still shopping at the mall when their defacement was discovered.

that he might like to thank the couple and share a cup of tea with them.

Ironically, because of the "planetary buzz," the vandalism of JonOne's *Untitled* caused the piece to go up in value. It is now speculated to be worth almost half a million dollars. Not to be left out of the hype, the marketing team for the *Street Noise* exhibition began featuring the vandalized painting, front and center, in their advertising material.

P/O/S/T couldn't have imagined the attention the accidental vandals would bring to their exhibition. In spite of the overwhelming popularity of the act, the gallery did put up a wire barricade in front of *Untitled* with a warning to any future copycats: Do Not Touch.

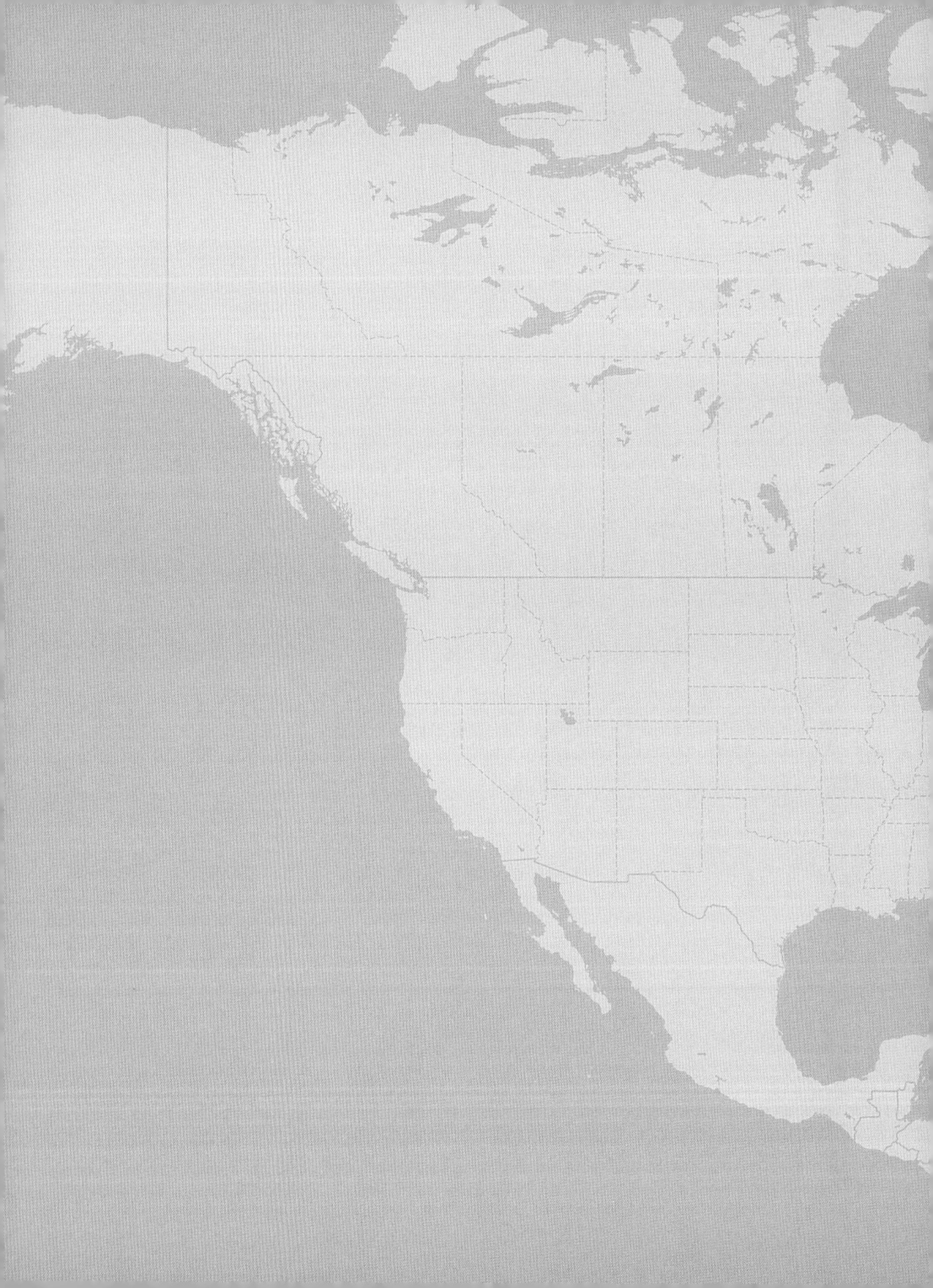

CHAPTER THREE
FORGERIES

EUROPE: ENGLAND

When: 1986–95

Where: London (Drewe) and Sugnall, Stafford (Myatt)

What: More than two hundred forgeries by Myatt in the style of nineteenth- and twentieth-century artists such as Georges Braque, Marc Chagall, Le Corbusier, Jean Dubuffet, Raoul Dufy, Alberto Giacometti, Albert Gleizes, Henri Matisse, Ben Nicholson, Nicolas de Staël, Graham Sutherland, and more, accompanied by fake provenances created by Drewe

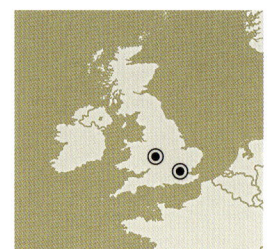

GENUINE FAKES

John Drewe and John Myatt perpetrated "the biggest contemporary art fraud the 20th century has seen," according to British police. What made this odd couple's work so insidious was not only Myatt's artistic skill as a forger, but also Drewe's infiltration of archives. While Myatt was forging art, Drewe was forging its provenance. Together, they literally and figuratively permanently altered the history of modern art.

In keeping with the typical profile of a forger, John Myatt was a painter who couldn't make it in his own right. Instead, he made his living as a part-time art teacher. In 1986, to supplement his income, Myatt started creating art that resembled the works of famous nineteenth- and twentieth-century artists—"genuine fakes," he called them. He advertised his work in *Private Eye* magazine. One of the readers to show interest was John Drewe.

Drewe told Myatt he was an officer of the Ministry of Defense, worked for British Intelligence, had earned a PhD, and had been a physics professor. Unbeknownst to Myatt, Drewe was born John Crockett in southern England in 1948. Childhood friends remember

him as an intelligent but average student, a hoarder of newspaper clippings and books, and a compulsive liar who didn't finish high school.

Drewe commissioned more work from Myatt and asked lots of questions about the art world. He wanted to know how it operated, what the process was for authenticating art, and which artists' work sold for the most money. At this time—the late 1980s—the art world was booming with record-breaking auction prices.

One day in 1986, Drewe took one of Myatt's paintings to Christie's, where they said it could be worth as much as $38,000. Myatt, a perpetually cash-strapped single dad, agreed to start painting works that Drewe would sell under false pretenses. Instead of genuine fakes, forgeries.

Drewe decided that, while Myatt was forging works of art, he would forge their provenance. Starting in 1989, Drewe masqueraded as a

Opposite: Henri Matisse's paintings of odalisques are in some of the great art museums of the world. This one, *Yellow Odalisque*, is not one of them. It is a forgery by John Myatt.

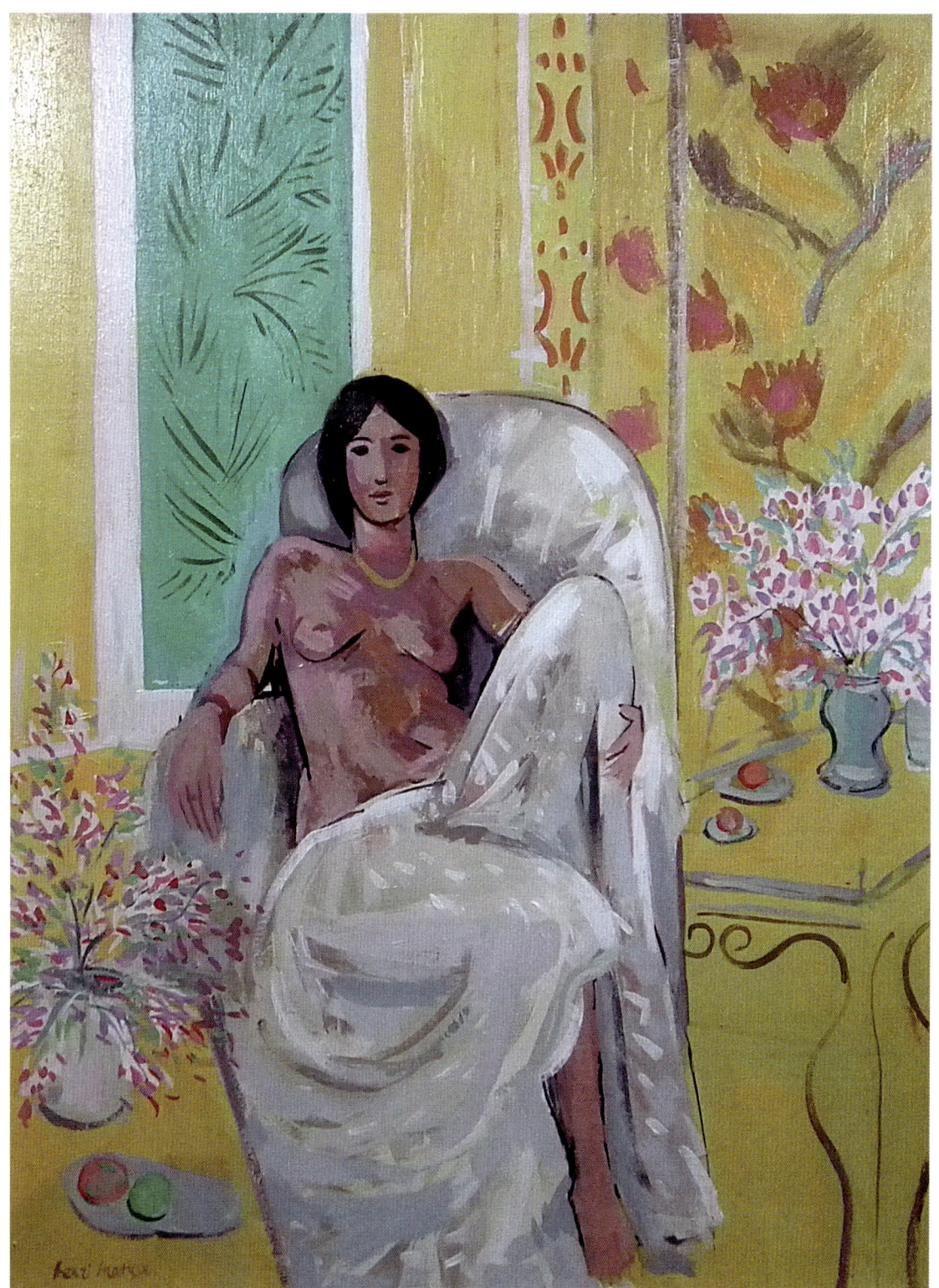

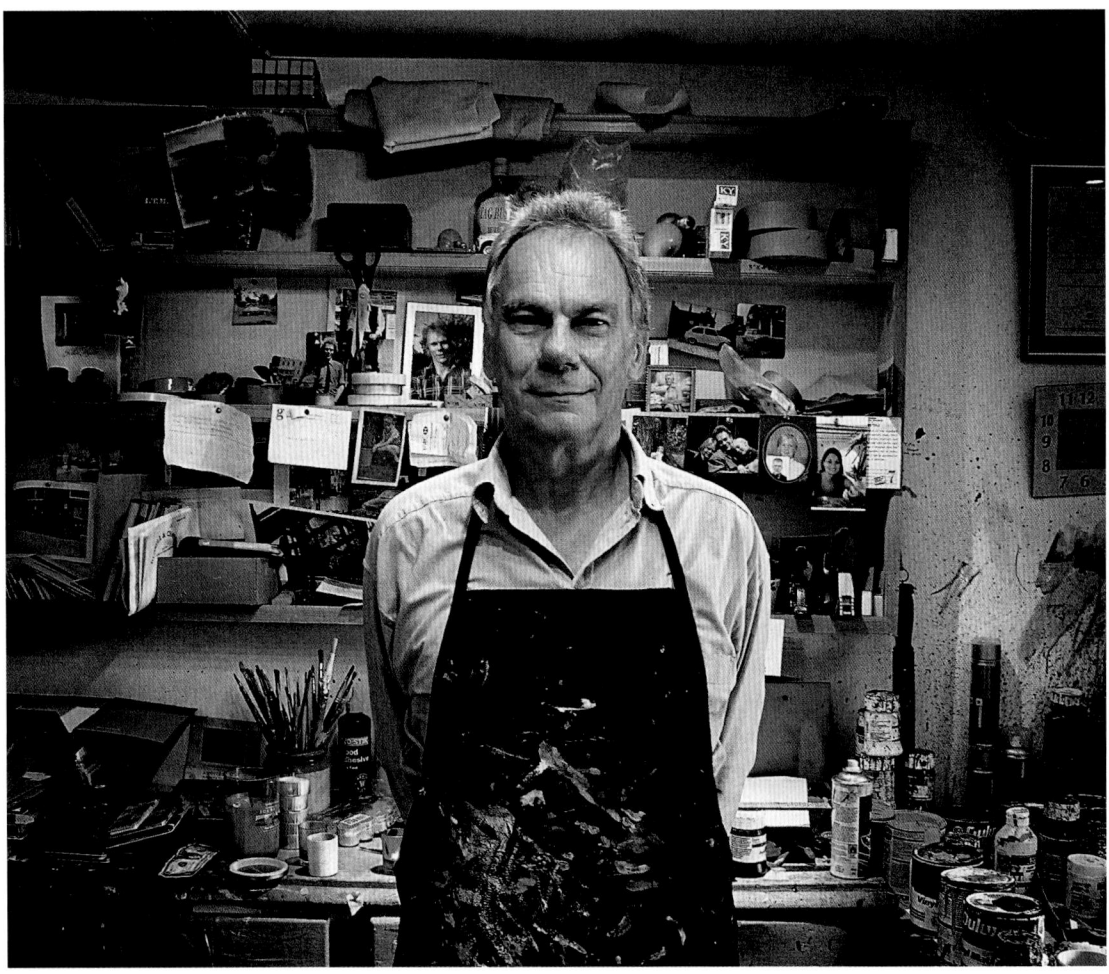

Above: John Myatt, shown here in his studio, won't identify which of his forgeries remain in circulation. He doesn't think anyone gains from knowing what's real and what's fake. Police believe 120 of Myatt's works are still out there.

wealthy art patron, scientist, and historian who wanted to write books about the history of high-profile London museums like the Institute of Contemporary Arts, the Tate, and the Victoria and Albert Museum. He needed access to the museums' archives. To grease the wheels, he donated money and forgeries by Myatt.

Museum archives are full of items related to provenance: old exhibition catalogues, letters written by the artist or patrons, bills of sale, invoices, photographs of the work hanging in various places, and much more. Drewe would steal these items and take them home, where he would create elaborate fictional provenances for Myatt's work, systematically insert the fake provenances for Myatt's forgeries into the existing official museum files, and then return them to the archives.

Using an old typewriter and a computer scanner, Drewe also created new pages for exhibition catalogues and catalogue raisonnés held in museum archives, folding Myatt's forgeries into the history of the art before restitching the book bindings. Someone researching one of Myatt's forgeries would find it recorded in one of the publications Drewe had infiltrated, along with a sterling provenance, just like a legitimate work of art.

Though the money was better than ever for Myatt, he became increasingly uneasy working with Drewe and decided to end their arrangement. He knew that Drewe had hoarded several of his forgeries and had a small stockpile to keep him busy for a while. Myatt went back to teaching art, tried to focus on his children, and stopped painting.

At this point, in 1995, Myatt and Drewe had been forging work for about nine years. There were over two hundred forged works by Myatt in circulation.

In September 1995, Scotland Yard detectives knocked on Myatt's door. Myatt cooperated fully and told detectives the whole story of Drewe and the forgeries. Detectives were shocked to find out Myatt's forgeries were done in emulsion paint mixed with personal lubricant (K-Y Jelly), materials that, if properly examined, would quickly reveal the paintings to be forgeries. Myatt helped Scotland Yard build their case against Drewe. He identified the forgeries he had painted that were already in the market, but police were able to track down only seventy-three of the two hundred.

With incriminating letters from Drewe's ex-wife and Myatt's cooperation, Drewe's home was raided by Scotland Yard, who found plenty of evidence for their case. Drewe, it transpired, was still the compulsive liar and hoarder his childhood friends remembered.

Unsurprisingly, Drewe did not cooperate and refused to admit any wrongdoing even after several days of interrogations. After bailing out, Drewe skipped town. When Scotland Yard re-apprehended him months later, he had a new cover story, explaining that he had been framed as part of a seven-nation government conspiracy that involved selling thousands of works of art to fund illicit arms trading.

When Drewe's lawyer refused to represent his conspiracy defense, Drewe represented himself. In February 1999, Drewe was sentenced to six years in prison for conspiracy to defraud, two counts of forgery, one of theft, and one of using a false instrument with intent.

Drewe was released after two years, but he was convicted again in 2012 for defrauding a seventy-one-year-old retiree out of her £700,000 life savings and sentenced to eight years in prison. Judge Alasdair Darroch said of him, "In my view you are about the most dishonest and devious person I have ever dealt with." Detective Constable Inspector Miki Volpe concurred, telling the *New York Times*, "He [Drewe] was certainly the most devious character I had ever come into contact within my service."

Myatt, on the other hand, was sentenced to just one year in prison and served only four months, earning him the nickname "Picasso." Once released, Myatt was able to reopen his "genuine fakes" business with gallery representation and even exhibitions of his work. He has also hosted and starred in two television programs in which he paints celebrities' portraits in the style of a famous artist, and hosts a self-explanatory series titled *Forger's Masterclass*.

What goes around comes around: Myatt has been paid by Scotland Yard to consult on art forgeries.

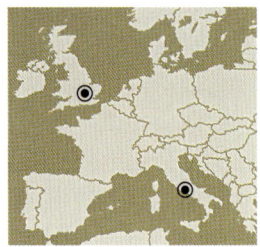

When: Primarily 1961–88

Where: London and Italy

What: Forgeries of Renaissance Old Master drawings as well as paintings and drawings by a range of artists such as Jan Bruegel the Younger, Jean-Baptiste-Camille Corot, Anthony van Dyck, Giovanni Battista Piranesi, and Peter Paul Rubens

EGGING ON THE EXPERTS

Eric Hebborn wrote, "Only the experts are worth fooling. The greater the expert the greater the satisfaction of deceiving them." And deceive them he did, by producing over a thousand forgeries that ended up in esteemed collections around the world. Hebborn's tangle of forgeries continues to cause chaos in the art world today.

Hebborn would have relished the mess. He played the shell game with experts, convincing them that legitimate works were actually his forgeries and also allowing them to attribute his forgeries to famed artists. Hebborn claims he never aimed to overtly deceive experts; he simply presented his work, and they authenticated it as they wished. In a 1991 documentary about him, Hebborn told the BBC "If they can't see it [the forgery], what kind of damned experts are they?"

Hebborn started out as most forgers do: wanting to be an artist in his own right. He was talented as a child, attended arts schools, and won prestigious awards. In his thesis, Hebborn duplicated the work of Old Masters. While working as a painting restorer in 1960, Hebborn met Sir Anthony Blunt, art historian

and Surveyor of the Queen's Pictures. Blunt told Hebborn that one of his drawings resembled the work of the French Baroque master Nicolas Poussin, on whom Blunt was an expert. A seed was planted. Blunt, who later confessed to being a Soviet spy, and Hebborn became life-long friends: master spy and master forger.

Hebborn's career escalated from there. He sold his first pencil drawings between 1961 and 1963, and eventually opened a gallery, where the real and the fake were exhibited as authentic works of art, and both were sold to unsuspecting collectors and curators. Though Hebborn's virtuosity itself was convincing, his forgeries also stood up to scientific testing. He was meticulous in using paper, wood, pigments, and other materials from the time period of the original.

In 1978, curator Konrad Oberhuber of the National Gallery of Art in Washington, DC, noticed that two drawings from Colnaghi (a gallery in London and frequent buyers of Hebborn's work) by two different artists were on the same type of paper. Concerned, Oberhuber contacted another curator, who noticed the same thing about a Colnaghi drawing in their collection. The jig was up. Though Colnaghi

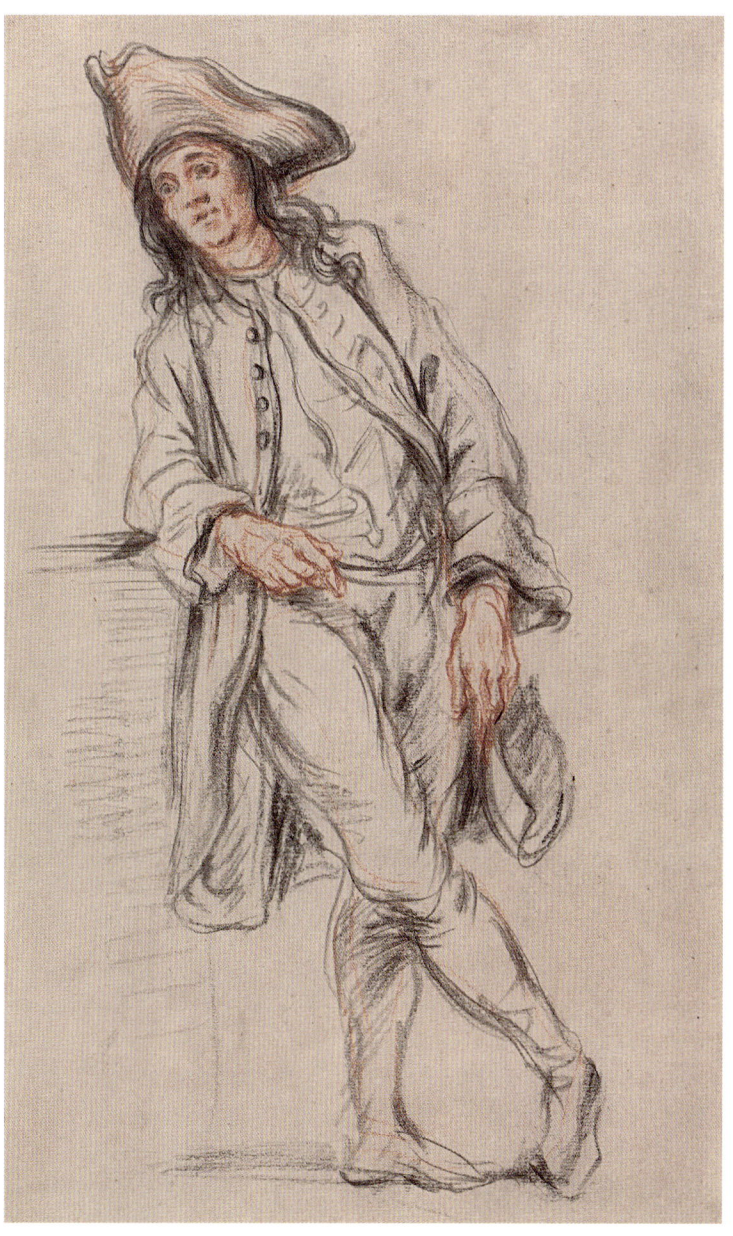

didn't name Hebborn publicly in the statement they issued, Hebborn confessed in his 1991 autobiography, *Drawn to Trouble: The Forging of an Artist*, that he had forged over five hundred works between 1978 and 1988. He also claimed "in no uncertain terms that there is no such thing as a fake, only fake experts and their fake labels."

Though never charged for his forgeries, Hebborn was happy to take credit.

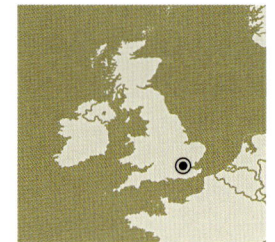

When: Early 1950s–1979

Where: London

What: More than two thousand forgeries in the style of a wide range of artists, including Edgar Degas, Edvard Munch, Samuel Palmer, Rembrandt van Rijn, J. M. W. Turner, and many more

SEXTON BLAKE RHYMES WITH "FAKE"

Forger Tom Keating relished adding "time bombs," a phrase he coined, to his paintings. With lead white, Keating underpainted words or phrases such as "Bollocks!" or "You've been had!" that revealed themselves if the forgery were X-rayed. Another trick of his was to mix paint with glycerin, so that if cleaned with solvent it would dissolve and ruin the painting, making the forgery obvious.

Keating wanted the art world to know that it and he had been cheated. As part of a rehabilitation program after Navy discharge, from 1944 to 1946 Keating studied art at Goldsmiths' College while working as an art restorer. Two of his bosses secretly sold his work as forgeries, profiting handsomely. When Keating learned of this, the self-proclaimed socialist developed a plan to expose predatory capitalism and punish art dealers who preyed on artists and the public.

He flooded the market with "Sexton Blakes." Sexton Blake was a fictional British detective whose name rhymed with "fakes," so Keating adopted this term for his forgeries. Keating painted in a wide range of styles and time periods, channeling artists like Modigliani, Rembrandt, Renoir, and more. He claimed he was possessed by the spirit of the Old Masters who worked through him.

Keating's downfall was his Sexton Blakes of Samuel Palmer, an English Romanticist. Many of Palmer's works were posthumously burned by Palmer's son. Keating decided to undo Palmer's son's mistake, churning out tons of "newly discovered" Palmers.

In 1976, journalist Geraldine Norman of *The Times* noticed the influx of Palmers and bribed Keating's brother-in-law to track him down. They met at Keating's studio where Keating shared his vendetta against the art establishment. A week later, Norman unveiled Keating as the Palmer forger. Ten days later, Keating replied in *The Times*, stating, "I do not deny these allegations. In fact, I openly confess to having done them." He then revealed that, in addition to the Palmer forgeries, he had also made at least two thousand others.

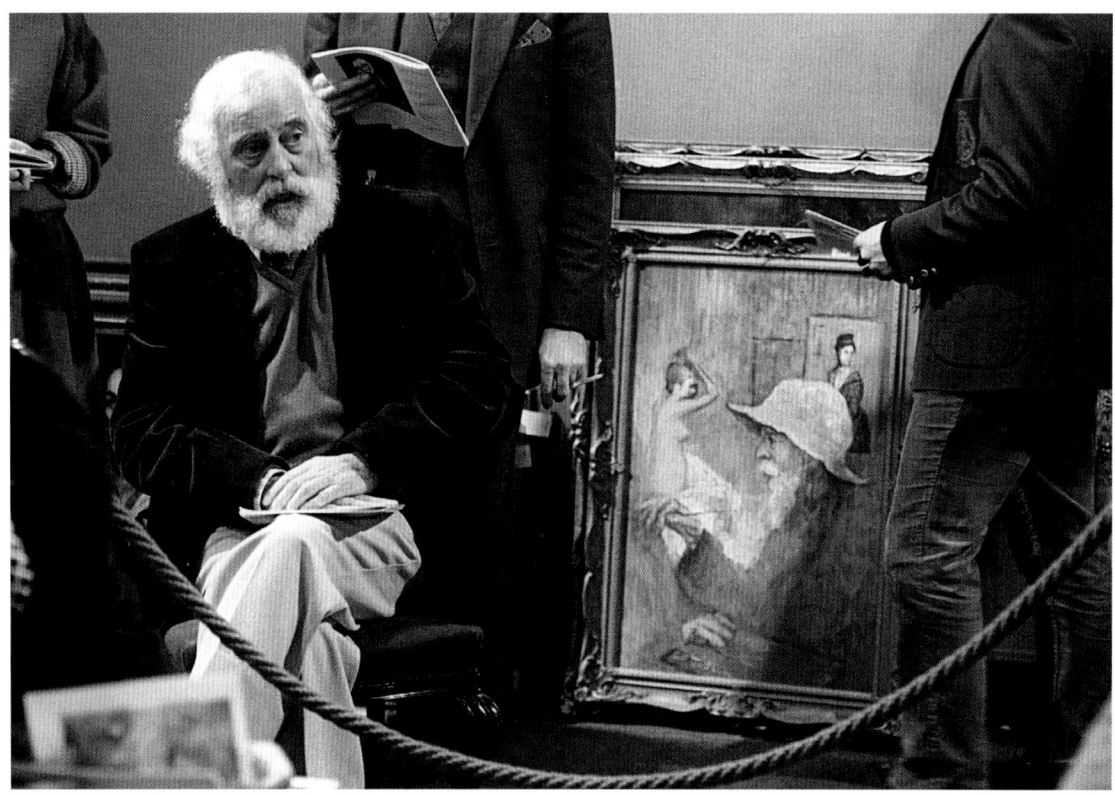

Above: Tom Keating, who once eschewed the mainstream art scene, sits beside his self-portrait at an auction of his work. The painting was one of 120 of Keating's pieces to be sold at Christie's London in 1983.

A year after that, Keating (with the help of Norman's husband) wrote a book about his secrets, *The Fake's Progress*, and in 1979, Keating and his wife, Jane Kelly, were put on trial. Kelly pleaded guilty, testified against Keating, and was sentenced to eighteen months. Keating pleaded not guilty and told the court that he never intended to deceive; he was simply trying to right a very wrong art market. In the middle of the trial, Keating was severely injured in a motorcycle accident and contracted pneumonia in the hospital. Doctors believed Keating wouldn't survive, and all charges against him were dropped. Keating, however, lived.

After his trial, Keating became an art-world darling, embraced by the very group he had railed against. At his trial, his paintings were sold in a gallery near the courthouse. At the age of sixty-six, Keating starred in an award-winning television series, *Tom Keating on Painters*, in which he taught viewers how to paint in the style of the great masters. Today, Keatings sell for thousands and still earn piles of money for art dealers. Keating, who died in 1984 at the age of sixty-seven, would be rolling over in his grave.

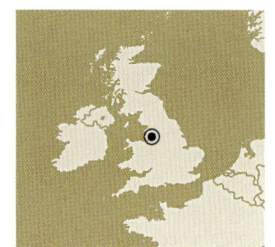

A FAMILY AFFAIR

Nicknamed "The Garden Shed Gang," because the forgeries were created in the family's backyard shed, the Greenhalghs created and sold a staggering array of forged art that included paintings, sculptures, and ceramics, made in pastels, metals, and stone, to name a few. The works represented art history from ancient Egypt to the modern period and ended up in prestigious museums and in the collections of world leaders like President Bill Clinton (who bought a bust of Thomas Jefferson) and the British royal family (who bought a medieval crucifix).

The gang included Shaun Greenhalgh, the artist; his parents, Olive and George, the sellers; and his older brother, George Jr., the family treasurer. The improbable squad was described by Scotland Yard as "possibly the most diverse forgery team in the world, ever."

Dubbed "The Artful Codger" by the press, Greenhalgh began replicating art at age thirteen, and by the time he was seventeen his forgeries would fool the elite art market. He sold a forged Degas drawing to Christie's and pocketed £10,000 from the sale. His half-man, half-goat sculpture, purportedly by Gauguin, was bought by the Art Institute of Chicago for $125,000 in 1997. An alabaster, supposedly ancient Egyptian carving called the *Amarna Princess* sold to Greenhalgh's beloved childhood museum, the Bolton Museum, for £439,676. The princess was aged with a slurry of tea and clay, and her curves were created using tools from B&Q, a UK home improvement store. On both works, Greenhalgh had used Araldite Rapid, a superglue.

Shaun Greenhalgh's forgeries were convincing, and so were the provenances that George Greenhalgh peddled to would-be buyers. George played the "helpless old man," showing up to auction houses sopping wet from rain, sometimes using a wheelchair, seemingly unaware of what his treasures were, who they were by, or what their potential value was. Buyers bought his act.

The Greenhalghs were on Scotland Yard's radar for years before the family was arrested on March 15, 2006, for peddling purported Assyrian reliefs to the British Museum. Olive, eighty-three at the time, and George, eighty-four, were both given suspended sentences and never served time due to their age and frail health. George

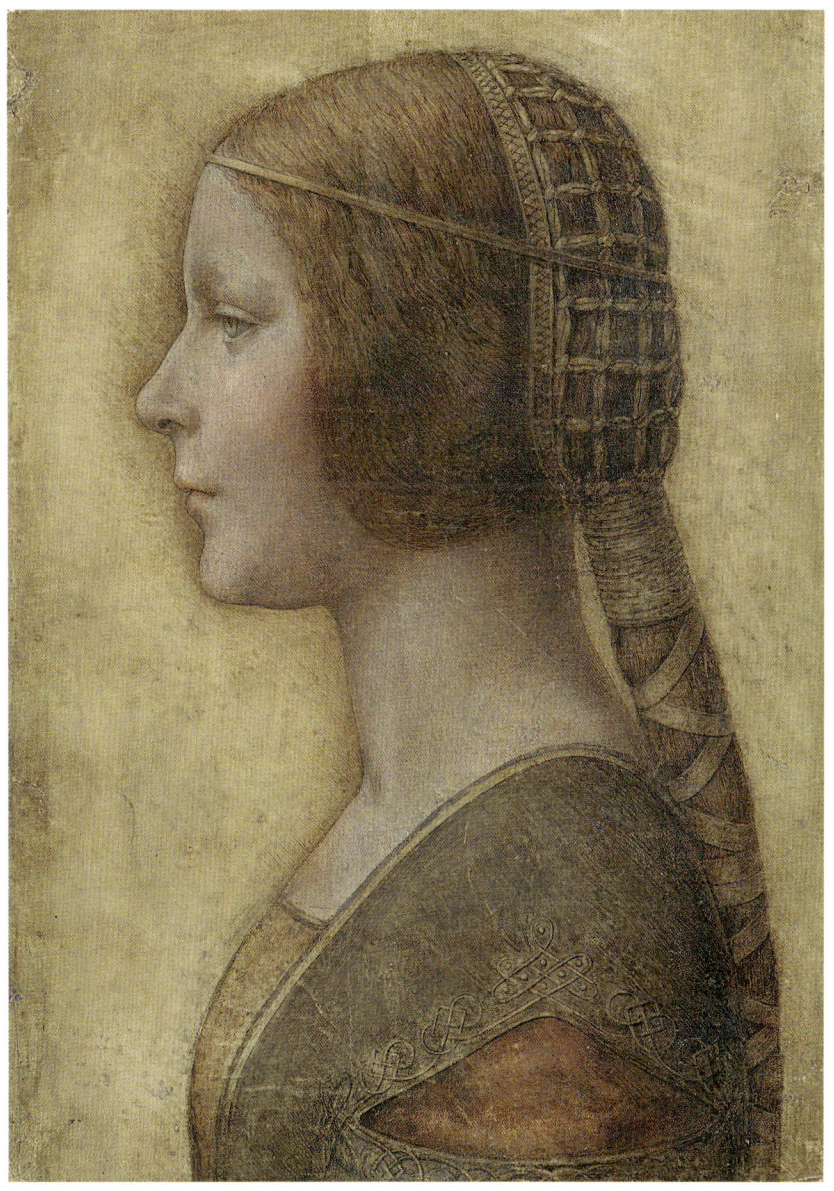

passed away in 2014 and Olive in 2016. George Jr. was given a six-month suspended sentence for his role. Shaun was sentenced to four years and eight months, during which he penned an award-winning autobiography, *A Forger's Tale: Confessions of the Bolton Forger* (2017). Post-prison, he starred in the TV program *Handmade in Bolton*. In 2017, Shaun expressed regret, stating in the *Guardian*, "I went the wrong way. I could have done something useful. If I could have my time again, I'd like to be a teacher at an art college."

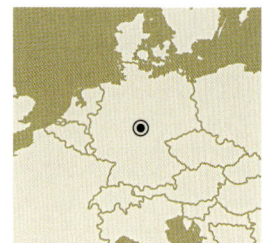

When: 1993–2010

Where: Germany

What: Forgeries of the work and provenance of lesser-known Expressionists, Surrealists, and Cubists, but also of big-name artists like Georges Braque, André Derain, Max Ernst, Fernand Léger, and Max Pechstein

BONNIE AND CLYDE WITH PAINTBRUSHES

After dabbling in forgeries, opium, hash, and LSD from the late 1960s to mid-1980s, Wolfgang Fischer's life changed in 1992, when he met Helene Beltracchi. Wolfgang married Helene and took her surname, and together they started a family and a thriving art-forgery business. The Beltracchis carefully invented a story for dealers, galleries, and auction houses: Helene inherited a substantial art collection from her grandfather, Werner Jägers, who had befriended a German-Jewish art dealer, Alfred Flechtheim. When Flechtheim fled Germany prior to World War II, he sold most of his collection to Jägers, a Nazi sympathizer, who would have been merely a teenager at the time.

Wolfgang and Helene didn't stop there. They created forged labels from Flechtheim's gallery, aging paper by soaking it in coffee and tea. They bought a camera from the 1920s and staged photos of Helene as her grandmother, Josefine, supposedly surrounded by Flechtheim's art (actually painted by Wolfgang), printing them on prewar paper. The Beltracchis scoured flea markets and antique shops for canvases and frames and carefully recreated pigments from the era. Wolfgang immersed himself in the artists' lives, like a method actor, engaging in in-depth research, practicing the artists' techniques, and visiting sites the artists had lived and worked in.

The Beltracchis were wildly successful. They enjoyed lavish parties, trips, and multiple homes around the world. Wolfgang's paintings ended up in the collection of the actor Steve Martin, in exhibitions at the Metropolitan Museum of Art, and in galleries, museums, and private collections around the world. The widow of Max Ernst, Dorothea Tanning, proclaimed one forgery to be the most beautiful picture that Ernst had ever painted. In a *Vanity Fair* profile, Helene said she and Wolfgang are 'still laughing about it'.

The law caught up with the Beltracchis in 2008 when a forgery of German Expressionist Heinrich Campendonk's missing painting *Red Picture with Horses* was chemically analyzed. The white paint was found to contain titanium, which was not used in 1914 when Campendonk

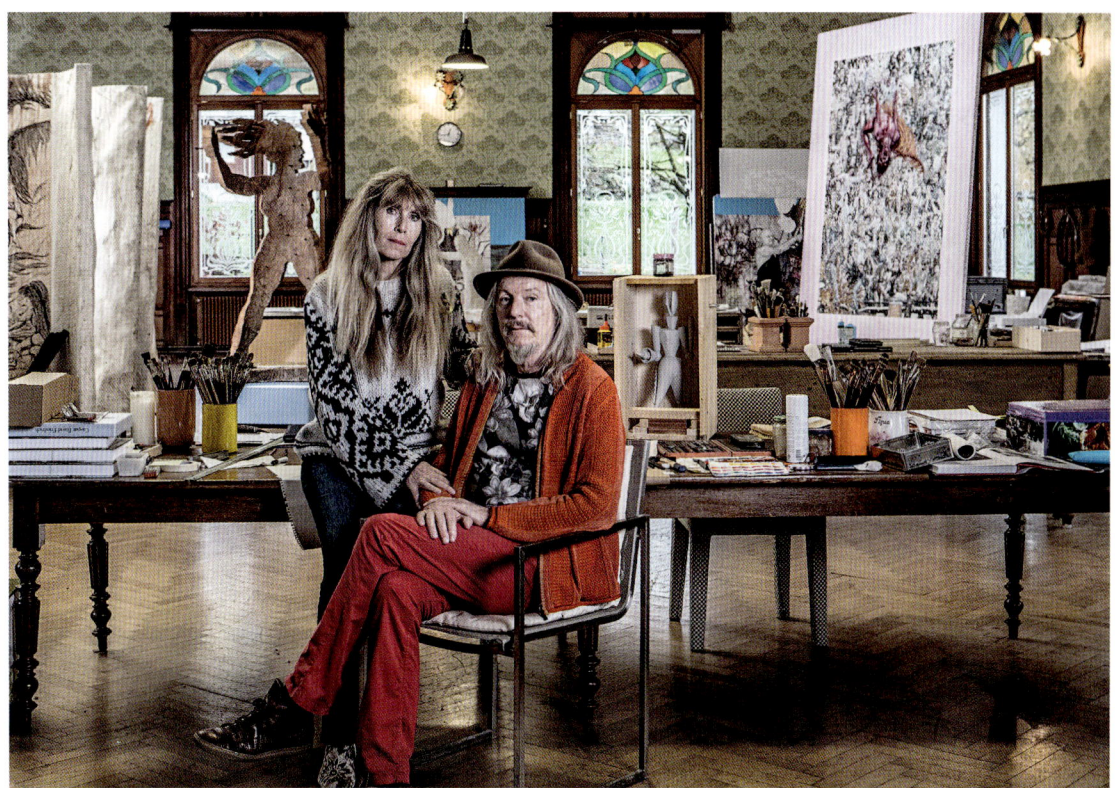

Above: Forgers Helene and Wolfgang Beltracchi. Ironically, in 2021, Wolfgang launched a series of NFTs, an "art form" supposedly impossible to copy. In 2023, the market crashed, making 95 percent of NFTs worthless, according to dappGambl.

would have painted the original. When creating the forgery, Wolfgang had run out of his hand-mixed white paint and substituted a premade one that failed to list titanium as an ingredient.

The Beltracchis were arrested in 2010 and sentenced in 2011 to terms in open jails. Wolfgang was given six years, of which he served just over three, and Helene four years, of which she served less than two. The trial connected the Beltracchis to only fourteen forged paintings, but they claim to have faked works from around fifty artists; their total forgeries might range from three hundred to thousands. The

Beltracchis have made an estimated $100 million from their schemes, making them some of the most lucrative forgers of all time.

Today, the Beltracchis remain unrepentant. They have starred in numerous TV episodes and a documentary, and they have authored books and had books written about them. Wolfgang still paints under his own name, and the BBC reports that he still takes in millions. One of Wolfgang's websites describes his forgery career as a "Robin Hood" tale; though he certainly stole from the rich, the websites never explain whether he gave to the poor.

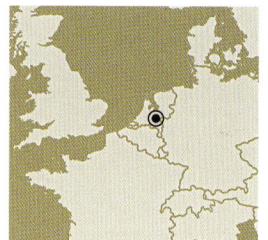

SEX, DRUGS, AND ART FORGERY

Supper at Emmaus, purportedly by Johannes Vermeer, made a dramatic entrance onto the art scene in 1936, with no previous record of its existence. Experts debate how many paintings can be attributed to Vermeer, but estimates range from thirty-four to thirty-seven. If it seems unusual that the newly discovered Vermeer was a religious painting when there are no other existing religious scenes in his oeuvre, your instincts are correct. Most of the Vermeers that exist today are of quiet, everyday scenes.

But *Supper at Emmaus* was not by the esteemed seventeenth-century Dutch master. It was actually painted in the same decade it first appeared by the vain, alcoholic, drug-addicted, opportunistic, scorned painter Han van Meegeren. It's staggering that anyone fell for these poor imitations. They have none of the magic of a real Vermeer: the figures are waxy and flat; the light is dull; the details are neither subtle nor wondrous. But critics, art historians, and museum directors saw what they wanted to see in Van Meegeren's forgeries: Vermeers.

Van Meegeren was a failed artist who stewed over the art world's dismissal. His work gained a measure of commercial success, but critics considered it saccharine and mundane. They applauded his ability to copy the Dutch masters but were convinced he had no original abilities. Van Meegeren planned revenge, and by the early 1930s, had started working toward the forgeries.

One of the great hurdles Van Meegeren had to contend with was time. A three-hundred-year-old painting has distinctive qualities that are hard to replicate: the canvas, nails, and wood of the stretcher need to reflect the age and region where it was painted. And, most damningly, the painting's surface would need to have the proper craquelure—the cracks that develop in hardened paint and varnish over hundreds of years.

Van Meegeren purchased antique wood, canvas, and nails, but at the time there was no known way to make oil paint look older. Through experiments, Van Meegeren made paint from the raw materials Vermeer would have used and made his own paintbrushes from badger hair, like Vermeer. He also added

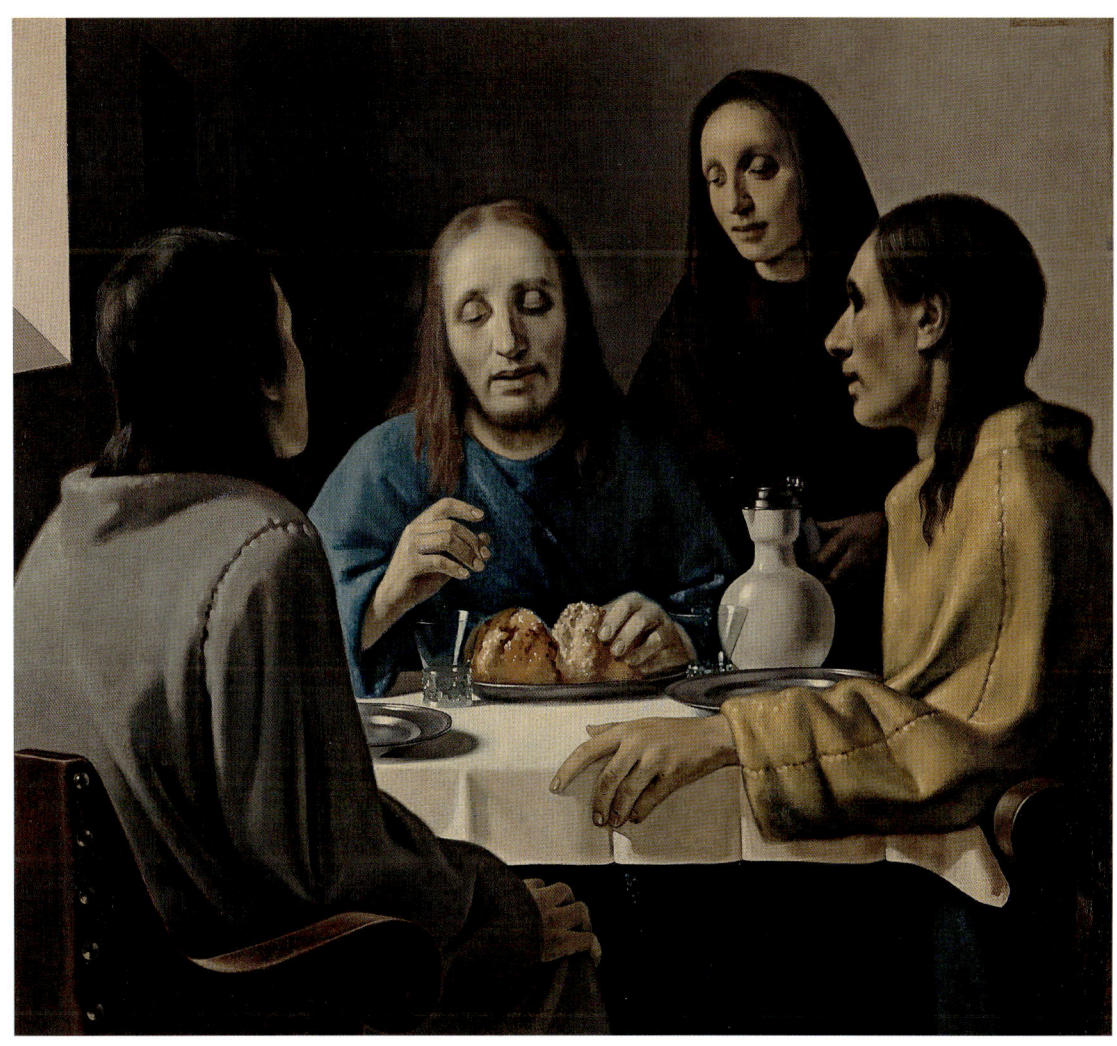

Above: *Supper at Emmaus* launched Van Meegeren's forgery career. Today, it is hard to imagine it ever fooled anyone. The Museum Boijmans Van Beuningen has four of Van Meegeren's forgeries, including this one.

Bakelite, a synthetic material that was essentially the first plastic, invented in the twentieth century, to his paint, which brought his forgeries into a realm of believability.

In 1936, Van Meegeren bought a seventeenth-century canvas from a gallery, scraped off the original paint, and created a scene from the Bible, *Supper at Emmaus*. Van Meegeren targeted two important art-world luminaries: Abraham Bredius, former director of the Mauritshuis museum at The Hague and one of the national authorities on Dutch painting, and Dirk Hannema, director of the Museum Boijmans Van Beuningen in Rotterdam. Duped and overcome with delight at their discovery of an unknown Vermeer, Bredius launched a vigorous campaign to have the work bought and donated to Hannema's Boijmans. With the profits from the sale (around $5 million today), Van Meegeren purchased an outlandish estate in Nice, France.

Hannema unveiled the Boijmans' new Vermeer to the public in 1938. It was resoundingly popular and declared to be one of Vermeer's most important works. The work is still at the Boijmans, but it is neither in a place of prominence, nor is it attributed to Vermeer.

Van Meegeren would go on to create six more Vermeer forgeries over the course of six years, selling them all for handsome profits. He became a caricature of someone who had too much money and didn't know what to do with it. He spent it on prostitutes, threw incredibly extravagant parties, and bought real estate like a mogul in addition to his other vices of smoking, drinking, and morphine.

During this time, Van Meegeren's forgery *Christ with the Woman Taken in Adultery* (1942) caught the attention of Hermann Göring, the Reich marshal, commander of the Luftwaffe, and second in command of the Nazis. Göring ended up trading 137 looted artworks for this one forged painting.

The link between Göring and Van Meegeren was uncovered in the chaotic aftermath of World War II. The Dutch provisional government was eager to prosecute anyone who had pillaged Dutch cultural property during the war, and they arrested Van Meegeren for selling what everyone thought was a piece of Dutch art history to Göring.

While in custody, Van Meegeren confessed he had not been in league with the Nazis—he had duped them. He explained his Bakelite concoction and his hoodwinking of the art world. Authorities were skeptical, and they asked Van Meegeren to prove it. They rounded up canvas, paints, and any other materials needed to produce an "original forgery of Vermeer." Between July and December of 1945, in front of reporters and witnesses, Van Meegeren literally painted for his life. The sentence for working with the Nazis was death.

After several months of work, the result was *Jesus Among the Doctors*. The legal team representing Van Meegeren had experts and scientists testify as to how he pulled off the forgery. A search of Van Meegeren's home confirmed a studio filled with forgery materials.

Almost ten years after Van Meegeren achieved success with his first forgery, *Supper at Emmaus*, he was found guilty of fraud and sentenced to one year in prison. While waiting to be transferred to jail, he was admitted to the hospital for chest pains, perhaps a complication of syphilis. Van Meegeren spent a month in the hospital and passed away there, having never completed a single day of his prison sentence. The Rijksmuseum acquired a plaster death mask of Van Meegeren's face. In the end, Van Meegeren did end up in a museum as himself.

Meanwhile, Göring was tried at Nuremberg and sentenced to death by execution. He ended up committing suicide while in jail but not before finding out that his beloved and prized Vermeer was a fake.

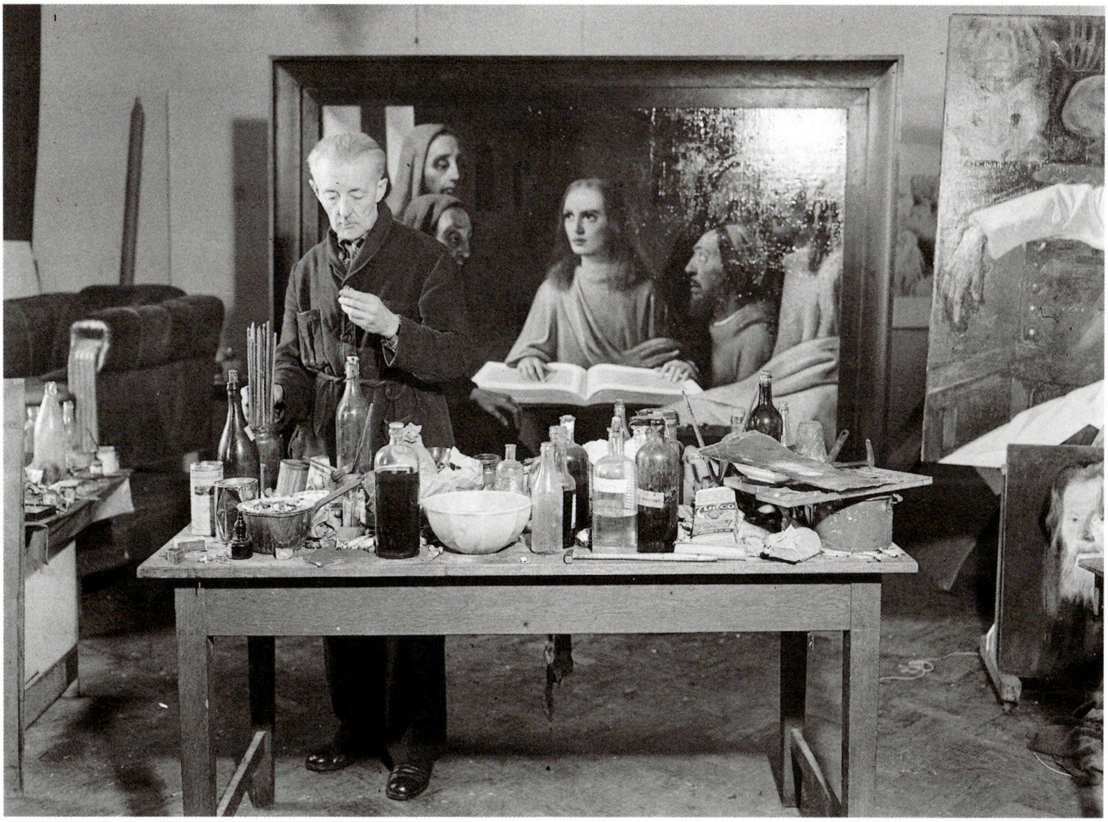

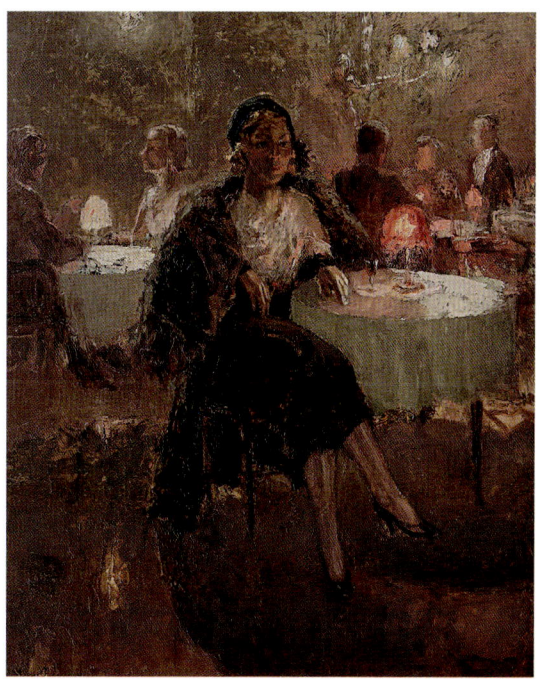

Above: Han van Meegeren is shown here painting *Jesus Among the Doctors* at his trial. From July to December of 1945, he worked in front of court-appointed witnesses and reporters to prove he was the Vermeer forger.

Right: Van Meegeren started his artistic career painting innocuous and bland genre scenes such as this one, *The Actress Clara Vischer-Blaaser in a Tea Room.* Art critics were not impressed.

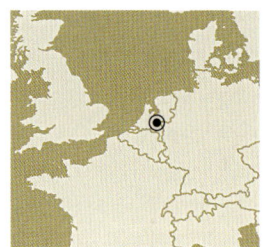

GIACOMETTIS GALORE

When asked about his forgery career, Robert Driessen described himself carefully, stating: "[I was] not making art. I was copying art. I'm not an artist."

At a young age, Driessen discovered he had a natural talent for art. At age sixteen in 1975, Driessen left home to sell paintings to tourists. His own original art brought little success, so Driessen started creating copies of Dutch Romantic painters and forgeries of the Expressionists. Art dealers encouraged this work, and Driessen thinks he sold at least a thousand, some of which may be hanging in museums.

Driessen saw an opportunity after learning how to cast bronze sculptures in 1987. Once he created a cast (which took a mere thirty to forty minutes), he could churn out forged sculptures and rake in the dough. In 1998, Driessen made *Annette*, his first Giacometti-style sculpture, which he named after Giacometti's wife.

Again, art dealers were interested, knowing full well the sculptures were forged. Driessen would go on to sell *Annette* for 25,000 German marks. For the next ten years, Driessen collaborated with two main dealers, Guido S.

and Lothar S., both of whom lived in Germany. The demand for the forged Giacomettis was so great that Driessen had to hire two assistants. This was much more lucrative than painting Dutch scenes for tourists. He drove a fancy car and rented a palatial villa with eleven bedrooms, six bathrooms, and three art studios. Driessen guesses that he made about 1,300 Giacometti sculptures, while Giacometti is believed to have made only five hundred himself.

In 2005, Driessen, with his wife and son, moved to Thailand, a country from which he knew he could not be extradited, and where the winters were less oppressive. Driessen occasionally returned to cast more Giacomettis until 2009 when he was detained by police at Frankfurt airport. Kept under close surveillance, Driessen did not visit his foundries and returned to Thailand, shaken.

A month later, Driessen's dealers in Germany warned him not to return. Soon after, Lothar was sentenced to nine years, and Guido to seven years and four months. German authorities raided their warehouse, where they found 831 bronze statues in the style of Giacometti and 171 plaster figures. The plaster figures were crushed

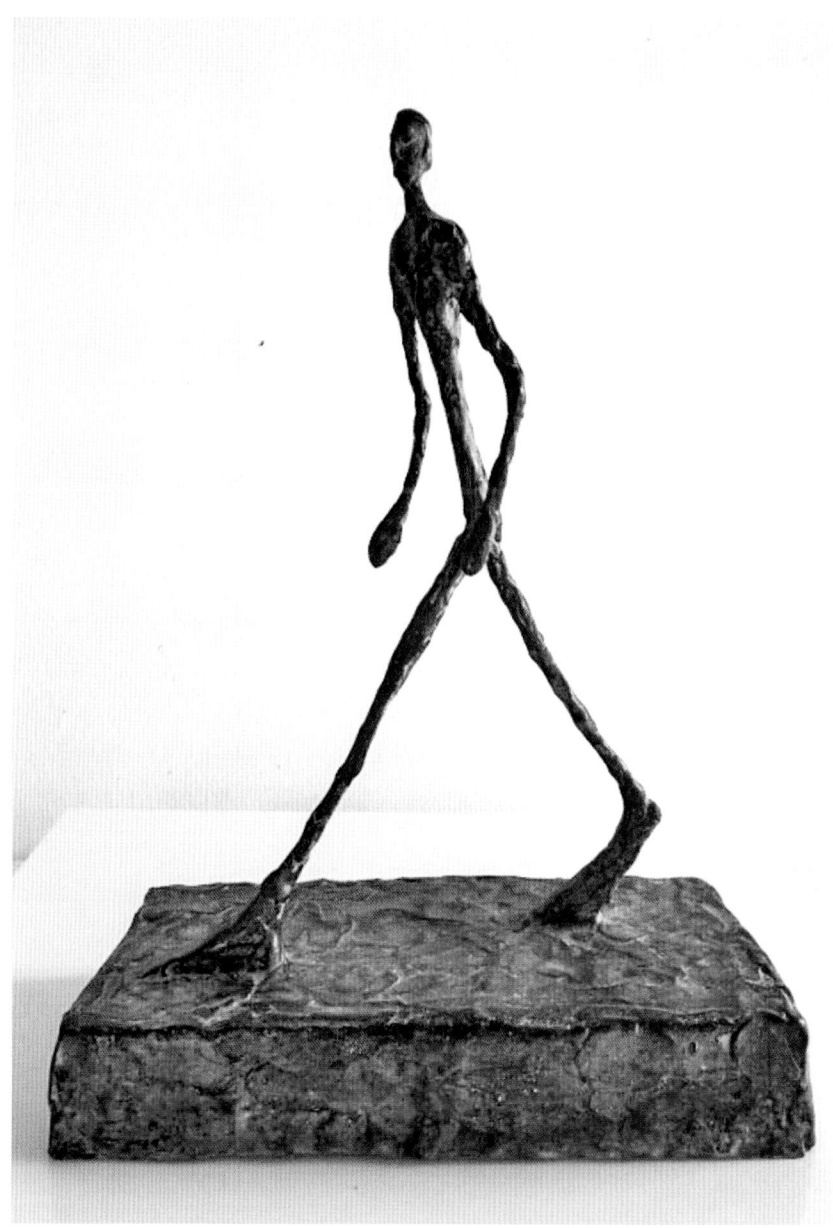

Right: Alberto Giacometti's haunting sculptures have become so famous and recognizable that they were featured on the Swiss 100-franc banknote from 1998 to 2016. This sculpture sure looks like a Giacometti, but it's a Driessen.

with a backhoe, and the sculptures were melted down into five tons of bronze that were used to make an ornate door in Abu Dhabi.

In 2014, Driessen visited Amsterdam, where he was caught, extradited to Germany, and tried and sentenced for forgery. Once released from jail, Driessen returned to Thailand, where he lives modestly, still selling Giacometti knockoffs, but with the important distinction that he signs them with his own name.

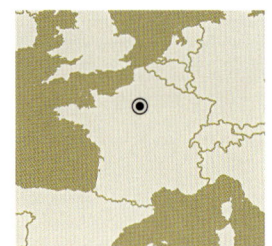

When: 1946–64

Where: Various locales around the world, beginning in Paris

What: Forgeries in the style of modern masters such as Henri Matisse, Amedeo Modigliani, Pablo Picasso, and Pierre-Auguste Renoir

F IS FOR FORGERY

Elmyr de Hory (born Elemér Albert Hoffmann) achieved legendary status as, according to Clifford Irving, "the greatest art forger of our time." His fascinating life has been detailed in books, film, and even a musical.

In spite of his fame, de Hory's definitive life story is unknown. He liked to embellish and invent, and couldn't be trusted to truthfully tell his own life story. Here are some things we know: de Hory was born in 1906 to a lower-middle-class Jewish family in Budapest. In the 1920s, he studied art in Munich, Transylvania, and Paris. After school, he was convicted not of art forgery but check fraud, counterfeiting documents, and falsely claiming an aristocratic title. After his stint in Transylvania, perhaps the title was "Count."

De Hory's career in forgery started in Paris in 1946, when he claimed that a wealthy woman mistook one of his drawings for a Picasso. He forged more drawings and partnered with an art dealer in Paris, then moved to Rio, and eventually to America in 1947.

In the US, some of de Hory's buyers, including a curator at Harvard's Fogg Museum and a Chicago art dealer, became skeptical. The FBI launched an investigation while de Hory fled to Mexico City in 1955.

De Hory snuck back into the US, where he met Egyptian-born con man Fernand Legros, striking up a business relationship that eventually also included the French Canadian Réal Lessard. The scheme was simple: de Hory would create forgeries and Lessard and Legros would peddle them.

Legros and Lessard had heard of the wildcatters of Dallas and Fort Worth, so they also headed west. Algur Meadows was an easy target. The inimitable oil tycoon and chairman of General American Oil was a shrewd businessman and fierce negotiator, but he was not well versed in the oily art world. Legros and Lessard sold Meadows the first of de Hory's paintings from the trunk of their car. Meadows

Opposite: Elmyr de Hory's *Hommage to Modigliani* closely mimics the hallmark features of a real Modigliani: elongated face, almond eyes, and graceful curves.

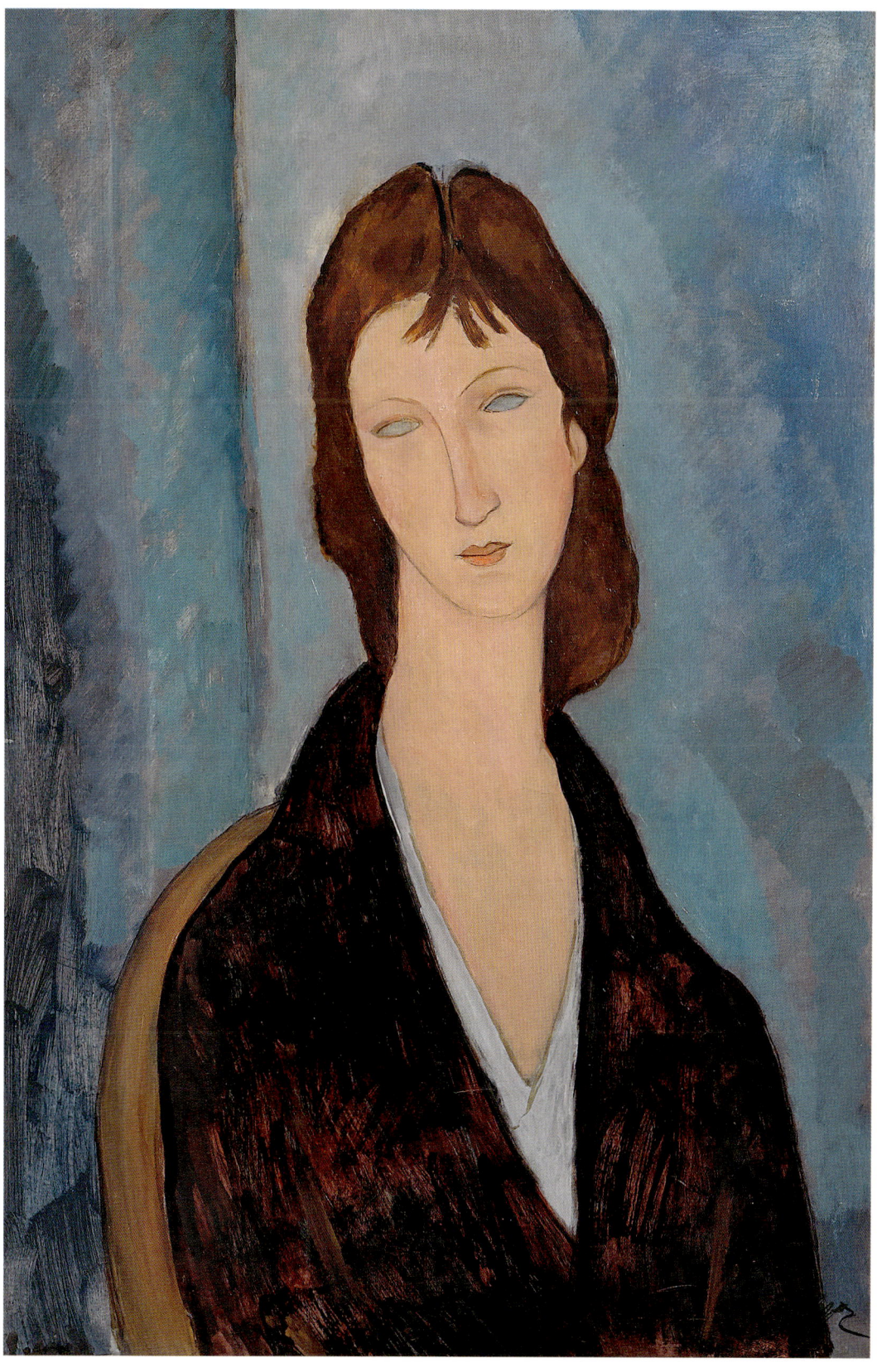

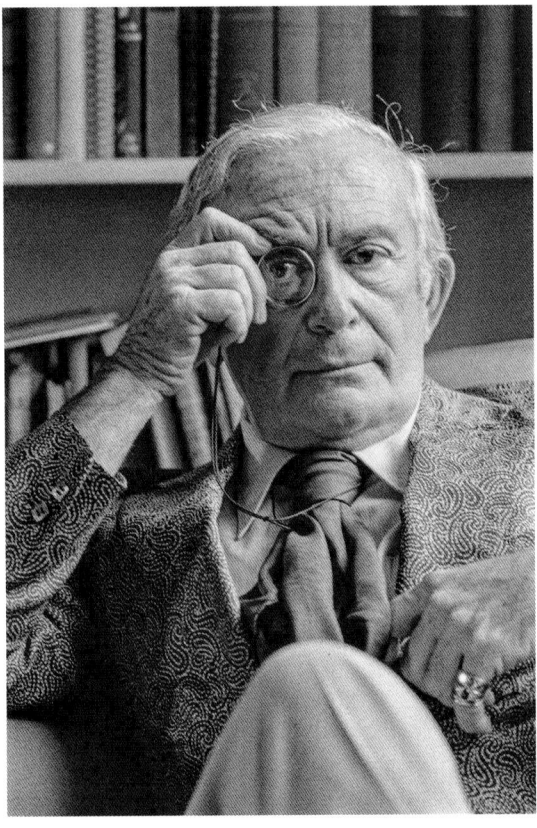

Above: Elmyr de Hory in 1973, sporting a monocle and a smart paisley jacket, looking every bit the aristocrat that he claimed to be.

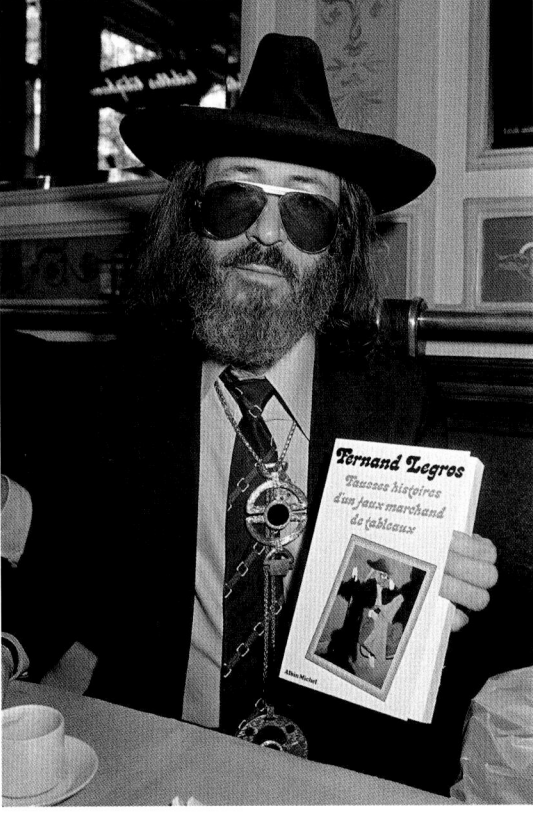

Above: Fernand Legros displays his 1979 book *Fausses Histoires d'un Faux Marchand de Tableaux* (False Stories about a Fake Art Dealer).

thought he took advantage of the two "peddlers," but the joke was on him.

Legros and Lessard were no dummies, putting forgeries up for auction and buying them under an assumed name to provide provenance. They copied stamps from art galleries, museums, and US Customs. They bought exhibition catalogues and inserted photos of de Hory's work to falsify the paintings' history.

During the 1950s and 1960s, de Hory forged more than a thousand works that were sold across five continents. Many have been removed from museums, but others have not. He forged so many Modiglianis that the director of the

Modigliani Project said they may never be able to compile a catalogue raisonné.

In the late 1970s, Meadows asked Dallas gallery owner Donald Vogel to sell a few of his paintings. Horrified at what he saw, Vogel was the first person to tell Meadows that his paintings were not originals.

At this point, the band had broken up. Legros and Lessard were in Paris, and de Hory was at his home in Ibiza.

Vogel and the Art Dealers Association of America traveled to Meadows's collection accompanied by two ardent pursuers of forgeries, one from each coast, known as the witch hunters of the east and west. Their verdict was that "of the 58 items … it is [our] opinion that 11 of them are or may be by the artists to whom they are attributed, and 44 are not by the artist to whom they are attributed."

After this indictment, Vogel wrote, "All hell broke loose." One of the members of the committee leaked details of their visit. Major outlets including the *New York Times* and NBC ran the story. In the UK, Princess Margaret allegedly spent time quizzing an American visitor about Meadows.

Meadows owned up to being duped and ponied up an additional $2 million for an actual, legitimate art dealer to buy him "the real things." But he wanted vengeance and demanded the trio be arrested. Legros was picked up in Rio in 1973, extradited to France, convicted of artistic and financial fraud, and sentenced to two years in prison and a $3,000 fine. He got out of most of it due to "psychiatric evidence." Legros might be better known if the creator of *Tintin*, Georges

Remi, had finished his last opus featuring a character based on Legros: Enddadine Akas, who aptly ran a network of forgers. The real Legros died of throat cancer in 1983 in France.

Lessard also did jail time but continues to live and paint in France, making money from a book about his experience called *L'Amour du Faux*, or "Love of Fakes."

De Hory managed to elude police for almost two years but eventually returned to Ibiza, where he was arrested. Spanish police couldn't prove de Hory had forged in Spain, so he was arrested for homosexuality and sentenced to two months in jail.

De Hory emerged a celebrity. Clifford Irving wrote a book, *Fake!*, and Orson Welles made a film about him, *F for Fake*, launching de Hory into the stratosphere.

His fame and happiness were short-lived—Spanish and French police reached an extradition agreement, and de Hory was to be tried in France. Fearing jail, he overdosed on sleeping pills in Ibiza on December 11, 1976.

Meadows referred to himself as "Mr. Sap," and according to *Life* magazine he "talked openly about being swindled and laughed along with his friends at his gullibility." Meadows joked that he might dedicate a "My Experience with Fake Paintings room" in his mansion.

If only more museums, galleries, and auction houses were as willing to publicly admit defeat, the art world would be a much more transparent place.

THE AMERICAS: USA

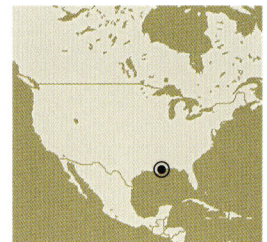

When: 1960s–2009

Where: New Orleans and Baton Rouge, Louisiana

What: Forgeries predominantly of Clementine Hunter, but also of the work of Paul Gauguin, Claude Monet, Pierre-Auguste Renoir, Alfred Sisley, and others

KITTY LITTER

When the Baton Rouge home of William and Beryl Toye was raided by the FBI in September 2009, neighbors had front-row seats to the spectacle. The FBI, followed by an animal control van, a fire truck, and an ambulance, spent over five hours combing the Toyes' home. They found (and smelled) much evidence of the Toyes' more than one hundred cats, sixty of which were buried in the backyard, each in their own coffin, hand built by William, in holes dug by Beryl. But what the FBI was really there for were the forgeries. The FBI carried out a parade of paintings, which they inventoried while neighbors watched. Next door, James Breedlove told the news, "It was quite a show actually." He added, "I had so many people come over, I could've sold tickets." The raid ended with Beryl in an ambulance; she spent a few days in the local psychiatric ward after trying to strike an FBI officer and threatening to kill herself.

William Toye met Beryl Spalding in New Orleans in 1967. Spalding, a tourist from England, headed home after meeting William, but soon returned after a courtship conducted via love letters. They realized they had a lot in common: both struggled with agoraphobia and wanted enough cats to require five tons of kitty litter a year. Over the years, Beryl claims she amassed an enormous collection of the work of Clementine Hunter, a plantation worker turned self-taught artist in Louisiana. Toye had little respect for Hunter's work, calling it "junk," and "really only good as dartboards," going so far as to break the wooden panels in two, sticking them in the trash, or letting their cats pee on them. When the cats used Beryl's collection of Hunters as a litter box, William said he was pleased as he felt the act improved the paintings.

Somewhere along the line, though, the Toyes realized that William was a good forger of Hunter's work. William had been forging other artists' work. He was also good at Monet's style, telling *Garden & Gun* in 2010, "Nobody does Monet better than me. If he were still alive and we both did a water lily painting, tell me the difference." Toye boasted that he knew the "secret formula" that Degas had used to sketch his famed ballerinas. Toye even skirted trouble for continuing to forge after having been accused but not prosecuted three times. William had learned to paint as a high-school dropout,

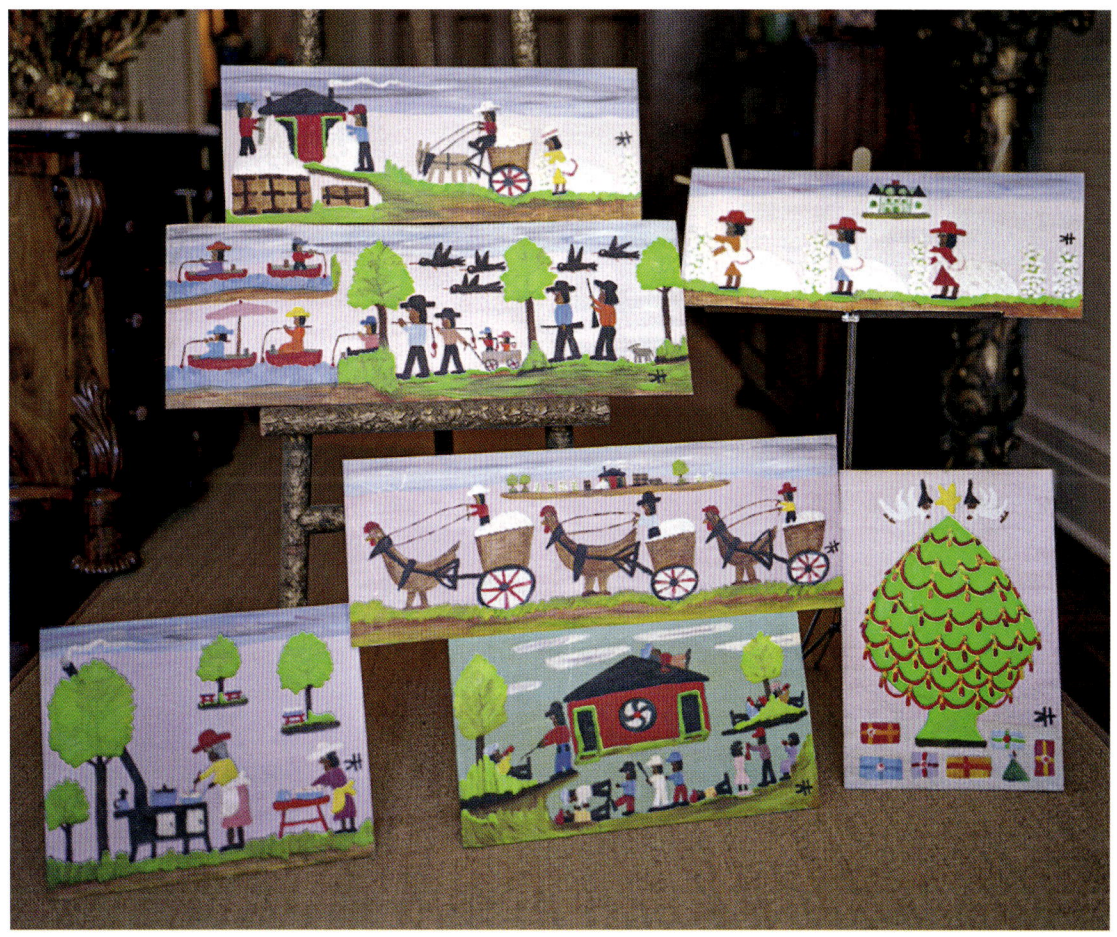

Above: Shown here are several of William Toye's forgeries of Clementine Hunter. Hunter, born in 1887, didn't start painting until the 1940s. She was prolific, producing between five and ten thousand pieces over forty years.

working on sets at the Metropolitan Opera House in New York City. After moving back to New Orleans in 1951, William continued to teach himself to paint and became quite adept as a mimic.

After the three separate fraud accusations, the Toyes' luck ran out. They were indicted for fraud in 2011, along with Robert Lucky, a New Orleans-based art dealer who was willingly (and knowingly) selling William's forgeries. In court, William and Beryl pleaded guilty but managed to avoid prison sentences, though they were each given two years' probation and made to pay back $423,393 to victims of their forgery scheme.

Never one to stand down, William, then seventy-nine years old, lashed out like a cornered cat at a press photographer outside of the courthouse, striking him twice with his cane.

When: 1985–2014

Where: Laurel, Mississippi

What: Forgeries of the work of a range of artists from the sixteenth to the twentieth century, including Charles Curran, Stanislas Lépine, Paul Signac, and Everett Shinn

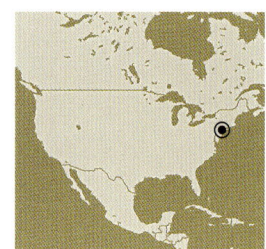

A PRIEST WALKS INTO A MUSEUM...

Mark Landis is an unlikely art forger who prefers to think of himself as a philanthropist. He attended art schools after his first nervous breakdown and a diagnosis of schizophrenia at the age of seventeen, where he learned during his art-therapy sessions at the hospital that he had a talent for painting and drawing.

Living in San Francisco in 1985, where he briefly owned a gallery, the thirty-year-old Landis wanted to please his mother. He whipped up a piece in the style of Maynard Dixon, a twentieth-century painter of the American West, and gifted it to the Oakland Museum of California in his late father's honor. The curator who received the gift was exceedingly grateful. When Landis showed his mother the letter of appreciation from Oakland, she was pleased, telling him she was proud. Between the curator's gratitude and his mother's approval, Landis was hooked.

Landis began to forge work by a wide array of lesser-known artists from the sixteenth to the twentieth centuries. His targets were mainly smaller, regional museums from Boston to Santa Fe, which lacked the resources for detailed forensic analysis. When scrutinized, Landis's forgeries were obvious. He used contemporary materials bought at his local art store in Laurel, Mississippi. Under a microscope, it was clear Landis had printed out a copy of an artist's already-extant work, pasted it onto a board, and painted over it. Plus, his canvases smelled suspiciously like the coffee he used to age his work.

Landis's cons weren't remarkable in terms of the work he copied, but rather for the personas he inhabited when donating his forgeries. Landis had numerous aliases and enjoyed dressing up like a Jesuit priest in full cassock when he visited museums.

From 1985 to 2007, Landis continued to donate to museums, except for a period of a few years when he had another psychiatric hospitalization and attended university for economics. After a donation attempt at the Oklahoma City Museum of Art in 2007, an eagle-eyed registrar, Matthew C. Leininger,

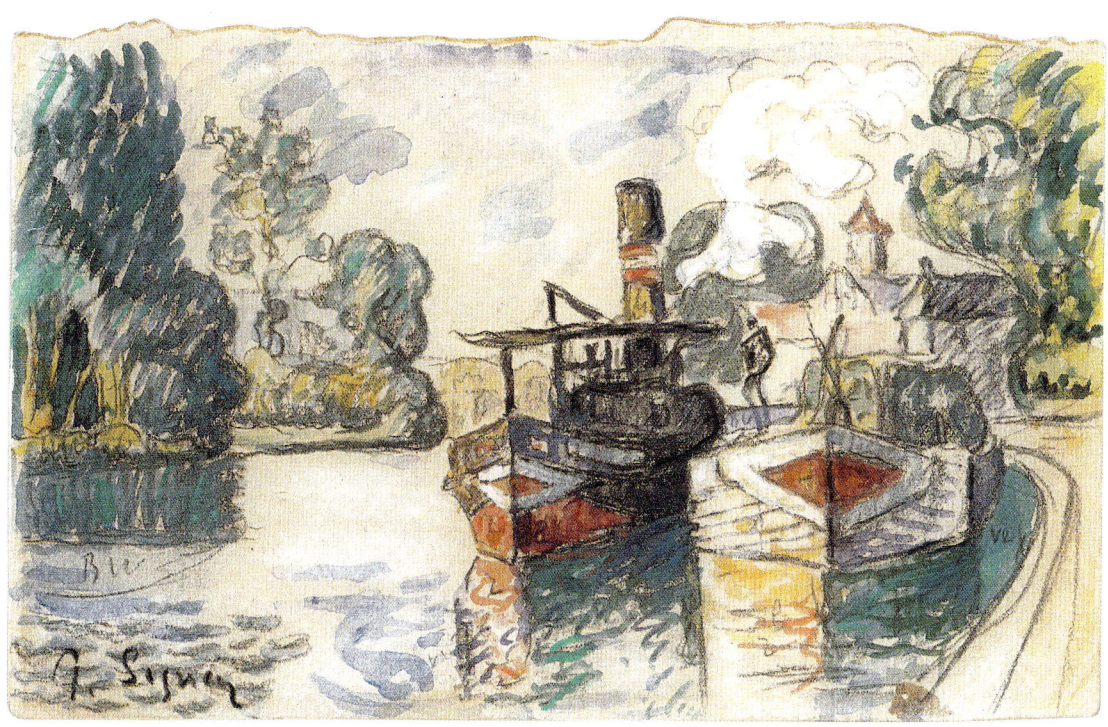

Above: A giver, not a taker, Mark Landis painted a copy of this watercolor by Paul Signac and tried to gift it to the Oklahoma City Museum. The original hangs in the Hermitage Museum in St. Petersburg, Russia.

noticed several inconsistences in the five pieces from Landis, who had claimed he wanted to sell them before his heart surgery (a compelling story, though false). Leininger reached out to his museum network and started putting together the puzzle pieces. Leininger discovered that Landis had donated over fifty forgeries to more than twenty museums. The FBI, which Leininger alerted, merely shrugged when asked about Landis's activities, saying he had not broken any laws. Hoping to expose Landis and get him to stop, Leininger organized an exhibition of Landis's forgeries titled *Faux Real* in 2012. Since then, Landis has also starred in a documentary about himself, *Art and Craft* (2014), and has started selling work in his own name.

Landis is a wholly unique forger in that he never once tried to sell his forgeries; he only ever donated his work. He never even tried to use any of his donations for tax refunds. Many other forgers seek some combination of money, power, fame, or revenge. Landis, on the other hand, seemed most driven by praise and encouragement, priceless things that can be given away for free.

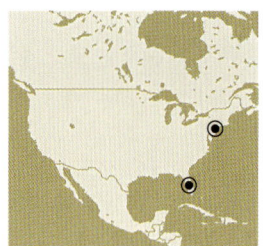

When: 1968–98

Where: New York City and Florida

What: Forgeries of sixteenth-century Flemish artists, nineteenth-century American masters such as Martin Johnson Heade, and eighteenth- and nineteenth-century sporting and maritime artists like James Buttersworth

BUYER BEWARE

Many art forgers might claim the title of "most prolific," but few advertise themselves as the "most lavishly compensated." Ken Perenyi claims this title in the Autobiography section of his website and for good reason. He estimates he made over a thousand forgeries in his thirty years of work and millions of dollars, at one point keeping $1 million in his own home safe.

As a teenager in New York City, he soaked up masterpieces at the Metropolitan Museum of Art and learned to appreciate the Old Masters. Perenyi taught himself how to paint after an artist friend, Tom Daly, loaned him oil paints and suggested he try to copy a Rembrandt from a book of fine-art prints. No one, including Perenyi, could believe how well it turned out. Perenyi credits his father for his instantaneous ability to mimic; his dad was a mechanic and instilled in Perenyi an interest in all things technical. His technical way of thinking about art would serve him well in his future career.

After bemoaning how expensive it was to find parts for his vintage Bentley, Daly gave Perenyi another book—this one about the

Dutch art forger Han van Meegeren (p. 188). Thus inspired, Perenyi sold his first forgery in New York City for $800. Exhilarated, he continued to perfect his craft, working by day as an art restorer where he could closely examine art that he would later forge. After noticing that nineteenth-century American artists were having a moment at auction, Perenyi chose to focus on second-tier artists from this era so as to avoid the close scrutiny that would come with impersonating the big names. Eventually, he would expand his strategy to include British maritime scenes. Perenyi had ambitions to break into the art world on his own terms as an Abstract Expressionist painter, but life (and bills) always got in the way, and forgery was a steady source of income.

Perenyi drew the line at creating fake provenances for his paintings. He left that

Opposite: Perenyi's biggest payday came from a forgery in the style of Martin Johnson Heade. In this piece, *After Martin Johnson Heade, Passion Flowers with Hummingbirds*, Perenyi tries to recreate the magic without breaking the law.

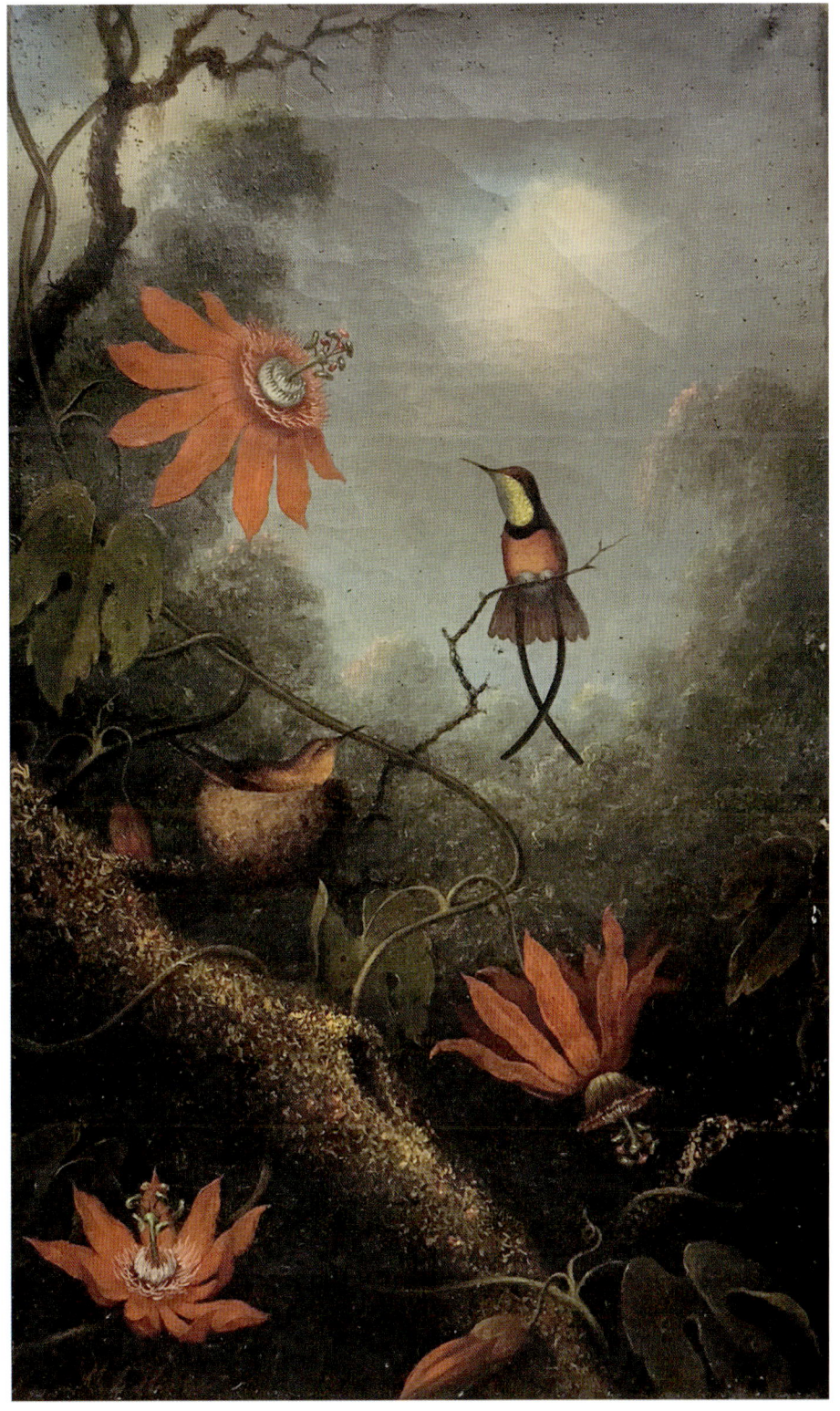

up to the auction houses or galleries in New York, London, and Washington, DC—all places Perenyi frequented. Perenyi wanted his art to stand on its own merits, not on an invented provenance.

The FBI started sniffing around Perenyi in 1998 when a forgery of his, a James Buttersworth maritime painting, ended up on a Bonham's postcard as an advertisement for an upcoming auction. A collector who had already bought a nearly identical Buttersworth by Perenyi called the FBI. Perenyi quickly pivoted, advertising himself as a mimic who, for a price, would create above-board forgeries and sign them in his own name, in the vein of John Myatt (p. 176). In spite of what was called "a mountain of evidence," the FBI let Perenyi be. The statute of limitations on his case expired in 2003 and, according to Perenyi, he still has no criminal record.

Perenyi also attributes his abrupt exit from illicit forgeries to the television program *60 Minutes*. In 1997, Perenyi tuned in to an episode highlighting the practice of ritual servitude. The program detailed the life of a seven-year-old Ghanaian girl, Brigitte, who had been kidnapped by her uncle and sold into slavery at a shrine in Togo in a system called *trokosi* as a way for her uncle to atone for his infidelity. Determined to rescue Brigitte, Perenyi brought money and a few of his forgeries to Africa. After Perenyi was ritually beaten with a eucalyptus branch while naked, the high priest insisted on both

TRICKS OF THE TRADE

Using magnifying glasses and an incredibly sharp, fine needle, Perenyi perfected a way of engraving cracks into oil paint to mimic the natural cracking that occurs over hundreds of years as paint hardens. Authentic craquelure also collects debris and dust, which Perenyi mimicked with yellow varnish sprinkled with dust. Creating a painting might take him a few days, but engraving and embellishing cracks could take weeks. Perenyi followed in the footsteps of other forgers, collecting period frames and scouring flea markets for antique canvases, nails, and paper. He had fake stamps and old inventory labels, and he made chalk marks on the backs of paintings to suggest that a piece had been auctioned in the past. Perenyi added his own flourishes as well: for example, as an art restorer, he knew that when a painting was examined under UV light, old oil paint glowed. Perenyi figured out that he could collect the varnish he was cleaning off an authentic painting and spray it onto his own forgeries. Then, voila—his forgeries also glowed!

Another added piece of authenticity was something Perenyi observed as a restorer. He would see paintings sprinkled with dozens, hundreds, maybe even thousands of black dots, no bigger than the tip of a needle. He learned that the high sugar content of oil paint attracts flies, and over hundreds of years, if a painting were improperly stored, flies could leave minuscule droppings all over the surface. Perenyi devised a way to mimic fly poop using epoxy glue, powdered pigment, and the tip of a needle.

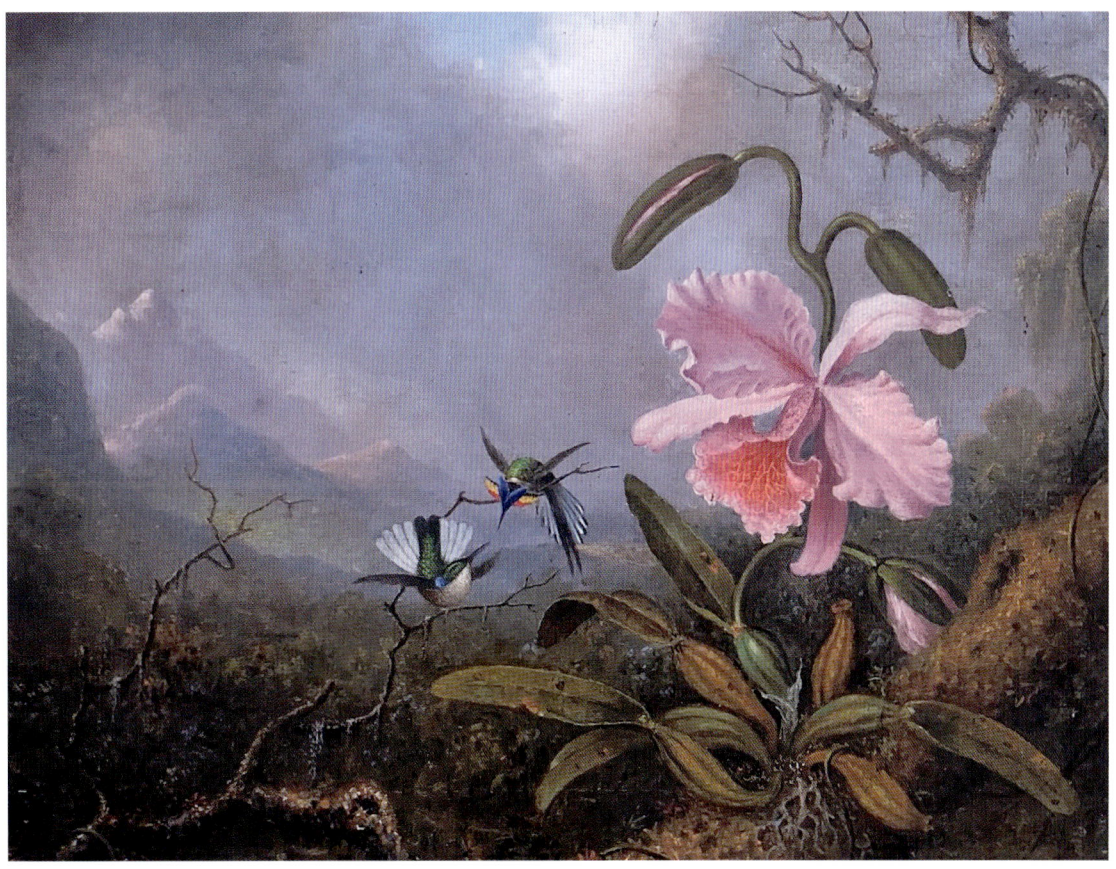

Above: Now squeaky clean and selling his own paintings, Perenyi advertises this piece on his website under the title *After Martin Johnson Heade, Orchid and Hummingbirds*.

a case of expensive whiskey and pills for his alcoholism. The priest also demanded $10,000. Perenyi obliged and eventually the young girl he had seen on *60 Minutes* came to America as his adopted daughter. As the process of adoption was formalized, Perenyi was under FBI investigation. He told *HuffPost* in 2017, "It was bachelor father—cooking, cleaning and juggling the FBI and sleepovers for my daughter! It was a bizarre life!" Today, Brigitte Perenyi is an award-winning documentary filmmaker, fighting to end the practice of *trokosi*.

Perenyi's life story was also given a film treatment when it was bought by RKO Pictures after he published his autobiography, *Caveat Emptor: The Secret Life of an American Art Forger*. When asked by the *New York Post* who might play him in a movie about his life, Perenyi shyly suggested "A young Johnny Depp."

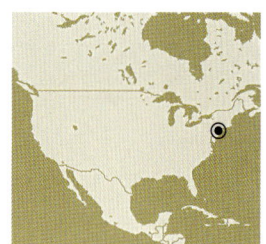

When: 1994–2008

Where: New York City

What: Forty forgeries in the style of Abstract Expressionist painters like Willem de Kooning, Robert Motherwell, Barnett Newman, Jackson Pollock, Mark Rothko, and Clyfford Still

SECRET SANTA

Freedman took the helm of the Knoedler, an art dealership founded in 1846 in New York City, in 1994, the same year Ecuadoran-born thirty-seven-year-old Glafira Rosales walked into the gallery with a previously unknown Mark Rothko painting. Freedman bought it from Rosales and resold it herself for millions more. Rosales, from Long Island, explained she had a wealthy but private friend, "Mr. X," who wanted to discreetly sell pieces from his sterling art collection. Between 1994 and 2008 Freedman would buy forty paintings Rosales claimed were made by Abstract Expressionist giants. The Knoedler would net more than $80 million from these sales, of which Freedman would keep around $10.4 million (in addition to her $300,000 annual salary). Behind closed doors, Freedman called Mr. X "Secret Santa."

By 2009, the FBI had begun investigating some disputed Robert Motherwell works sold by the Knoedler. Elsewhere, Pierre Lagrange was raising hell: he had bought a Jackson Pollock from Freedman in 2007 for $17 million, and in 2011 forensic testing showed that the painting's yellow paint was made in 1970, decades after

Pollock was purported to have splattered it on the canvas. Learning this, Lagrange demanded that the Knoedler give him his money back or he would take them to court. The Knoedler replied by brusquely shutting down. The gallery would not reach its 166th birthday.

Lagrange's lawsuit inspired others, notably the 2012 suit by the De Sole family, who had bought what they believed was a Rothko from the Knoedler in 2004 for $8.3 million. After a dramatic few weeks in court where the once-precious painting was, according to *Artnews*, "handled roughly, like a piece of cardboard," Freedman settled out of court before having to testify, leaving many to believe that the truth would have been far more damaging than her settlement.

In 2013, Rosales spilled the beans: none of the paintings were by the Ab-Ex greats; they were by an elderly Chinese immigrant named Pei-Shen Qian living in Queens. Rosales and her boyfriend, José Carlos Bergantiños Díaz, discovered Qian in the early 1990s. Qian was a floundering artist whom Rosales (Díaz denies being involved) offered from a few hundred to a few thousand dollars for each painting he made.

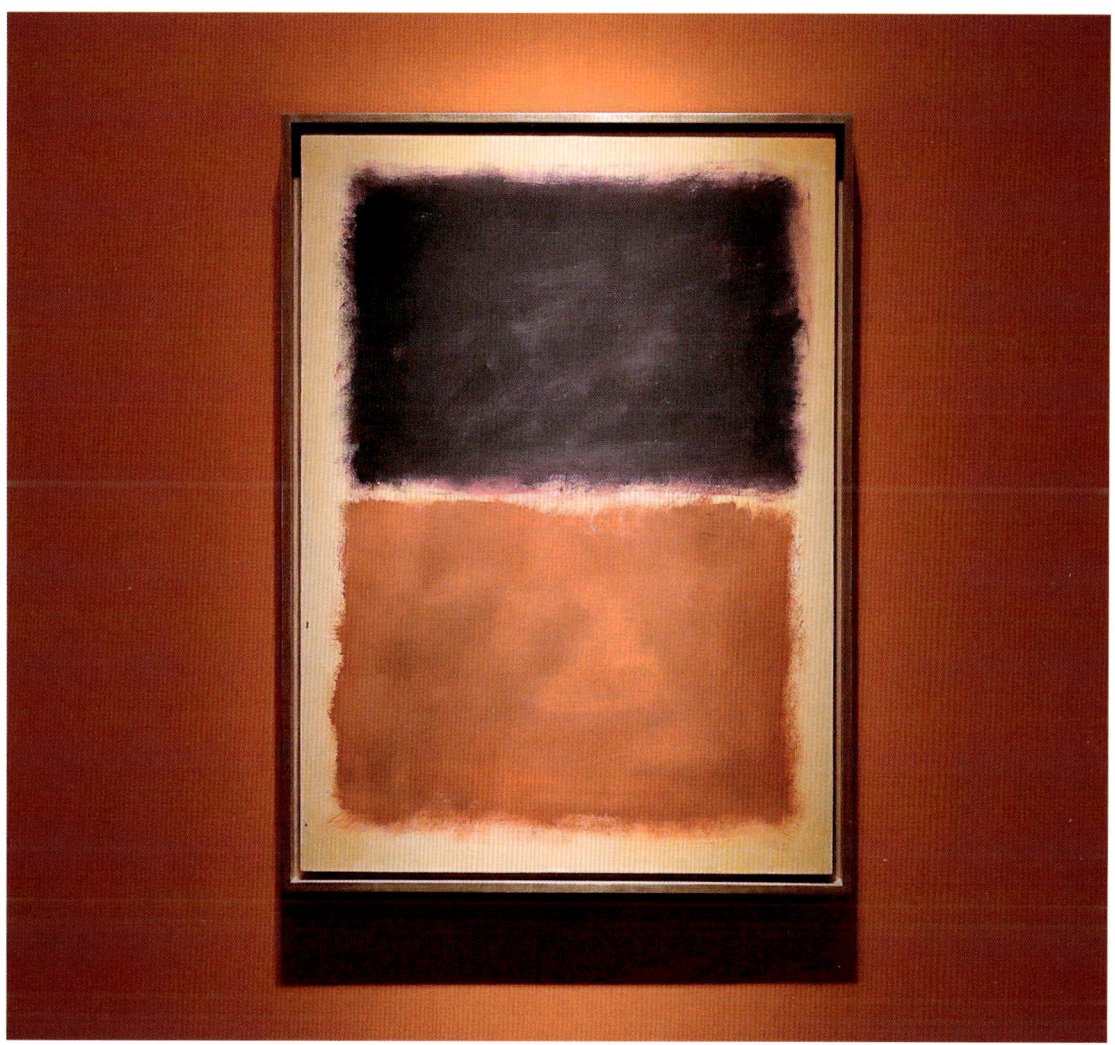

Above: A painting in the style of Mark Rothko. Although scientific analysis didn't raise any alarms, the sketchy provenance should have been a clue that this canvas was not what it purported to be.

Qian claims he had no idea the forged work on which he signed other artists' names was being sold for millions.

Díaz fled to Spain and Qian to China. Rosales was left holding the bag. She spent three months in jail, after which she continued serving house arrest and supervised release. As of 2017, Rosales, forced to forfeit her assets to the government, was working as a busser in a restaurant.

In *New York Magazine*, Freedman referred to herself as Rosales's "central victim." Today, Freedman runs her own space, Freedman Art, in New York City. As Ken Perenyi (p. 202) warned in the title of his autobiography: *caveat emptor*.

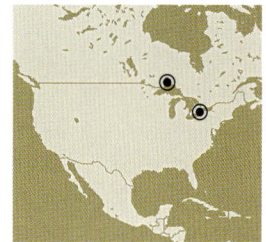

IT'S ALL BEEN DONE BEFORE

Norval Morrisseau, an artist from the Bingwi Neyaashi Anishinaabek First Nation, was known by other names and titles: Miskwaabik Animiiki (Copper Thunderbird), a name given to him by a medicine woman when he was close to death at age nineteen, a name (along with Norval Morrisseau) with which he signed his paintings; "Picasso of the North," a moniker used to promote Morrisseau during an exhibition in France in the late 1960s; and *mishomis* (grandfather) of contemporary Indigenous art in Canada. Morrisseau was a founder of the Woodlands school and a member of the Indigenous Group of Seven, the Order of Canada, and the Royal Canadian Academy of Arts. He was the first Indigenous artist to have a retrospective at the National Gallery of Canada in 2006; a year after that he died of Parkinson's disease, aged seventy-five.

Morrisseau's distinctive paintings—in bright colors outlined with thick black paint—told stories of Anishinaabek legends; of the tensions between being Indigenous and Canadian,

Christian, and Anishnaabe; of existential and spiritual dilemmas; and of humankind's relationship with nature. Morrisseau believed his medicine paintings could heal people with their energy. In spite of this, he struggled with alcoholism and drug addiction throughout his life. In 1973, Morrisseau was arrested for public intoxication and jailed for six months; he was given an extra cell to use as a studio, where he continued painting during his incarceration.

Others took advantage of Morrisseau and saw an opening to make money. Three groups began forging Morrisseau's work. The first, a Thunder Bay-based assembly line, was launched by David Voss in 1996. The second, also in Thunder Bay, was started in 2002 by Gary Lamont, a repeat sexual offender, who roped Morrisseau's nephew, Benjamin "Benjie" Morrisseau, into the scheme. The third, led by Jeffery Cowan in Southern Ontario, began in 2008. These forgery rings would create so many facsimiles that some experts believe that Morrisseau forgeries outnumber originals by a ratio of 10:1. Authorities think these rings, using child labor

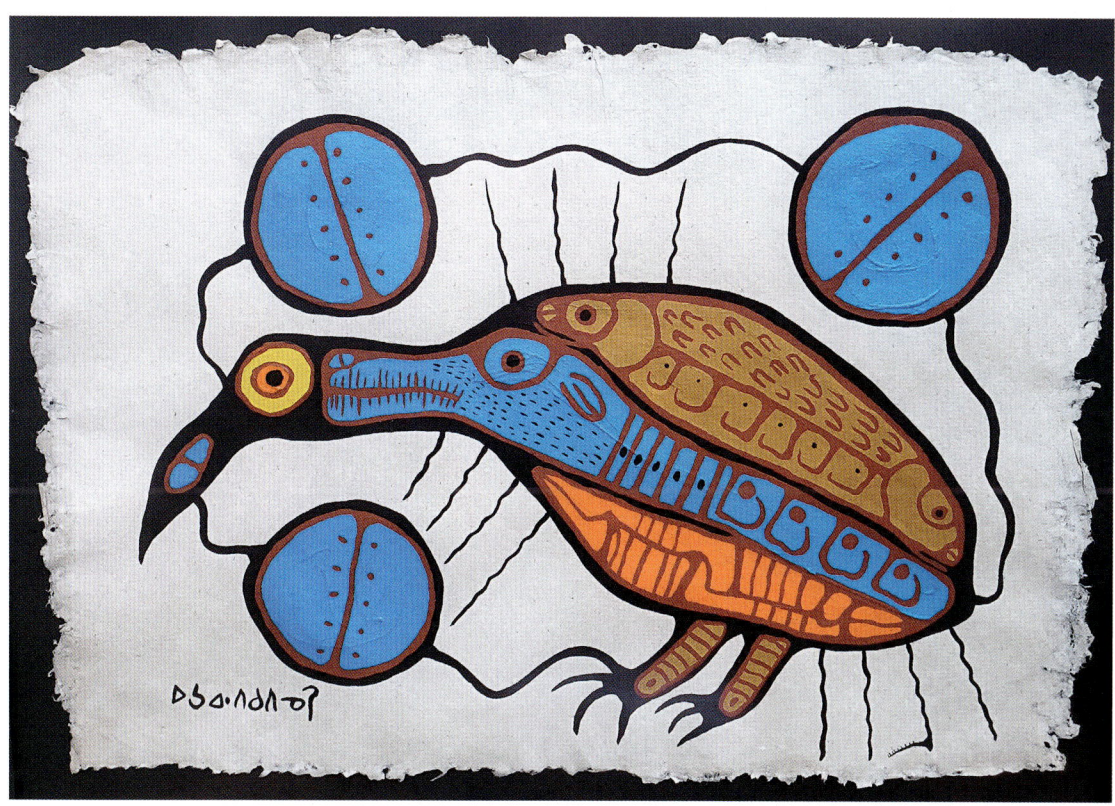

Above: Norval Morrisseau's distinctive paintings were characterized by Anishinaabe symbolism, vivid and bold colors, thick black outlines, and dynamic but balanced compositions, as in this totem of a fish, a bear, and a loon.

and often headed by and comprised of friends or family of Morrisseau, churned out somewhere between 4,000 and 6,500 forgeries, each selling for an average of 15,000 Canadian dollars. The schemes could have netted as much as 100 million Canadian dollars, making it "the biggest art fraud in world history," according to Thunder Bay police detective Jason Rybak.

One of the victims of the Morrisseau fraud rings was Kevin Hearn, the keyboard player and guitarist of Canadian band Barenaked Ladies. In 2005, Hearn bought a Morrisseau for 20,000 Canadian dollars in Toronto and wanted to loan it to the Art Gallery of Ontario, whose curator told him that it was forged. Hearn's humiliation and frustration helped launch a cinematic exploration into the allegations of fraud around Morrisseau's work. The documentary, *There Are No Fakes*, caught the attention of Thunder Bay Police, who launched a two-plus-year-long investigation with the Ontario Provincial Police. The result: eight suspects, including Morrisseau's nephew, were arrested and charged. Though sentences have not yet been doled out, no doubt, none of the forgers will be given a separate cell to continue painting their forgeries.

ASIA, PACIFIC, AND AFRICA: CHINA

When: 2004–6

Where: Guangzhou, China

What: Theft and copying of paintings by seventeenth- to twentieth-century Chinese artists from the collection of the Guangzhou Academy of Fine Arts

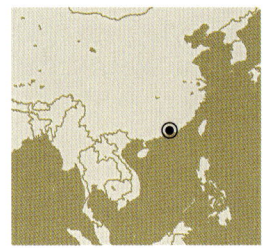

A COPYCAT AND A THIEF

From 2003 to 2006, Xiao Yuan was the chief librarian at an art gallery within the library of the Guangzhou Academy of Fine Arts. The art gallery operated much like the library: staff, faculty, and students at the university could check out works of art just like they could check out books.

Yuan, who had written several books about Chinese art, says that, in a sea of book librarians, he was the only one to know anything about the art at the gallery. Because of this, Yuan, who wore shorts at his video-recorded trial at the Intermediate People's Court in Guangzhou in 2015, admitted he was "very greedy and tempted" after noticing on his first day at the job that many of the paintings in the collection were clearly forgeries. With this awareness and his newfound authority as the chief librarian, Yuan said, "Now I had the keys, and I could do it too."

A year into his new role, Yuan started using those keys to enter the library on weekends. He took home lesser-known paintings, staying clear of artists that scholars would be most familiar with. Using paper and ink from centuries past, Yuan painted identical copies and then replaced the missing paintings with his own copies.

Between 2004 and 2006, Yuan copied 143 paintings from the library and started selling the originals to auction houses. During this time, prosecutors estimate he made nearly 34 million yuan (about $5.5 million) selling 125 paintings. When arrested, he still had eighteen of the university's paintings in his possession, which were thought to be worth almost double the 70 million yuan ($11 million) he had earned from his previous sales.

Yuan ceased his scheme when he was moved to another gallery in 2006. A former Guangzhou Academy of Fine Arts student noticed the university's seal on a painting for sale at an auction in Hong Kong in 2010. Yuan's house of cards fell after that. In 2011, he was arrested and charged with corruption. As of 2015, he was yet to be sentenced.

In an ironic twist, Yuan complained in court that he had revisited the gallery years after his time working there only to find that many of his own copies had been replaced by someone else's copies. Of his discovery, he said, "I realized that paintings I had substituted ten years ago had been substituted again. I could tell right away they weren't mine. The quality was too low.

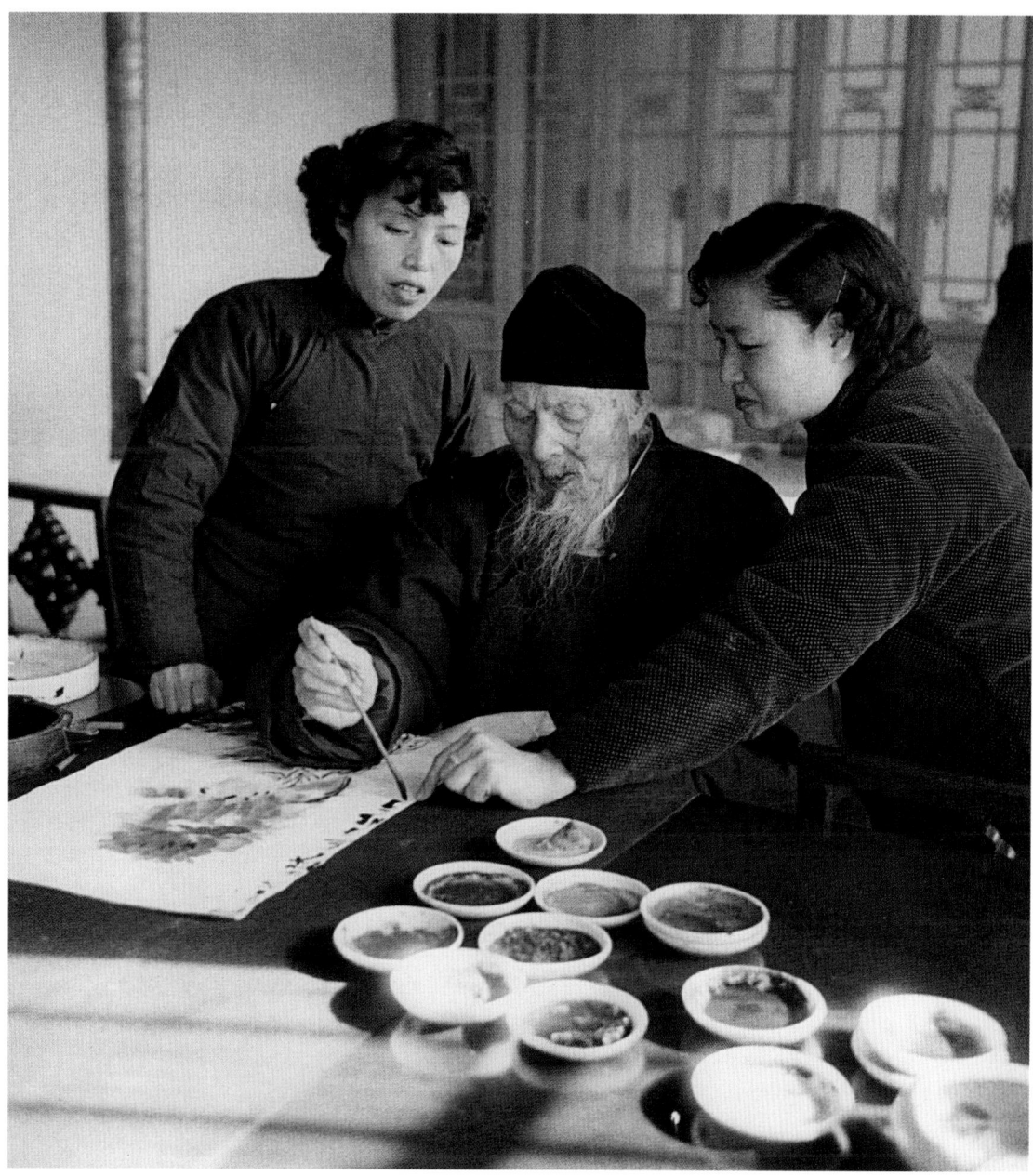

I pointed this out to people, but they didn't pay any attention."

One has to wonder how Yuan felt having his own work copied. He will, no doubt, have a lot of time to think about it behind bars.

Above: Qi Baishi, a pillar of Chinese art, is shown here in his studio, painting a scroll. Qi was one of the famed artists featured in the Guangzhou Academy of Fine Art's collection.

REFLECTIONS ON ART CRIME

Art critic Holland Cotter once responded to the sentiment that art represents humanity at its best by saying, "it also represents us at our worst." After writing this book, I think the same can be said about art crime. Though art crimes might generally seem to involve the worst of humanity, they can also represent its best— though sometimes art criminals are not easily classified.

The Worst

Undeniably, as I researched thefts, vandalism, and forgeries, I was struck by the incontestable worst of humanity: thieves who destroy great human achievements; vandals who climb with sharp cleats onto the shoulders of others to have their fifteen minutes of fame; and forgers who falsely, selfishly, and undeservedly forever alter the history of art and insert themselves within it. But I was even more disillusioned by the actions of the art world's gatekeepers. Their greed, pridefulness, selfishness, and mercilessness were hard to digest.

Before I began writing, I thought that "Vandalism" would be the most disturbing chapter of this book to research and write. According to Christopher Cordess and Maja Turcan, art vandalism has long been associated with the "mentally unstable." In their seminal 1993 article "Art Vandalism," they cite the frequency of vandals later committing suicide, which mirrors a pattern seen in murders and other crimes of passion. Furthermore, the frequency of attacks on images of women, as discussed by Cordess and Turcan, left me a bit hopeless.

I was surprised that "Forgery," not "Vandalism," was the most distressing chapter for me. In a 1999 *New York Times* article by Peter Landesman, an art dealer described the art world as "a shark-infested business", and

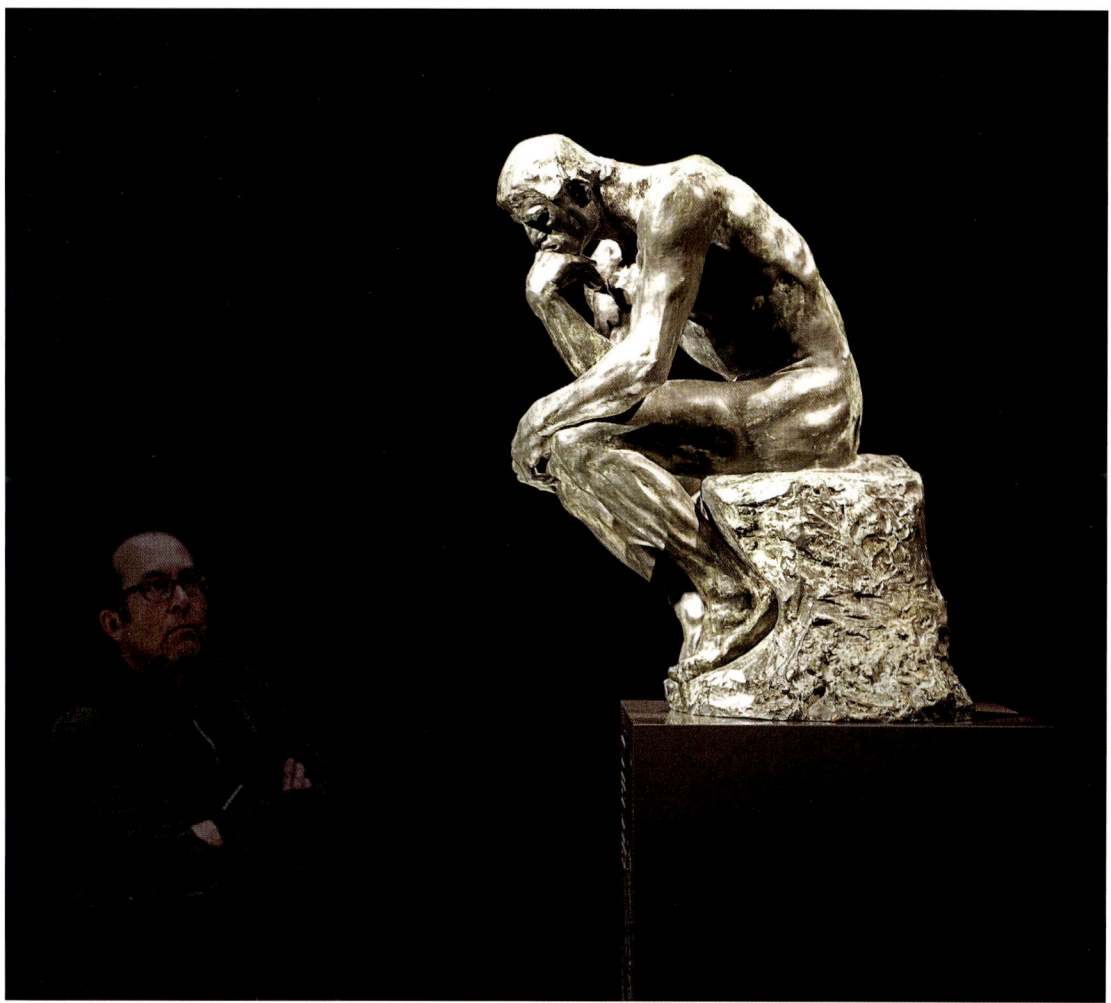

Above: After being stolen in 2007 and disfigured by thieves who wanted to melt him down for his parts, *The Thinker* returned to the Singer Laren Museum in 2011 after extensive conservation work. Here, a visitor contemplates the sculpture at a homecoming exhibition titled *The Thinker Thinks Again.*

I think my anguish can be best summed up in a similar way. I would add that there always seems to be blood in the water even before the sharks circle. I was struck by how damaging pride and greed are from start (the forger) to finish (whomever made money from authenticating and selling the forgery). To be honest, I am far more disturbed by the lack of accountability on the art world's side of the process than on the forgers' side. It is ironic that in a market built on looking at objects, there remains a lot of conscious blindness.

The Best

So, there we have it: art crime at its worst. But at its best? There are countless tales throughout the history of art crime of heroes acting

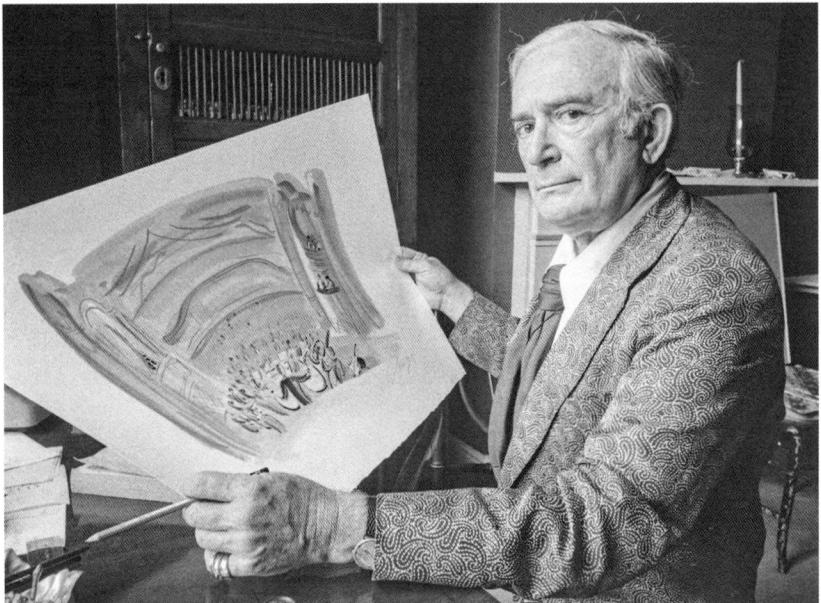

Left: Elmyr de Hory, art forger extraordinaire (p. 194), brandishes one of his paintings done in the style of the Fauvist artist Raoul Dufy. This photo was taken in 1973, the same year de Hory would star in Orson Welles' *F for Fake*.

valiantly, from art-crime detectives who have recovered stolen art in undercover stings (p. 84); to reporters (p. 182), researchers (p. 180), and registrars (p. 200) who have followed their instincts and clues to reveal serial forgers; to art conservators who have saved many a work of art from destruction (p. 158). Thieves, forgers, vandals, and crooked dealers get the majority of attention in the press, but our better art-world angels are the people who have saved art for us so that it can live another day. Even though it could be argued that art can save us, art cannot save itself. I thank the many unsung heroes who have preserved our ability to commune with art. I hope, someday, to write a book focused on these stars.

The Not Easily Classified

In a third category, somewhere hanging between the balance of the worst and the best, are those who seem to defy categorization: thieves who stole to bring attention to injustice (p. 20); vandals who fought for equality (p. 136); forgers who didn't care about money but exposed the art world as a rotten place (p. 182); and thieves who seemed to love and appreciate art more than the multimillionaires who could afford it (p. 94). What do we make of these people? By Conklin's definition, they were all engaged in criminally punishable acts involving art. But clearly certain art criminals felt justified in their actions.

Below: The soggy note left at the Loo-vre (nicknamed thus because it was a public toilet) in Manchester, where three paintings were recovered after being stolen from the Whitworth Art Gallery in 2003 (p. 26).

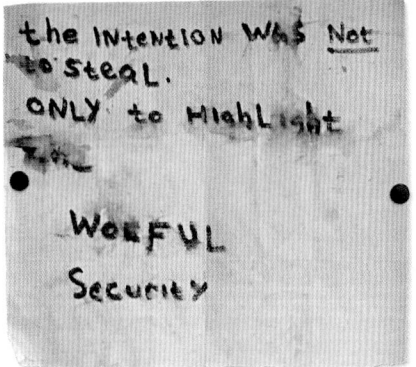

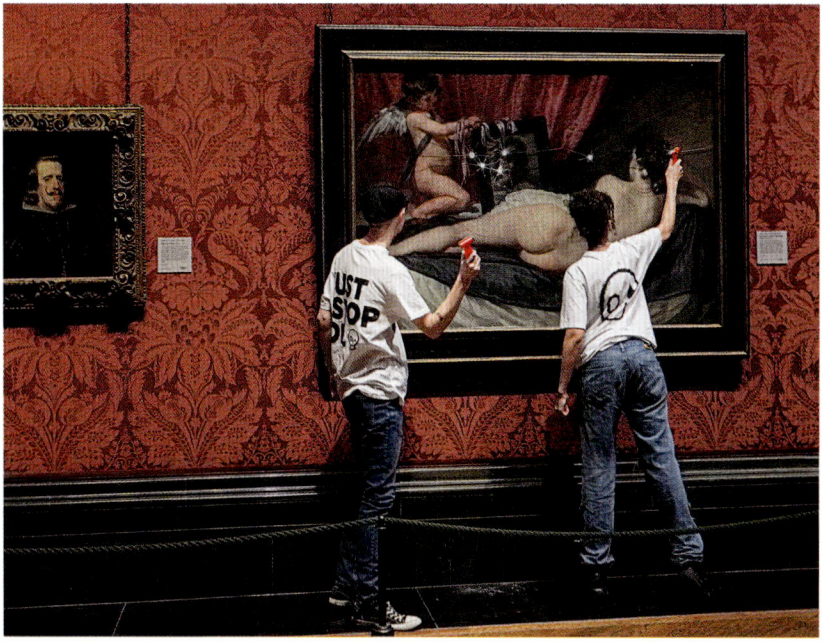

Right: Echoing Mary Richardson's 1914 social-justice-inspired vandalism of *The Toilet of Venus*, Just Stop Oil protestors used Velázquez's painting to highlight their cause in 2023 (p. 139).

I was surprised to discover that some people were trying to make positive change in the world by committing art crimes (however misguided their approach). Writing about the historical precedent of vandals such as Mary Richardson (p. 136) made me think about the recent spate of climate-change protestors in art museums—though these activists have not (yet) gone nearly as far as Richardson did with '*The Rokeby Venus*'. Thinking about and comparing these acts of consciousness is something I would like to look into further with more nuance, empathy, and care.

In closing, I encourage you to go to a museum, go to a gallery, or go to a sculpture park to see art in person. Better yet, go with someone you love and talk about what you see, what it means to you, and what it might mean for us in the world. You never know when that painting, that sculpture, that banana might not be there anymore, so enjoy it while you can. Do what you can to show your appreciation for the institution where it is preserved, for the people who steward our heritage, and for the art itself. However, resist the urge to kiss it with red lipstick (p. 146), no matter how overcome you might feel. That stuff can really leave a mark.

REFERENCES

CHAPTER ONE: THEFTS

The Disappearing Duchess: A Love Story
Macintyre, Ben. "The Disappearing Duchess." *New York Times*, July 31, 1994.

Luck of the Irish
Lonergan, Aidan. "How Two Irish Students Stole a Priceless Masterpiece from London's Tate Gallery—and Got Away with It." *Irish Post*, April 6, 2017. https://www.irishpost.com/life-style/two-irish-students-stole-priceless-masterpiece-londons-tate-gallery-got-away-117360.
National Gallery, London. "The Hugh Lane Bequest: The Story of Masterpieces Collected by Sir Hugh Lane." Accessed November 30, 2023. https://www.nationalgallery.org.uk/about-us/history/collectors-and-benefactors/sir-hugh-lane.

Stealing Art for Free TV
Hirsch, Alan. *The Duke of Wellington, Kidnapped!: The Incredible True Story of the Art Heist that Shocked a Nation.* Berkeley, CA: Counterpoint, 2017.
Nairne, Sandy. *Art Theft and the Case of the Stolen Turners*. London: Reaktion Books, 2011.
Grant, Thomas. *Jeremy Hutchinson's Case Histories: From Lady Chatterley's Lover to Howard Marks.* London: John Murray, 2016.

Why2K?
Lyall, Sarah. "Art World Nightmare: Made-to-Order Theft; Stolen Works Like Oxford's Cézanne Can Vanish for Decades." *New York Times*, February 3, 2000.

The Loo-vre Caper
Bailey, Martin. "A Stolen Van Gogh Drawing Recovered Outside a Public Lavatory 20 Years Ago Goes on Show." *Art Newspaper*, November 24, 2023. https://www.theartnewspaper.com/2023/11/24/a-stolen-van-gogh-drawing-recovered-outside-a-public-lavatory-20-years-ago-goes-on-show-royal-academy-london-whitworth.

Royal Flush
Harper, Tom, and Grant Tucker. "Blenheim Palace's £1m Golden Loo Stolen after Owner Pooh-Poohed the Risk." *Sunday Times* (London), September 15, 2019. https://www.thetimes.co.uk/article/blenheim-palaces-1m-golden-loo-stolen-after-palace-pooh-poohed-the-risk-n9f3bf5ff.
Soto, Kaly. "Golden, Going, Gone: 18-Karat Gold Toilet Is Stolen." *New York Times*, September 14, 2019. https://www.nytimes.com/2019/09/14/world/europe/golden-going-gone-18-karat-gold-toilet-is-stolen.html.
Lally, Catherine, Dominic Kenneny, and Boer Deng. "Thieves the real artists, says gold toilet's creator." *Times* (London), September 16, 2019. https://www.thetimes.co.uk/article/gold-toilets-creator-says-the-thieves-are-the-real-artists-gggk63xfl.
"Artist Behind £4.8m Gold Toilet Praises Thieves Who Have Taken It." Sky News, September 15, 2019. https://news.sky.com/story/solid-gold-toilet-stolen-from-winston-churchill-birthplace-blenheim-palace-11809266.

The Takeaway Rembrandt
Harris, Gareth. "Attempted Robbery of Rembrandt Paintings at Dulwich Picture Gallery." *Art Newspaper*, November 14, 2019. https://www.theartnewspaper.com/2019/11/14/attempted-robbery-of-rembrandt-paintings-at-dulwich-picture-gallery.

"This is Just Practice"
Seenan, Gerard. "Thieves Steal Priceless Art 'for Status, Not Profit.'" *Guardian*, December 27, 2003. https://www.theguardian.com/uk/2003/dec/27/arts.artsandhumanities.

A Welcome Mat for Art Thieves
Amore, Anthony M. *The Woman Who Stole Vermeer: The True Story of Rose Dugdale and the Russborough House Art Heist*. New York: Pegasus Crime, 2021.

The Theft That Made The *Mona Lisa*
Zug, James. "Stolen: How the Mona Lisa Became the World's Most Famous Painting." *Smithsonian Magazine*, June 15, 2011. https://www.smithsonianmag.com/arts-culture/stolen-how-

the-mona-lisa-became-the-worlds-most-famous-painting-16406234.

Hales, Dianne. *Mona Lisa: A Life Discovered*. New York: Simon & Schuster, 2015.

The Spider-Man Theft

Agence France-Presse. "'Spider-Man' Burglar on Trial over €100m Paris Art Theft." *Guardian*, January 30, 2017. https://www.theguardian.com/world/2017/jan/30/spider-man-burglar-on-trial-over-100m-paris-art-theft.

Halpern, Jake. "The French Burglar Who Pulled Off His Generation's Biggest Art Heist." *New Yorker*, January 7, 2019. https://www.newyorker.com/magazine/2019/01/14/the-french-burglar-who-pulled-off-his-generations-biggest-art-heist.

The Pathological Thief

Finkel, Michael. "The Secrets of the World's Greatest Art Thief." *GQ*, February 28, 2019. https://www.gq.com/story/secrets-of-the-worlds-greatest-art-thief.

Sharp, Sarah Rose. "World's Most Successful Art Thief Told His Secrets in a GQ Interview." *Hyperallergic*, March 6, 2019. https://hyperallergic.com/488222/worlds-most-successful-art-thief-told-his-secrets-in-a-gq-interview.

Holmes, Helen. "The World's Most Prolific Art Thief Has Just Explained His Motivation." *Observer*, February 28, 2019. https://observer.com/2019/02/the-worlds-most-prolific-art-thief-has-just-explained-his-motivation.

Finkel, Michael. *The Art Thief: A True Story of Love, Crime, and a Dangerous Obsession*. New York: Alfred A. Knopf, 2023.

The Lost Sheep

Charney, Noah. *Stealing the Mystic Lamb: The True Story of the World's Most Coveted Masterpiece.* New York: PublicAffairs, 2010.

There Is a Criminal Touch to Art

Beisswanger, Lisa. "Art Theft as Artwork." *Schirn Magazine*, November 1, 2016. https://www.schirn.de/en/magazine/context/ulay/ulay_carl_spitzweg_neue_nationalgalerie_berlin_criminal_touch_art/.

Wanted

Scherf, David, and Martin Gayford. *Lucian Freud: The Copper Paintings.* Hamburg, Germany: Less Publishing, 2021.

Smee, Sebastian. *The Art of Rivalry: Four Friendships, Betrayals and Breakthroughs in Modern Art*. London: Profile Books, 2017.

Tate. Catalogue entry for *Francis Bacon*, by Lucian Freud, 1952. Accessed December 18, 2023. https://www.tate.org.uk/art/artworks/freud-francis-bacon-n06040.

Stealing "The *Mona Lisa* of Sculpture"

Fleishman, Jeffery, and Sonia Yee. "Masterpiece Is Stolen from a Vienna Museum." *Los Angeles Times*, May 12, 2003. https://www.latimes.com/archives/la-xpm-2003-may-12-fg-bigtheft12-story.html.

The Resurrection of a Stolen Masterpiece

Kimbell Art Museum. Catalogue entry for *Christ and the Woman of Samaria*, by Guercino, c. 1619–20. Accessed December 18, 2023. https://kimbellart.org/collection/ap-201001.

Work in Progress

Charney, Noah. "The Maltese Priest and the Kidnapped Caravaggio." *Salon*, December 4, 2016. https://www.salon.com/2016/12/04/the-maltese-priest-and-the-kidnapped-caravaggio-the-amazing-true-story-of-the-scrappy-octogenarian-who-busted-an-audacious-art-heist.

Russell, John. "Caravaggio at Met, an Age Comes to Life." *New York Times*, February 8, 1985.

Holland's Most Stolen Artist

Siegal, Nina. "As Stolen Van Goghs Return to View, a Thief Tells All." *New York Times*, March 19, 2017. https://www.nytimes.com/2017/03/19/arts/design/van-gogh-museum-theft-octave-dunham.html.

Slash and Dash in Sweden

"Stolen Renoir Recovered." BBC News, April 6, 2001. http://news.bbc.co.uk/2/hi/entertainment/1263808.stm.

Chip on the Shoulder

"The Thief Who Stole a $35,000 Statue from the Phillips Collection." UPI (United Press International), January 12, 1983. https://www.upi.com/Archives/1983/01/12/The-thief-who-stole-a-35000-statue-from-the/7759411195600/.

"Was Stolen Statue a Lesson in Security?" *Beaver County Times*, January 14, 1983.

Daylight Robbery

Shapira, Ian. "Baltimore Museum of Art Argues in Court Papers for Return of 'Flea Market' Renoir." *Washington Post*, June 5, 2013. https://www.washingtonpost.com/local/baltimore-museum-of-art-argues-in-court-for-return-of-renoir/2013/06/05/22b4e4e8-cdea-11e2-8845-d970ccb04497_story.html.

"FBI Closes Investigation into Theft of 'Flea-Market' Renoir as Painting Returns to Public

View." *Baltimore Sun*, March 27, 2014. https://www.baltimoresun.com/2014/03/27/fbi-closes-investigation-into-theft-of-flea-market-renoir-as-painting-returns-to-public-view-2/.

A Couple of Unlikely Thieves
Knight, Christopher. "Commentary: A Stolen, Horribly Damaged De Kooning Painting Gets the Getty Conservation Treatment." *Los Angeles Times*, May 31, 2022. https://www.latimes.com/entertainment-arts/story/2022-05-31/commentary-stolen-de-kooning-painting-getty-conservation/.

An Unclaimed $10 Million Reward
Feeney, Mark. "Isabella Stewart Gardner Was 'the Brightest, Breeziest Woman in Boston.'" *Boston Globe*, January 15, 2012. https://www.bostonglobe.com/2012/01/15/isabella/nOQtDqE1Ou3zWyhhyjrzzI/story.html.

Pore, Jenny. "The Orchid Habit: Under the Spell of the Cymbidium." Isabella Stewart Gardner Museum, January 24, 2023. https://www.gardnermuseum.org/blog/orchid-habit-under-spell-cymbidium/.

Boser, Ulrich. *The Gardner Heist: The True Story of the World's Largest Unsolved Art Theft.* New York: Harper, 2010.

A Dalí Fever Dream
Fanelli, James. "The Great Rikers Island Art Heist." *Esquire*, October 11, 2018. https://www.esquire.com/news-politics/a22854081/rikers-island-stolen-salvador-dali-painting.

The Skylight Caper
Henson, Jim, dir. T*he Great Muppet Caper.* 1981; Burbank, CA: Buena Vista Home Entertainment, 2005.

Roaring Lion Escaped
Feldman, Ella. "Hotel Discovers Its Famous Churchill Portrait Was Swapped with a Fake." *Smithsonian Magazine*, August 29, 2022. https://www.smithsonianmag.com/smart-news/churchill-portrait-stolen-from-canadian-hotel-180980644.

Bermuda's Lost Crown Jewels
"The Tucker Cross." Teddy Tucker (website), accessed December 18, 2023. https://www.teddytucker.com/articles/2017/9/25/tucker-cross.

The Deception of Paint
Kirov, Blago. *Henri Matisse: Quotes and Facts.* Scotts Valley, CA: CreateSpace Independent Publishing Platform, 2015.

Stolen Art for Christmas
Shortland, Anja. *Lost Art: The Art Loss Register Casebook, Vol. 1.* London: Unicorn, 2021.

"The Pain Passes but the Beauty Remains." *Experiment Station* (blog), Phillips Collection, July 27, 2012. https://blog.phillipscollection.org/2012/07/27/the-pain-passes-but-the-beauty-remains/.

The Face That Would Haunt Melbourne
Fortescue, Elizabeth. "The Shocking Story of a Picasso Painting That Was Brazenly Stolen and Held at Ransom by the 'Australian Cultural Terrorists.'" *Art Newspaper*, June 9, 2022. https://www.theartnewspaper.com/2022/06/09/the-shocking-story-of-a-picasso-painting-that-was-brazenly-stolen-and-held-at-ransom-by-the-australian-cultural-terrorists.

Judd, Bridget. "A Picasso Painting Was Stolen from a Melbourne Gallery—and We Still Don't Know Who Did It." ABC News, September 19, 2019. https://www.abc.net.au/news/2019-09-14/retrofocus-picasso-weeping-woman-famous-unsolved-art-heist/11498936.

April Fool's Day Disaster
Rea, Naomi. "Dark-Web Shoppers Are Bidding $350,000 in Bitcoin for a Stolen Painting—and It's Likely a Fake." Artnet News, November 28, 2017. https://news.artnet.com/art-world/new-zealand-art-center-director-dubs-dark-web-lindauer-hoax-1161812.

"Lindauer Paintings Stolen during Art Gallery Burglary Recovered by Police." *NZ Herald*, December 7, 2022. https://www.nzherald.co.nz/nz/lindauer-paintings-stolen-during-a-burglary-recovered-by-police/URTUBVEOPFGX3DWY6BKOSNAB7Y/.

A Matryoshka Doll of Art Crime
Weiser, Benjamin. "In Art Theft Case, Defense Finds Beholder Who Is Not Impressed." *New York Times*, January 17, 1998.

CHAPTER TWO: VANDALISM

Votes (and Vandalism) for Women
Carr, Dawson. *Velázquez.* London: National Gallery, 2006.

"Rokeby Venus: The Painting That Shocked a Suffragette." *Magazine Monitor* (blog), BBC News, March 10, 2014. https://www.bbc.com/news/blogs-magazine-monitor-26491421.

Sharpe, Emily. "Art and the Appetite for Destruction: Histories of British Iconoclasm on Now at Tate Britain." *Art Newspaper*, October 1, 2013. https://www.theartnewspaper.com/2013/10/01/art-and-the-appetite-for-destruction-histories-of-british-iconoclasm-on-now-at-tate-britain.

"Deeds not Words," Women and the Vote, UK Parliament, accessed December 18, 2023. https://www.parliament.uk/about/living-heritage/transformingsociety/electionsvoting/womenvote/overview/deedsnotwords/.

Gamboni, Dario. *The Destruction of Art: Iconoclasm and Vandalism since the French Revolution.* London: Reaktion Books, 2007.

"TIME 100 Persons of the Century." *Time*, April 13, 1998. https://content.time.com/time/magazine/article/0,9171,26473,00.html.

"'Women Didn't Get the Vote by Voting; It's Time for Deeds Not Words'—Just Stop Oil Supporters Smash Suffragette Painting." Just Stop Oil, November 6, 2023. https://juststopoil.org/2023/11/06/women-didnt-get-the-vote-by-voting-its-time-for-deeds-not-words-just-stop-oil-supporters-smash-suffragette-painting.

Fraser, Matthew. *Monumental Fury: The History of Iconoclasm and the Future of Our Past*. Amherst, MA: Prometheus Books, 2022.

Not What He Signed Up For

"Mark Rothko Painting Defacement: Man Arrested." BBC News, October 9, 2012. https://www.bbc.com/news/uk-england-london-19879650.

Luke, Ben. "Anish Kapoor: Attack on Tate's Rothko Painting Was Simply Vandalism." *Standard*, October 10, 2012. https://www.standard.co.uk/culture/exhibitions/anish-kapoor-attack-on-tate-s-rothko-painting-was-simply-vandalism-8203598.html.

Lerner, Ben. "Damage Control: The Modern Art World's Tyranny of Price. *Harper's Magazine*, December 2013. https://harpers.org/archive/2013/12/damage-control.

Hess, Barbara. *Abstract Expressionism*. Cologne: Taschen, 2006.

Best Case Scenario: A Prison Sentence

Seaton, Jillian Elizabeth. "Touching the Void: The Museological Implications of Theft on Public Art Collections." Dissertation, University of Edinburgh, 2014. https://era.ed.ac.uk/handle/1842/957.

Jackson, Penelope. *Females in the Frame: Women, Art, and Crime*. Cham, Switzerland: Palgrave Macmillan, 2020.

Let Her Eat Cake

"Salvador Dalí on Why People Attack Leonardo's 'Mona Lisa,' in 1963: From the Archives." ARTnews, October 23, 2019. https://www.artnews.com/art-news/retrospective/salvador-dali-mona-lisa-essay-13450.

Torchinsky, Rina. "A Man in a Wig Was Detained after Throwing a Piece of Cake at the Mona Lisa." NPR, May 30, 2022. https://www.npr.org/2022/05/30/1102044111/man-throws-cake-at-mona-lisa-the-louvre.

Sealed With a Kiss

"French Woman Leaves Lipstick Kiss on $2m Artwork." CBC News, July 23, 2007. https://www.cbc.ca/news/entertainment/french-woman-leaves-lipstick-kiss-on-2m-artwork-1.663749.

"Woman Fined for Kissing Painting." BBC News, November 16, 2007. http://news.bbc.co.uk/2/hi/entertainment/7098707.stm.

Plato. *Plato's Phaedrus*. Translated by R. Hackforth. Cambridge: University Press, 1952.

Arlett, Megan J. "A Preliminary Theory on Kissing." *Pinch*, November 15, 2019. https://www.pinchjournal.com/blog-posts/apreliminarytheory.

Willful Damage

"A Secret Varnish: Restoration Photographs of *The Night Watch* from 1911." RKD—Netherlands Institute for Art History, August 21, 2020. https://rkd.nl/en/about-the-rkd/coming-soon/news/890-a-secret-varnish-restoration-photographs-of-the-night-watch-from-1911.

"Rembrandt's 'The Night Watch' Slashed." *New York Times*, September 15, 1975.

"Rembrandt's 'Night Watch' Painting Vandalized." *Los Angeles Times*, April 6, 1990. https://www.latimes.com/archives/la-xpm-1990-04-06-mn-973-story.html.

Who's Afraid of a Repeat Art Vandal?

Schreyach, Michael. "Beholding *Adam*: Scale and Standing," Tate Research Publication, 2018. https://www.tate.org.uk/research/in-focus/adam/beholding-adam.

Flotsam and Jetsam

Nash, Jørgen. *Havfruemorderen krydser sine spor: Erindringer på fast gerning*. Olso, Norway: Aschehoug, 1997.

"Little Mermaid: Copenhagen Statue a Target for Vandals." BBC News, June 15, 2017. https://www.bbc.com/news/world-europe-40293396.

The Seven Mysteries of Laszlo Toth

Brownlee, John. "Hey, Whatever Happened to Laszlo Toth?" *Wired*, December 11, 2006. https://www.wired.com/2006/12/hey-whatever-ha.

Acid Rain

Russell, John. "Healing a Disfigured Rembrandt's Wounds." *New York Times*, August 31, 1997.

"Restoration." *Spokesman-Review*, October 14, 1997. https://www.spokesman.com/stories/1997/oct/14/restoration/.

No Eyes, No Mouth, No Beauty!
Kishkovsky, Sophia. "Russian Guard Who Doodled on $1m Painting Speaks Out: 'I'm a Fool, What Have I Done!'" *Art Newspaper*, February 11, 2022. https://www.theartnewspaper.com/2022/02/11/russian-guard-who-doodled-on-dollar1m-painting-speaks-out-im-a-fool-what-have-i-done.

Now Showing: American Graffiti
"'Guernica' Survives a Spray-Paint Attack by Vandal." *New York Times*, March 1, 1974.
"Vandal Sprays Picasso Mural: Priceless Work Attacked Here." *Daily News*, March 11, 1974.
"Tony Shafrazi Defaces 'Guernica' Again." *Vulture*, May 12, 2008. https://www.vulture.com/2008/05/tony_shafrazi_defaces_guernica.html.

Bombs Away
Alighieri, Dante. *The Inferno*. Translated by Anthony M. Esolen. New York: Modern Library, 2002.

Heartbreak ~~Hotel~~ Museum
Cummings, Tommy. "Works of Ancient Art Destroyed at DMA in Overnight Break-In." *Dallas Morning News*, June 2, 2022. https://www.dallasnews.com/arts-entertainment/visual-arts/2022/06/02/5-million-of-ancient-art-destroyed-at-dma-in-overnight-break-in.
Bever, Lindsey. "Man Breaks into Dallas Art Museum, Damages Ancient Artifacts, Police Say." *The Washington Post*, June 3, 2022. https://www.washingtonpost.com/nation/2022/06/03/dallas-museum-art-vandalism/.

Vandalism Via Vomit
Nicole, Corinna. "Artists Who Vandalized Art to Create a New Work of Art." Owlcation, November 17, 2023. https://owlcation.com/humanities/Artists-Who-Vandalize.
Depalma, Anthony. "Student Says Vomiting on Painting Was an Artistic Act." *New York Times*, December 4, 1996.

Yes, We Have No Bananas!
Hawkins, Derek. "A Rogue Artist Ate the $120,000 Duct-Taped Banana at Art Basel. 'It's Performance,' He Said." *Washington Post*, December 8, 2019. https://www.washingtonpost.com/arts-entertainment/2019/12/08/rogue-artist-ate-duct-taped-banana-art-basel-its-performance-he-said.
Taylor, Elise. "The $120,000 Art Basel Banana, Explained." *Vogue*, December 10, 2019. https://www.vogue.com/article/the-120000-art-basel-banana-explained-maurizio-cattelan.
Noh, Hyun-soo. "Experience: I Ate a $120,000 Banana." *Guardian*, June 23, 2023. https://www.theguardian.com/lifeandstyle/2023/jun/23/experience-i-ate-a-120000-banana.

Accidental Vandals
"John 'JonOne' Perello." Kolly Gallery, accessed December 18, 2023. https://www.kollygallery.ch/jonone-artist.
"Graffitied Graffiti." *Korea JoongAng Daily*, March 30, 2021. https://koreajoongangdaily.joins.com/2021/03/30/imageNews/photos/jonone-graffiti-mural/20210330172500515.html.
Kwon, Junhyup. "A Couple Defaced a $450,000 Painting, and the Artist Is Fine with It." *Vice*, April 14, 2021. https://www.vice.com/en/article/xgxq9a/korea-art-defaced-jonone.

CHAPTER THREE: FORGERIES

Genuine Fakes
Bailey, Martin. "'The Biggest Contemporary Art Fraud of the Century.'" *Art Newspaper*, March 1, 1999. https://www.theartnewspaper.com/1999/03/01/the-biggest-contemporary-art-fraud-of-the-century.
Amore, Anthony M. T*he Art of the Con: The Most Notorious Fakes, Frauds, and Forgeries in the Art World*. New York: St. Martin's Press, 2016.
Landesman, Peter. "A 20th-Century Master Scam." *New York Times*, January 18, 1999.

Egging on the Experts
Mount, Harry. "As 200 of His Art Works Go on Sale... How Many of This Master Forger's Fakes Are Hanging in Our Galleries?" *Daily Mail*, October 20, 2014. https://www.dailymail.co.uk/news/article-2799515/as-200-art-works-sale-master-forger-s-fakes-hanging-galleries.html.
Eric Hebborn: Portrait of a Master Forger. Aired November 8, 1991, on BBC One.
Hebborn, Eric. *Drawn to Trouble: The Forging of an Artist*. Edinburgh: Mainstream Publishing, 1991.

Sexton Blake Rhymes with "Fake"
"London Painter and Restorer Admits Flooding Art Market With Forgeries." *New York Times*, August 21, 1975.
Keating, Thomas F., Frank Norman, and Geraldine Norman. *The Fake's Progress*. London: Hutchinson, 1977.

A Family Affair

O'Neill, Sean. "The £10m Art Collection That Was Forged by a Family in Their Garden Shed in Bolton." *Times* (London), November 17, 2007. https://www.thetimes.co.uk/article/the-10m-art-collection-that-was-forged-by-a-family-in-their-garden-shed-in-bolton-vshhxzq25rv.

Parkin, Simon. "'I Wasn't Cock-a-Hoop That I'd Fooled the Experts': Britain's Master Forger Tells All." *Guardian*, May 27, 2017. https://www.theguardian.com/artanddesign/2017/may/27/wasnt-cock-a-hoop-fooled-experts-britains-master-art-forger.

Greenhalgh, Shaun. *A Forger's Tale: Confessions of the Bolton Forger*. London: Allen & Unwin, 2017.

Bonnie and Clyde with Paintbrushes

Hammer, Joshua. "The Greatest Fake-Art Scam in History?" *Vanity Fair,* October 10, 2012. https://www.vanityfair.com/culture/2012/10/wolfgang-beltracchi-helene-art-scam.

"The Ex-Con Artist Now Making Millions." BBC News, May 9, 2015. https://www.bbc.com/news/av/entertainment-arts-32671112.

"Wolfgang Beltracchi." The Greats by Beltracchi (website), accessed December 18, 2023. https://www.greats.art/beltracchi.

Giacomettis Galore

Cacouris, Christina. "An Interview with Art Forger Robert J.C. Driessen." Artnome, September 24, 2019. https://www.artnome.com/news/2019/9/24/an-interview-with-art-forger-robert-jc-driessen.

F Is for Forgery

Irving, Clifford. *Fake! The Story of Elmyr de Hory, the Greatest Art Forger of Our Time*. New York: McGraw-Hill, 1969.

Vogel, Donald S. *Memories and Images: The World of Donald Vogel and Valley House Gallery.* Denton: University of North Texas Press, 2001.

Lessard, Réal. *L'amour du faux*. Paris: Librairie Générale Française, 1989.

Legros, Fernand. *Fausses histoires d'un faux marchand de tableaux*. Paris: A. Michel, 1979.

McWhirter, William A. "The Swindling of an Art-Loving Millionaire: How Algur Hurtle Meadows Was Duped into Buying a $1.5 Million Collection of Paintings That Have Mostly Been Judged Fakes." *Life*, July 7, 1967.

Kitty Litter

Bradley, John Ed. "The Talented Mr. Toye." *Garden & Gun*, April/May 2010. https://gardenandgun.com/feature/the-talented-mr-toye.

Buyer Beware

"Autobiography: Ken Perenyi." Ken Perenyi (website), accessed December 18, 2023. https://www.kenperenyiart.com/blank-page.

Perenyi, Ken. *Caveat Emptor: The Secret Life of an American Art Forger*. New York: Pegasus Books, 2013.

Harper, Janice. "A Tale of Art Forgery, Sex Slavery and Single Parenthood." *HuffPost*, October 10, 2013. https://www.huffpost.com/entry/a-tale-of-art-forgery-sex_b_4073738.

Cahalan, Susannah. "Confessions of a Forger." *New York Post*, July 22, 2012. https://nypost.com/2012/07/22/confessions-of-a-forger/.

Secret Santa

Miller, M. H. "The Big Fake: Behind the Scenes of Knoedler Gallery's Downfall." *ARTnews*, April 25, 2016. https://www.artnews.com/art-news/artists/the-big-fake-behind-the-scenes-of-knoedler-gallerys-downfall-6179/.

Panero, James. "'I Am the Central Victim': Art Dealer Ann Freedman on Selling $63 Million in Fake Paintings." *New York*, Intelligencer, August 27, 2013. https://nymag.com/intelligencer/2013/08/exclusive-interview-with-ann-freedman.html.

It's All Been Done Before

Robertson, Carmen. "Norval Morrisseau: Picasso of the North." Art Canada Institute—Institut de l'art Canadien, accessed December 18, 2023. https://www.aci-iac.ca/the-essay/picasso-of-the-north-by-carmen-robertson.

White, Patrick, and Willow Fiddler. "Police in Ontario Charge Eight in Norval Morrisseau Art Fraud Investigation." *Globe and Mail* (Toronto), March 3, 2023. https://www.theglobeandmail.com/canada/article-norval-morrisseau-art-fraud/.

Kastner, Jamie, dir. *There Are No Fakes*. Toronto: Mongrel Media, 2019. https://www.therearenofakes.com/.

A Copycat and a Thief

Ramzy, Austin. "Out-Faking the Fakers: Chinese Librarian Proud of Forged Masters." *New York Times*, Sinosphere, July 22, 2015. https://archive.nytimes.com/sinosphere.blogs.nytimes.com/2015/07/22/out-faking-the-fakers-chinese-librarian-proud-of-forged-masters/.

INDEX

PICTURE CREDITS

Key: top = t; bottom = b; left = l; right = r; m = middle

Front cover © Popperfoto/Getty Images. **Back cover** © Isabella Stewart Gardner Museum/Photo © Sean Dungan/Bridgeman Images.

Frontis Bruce Postle/Fairfax Media, MEAA. **6** Universal History Archive/Universal Images Group/Getty Images. **13** Reproduced by permission of Chatsworth Settlement Trustees/Bridgeman Images. **14** Library of Congress, Washington, D.C.; Prints and Photographs Division. **15** Still Light/Alamy Stock Photo. **17** Popperfoto/Getty Images. **19** National Gallery, London/Bridgeman Images. **20** Sailko, via Wikipedia (CC By 3.0). **22** Keystone/Hulton Archive/Getty Images. **25** © Ashmolean Museum/Bridgeman Images. **27** Whitworth Art Gallery/Getty Images Entertainment /Getty Images. **29** Lindsay Lipscombe/Alamy Stock Photo. **31** Dulwich Picture Gallery/Bridgeman Images. **33** Fine Art Images/Heritage Images/Getty Images. **34** © Alfred Beit Foundation, Russborough. **36** PA Images/Alamy Stock Photo. **37** ©National Museums NI, Ulster Museum Collection (BELUM.U2017.10, *The Cornfield*, Jacob van Ruisdael). **39** Musée du Louvre, Paris/Bridgeman Images. **40–41** Roger Viollet/Getty Images. **43** Musée d'Art Moderne de la Ville de Paris, Paris/Bridgeman Images. **45** After Sotheby's auction catalogue *The Collection of the Margraves and Grand Dukes of Baden, vol. 5: Paintings & Prints*, No. 2275, Wikipedia (PDM). **47** Prisma Archivio/Alamy Stock Photo. **49** Rijksmuseum, Amsterdam (SK-A-1595). **51** Rob Mieremet/National Archives of the Netherlands/Anefo (PDM). **53** Ulay: Courtesy the artist, Copyright Ulay Foundation. **54** © Archiv Gerstenberg/ullstein bild/Getty Images. **55** Danvis Collection/Alamy Stock Photo. **57** Bridgeman Images © The Lucian Freud Archive. All Rights Reserved 2023. **59tl, 59tr** © Tate. **59b** Hamburger Kunsthalle, Hamburg/Bridgeman Images. **61** © KHM-Museumsverband. **62** (Herbert Pfarrhofer/EPA/Shutterstock. **64** Cuppoz, via Wikipedia (PDM). **67l** The Yorck Project, Directmedia Publishing GmbH (2002). **67r** Ricci-Oddi Gallery, Piacenza/The Picture Art Collection/Alamy Stock Photo. **69r** Picture Art Collection/Alamy Stock Photo. **69l** Heritage Images Partnership/Alamy Stock Photo. **71** Fine Art Images/Heritage Images/

Getty Images. **73** David Gee/Alamy Stock Photo 4. **74** Uffizi Gallery, Florence (PDM). **77** Van Gogh Museum, Amsterdam/Bridgeman Images. **78** The Yorck Project, Directmedia Publishing GmbH (2002) **81** Richard Mortel, via Wikipedia (CC BY 2.0). **82l** Photograph Stig B. Hansen, NTB/SCANPIX/Alamy Stock Photo. **82r** AP Photo/ SCANPIX/Alamy Stock Photo. **85l** Nationalmuseum, Stockholm(NM 5324) /Erik Cornelius, via Wikipedia (PDM). **85tr** PHAS/Universal Images Group/Getty Images. **85br** Penta Springs Limited/Alamy Stock Photo. **86** © Worcester Art Museum/Bridgeman Images. **88** © Worcester Art Museum/Bridgeman Images. **89** © Rick Cinclair—USA TODAY NETWORK. **91** The Phillips Collection, Washington D.C. **93** The Potomack Company, Alexandria, VA/Art Collection2 /Alamy Stock Photo. **95** Gift of Edward Joseph Gallagher, Jr.; The University of Arizona Museum of Art, Tucson. **96** Collection of The University of Arizona Museum of Art, Tucson. **98** © Isabella Stewart Gardner Museum/Bridgeman Images. **100** © Isabella Stewart Gardner Museum/Photo © Sean Dungan/Bridgeman Images. **101** © Isabella Stewart Gardner Museum/Bridgeman Images. **103** Leonard Detrick/NY Daily News Archive/Getty Images. **105** Gift in memory of Mr. and Mrs. William F. Angus, Montreal Museum of Fine Arts; Photo MMFA. **107** Gift of Miss Jean Scott, Montreal Museum of Fine Arts; Photo MMFA. **109** © Photograph By Yousuf Karsh, Camera Press London. **111** The Royal Gazette, Bermuda, copyright unknown. **112** Courtesy of Wendy Tucker, www.teddytucker. com. **115** Marlborough Graphics, London/Bridgeman Images. **117** Museo Nacional de Bellas Artes, Buenos Aires/Bridgeman Images. **119** Museus Castro Maya/IBRAM/MinC, Rio de Janeiro. **121** National Gallery of Victoria, Melbourne/Bridgeman Images. **122** Bruce Postle/Fairfax Media, MEAA. **123** Rob Leeson/Fairfax Media, MEAA. **125** Courtesy of New Zealand Police. **127** After *L'Illustration*, 22 December 1860, Wikipedia (PDM). **129–130** James Tourtellotte, via Wikipedia (PDM). **131** Kunsthalle Bremen, via Wikipedia (PDM). **132** Younes Mahmoud Ahmed/agefotostock/Alamy Stock Photo. **137t** National Gallery, London/Bridgeman Images. **137b** Chronicle/Alamy Stock Photo. **138** Museum of London/Heritage Images/Getty Images. **141** Ben Stansall/AFP/Getty Images. **143** © Photo Josse/Bridgeman Images. **145** David Cantiniaux/AFPTV/AFP/Getty Images. **147** David Lees/Getty Images. **149t** Rob Bogaerts/National Archives of the Netherlands/Anefo (PDM). **149b** Rijksmuseum, Amsterdam: (SK-C-5). **151** Collection Stedelijk Museum Amsterdam (A

28310, A 35917). **152** W. Charewicz/Keystone/Getty Images. **154** Brian Bergmann/SCANPIX, Denmark/AFP/Getty Images. **155** Ida Marie Odgaard/AFP/Getty Images. **157** Bettmann/Getty Images. **159t** Alexander Demianchuk/Reuters/Bridgeman Images. **159b** Hermitage Museum, St. Petersburg/© Scala, Florence. **161** Newsflash © the artist. **163** New York Daily News/Getty Images. **165** Photo Cleveland Press Collections, courtesy of the Michael Schwartz Library Special Collections, Cleveland State University, http://ClevelandMemory. org (PH2000.000PRE) **167** Images courtesy of Dallas Museum of Art. **169** Museum of Modern Art, New York/Digital Image © 2013 MoMA. N.Y./Scala, Florence. **171** Eva Marie Uzcategui/Reuters. **173** Minwoo Park/Reuters. **177** Courtesy of Washington Green/Castle Fine Art. **178** Ak Suggi/Washington Green/Castle Fine Art. **181** National Gallery of Art, Washington D.C. **183** PA Image/Alamy Stock Photos. **185** VCG Wilson/Corbis/Getty Images. **187** 13Photo/Vera Hartmann. **189** Museum Boijmans Van Beuningen, Collection, Photo Studio Tromp. **191t** Koos Raucamp/National Archives of the Netherlands/Anefo (PDM). **191b** Private collection; previous collection Simonis & Buunk Art Dealers, The Netherlands. **193** Courtesy of Robert Driessen. **195** Koller Auctions, Zurich. **196l** Evening Standard/Hulton Archive/Getty Images. **196r** Laurent Maous/Gamma-Rapho/Getty Images. **199** © Erika Larsen. **201** Courtesy of Mark Landis. **203** © 2023 by Ken Perenyi. **205** © 2023 by Ken Perenyi. **207** Patrick Semansky/Associated Press/Alamy Stock Photo. **209** Permissions by The Norval Morrisseau Estate Ltd, OfficialMorrisseau.com. **211** Phillip Harrington/Alamy Stock Photo. **213** Toussaint Kluiters/AFP/Getty Images. **214t** Evening Standard/Hulton Archive/Getty Images. **214b** Manchester Police/PA Images/Alamy Stock Photo. **215** Kristian Buus/In Pictures/Getty Images.

Additional copyrights
43l Leger © ADAGP, Paris and DACS, London 2024. **53** ULAY © DACS 2024. **95** De Kooning © The Willem de Kooning Foundation/Artists Rights Society (ARS), New York and DACS, London 2024. **103** Dali © Salvador Dali, Fundació Gala-Salvador Dalí, DACS 2024. **115** and **119** Matisse © Succession H. Matisse/DACS 2024. **121** and **163** Picasso © Succession Picasso/DACS, London 2024. **141** Rothko © 1998 Kate Rothko Prizel & Christopher Rothko ARS, NY and DACS, London. **151** Newman © The Barnett Newman Foundation, New York/DACS, London 2024. **173** JonOne © ADAGP, Paris and DACS, London 2024.